WITHDRAWN

D1542979

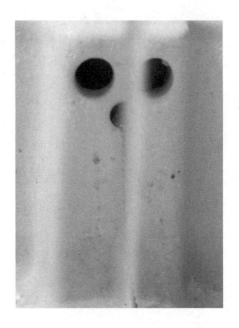

Even in its most hallucinatory
conditions of satisfaction, the ego senses
that something may be missing;
it becomes insecure and must start up
the machinery of testing.

3000 800059 05501
St. Louis Community College

Florissant Valley Library
St. Louis Community College
3400 Pershall Road
Ferguson, MO 63135-1499
314-595-4514

The Test Drive

AVITAL RONELL

With Photographs by Suzanne Doppelt

University of Illinois Press
Urbana and Chicago

Copyright © 2005 by the Board of Trustees of
the University of Illinois. All rights reserved.

The bust of Robert Boyle reproduced on pages
89, 90, is from The Royal Collection © 2004,
Her Majesty Queen Elizabeth II. The Prints on
pages 204 and 205 are from the archives of the
Library of Congress, Prints and Photographs
Division (ppmsca 02508 and cph 3b39407).
The photograph on page 206 is from the NOAA
Photo Library, NOAA Central Library; OAR/ERL/
NSSL, image catalog ID nss10017. All other
photographs are © 2004 by Suzanne Doppelt.

This project was supported in part by a grant
from the New York University Research Challenge Fund Program.

Manufactured in the United States of America
1 2 3 4 5 C P 5 4 3 2 1

⊗ This book is printed on acid-free paper.

Library of Congress Cataloging-in-Publication Data
Ronell, Avital.
p.   cm.
The test drive / Avital Ronell.
Includes bibliographical references and index.
ISBN 0-252-02950-X (cloth : alkaline paper)
1. Methodology. 2. Testing. I. Title.
BD241.R598   2004   101–dc22   2004007218´

For my incomparable teacher
and friend
JACQUES DERRIDA

Zu lieben ist gut: denn Liebe ist
schwer. Liebhaben von Mensch zu Mensch,
das ist vielleicht das Schwerste, was
uns aufgegeben ist, das Äusserste, die letzte
Probe und Prüfung, die Arbeit, für
die alle andere Arbeit nur Vorbereitung ist.
— Rainer Maria Rilke, *Briefe I,*
May 14, 1904

[It is good to love, for love is hard.
Tenderness from one person to another is
perhaps the most difficult task assigned
to us – the most extreme, the final test and
examination, the work, for which
all other work is only
a preparation.]

Contents

The Test Drive

Und wenn die Prüfung
Ist durch die Knie gegangen,
Mag einer spüren das Waldgeschrei.
— Hölderlin, "The Ister Hymn"

[And when the trial
Has passed through our knees,
May someone sense the forest's cry.]

Part I
Proving Grounds

Dreams and beasts are two keys by which we are to find out the secrets of our nature. They are our test objects. – Ralph Waldo Emerson

But what contributes most of all to this Apollonian image of the destroyer is the realization of how immensely the world is simplified when tested for its worthiness of destruction. This is the great bond embracing and unifying all that exists. – Walter Benjamin

I always want to test everything to the point of death. Beyond. – Kathy Acker

TESTING 1 On Being Tested

Whether you mean to prove that you can do it, or we are driven by what Maurice Blanchot calls "the trial of experience," and he submits himself endlessly to Nietzsche's loyalty tests, or she is a runaway replicant whose human factor is being scrutinized, or the sadistic coach has us revving up for an athletic contest; whether you are entering college, studying law, or trying to get out of an institution; whether they are giving you the third degree; whether you are buffing up on steroids, or she had unprotected sex, or he doesn't know what he has but he's fatigued and nauseated; whether they have to prove their mettle or demonstrate a hypothesis or audition for the part, make a demo, try another way, or determine paternity; whether you roll back to the time of the Greeks who first list their understanding of *basanos,* or to the persecution of witches and press forward to push out the truth in the medium of torture and pain: it seems as though everything – nature, body, investment, belief – has needed to be tested, including your love. What is the provenance of this need to torture, to test? A link between torture and experiment has been asserted ever since Francis Bacon; yet, what has allowed acts and idioms of testing to top out as an essential and widening interest, a nearly unavoidable *drive?*

A kind of questioning, a structure of incessant research – perhaps even a modality of being – testing scans the walls of experience, measuring, probing, determining the "what is" of the lived world. At the same time, but more fundamental still, the very structure of testing tends to overtake the certainty that it establishes when obeying the call of open finitude. An unpresumed fold in metaphysics, testing – that is, the types and systems of relatedness that fall under this term – asserts another logic of truth, one that subjects itself to incessant questioning while reserving a frame, a trace, a disclosive moment to which it refers.

There is nothing as such *new* about the desire bound up in the test; yet the expansive field or growing promiscuity of testing poses novel problems and complicates the itinerary of claims we make about the world and its contractions, the shards of immanence and transcendence that it still bears. Our contract with Yahweh, whether piously observed or abominated, involves the multiplication of test sites. Shortly after completing his *Critique of Judgment*, Kant, in response to a public questionnaire, examined the problem of testing the faith of theology students.[1] Can faith be tested or is it not the essence of faith to refuse the test – to go along, precisely on blind faith, without ground or grade? Or again, perhaps the Almighty Himself has proven time and again to be addicted to the exigencies of testing. If God can be said to have a taste for anything, then it may well be located in the incontrovertible necessity of the test. No one is not tested by God, at least by the God of the Old Testament who showed a will to perpetual pursuit, perpetual rupture. Even the satanic beloved, who got away or was kicked out (depending on whether you are reading the satanic version of Goethe or God), became a subsidiary testing device for the paradisiacal admissions policy. In German, *Versuch* unites test with temptation – a semantic merger of which Nietzsche makes good use. The devil is the visible mark of a permanent testing apparatus. It is one name for an operation that engages the frazzled subject in a radical way.

The figure of the test belongs to what Nietzsche saw as our age of experimentation. Nietzsche's work can be seen to pivot around different appropriations of testing, and it is for this reason that I want to look at it more closely while tracking the phenomenon that appears to have flown beneath philosophical radars. Even where testing is mentioned in contemporary thought – the astounding commentaries of key theorists and philosophers tend to make mention but not use of the term's potentialities – it does not necessarily become an object of inquiry or a field of discovery, of anxious discrepancy. Husserl steps on the brakes at a moment when the question of testing emerges in his reflections on science; in any case, he swerves around Nietzsche, nearly hitting him but leaving him unmarked in the *Crisis*. Nietzsche, for his part, introduces the experimental turn in the most personal among his books, *The Gay Science*. Still, the last philosopher being and becoming who he is (that is, according to the ticking of the eternal return: Nietzsche, ever becoming who he will have been) at once announces and denounces this emergence. We must never lose sight of the Nietzschean ambivalence toward experimentation. With his future-seeing night goggles and his sensitive little radar ears he sensed that test sites would make the wasteland grow and foresaw the

6

concentration camp as the most unrestricted experimental laboratory in modern history, a part of the will to scientific knowledge.[2]

At the same time, though time has stood still, life as knowledge, Nietzsche hoped, would not be at best a bed to rest on or a slouch of leisure, but would embrace dangers, victories, heroic feelings. Nietzsche noted science's capacity for making immense galaxies of joy flare up. "So far, however, science deprived man of his joys, making him colder, more like a statue, a stoic."[3] Nietzsche addresses his pressing demand to the science of the future. He asks that it account for its peculiar production of meaning, for its place and pace in human existence. In a sense Nietzsche set out to find a structure of possibility that reaches beyond life's "what is" while maintaining his irrefragable investment in the world. It is important to remember that Nietzsche had no getaway car that would take him to a mystified Elsewhere, though he reverted to the daring and dashing rhythm of mortal existence first scanned by the Greeks. Still, he did not establish the rights of a world-beyond or appeal for credit to a transcendental loan shark. Whatever his faults, he did not shirk his sense of responsibility to this world, here and now, which invited trouble on many levels and in different areas of his fractured thought. The effort to secure the time zone of the here-and-now was not the least of his problems, especially after Hegel had ditched it in favor of another temporal enterprise. Like Husserl after him, though they by no means formed a partnership, the urgency he sought to address concerns "not the scientific character of the sciences but rather what they, or what science in general [including scholarship], had meant and could mean for human existence [*menschliches Dasein*]."[4] In order to think the world rigorously, one can no longer turn one's face from the pressure points of science, no matter how invisible, recondite, or elusive their impressions are. Reading and contesting Heidegger's statement that science falls short of thinking ["die Wissenschaft denkt nicht"], Derrida links science to mourning and memory.[5] Lacan builds his *Ethics of Psychoanalysis* under the horizon of scientific encroachment: it is always there, ready to erupt, amaze, or blow you away.[6] It holds sway but often in the mode of denial, as if one could walk or turn away from the sway of the scientific pregivenness of our modernity. Yet where is it? What is it? How does Nietzsche construe the possibility of a science that also bears the force of interminable resistance?

Beyond its meaning for human existence, there is the question of science's self-understanding. In a manner reminiscent of the genealogical probe, Husserl traces a mutation in the formation of meaning "which was originally vital, or rather of the originally vital consciousness of the task which gives rise to the methods, each with its special sense."[7] Scientific method is handed down, as is the progressive fulfillment of the task as method, an art (*techne̅*); "but its true meaning cannot be handed down with it."[8] Science can master the infinity of its subject matter only through the infinite pursuit of its method and can master the latter infinities only by means of a technical thought and activity that are empty of meaning. A theoretical task and achievement like that of a natural science (or any science of the world) "can only be and remain meaningful in a true and original sense *if* the scientist has developed in himself the ability to *inquire back* into the *original meaning* of all his meaning-structures and methods, i.e., into the *historical meaning of their primal establishment*, and especially into the meaning of all the *inherited meanings* taken over unnoticed in this primal establishment, as well as those taken over later on."[9] Husserl adds this caveat: "But the mathematician, the natural scientist, at best a highly brilliant technician of the method – to which he owes the discoveries which are his only aim – is normally not at all able to carry out such reflections."[10] The scientist, limited to a circumscribed sphere of inquiry and discovery, does not know at all that everything these reflections must clarify "is even in *need* of clarification, and this for the sake of that interest which is decisive for a philosophy or a science, i.e., the interest in true knowledge of the *world itself, nature itself.*"[11] He concludes his elaboration: "And this is precisely what has been lost through a science which is given as a tradition and which has become a *techne̅*, insofar as this interest played a determining role at all in its primal establishment. Every attempt to lead the scientist to such reflections, if it comes from a nonmathematical, nonscientific circle of scholars, is rejected as 'metaphysical.'"[12] The philosophical needs – "philosophicomathematical," "philosophicoscientific" – that are aroused by historical motives are largely unseen "and thus not at all dealt with."[13] There is a vast area of scientific activity that is simply not submitted to the rigors of reflection or that aggressively risks sinking into the autism of one or another form of closure. The scene of this repression, which arguably governs our Dasein, is what needs to be addressed. This scene does not constitute science's outside but troubles its inner workings, pointing at times to a forgotten or displaced germ, a desire, an original need or sense of lack – what both Husserl and Nietzsche would agree belongs to the precincts of an original intensity, circumscribing that which in science is on the side of life. Even so, we are not concerned only with uncovering an original vitality but with listening to the future that science portends. In this context, science might be regarded as a kind of questioning, a structure of exposure that often forgets to turn back on itself in order to interrogate its vital impulses and philosophical point of origin. The severance of philosophical reflection and scientific endeavor is as artificial as it is dangerous. My purpose is not to make general pronouncements about the estrangement of science from philosophy. I regard both fields of articulated meaning with skepticism and on this matter must hold to the Flaubertian irony of non-conviction. Science and philosophy have failed us. But that is another story.

The test, which belongs at once to scientific and philosophical protocols but, joining what it severs, does not hold exclusive rights in either domain, leverages some of the discursive intensities that have formed around the issues at hand. It is made to stand in this work for a permanent innovation, introducing a new relation between *technē* and *epistēmē*. At the same time the experimental turn, which houses the test and gives shape to its particular contours, transgresses, in breaking down and disassembling the ground of a tradition, the limits of knowledge and technicity or method. Though articulated with unique precision by Nietzsche, the experimental turn should not be seen as the oriented homogeneity of becoming. By its very nature, it interrupts itself, discontinues itself.

Essentially relational and not static, testing admits of no divine principle of intelligibility, no first word of grace or truth, no final meaning, no privileged signified. How can such a phenomenological line-up of serial "no"s concern us today or speak to our needs? There is something on the order of absolute risk that compels our attention, something that, risking the knowable, requires extreme vigilance and establishes the condition of responsibility and decision. True responsibility, the kind that Dostoevsky, cited by Levinas, sees as always excessive – one is never responsible enough, I am more than anyone else responsible for the other – depends on a self-testing that is never satisfied with its results, never finished with exceeding itself. Nor can it rely upon the reassuring precepts of a determined knowledge.[14]

The multiple disengagement to which the test attests takes us in the direction of the unknown, situated as it is in what Husserl might term an open infinitude. The test asserts that which is threatened from its first tracing or in any case points to a vacancy, an irregularity that no trace can stabilize. The space of what I am calling the *test drive* is circumscribed by an endless erasure of what is. In the context of Nietzsche's reflections on the experimental turn or what in *The Gay Science* he locates as the "experimental disposition," the concept of *rescindability* is introduced to express the fundamental mobility of thought given over to constant disturbance. Nietzsche is concerned with a structure or concept – though these terms in turn wear thin, throwing us into the rut of paleonymy – of the scientific trial, of that which makes us fail, rewind, and start again; still, Nietzsche operates the decimation of scientific thought by trial without downgrading the performance of failure – without having to bow to his Lordship, as he says, quivering with fear because only failure and erasure have been the returns of the day. But failure cannot be pegged or evaluated as such; it gets absorbed into the heat of testing, becoming its supreme articulation in a movement that provokes ruptures without interruption – or ruptures that do not interrupt. The movement that interests Nietzsche duplicates itself interminably, recurrently fissures itself, and contradicts itself without remaining the same, without yielding to any dialectic. It is as if the test held together the absolute immanence of which Seneca had spoken, the immanence of death at every instant.

As disappropriating forms of experience, testing and experimentation are related inextricably to acts of negating and affirming. From the selective science of the eternal return to Zarathustra's trials, to the experimental language shots of the aphoristic style and the makeovers of Nietzsche's different signatures, Nietzsche put his corpus on the line, exposing it to the experience of permanent dislocation. At any given moment, his test-writing interrupts any *presentable* determination and provokes instead an instantaneous dissociation from the present, what Derrida calls a *différance* in being-with-itself.[15] Split up, fractured, essentially incomplete in the way it runs its protocols, the experimental disposition cannot count on impassable borders to rein it in but runs on excess, trespass, and essential instability. There is another way to translate the resistance to presence that Nietzsche scrupulously structures. Dionysus is the god of the test – of transformations; as that which pounces on the momentary unity of mul-

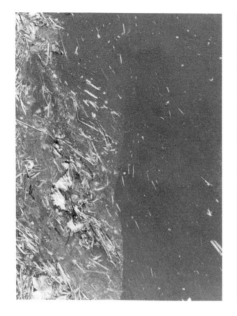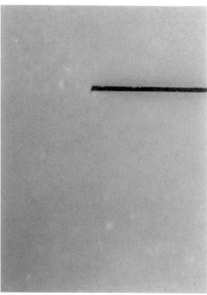

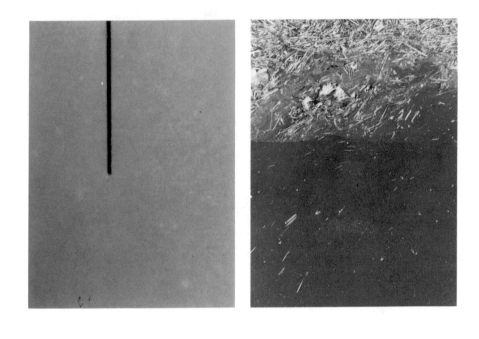

tiplicity, he rules a force that affirms multiplicity and is affirmed of it. Not one to invade a zone of presence, Dionysus keeps passionately quiet: to gain time, to hide himself, to take another form and to change forms. In the end, "Ariadne's Complaint" establishes a fundamental relationship between a way of questioning and the divinity hidden behind every question. Even where the field gets heavily technologized.

Testing, which could be seen as the thrownness of technology, traverses many sectors of existence and does not begin as an explicitly technological life-form. Whether we are speaking of abandoned being (abandoned in the desert, on the cross, at home, or on the streets) or discursively bolstered being (socially pinned, legally inscribed, politically activated) – or where these formations meet and intersect – these skids on the path of becoming tend to assume the character of a test. Very often literature understands the dilemma of tested being on which it bases some of its most harrowing narrations. Kafka constructed his test sites with a striking sense of urgency. From his narrative "The Test" to the interminable *Trial* and "The Penal Colony" – or even Gregor trying out his little legs, the hunger artist weighing in, and K. testing the limits of intelligibility in *The Castle* territory, to the contested medical gaze in "A Country Doctor," and the father's pop quiz at the end of "The Judgement" – Kafka submitted language to the test of its limits as his figures probe for reference, often under torture. The link between testing and torture is given ample consideration in Kafka's works, relating his passion in more ways than one to that of Bacon. Still, a history of lacerated disclosure begins with the Greeks' notion of *basanos,* relating truth to torture, binding a strictly constellated confluence of acts that I study. Perhaps one of the great test cases in Kafka occurs in a story where essentially nothing happens except that a man is made to wait. In the parable "Before the Law" a man waits to be admitted to the law. He grows old and blind as he waits. He stoops. His only interlocutor, besides the flea on his collar, is the doorman, a gatekeeper who in a sense administers the exam without bothering to evaluate the results. It is fair to say that there are no results, just an interminable trial, a series of deferrals and man's marked relation to the law as nonpresence. The law doesn't show up; the man never arrives. Refusing itself, the law does not manifest. Maybe that is the nature of the law, to withhold presencing, except in the parceled out form of representatives – cops, security guards, a judge, surveillance cameras, the lease you signed. Endless metonymies of what never takes place as an essence; there is no place where one could find the law, dashing the only hope of the man from the country. The story in which nothing happens, and only a relation is established, a relation without contact and around which everything is demobilized, tests the patience of the being, man. The man from the country is infinitely patient. He waits. His test consists in not knowing that he is being tested. This man, this hick as concerns the law of testing, could be Odysseus, Rousseau, you or me.

TESTING 1,2   Why Science Amazes Us

I write from a philosophical need – such needs still exist – to respond to the question of testing. The problem is that the test has not yet become a philosophical question, though it belongs to an ever-mutating form of questioning. As that which legitimates and corroborates or, conversely, as that which carries the considerable burden of delegitimating assumed forms of knowledge or legal, pharmaceutical, screen, and other decisive claims of an epistemological or projective order, the test at once affirms and deprives the world of confidence; it belongs to a specific sequence of forces that not so much annihilates as it disqualifies. This force constitutes an often invisible border in the land of negation. Still, in one of its forms the test manifests the luxury of destruction. Let me hold off on that for now; we'll get there soon enough. Until then, think of the test as that which advances the technological gaze as if nothing were.

According to Nietzsche, science alone is forbidden by God: the Almighty manifested time and again His mortal terror of science. Faith is a veto against science.

The subtitle to this work could have been "Why Science Amazes Us." My question is urged by a sense of awe and amazement: it comes from a place of sheer stupefaction. This is a place, or mood, that has a long philosophical heritage, beginning with the ancient Greeks, so it is perhaps an inherited mood, a citational stance, part of a strictly determined circuit. Stupefaction and astonishment open the scene of any possible knowing, even where knowledge emerges from an avowed epistemological deficiency – I want to say simply that science truly amazes us. It fascinates. Which is to say, also, it blinds us and may itself be blinded to its own trajectories, axiomatic presuppositions, procedures, and premises; not to speak of the unmarked status of scientific desire, whether in crisis or, on the contrary – but this is not a contradiction – self-assured and well funded, state supported. So much blindness compels an inward turn, or at least a staggering movement toward something like a philosophical outside. In What Is Called Thinking? *Heidegger says, we blink.*

The suspicion cast upon science's recalcitrance when it comes to reflecting upon its essential nature echoes an old philosophical prejudice. Philosophy has introduced the topos of scientific blindness with good reason; yet, this is not the relationship or vintage from which I come. Science has posited, thought, discovered, and repressed the viability of our life-forms in recognizable and, sometimes, disfigured yet familiar ways – such observations or similar indictments are no longer at issue, and polemical turf wars actually cover up the ground they are probing. Besides, it may be the case that we are still not thinking, all of us. At this point I choose simply to retain the sense, the mood, the spark of dissipation and giddy alienation of astonishment: I want to sustain a level of questioning and reflection within a domain that is not meant to be against or about science. These reflections are offered by – what shall I say? – an admittedly driven yet nonetheless poetic, if often scholarly, sensibility that seeks to understand without appropriation, to grasp without the use of her claws.

At one point Nietzsche sees the experiment freeing us from the constraints of referential truth. Science amazes him, though a reactive tendency to reduce itself to calculative efficacy also lands it squarely in his repertoire of illusions, dissembling interpretations, and masks. He redirects science to art, ligaturing an ancient complicity.

For my part I am neither averse to nor obsessed by science – options that seem useless. I feel the weight that presses upon our bodies, our embarrassed sense of promise and emptiness and connection to world, the tests to which I am put and others have to endure – tests by which that being, still tagged as human, nowadays receives definition. One has every right, in fact it is a duty, to ask of science if it is capable of devoting itself to securing the conditions for thinking joyousness and the affirmation of life. (Those conditions are not to be construed as simplistic or regressive-utopian, as anyone who has been circuited through psychoanalysis realizes.) Or is science really only able in the end to promote the glacialization, the sterilizations, the steely calculative grid of the technological dominion, allied as it is with the persistent menace of world loss and money-eating privilege? One does not have to be a withering Marxist, a vegan or ecomilitant to see that there are all too few scientific activists in our midst, not enough care around its effusions.[16] Yet science amazes me.

For a long while I contemplated as subtitle "The Price We Are Paying for Science" – along the lines of Nietzsche's statement, "the price we are paying for Wagner." I have to assume that the price tags are still showing as I drive the investigation through the back roads of scientific experimentation and diverse cartographies of rupture. As some of the chief inflections and folds indicate, testing will be put in communication with the rhetorical figure of irony. I have not found much in the philosophies of science or in scientific discourse on irony as a decisive rhetorical calibration for the fate of the test. Even though testing is dead serious, its performance can be understood to rely on advanced theories of ironic velocities, whose fissional burnouts are every bit as deadly. It is no mere coincidence that Nietzsche, supreme ironist, leads the investigation into our experimental culture – or that Romantic ironists gathered around the Schlegel brothers tested the aesthetics of taste and the politics of democracy when launching their journal, the Athenaeum. Both irony and testing involve a certain tolerance for risk-taking and fuel the warping edges of temporal acceleration. Both produce novel experiences of breakdown and disruption. One can try to pull the brakes and recuperate irony's unpredictable consequences, shrinking back from an awareness of its destructive propensities – this is the case of Peter Szondi and Wayne Booth[17] – or one can try to ride it like a rodeo beast, until one is thrown off, dashed, kaput. It is necessary to retain the hypothesis that in the end irony, like testing, blows us away.

TESTING 1,2,3 Controlled Experiment

There was a time when philosophy and science were into each other, about and on each other. The one could not do (or be) without the other: a passionate affair of fusional desire. There are still communications, custody battles, visitations, shared holidays in art works and on academic panels. But the solid commitment has been broken in ways that intrude on the course of "serious living" as Husserl says. The youngest son of the remembered union,

Husserl was perhaps the one most freaked out by the historical split. In an-
other time zone Mary Shelley had already inscribed the disaster of such a
split – between thought and science, between the literary and technological
ways – in the creation of the unforgettable unnameable, the monster that
came to be known as Frankenstein. For his part, Husserl urged caution when
it came to advocating a rapprochement of the severed pair. "It is a mistake,"
he wrote, "for the humanistic disciplines to struggle with the natural sciences
for equal rights. As soon as they concede to the latter their objectivity as self-
sufficiency, they themselves fall prey to objectivism."[18] *Literary and philo-*
sophical studies, art and art criticism, risk getting sucked in by the ruling
scientific claims, the alienating authority of what Husserl calls "objectivism."
The attitude that science gives us, this Einstellung, *is life-depleting and*
aura-sapping. It has left a toxic residue of uninterrogated policies, now be-
come decisive. The delusion of self-sufficiency, a mark of the self-evisceration
of the sciences detached from their reflective ground and forgotten abysses, is
dangerous for us all, blocking vision and eclipsing futurity. So Husserl, more
or less. Upgraded by historicity. The other one, Nietzsche, cried: "The waste-
land grows."[19] *Still, I am not about gloom and doom but want to heed what*
Husserl and others, some whose names you do not know, say about "man's
now unbearable lack of clarity about his own existence and his infinite
tasks."[20] *This may sound old-fashioned, that is to say, pre-Freudian, ante-*
Bataillean, post-Enlightenment, and so forth. For who today hungers for
clarity as if darkness did not send out its own special light, perhaps a solar
storm of another order? And who today would restrict her rhetorical-
existential quiver to "man"?

Here is the question that I bring to the table: Why has the test – throughout
history, and perhaps most pervasively today – come to define our relation to
questions of truth, knowledge, and even reality? It is not a matter of choosing
between a science of fact and a science of essence – between an account of
why things are actual rather than possible. Nor is it simply a matter of tech-
nological self-understanding, as if the scientific reflection on its own proce-
dures and premises could satisfy a philosophical hunger. The term "subject
position" would not cover the calamity of the field that encompasses the will
to test. At times my said subject position seems reduced to that of a shivering
rabbit, or less glamorously fragile, to that of a rat, prodded and probed, sec-
tionalized and cornered by the technological feeler. As a receptor to the inva-
sive demand my little rabbit ears are shaking – a figure conjured by Heideg-

ger to represent exemplary listening. I do not know if my listening device is exemplary, nor do I insist on sustaining the pathos that propels the images gathered in this place. Like a good Nietzschean, I am attuned to the conflicting valuations, the gains and losses, of the phenomena under consideration. I am not insensitive to the liberating potential of testing one's ground, which is to say, of recanting one's certainties, throwing off the security blankets of time and history.

There is something about the relationship to truth that depends on the test. Why is it, for example, that the most pressing ethical and political issues of our day increasingly seem to have more to do with testing than with other names for questioning, hesitation, and certainty? The test drive covers a lot of ground and splits off into different, though related, semantic fields. There are moments of local or functional reduplication, overlap and support. One side of testing is as assertive in its findings as the other is vulnerable when counting its losses. There is the test that stands its ground, standardized, and equipped with irrefutable results. So it claims and so it stands. There is the other test that crashes against walls, collapses certitudes, and lives by failure – lives by dying or, at least by destroying. All sorts of issues come to the fore, including those institutions and acts that deal with norms and establish boundaries and those that rely on expertise, or, in a court of law, on expert witnesses. The one register of testing offers results – certitudes – by which to calculate and count on the other (including the self as other, as tested other). Another register consistently detaches from its rootedness in truth: self-dissolving and ever probing, it depends on boundary-crossing feats and the collapse of horizon. It implicates a politics of risk that Nietzsche has shown, on one page, to be linked to a concept of freedom. On the next page, he characteristically contradicts himself, paying the price for science by pointing to the gravest risks ascribable to the culture of the Versuch, the test or trial. The two principal registers do not lead separate lives in the world according to Nietzsche but imply and breach one another at several critical junctures of his thought.

Even if we take the simple question of experimental testing – which touches everything from recent warfare (the unending Gulf War being a privileged instance here) to urban planning, military strategy and national security, space, medical, and reproductive technologies, the aporias of ethics, drug and polygraph testing, the steroidal tests of Olympic Games, and all the various means of measuring and testing that support, among so many others, political, religious, and educational institutions, it is not difficult to see that this mode of testing involves a thoroughgoing reconstitution and reconceptualization of the subject. The test has everything to do not only with the way the policing of political sites and bodies take place but also with the experienceability and constitution of reality in general, especially since the elliptical circuit that now has been established between testing and the real often works to cancel the difference between them.

Ever since Freud introduced the crucial concept of reality-testing, the authority of reality has not only been undermined, but its status has been submitted to various testing apparatuses whose character and significance still need to be investigated. The French psychoanalyst Jacques Lacan has linked testing to the subject's creation of a first "outside" – a space that is no longer the same as "reality." Though the pervasive figure of testing is a peculiarly modern phenomenon, its precedents and models should not be ignored.

This study of our compulsion to test explores the ways in which the test comes to require an unprecedented colloquy of witnesses, evidence, repeatability, and an entire network of apparatuses meant to enforce the test and its findings. Beginning with the Greeks and moving through several indices of an often sublimated and subterranean logic (a logic that binds testing to violence), let us consider the important controversy surrounding the conflicting views in natural philosophy of Robert Boyle and Thomas Hobbes, which in many ways led to the mechanisms of laboratory testing as we know it today, the Nietzschean and Freudian models of experimental testing, and the general philosophical if not parental question of how we come to acquire knowledge. In so doing, I will focus on the ways in which the test – and in particular the rhetoric of testing – has restructured the field of everyday and psychic life. Whether clearly stated or largely disavowed, models of testing inform diverse types of social organization, legitimating crucial and often irreversible discursive tendencies and mandating critical decisions. In terms of the political implications of testing, one need only consider the way wars are waged on material sites and objects, and the way the state uses drugs in order to take possession of the body. Testing means, among other things, that your pee belongs to the state or to any institution or apparatus that thrives on the new civic readability. It is my duty to bring us back to the more original unreadability of your urine sample, or, at least, if I am unable to restore your pee to its proper place, to trace the contours of the complicated extravagance of testing.

 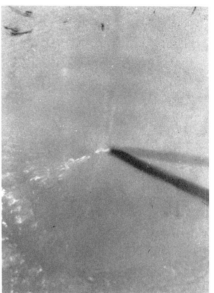

Prototype A

Testability and the Law

Within the long philosophical trajectory that could be plotted from Plato to Derrida, the figure of testing has put in strong though often unmarked appearances. Philosophy as a rigorous science received its golden gloves in German idealism but it first became attached to a particular brand of critical tapping when Plato arraigned the *hypotheton*. Plato's move was not detected until it was seized by a Protestant sensibility – Hermann Cohen. He is on site to manage the operations of the proven ground. From now on the reality of Being must be submitted to proof by scientific method. Among other things, Cohen puts the "protest" back in Protestant. In a related manner, and building on his observations, I would like to put the "test" back in Protestant. The way back calls for corroboration between Plato and German philosophy on the relationship of truth to testing. Questions bearing on certainty and doubt, and on different registers of truthfulness or authenticity, influence the course of our investigation. In a significant essay concerning the relationship between Judaism and Germany, Derrida gives focus to a key element of testing: the hypothesis. "The most fundamental determination, however, one which is to be found in Plato but has nevertheless been covered up and neglected throughout the renewals of Neoplatonism and the Renaissance, the one which founded idealism as a scientific project and a method, is the hypothesis, the concept of hypothesis."[21] Recasting the Platonic Idea, Cohen establishes a link between the Platonic concept of hypothesis and Kepler's astronomy and physics. Cohen's decision to zero in on the hypothesis provides a strategic opening, for it allows him to profile the German spirit in its becoming, situating its place as the moral consciousness of philosophy and science. Briefly, his reinterpretation of Platonic *logos, eidos,* and the *hypotheton* allows Cohen to newly appraise the Lutheran Reformation, opposing it to the French *Lumières,* which, unlike the *Aufklärung,* failed to oppose the Catholic Church. "In allying itself with critical science, with the hypothesis, with doubt, with the history of knowledge, with the putting-in-question of institutional authorities, and so on, 'the Reformation placed the German spirit at the center of world history.'"[22] Ushering in the German spirit, Cohen's critical tactic of foregrounding the hypothesis in Plato allows him to supplant the naïve ontology of the Idea in favor of its methodological and scientific interpretation: "For philosophical (that is, German) idealism must be a project of scientific philosophy: not science itself but philosophy as scientific (*wissenschaftlich*). Such is the answer to the question: 'What meaning (*welche Bedeutung*) does it have for the characterization of the German spirit that the idea should be known only as Being or as hypothesis?'"[23] Derrida reviews the implications of what he calls "a subtle wrinkle" in the meaning of Being.

According to Cohen, it is owing to the concept of hypothesis that Kepler was able to develop his astronomy and mechanics: "it is through Kepler that German thought was able to make out of the authentically scientific *idealism*, founded upon the Idea as hypothesis, the moving force of science."[24] The interpretation of the Idea as hypothesis is for Cohen an inaugural one that sets off another history of philosophy, another relatedness to Being: "Being is not grasped as an immediate datum – a prejudice on which sensualism is founded – but it is thought as a universal project, as a problem that scientific research must solve and whose reality it must prove. As hypothesis, the idea is then by no means the solution of the problem but only the exact definition of the problem itself."[25] Derrida links this move to the text of Husserl, which, when diagnosing the crisis of European sciences, defines the infinite task at hand. What Cohen proposes, under the rubric of hypothesis, is "indeed a determination of the idea as an opening to the infinite, and infinite task for 'philosophy as a rigorous science.'"[26] Let us review the pertinent passages in which Cohen states his position:

> Consequently, nor is it true a priori and in itself, still less is it the final truth; on the contrary, it must undergo the test of its own truth to be decided by this test alone.
>
> That is why, in order to designate this method of the idea, Plato used another expression: that of rendering account (*Rechenschaftsablegung*) (*logon didonai*).
>
> The idea (*Idea*) is so far from being synonymous with the concept

(*eidos* = *logos*) that it is only thanks to it and to the account it renders that the concept (*logos*) itself may be verified.[27]

The idea, dissociated from mere concept, will lead Cohen to Kant, whom he sees as having the closest affinity among existing philosophers with Judaism. Cohen puts an ethical demand on scientificity. Truth cannot be dogmatically asserted but must each time be ascertained, produce its own justification, "undergo the test of its own truth." Ontologically demoted, truth becomes secondary to itself, for only the test has the right to decide and approve the truth that must first submit itself. *Logos*, the concept, owes its authority to a still higher authority: that of the test. Thus the test inserts an irreversible ethical consciousness in scientific thought, allowing for a procedure that bears prodigious historical consequence: "One understands now what depth this truly authentic interpretation of idealism reveals and guarantees to the deontological consciousness of scientific thought. . . . This procedure is the prejudicial condition of any authentic science and, therefore, of any philosophy, any scientific fecundity; but for all that, it is no less the condition of any natural thought in life in general, as in the historical conduct of peoples."[28] The procedure described by Cohen and ascribed to the core of a vital ethical stance staves off all Dionysian or *Sturm und Drang* types of excess, leading instead to an exemplary sobriety with which he associates the classical apex of philosophical and scientific endeavor:

> This sober lucidity is the deep, true, meaning of German idealism, which has always been the mark both of its science and its philosophy in their classic productions.[29]

The demand for hypothesis, the induction of truth as testing, and the emphasis on science in *Deutschtum und Judentum* is, as Derrida points out, peculiarly Protestant or related to that which, in the protest movement that once described it, was capable of converting authority to its hypothetical genesis. Linked to the necessity of conversion, hypothesis and testing band together to undermine dogma. In spirit, then, the Reformation is the legitimate heir to Platonic hypotheticism, involving as it does "respect for the hypothesis, cult of the doubt, suspicion towards dogma (and if you prefer also towards *doxa*) and towards institutions based on dogma, a culture of interpretation but of a *free* interpretation, one which, in its spirit, at least, tends to liberate itself from any institutional authority."[30] Historically speaking, the Reformation installed a specific test site to the extent that it allowed nothing to stand as given or unchallenged. It required in principle a capacity for thoroughgoing conversion based on accountability. Things had to be justified, reexamined, questioned, and accounted for. Authority could no longer sustain itself absolutely but had to be submitted to review. "The Reformation wants to render an account and justify (*logon didonai*). It holds nothing as established, it submits everything to an examination. To render an account of, and to justify, the rendering of reason (*Rechenschaft*) and justification, this is the slogan (*Schlagwort*) of the Reformation. It is the exercise of the logos, of the *logon didonai,* or, in Latin, of the ratio, the *rationem reddere*."[31] Henceforth, justice and justification will be inextricably linked and made to answer for themselves by the insistent irritation of hypothetical testing.

On yet another level of reference and urgency, the test and its morph into the motif of testability stay lodged within the very possibility of justice. The empirical instances of testing call up poignant narratives and can have a bearing on everything from whom you'll go on a date with to proving your case after indictment. The falsely accused await the DNA test or its analogy in order to stand a chance of release. Theoretically, significant debate has been prompted by the question of the test's admissibility into a court of law. Recalling the dubious résumé of the professional gatekeeper in Kafka, the issue arises of whether a judge can be deemed an appropriate gatekeeper for scientific evidence. Science and law meet on philosophical grounds. The nature of the charged encounter grounds the cases of *Daubert v. Merrell Dow Pharmaceuticals, Inc.,*[32] which revolutionized scientific evidence law, and *Frye v. United States,*[33] which tries to determine what counts as an admissible subject of testimony by scientific experts. The case has attracted considerable interest, demonstrating, as noted by Bert Black et al., "the crucial role science plays in modern litigation."[34] The Daubert case pulled "twenty-two amicus briefs from over one hundred organizations and individuals and filled the Supreme Court to overflowing the day it was argued."[35] It has been considered "the most important case on the admissibility of scientific evidence."[36] In a substantial article that asserts the need for a philosophical understanding of the stakes at hand, Adina Schwartz argues that the Supreme Court's decision in *Daubert*, which she finds theoretically misguided, cannot be corrected simply by returning to the *Frye* standard. What is required, rather, is a thoroughly philosophical approach to the weighted issues in question. Facts, she reminds us, are theory-laden.[37] This is why law needs to have passed the prerequisite theory courses, especially where the evaluation of science is concerned. "While *Daubert v. Merrell Dow Pharmaceuticals, Inc.* revolutionized scientific evidence law, this decision was based on a fundamental misunderstanding of the history and philosophy of science."[38] The theoretical issue at hand is manifold and entails at least three major subdivisions: What is the relationship of law to science? Can a judge preside over scientific evidence without relying on scientific expertise? What constitutes scientific expertise? Based on philosophical axioms, the *Frye* case nonetheless exhibits vague notions of the relevant scientific community and "of general acceptance [that] has allowed judges to pay lip service to *Frye*, yet base admissibility decisions on their own substantive judgments and/or personal biases."[39] Schwartz's aim is to circumvent the surreptitious violation of *Frye*'s core dictate of judicial deference to scientists. Her critique interrogates *Daubert*'s unanimous holding that, as a matter of statutory interpretation, the Federal Rules of Evidence superseded *Frye*: "Under both *Daubert* and *Frye* a jury is permitted to hear proposed scientific testimony only if a judge determines beforehand that the testimony pertains to genuine science. Contrary to *Daubert*'s assumption that judges can make such determinations without deferring to scientists, the history and philosophy of science show that it is in principle impossible for judges, or anyone else outside the scientific community, to rationally decide whether science is being done."[40] Schwartz, for her part, establishes an exclusive scientific community by appealing to the extra-scientific discursive neighborhoods of history and philosophy. But I'm not going there – the deference that scientists require can be left to their negotiations with the judges whose capacity to determine the adequacy of a restricted number of utterances is being questioned. In order to bring some viable definition to these issues, Schwartz focuses on the problem of testability. She does so by way of a philosophical critique of falsifiability, namely, by critically reviewing Karl Popper's project.[41] Let us briefly follow her argument.

To gain momentum on her argument, Schwartz reminds us that Marxist and Freudian theories as well as the psychological theories of Alfred

Adler were the immediate targets of Popper's philosophy of science.[42] After World War I, many of Popper's fellow Viennese intellectuals welcomed these theories as genuine sciences. Ever the adversarial contender, Popper "concluded that each was more like a religion held by true believers and contrasted these pseudo-sciences with what he took to be the exemplary science: physics – in particular, the theory of relativity."[43] One of Popper's principal questions concerned "the problem of demarcation," what he saw as the primary task of epistemology.[44] A theory of knowledge should be able to answer: "When should a theory be ranked as scientific?" or, "Is there a criterion for the scientific character or status of a theory?"[45] Falsifiability provided Popper with a criterion, with a response to the problem of demarcation. Opposing other philosophers of the milieu, Popper offered that science cannot be distinguished from metaphysics or pseudo-science in terms of confirmation by experience or observations. "Rather, Popper claimed that the hallmark of a metaphysical theory – such as Marxism, psychoanalysis, or Adlerian psychology – is that it leaves its adherents free to transmute any seemingly refuting observation into a confirming instance."[46] Popper, who equated "falsifiability" with "refutability" or "testability," claimed that "not the verifiability but the falsifiability of a system is to be taken as a criterion of demarcation . . . it must be possible for an empirical scientific system to be refuted by experience."[47] Schwartz emphasizes that science for Popper "was supposed to be distinguished from pseudo-science by whether it was testable in theory, not by whether testing was technically possible or practically feasible, much less by whether actual testing had been done."[48] She proposes that *Daubert* stands on philosophically weak ground and cannot be used to supplant *Frye:* "In contrast, *Daubert's* discussion of whether a theory or technique 'can be (and has been) tested' is consistent both with a testability criterion and with the notion that actual testing must have occurred in order for a theory or technique to count as scientific. *Daubert's* ambiguity notwithstanding, a critique of testability suffices to establish the philosophical untenability of *Daubert's* alternative to *Frye.*"[49] She is cautious about allowing carelessly asserted distinctions to abide. Where Popper endeavored to "draw a clear line"[50] between them, Schwartz argues against the possibility of an "adequate, clean distinction between science and pseudo-science."[51] At this point I need to relinquish custody of the legal questions that confront us in order to focus on the philosophical points urged by Schwartz. As the relation of science to the law becomes more pressing, one of the principal areas of inquiry begins to concern the per-mutations of testing, whether empirically or theoretically based, and yet, as Schwartz has argued, the empiricalness of scientific suppositions can-not in any case stand alone. This is why it is necessary to be philosophi-cally aggressive with the law.

Schwartz's article does not limit itself to issues of statutory interpreta-tion but concerns legal enactments of scientific grammars and behaviors. She allows that the *Daubert* Court correctly interpreted the Federal Rules of Evidence; nevertheless, the *Daubert* standard relies on a "mythical con-ception of scientific activity."[52] Proposing a reconfigured understanding of scientific activity, "which should be adopted by both state and federal courts," she argues that the greatly maligned *Frye* standard "is grounded in fundamental philosophical insight" that, she suggests, ought to be pre-served.[53] *Daubert* imputes to judges the authority to determine whether expert testimony is genuinely scientific, that is, whether the scientific method was followed in elaborating the theory or technique at issue: "While *Daubert* suggests four factors that judges may appropriately con-sider in this determination, only one of the factors is plausible. The factor is the falsifiability criterion that the *Daubert* majority explicitly adopted from philosopher Sir Karl Popper: 'The criterion of the scientific status of a theory is its falsifiability, or refutability, or testability.'"[54] Schwartz, however, indicates that Popper's effort to fix an Archimedean standpoint from which to judge whether science is being done has been seriously undermined by subsequent philosophers and historians of science. One significant example would be that of philosopher Carl G. Hempel who in the early 1950s refuted the possibility of establishing the strict demarca-tions that Popper advocates. Despite its intuitive plausibility, the idea of testability, he offers, "can never be developed into an adequate criterion for distinguishing between science and pseudo-science."[55] Thus Hempel introduces the notion of "under-inclusiveness", which is used in order to show that no singular statement can be entirely falsified. The falsi-fiability criterion shares the same features and hence the same problem as those of the verifiability criterion. "The negation of any singular or exis-tential statement (e.g. 'there is at least one unicorn') is a universal state-ment ('there are no unicorns'). No matter how many conforming ob-servations are made of this universal statement, non-conforming events remain logically possible."[56] The falsifiability criterion is under-inclusive because "it excludes all singular statements from the class of empirically meaningful or scientific statements." There is yet another problem facing testability, regardless of whether or not it conforms to the figures of verifiability or falsifiability. Testability depends on a distinction between sentences that are to be tested and sentences that serve as the test. The works of Imre Lakatos and Hilary Putnam remind us that Hempel himself did not observe a strict separation between conditions of theory or fact, which means, among other things, that the sentences that are supposed to serve as the test are themselves in need of testing.[57] The conclusion drawn by Hempel concerning the fragility of that which does the testing is what we would like to hold on to as these investigations get under way. Hempel's critical observations indicate a need for consistent meta-testing, for putting the test to the test without at any given point relaxing any of the terms that allow for serious testing. The very apparatuses or sentences or signifiers that are said to administer the test and remain accountable for its constitution must themselves renounce a place of external stability in regard to testing. This inevitable complication designates yet another dimension of the policies of submission to which the test is theoretically bound.

The observations generated by Hempel and other commentators were called together in response to the criterion of falsifiability established by Popper. Yet the instabilities to which they point already exist in Popper's text, which relentlessly tests its asserted premises and thus in a sense "proves" Hempel's thesis on the inner margin of the work he questions. In this light another question emerges with the problems set up by Popper in Schwartz's legal brief. When Schwartz urges that Popper's work be viewed as discredited, she argues so with precise legal aim. Perhaps failing a text works well within a specified goal or limited framework – when one in fact avoids *reading*. Reading law may put the stop on reading, a lesson painstakingly taught by the lawyer Franz Kafka. In the interests of understanding the legal and theoretical debate around the question of testability, I would like to revert to Popper's text, if only to see how it defends itself even when discredited by a powerful legal brief. What, in any case, does it mean to dismiss a work – by which I mean a legitimately probing and self-critical articulation of thought?

In the context of *reading* or *citing* a work, whether or not one intends to instrumentalize its "content" for the purpose of meeting a stated aim, one still needs to consider the justice of dismissal, and whether it is truly possible to dismiss a genuine work, idea, or insight. One needs to interrogate the status of dismissive acts when they seek to annul significant theoretical work, as if one could successfully efface their uncontrolled borders and covert effects. Can thought, even when disrupted by its own rhetorical support systems or external review committees, be simply rendered nonviable? To be sure, Popper's invectives pose a number of problems that appear to call for outside intervention. Einstein himself wondered, in the case of a proposed imaginary experiment, whether Popper was not insisting too greatly on purity ("I have looked at your paper, and I largely [*weitgehend*] agree. Only I do not believe in the possibility of producing a 'super-pure case'").[58] A disagreement does not amount to a gesture of wholesale dismissal, however, and is fair game in the politics of scientific and philosophical inquiry.

Though on a fairly straightforward discursive level Popper stood his ground, there are moments in his work that are rich with ambiguity and seem to turn against his own legendary semantic severity. He had a penchant for ordering things in such a way as to exclude substantial domains of inquiry from science. This is not the place to go into the details of theoretical objections with which his work was met, nor even to ride above the rhetorical undertow of Popper's assertions, but I would like to point out a few instances pertinent to our discussion, if only to show how a text ineluctably submits itself to the uncompromising test of its stated premises. Testing may occur by means of the ironization or allegorization of the staked intention or textual assemblage, which is to say that significant pressure is put on scientific understanding by the positing feats of language. Many scientists and their historians tend to be impatient with the considerable burdens of linguistic positing, but they too revert to the lexicon of sentences, proposition, and statement in order to clarify the stakes at hand. Despite the outward displays of staged skirmishes and disputed principles, the overlapping fields concede the significance, if also the compulsory skittishness, of the linguistic acts on which they depend for their intricate elaborations and self-justifications. Let us take a brief look at the way Popper's problematic statements subvert and betray themselves by virtue of an internal testing mechanism.

The value of scientific argument no doubt transcends the materiality of what we call a paper, a report, or a book. Yet from the moment truth relinquishes its hold on substance or recedes from the metaphysical set, one has forfeited the rights that rely upon any such imputed transcendence. It may or may not matter to a scientist or philosopher, but the way an argument is constituted and bound by a book says something about its particular level of sense-making claims. No mark is as such simply irrelevant or marginal. Assuming that a book begins at the beginning – a falsifiable claim, but a common enough assumption – and that there is an implicit hierarchy of marks that have some bearing on what is to come and what is asserted in the rest of the book, then the way it presents itself is of some consequence. Let us consider how Popper opens his argument in one of his frequently cited works. The *Logic* is fronted by a quote from the Romantic poet and novelist Novalis. Allow a literary critic to contemplate this apparently innocuous fact. What is the fate of a scientific work prompted by a poetic word? Popper convokes Novalis at the opening. We need to wonder whether the quote reads and semantically engulfs the book or is read by the book to follow – how the fact of this quote corroborates or reroutes the major trajectories that the work proposes. A work on hypothetical thought, it is headed up by these words: "Hypotheses are nets: only he who casts will catch." This saying indicates the outer boundary to which the work is held. How would Popper situate such an initiatory utterance? Should it be located outside or inside the body of the text, at the core of its argument or on the sidelines, an ornament placed on the gateway, at the rim of the meaning it seeks to produce? How does it influence the flow of the purported inside or inner margin of asserted meaning? Does it perhaps belong to the playoffs between science and pseudo-science or is there yet another domain of scientific inquiry that supersedes or lags behind these crucial determinations?

In any case, the work, set on its way with a quote from Novalis, exhorts us to consider what it means to open the scientific interrogation with a poetic utterance. It tempts one to ask: Will poetry have been the ultimate authority, the meta-science, or merely an arbitrary punctuation mark? Even a punctuation mark can make or break an intended meaning, however. It is as if Popper were inching close to Nietzsche in the beginning, casting science near art. Yet who is casting and who is catching? Since Popper is known for catching pseudo-scientists in the act, it is peculiar that he should start out on his fishing expedition with this quote. Perhaps, more ironically cast, the appeal to the poets links Popper to Freud who turned, at crucial moments in the elaboration of his scientific demonstrations, to the validating prestige of Goethe. Thus the most authoritative scientific axioms are, in both these cases, cosigned by poetic insight. Since that signature lives on the edges of the work, framing and maintaining it, its power of assertion needs to be preserved. It is not as though one could simply peel off the poetic entry to the work, since this utterance, whether expected to remain sheerly ornamental or not, continues to effect its own community of meaning; this community unavoidably encroaches on the neighborhood of pure science. It is as though, from the get-go, Popper will have indicated a subversive layering to the reading prospectus of a work that replicates while shredding the ancient eviction notice for the pseudo or poetic figure that strains philosophical inquiry and faults scientific purity.

The second beginning to the book, a few pages later (the early pages are unnumbered) bears witness to this sentence:

> There is nothing more necessary to the man of science than its history, and the logic of discovery … the way error is detected, the use of hypothesis, of imagination, the mode of testing. – Lord Acton

OK, the "*man* of science." I'll let it slide. I will not move to send the malefactors under study to a political correctional facility. I am hardly the first to note the masculinist pulse of scientific habits. Let us stay with them, asking whether they are not necessary to the way science has been thought, and allow them to perform their own critique, perhaps provoking a crisis in the sphere of scientific self-understanding. What interests me in Popper's work at this juncture involves the relation of the logic of discovery to the mode of testing that Lord Acton favors. The relation to testing that holds sway in the *Logic*, though couched in appreciably different language than the usage made by Freud, shares some basic assumptions with psychoanalysis. Under a more philosophical light, it reflects the temporal insistence of the test advocated by Nietzsche and implemented in Freud. In fact, the critical attitude espoused by Popper would be comfortably accommodated by both presumed adversaries. Lord Acton sets the stage for evaluating the logic of discovery in terms that culminate with modes of testing. These terms are linked to error detection, hypothetical procedure, and the imagination, which weld scientific endeavor to the more poetically receptive faculties. Let us take a closer look at this mapping, which serves to orient Popper's chief discursive formations.

In the preface of 1959, Popper – taking on the neighboring language analysts (he chides them for ditching cosmology and for forgetting science's effort to understand the world) – equates the rational attitude with the critical attitude. Adjusting the coordinates supplied by Lord Acton, he puts the test drive into gear: "The point is that, whenever we propose a solution to a problem, we ought to try as hard as we can to overthrow our solution, rather than defend it. Few of us, unfortunately, practise this precept; but other people, fortunately, will supply the criticism for us if we fail to supply it ourselves."[59] The advocated scientific stance, then, involves the strength to try to overthrow rather than to establish the solution at which thought arrives. The point is to let go in good faith of the massive defense mechanisms that attend thought, to allow if not to provoke the dissolution of the solution, to affirmatively invite failure by losing the attachment to a solution made in service to a dogmatic principle. The witty Viennese philosopher makes it a point to remind us that if the individual does not engage the self-decimating operation, others will do it for us. The mutually destructive community of scientific discovery should incorporate the critical assault into its method. If these terms seem overly dramatic, they are derived from the nearly military strategic deployment of language that Popper's text sustains. His textual maneuvers involve defense buildup and the overthrow of a governing thought. He allows for guerilla raids made on presumed acquisitions, incessantly clearing the way, deposing and posing new regimens. Yet, in the end, the violent introject answers to a peaceful place. The necessity of attacking one's own solution to a problem comes from the communitarian aspect of thought, or, if this sounds like too much of a hippie scene suddenly descending on the grounds of Popper's logic, the fate of rational discussion depends on the endless calibration of the singular-plural, the shared nature of scientific work. Science has to remind itself of its shared predicament, of keeping the channels open and inviting the flow of communication – even, one might say, of a yet unrealized communism on which rational discussion thrives. It must vigilantly guard against the danger of autistic shutdown: "If we ignore what other people are thinking, or have thought in the past, then rational discussion must come to an end, though each of us may go on happily talking to himself. Some philosophers have made a virtue of talking to themselves; perhaps because they felt that there was nobody else worth talking to."[60] Popper advises that only God should occupy such an exalted monological speech realm: "No doubt God talks mainly to himself because he has no one worth talking to. But a philosopher should know that he is no more godlike than any other man."[61] It is noteworthy that Popper thinks that God is not talking to him, or to the devil, or that God even talks monologically (rather than just orders communities and the designated drivers of his word and world). God is the only experimenter, in any case, that is not bound by the communicative imperative espoused by Popper. To communicate is to be prepared to be overthrown. And even when one is overthrowing one's own solutions, this can occur only in terms of an incorporated community of others. Bound and beholden, one does not stand alone – there is no mystified privilege of a lone genius or soliloquizing discoverer here.

THE LITMUS TEST   Popper describes a scientist as a theorist or experimenter who puts forward statements, or systems of statements, and tests them step by step: "In the field of the empirical sciences, more particularly, he constructs hypotheses, or systems of theories, and tests them against experience by observation and experiments."[62] For the purpose of looping his argument back to the particulars of theoretical testing, it is useful to look at "Corroboration, or How a Theory Stands up to Tests" – a section that poses, among other things, a linguistic dilemma. Theories, contends Popper, are not verifiable but they can be "corroborated." Displaced and to a notable extent socialized, the degree of truth required for scientific viability is set to a different epistemic logic, one of tentative corroboration. Following probability logic, Popper recognizes that until now the whole problem concerning the probability of hypotheses has been misconceived: "Instead of discussing the 'probability' of a hypothesis we should try to assess what tests, what trials, it has withstood; that is, we should try to assess how far it has been able to prove its fitness to survive by standing up to tests. In brief, we should try to assess how far it has been 'corroborated.'"[63] In order to determine the survival of a hypothesis, he effects a shift from the projective tendencies of probability to the evaluative assessments of tests. Yet something distracts the course of an assertion; the disruption seems minor but soon enough bloats into a significant quandary. In a footnote Popper points out that Rudolf Carnap had translated his term "degree of corroboration" ("Grad der Bewährung"), which he had first introduced into the discussions of the Vienna Circle, as "degree of confirmation."[64] The term "degree of confirmation" became widely accepted. "I did not like this term because of some of its associations ('make firm'; 'establish firmly'; 'put beyond doubt'; 'prove'; 'verify': 'to confirm' corresponds more closely to *erhärten* or *bestätigen* than to *bewähren*')." The translation risked hardening the confirming moment into a concept and overstated the commitment to a final result, a definitive outcome. After consulting with a fellow professor, Popper proposed in a letter to Carnap to use instead the word "corroboration." "But as Carnap declined my proposal, I fell in with his usage, thinking that words do not matter. This is why I myself used the term 'confirmation' for a time in a number of my publications."[65] He soon rues his decision to capitulate to his colleague's linguistic tyranny and to "take words so lightly."[66] Popper realizes that he was in error because words, it would seem, do matter: "Yet it turned out that I was mistaken: the associations of the word 'confirmation' did matter, unfortunately, and made themselves felt."[67] The irony of the dilemma is not slight, for Popper had tilted and prefaced his book so as to undermine the overemphasis placed on words by the language analysts. The characters from across the linguistic street, being so concerned about language, do not pay sufficient attention to the growth of scientific knowledge. In this marginal pocket of his own elaboration, we see how scientific knowledge has been compromised by under-emphasis in terms of language usage. One wrong word can put a dent into the whole enterprise and stunt scientific growth. For his part, Popper had introduced the terms "corroboration" and especially "degree of corroboration" because he wanted a "*neutral* term to describe the degree to which a hypothesis has stood up to severe tests, and thus 'proved its mettle.'"[68] In corroboration, hypothesis takes more of a beating and must continually stand up for itself without the support of substantial safeguards: hypothesis must dispense with the hint of finality that is reserved for confirmation.

Hypotheses bear a relation to law; at the same time they depend on the provisional status of verification. The scientist is ever on the verge of being busted, detained, or taken over. Popper makes a point worth noting when he addresses himself to the so-called verification of hypotheses:

"the fact that theories may not only be improved but that they can also be *falsified by new experiments* presents to the scientist a serious possibility which may at any moment become actual."[69] Opting for the immutability of natural processes or the "principle of the uniformity of nature," his predilection for purity comes to the fore once again, "but never yet has a theory had to be regarded as falsified owing to the sudden breakdown of a well-confirmed law. It never happens that old experiments yield new results. What happens is only that new experiments decide against old theory. The old theory, even when it is superseded, often retains its validity as a kind of limiting case of the new theory."[70] Hence the emphasis in Popper's elaboration on the domain of the experiment and the grammar of testing. While new experiments will decide the fate of a given theory, their edges are determined by the rule of law to which they are subjected. It seems as though, throughout the argument, Popper were bent on safeguarding law, keeping it free from the implications of experimental incursions and restricting the degree of mutual destructiveness that the experiment could initiate. The question arises of whether laws have free range at all times and would not be taken down or seriously fractured by the explosive mobilities of new experiments. The laws of physics seem immutable and hypotheses, as Husserl noted, do not themselves simply vaporize with proof or refutation. Still, Popper relies significantly on metaphysical, if not pseudo-scientific structures, in order to drive his point home. Like Nietzsche he pits science against metaphysics, yet he runs home to mommy metaphysics in order to keep the existential horizon intact or – this may seem paradoxical but it's not – he runs to mommy in order to assure the sovereignty of paternal law. Though Popper often rails against metaphysical presuppositions, in this slippery phase of his thought he avows faith in (rather than knowledge of) the prime backing – that of metaphysical support. The above argument, he writes, "expresses the metaphysical faith in the existence of regularities in our world (a faith which I share, and without which practical action is hardly conceivable)."[71] At the very moment he tries to impose law, he slips up; when the law comes down, it exposes the ground of sheer scientificity to be rooted in faith and metaphysics. Surely language analysis would have provided more muscle.

Perhaps Popper's boldest statements, and those most relevant to this study, occur when he demarcates the space of scientific discovery. Writing of the epistemological aspects proper to it, Popper asserts what science is not. In a Goethean manner, Popper is able to see that even though science cannot attain to truth or its substitutes, the scientific urge is driven by a desire to know, by what Faust and Popper recognize as *striving* – a disposition that is independent of results and irresponsible, in an affirmative way, to its origin.

> Science is not a system of certain, or well-established, statements; nor is it a system which steadily advances toward a state of finality. Our science is not knowledge (*epistēmē*): it can never claim to have attained truth, or even a substitute for it, such as probability.
>
> Yet science has more than mere biological survival value. It is not only a useful instrument. Although it can attain neither truth nor probability, the striving for knowledge and the search for truth are still the strongest motives of scientific discovery. We do not know: we can only guess. And our guesses are guided by the unscientific, the metaphysical (though biologically explicable) faith in laws, in regularities which we can uncover – discover.[72]

Popper practices the labor of the negative, stating steadily what science is not. He puts the drive in reverse when seeking nearly psychologistic motivation for the thereness of regularities. What science refers us to is the perpetual motion of a striving that takes off from metaphysical faith, from the restless probes of the unscientific propulsion. Unlike his designated nemeses – psychoanalysis, Marxism, language analysis – Popper does not struggle with the metaphysical foundations of thought or the signifying limits that bind the scientific space of articulation. He does not take the leap of faith outside of faith but ventures more of a jump that lands where it started. "We do not know: we can only guess." Faith in laws is now amended to include a biological component motored by metaphysics. It is as though we were biologically prodded to assert metaphysical faith. Contemporary science is rooted in the kind of guesswork described by Bacon, consisting of "anticipations, rash and premature," and of "prejudices."[73] Despite his asserted advances, Popper's recovery of Bacon's "*anticipatio*" makes it perform according to valences that continue to be similar in tenor to those held by Bacon.[74] Both Bacon and Popper prepare scientific thought with purges and cleansing activities so that the work to come can attain an ascertainable level of purity. For Bacon, the mind has to be purged of anticipations, idols, and prejudices before it can apply itself to an untainted reading of nature. Thus, to prepare the mind for "the intuition of the true *essence* or *nature* of a thing, it has to be meticulously cleansed of all anticipations. . . . For the source of all error is the impurity of our own minds."[75] Bacon's "anticipation" means "almost the same as 'hypothesis' (in my usage)."[76] The primary function of eliminative induction is (as with Aristotle) to assist in the purification of the mind. Purging the mind of prejudices is viewed by Bacon as a kind of ritual, a letting go and meditation prescribed for the scientist who wants to approach the Book of Nature. Naturally, Popper is drawn to the purification ritual in which his own work is quietly invested in order to dissolve the stubborn dimension of precomprehension that informs the scientific gaze. Yet on the loudspeaker he is perhaps less obsessional than Bacon – that is, he proves to be more tentative, more probing, and even, anticipating Nietzsche, more free-spirited. He can afford to move about more freely than Bacon, whom he admires and translates in his own way (anticipation = hypothesis), because he can rely on a lucid form of control, something linked to sobriety. Thus what brings the logic of scientific discovery to a level of sustained sobriety is the test, which comes equipped with its very own recovery program:

> But these marvelously imaginative and bold conjectures or "anticipations" of ours are carefully and soberly controlled by systematic tests. Once put forward, none of our "anticipations" are dogmatically upheld. Our method of research is not to defend them, in order to prove how right we were. On the contrary, we try to overthrow them. Using all the weapons of our logical, mathematical, and technical armoury, we try to prove that our anticipations were false – in order to put forward in their stead, new unjustified and unjustifiable anticipations, new "rash and premature prejudices," as Bacon derisively called them.[77]

The test allows for the maximum freedom of scientific venturing and invites, within its borders, the free play of wholly unjustifiable conjecture. The test promotes incessant field days for the riotous or tentative spin of an unjustifiable conceptual urge. At the same time it serves the function of reality principle to science's pleasure principle, limiting and ordering the possible as it answers the call of the impossible. With Popper's marked usage of such terms as the "unjustified" and "unjustifiable," we sense that science wants to stake out for itself a domain of activity that need not respond to the exigencies of justifiability. The related theme of justice derives from the subterranean semantics of Popper's elaboration. In terms of a politics and ethics of scientific striving – something prompted by Mephistophelean instigation – what turns out to contain the necessarily excessive movement of prejudice and the unjustifiable, what overthrows these excesses in the end, is apparently the test. The test functions at once as a free zone and a regulator, an instance of merciful law.

One level of ethicity that is neither broached by Popper nor subjected to a fracturing semantics involves the play of gender. In a somewhat defensive move, the scientific philosopher justifies what turns out to be the aggression of unjustified anticipations and speculative thought. Nature is cast in the feminine ("Bold ideas, unjustified anticipations, and speculative thought, are our only means for interpreting nature: our only organon, our only instrument, for grasping her. And we must hazard them to win our prize").[78] The projective metaphysics of a veiled Nature from whom a truth must be pulled is old news by now. But the inevitable molestation of the recalcitrant force field – Nature or the Book of Nature – is what in the end comes under the dominion and is in a certain way resisted by the test. Although this system of testing requires the violence of which it is also a critique, it consistently puts the intrusive scientist in his proper place, throwing him off, that is, and unseating him as he thrones on momentary certitudes. If he wants to be counted in, the true scientist must be willing to be discounted and cut down to size, ever and again. The point is that a true scientist must be willing to hazard refutation, to be exposed and rebuffed or to "not take part in the scientific game."[79] Testing and intrusively probing, he is himself put down by the test that shows a guarded complicity with a femininely marked Nature. If testing is the basic organon of the scientist – and not only an intermediary step of investigation – he not only seeks to control nature by testing but is himself incessantly controlled by it.

In the final analysis Popper comes down on the side of the tentative affirmation. Even so, he can have it both ways, since there is no inherent threat hovering on the horizon of his observations. The risk-taking advocated by him is not absolute owing to the fact that in the end something vital is held together by the test. The test here guarantees a grounding, however friable or tentative. Testing diverges here from its Nietzschean facet, where it implicates explosive and nonrecuperable loss, a destruction without recovery. Popper, on the contrary, pulls back from the extremist insight exploited by Nietzsche. On the side of the tentative, Popper nonetheless hangs on to the solidity of the test, its capacity to renew and revitalize itself and above all to guarantee a kind of metaphysical permanence or, at least, continually to reaffirm the Goethean "Dauer im Wechsel," establishing time and again the permanence residing within mutability. Reading into the twilight of the epistemological idols, Popper concludes:

The old scientific ideal of *epistēmē* – of absolutely certain, demonstrable knowledge – has proved to be an old idol. The demand for scientific objectivity makes it inevitable that every scientific statement must remain tentative for ever. It may indeed be corroborated, but every corroboration is relative to other statements which, again, are tentative. Only in our subjective experiences of conviction, in our subjective faith, can we be "absolutely certain."

With the idol of certainty (including degrees of imperfect certainty or probability) there falls one of the defences of obscurantism which bar the way of scientific advance. For the worship of this idol hampers not only the boldness of our questions, but also the rigour and integrity of our tests. The wrong view of science betrays itself in the craving to be right; for it is not his possession of knowledge, of irrefutable truth, that makes the man of science, but his persistent and recklessly critical quest for truth. . . . Science never pursues the illusory aim of making its answers final, or even probable. Its advance is, rather, towards an infinite yet attainable aim: that of ever discovering new, deeper, and more general problems, and of subjecting our ever tentative answers to ever renewed and ever more rigorous tests.[80]

There is much to appreciate and retain in Popper's observations. Every scientific statement must relinquish its hope for permanence or its craving to be right – a narcissistic crisis for the scientific ego. Resisting closure, science disrupts its own narcissistic aim, frustrates and interrupts itself, refusing to settle into a fixed place. Even probability has to be given up as a subsidiary branch of truth or its purported temporality. Every answer remains tentative and calls for "ever more rigorous tests." Popper goes very far, careful not to exceed the limits he has faithfully established. The test is posed as the answer to the answer, as meta-answer, and is never considered from the angle of a possible collapse. In other words, the test, on which Popper's understanding of scientificity is based, is never itself interrogated. Or if it does indicate specific functional variations in his usage (where words do and do not matter depending on where he's aiming), the test is perhaps not ambiguated enough or viewed in terms of its inherent fragility.

In the same breath Popper proves able to invoke the "boldness" and "reckless critical" disposition of the essential scientist and offer these traits as a stabilizing force. In response to Popper, I have a few questions. Can the test be conceptually contained? Can it serve reliably to fix the limit and situate the law? Does it belong to what Nietzsche would designate as the Apollonian domain of existence? Even where Popper indicates sobriety, he inadvertently allows for the quick encroachment of imagination, the overflow of inspiration, or a sudden surge of unrestrained speculative ideas. So how sober is sober and who's taking the breathalyzer (another test)? I suppose my main question concerns the safe deployment of recklessness that Popper's argument unflinchingly advances. Ever since Walter Benjamin, and Nietzsche before him, one cannot assume that the reckless critical stab will draw no blood or fail to subvert itself, bringing down the whole house of science. Somehow, tentative is not tentative enough in Popper. The remaining question at this point is, Why doesn't he consider the dark side of these heroics? Allergic to psychoanalysis and to those who are felled by the subtle intricacies of language, Popper resists *reading* his own insights. The disturbing implications of striving, quest, and craving that Goethe problematized and Popper simply takes over – without the static – limit the scope of his otherwise outstanding inquiry. There is no down or dark side to scientific striving, no posthumanist defect to be anticipated. Not a trace of the humanist demons that haunt the scientific project. Science remains prepolitical, prepsychotic, one might say, and nonhostile, a safe place for human endeavor. As it stands, the test in Popper, a scientific guarantor of paramount importance, is posed as a successful restraint, as a good breast in a discursive world that has not heard of the rumored diffusion of effects of the bad breast – the other breast that (since at least the earthquake of Lisbon that made Kant tremble) Nature proffers.

Prototype B

Test Tube Grammatology

Popper was not the only one. Practicing avoidance strategies with regard to his own uninterrogated object, Popper projected subtle turbulence and massive inadequacy on the competition, on the neighboring scientists of Vienna. But let us move on, beyond the projection booth, to the extent that such a move is possible. In philosophy as in science, testing is inextricably linked to the experimental disposition. Having established some general theoretical parameters in which to situate the test drive, I want briefly to look more closely at the unfolding scene of the experiment – a scene strongly endowed by the narratives of scientific practice. An examination of experimental systems will allow us to follow the particulars of Bacon's *anticipatio* and Popper's understanding of hypothesis, inviting us to ask further, What constitutes a scientific object? I also want to underscore the extent to which fiction, narrative contingency, and *différance* inform the experimental effort. The experiment, too, is a Saying, a stammer that trails behind the telling of story: "Typically, an experimental system contains *more stories* than the experimenter at a given moment is trying to tell with it."[81] Thus a footnote appears to upend a significant story that is winding down by telling the tale of its own excess. The tale recounts the following adventure: a transfer RNA has remained an intermediate in the metabolic chain of protein synthesis; however, it finds itself marginalized by becoming the molecule that *translates* genetic information into protein function. The suspense is heart-stirring. Hans-Jörg Rheinberger has traced the implementation, between 1947 and 1954, of an *in vitro* system of protein synthesis at the medical laboratories of the Collis P. Huntington Memorial Hospital of Harvard University, Massachusetts General Hospital. His work, *Experiment, Difference, and Writing*, helps to consolidate a number of points that I want to emphasize and pursue. For his part, Rheinberger follows the experimental drama, and its attendant peripeteias, of protein synthesis; in so doing, he pulls on some of the threads that hold together the fabric of codified scientific investigation. He starts at the beginning of an exploratory investigation that might take place in any lab. Questioning what it means when we say that something is "in the air," or the significance of a "discovery" that has a collective starting point, he points to the peculiar status of the scientific object, what he chooses to call the "epistemic thing." Even where the scientific object exhibits elements of a physical structure – a chemical reaction, a biological function whose elucidation is at the center of the investigative effort – its nature is elusive. The scientific object at no point has the character of a presence that could be fixed from the beginning; "it represents itself in a characteristic, irreducible vagueness, which is inevitable since it translates the fact that one does not exactly know what one is looking for."[82] Rheinberger cites Derrida's thinking of *différance* for the purpose of interpreting the experimental scene, its essential graphematic structure, or what he also calls "experimental *écriture*." Part of an inscription apparatus, experimental *écriture* impugns simple oppositions such as those that tend to hold sway in philosophies and histories of science which assume strict divisions between theory and praxis, object and inscription, or representation and inscription. Concerning the assumed fixity of the scientific object, he writes that it "has the precarious status of being, in a way, absent in its experimental presence."[83] It is not as though the object had to be lured from a hiding place, that it is merely veiled or concealed "and could be brought to the fore through sophisticated manipulations. On the contrary, as an *epistemic* thing, it is yet in the process of becoming materially defined."[84] Having no autonomous existence as such, the object is not detachable, independent, or precedent to experimental activity: "It is the process of setting up the experimental system that constitutes the scientific object: it is not given from the beginning."[85]

Monopolized by non-presence, the experimental system runs on deferral and the unpreventable emptying of its object. In a manner recalling some of Gaston Bachelard's formulations, the experimental system is seen as having a double rapport to its productive potentials to the extent that it simultaneously exhibits both possibilities and obstacles. Bachelard introduced the notion of "epistemological obstacle" in order to fix the inherent resistance to immediacy in the scene of the experiment, to drive a wedge into what we think the scene can yield materially. Such resistance, slow-going and given to stagnation, put a drag in the pace of the scientist's knowledge-gathering intensities: "this is neither to consider external obstacles such as the complexity and fugacity of the phenomena nor to incriminate the weakness of the senses and the human mind: it is in the act of getting knowledge itself, intimately, that slowness and troubles appear in a kind of functional necessity. It is here that we will show causes of stagnation and even regression, it is here that we will reveal causes of inertia, which we will call epistemological obstacles. The act of obtaining knowledge of the real is a light that always somewhere casts shadows. It is never immediate and plain."[86] In *The New Scientific Spirit,*[87] Bachelard considers the "scientific real" or what Rheinberger calls "the scientific object" or "the epistemic thing," which he relates to graphematic activity, as consisting in "a noumenal context suitable for defining the axes of experimentation."[88] Enlarging the scope of what throws itself in the way of epistemological momentum, Rheinberger suggests that language itself may "present itself as an *obstacle* to what is going to be expressed," limiting and containing what can be discovered or known.[89] In this way he offers a response to some of the reigning views – expressed in this investigation by Popper as well as Hempel – that characteristically leave the unpredictable quality of linguistic positing out of the range of experimental activity.

Rheinberger considers specific temporal capacities in the different qualities of experimental research. He espouses a view of the research system and its formal dynamics as a "future-generating machine," and as a "tracing-game" – something that he links to Derrida's invention of differance as "a strategy without finality: one could call this blind tactics, empirical probing."[90] A research experiment is a device, according to Rheinberger, that brings forth something unknown – "in fact, something which does not even exist in the form in which it is going to be produced. What makes it a research experiment and not simply a trial is that the unknown is brought forward under conditions which allow its identification as something *new* with respect to a piece of already-modeled nature, the latter being implemented in the technical tools and used to set up the experimental system."[91] The trial works with what is known and continues to be bound to the experimental storehouse of knowledge as well as its intentionality. A research experiment, like that which exceeds even the familiar contours of monstrosity, contains the threat of pure imminence; it belongs to the future of its elaboration and, being wed to novelty, cannot be said to fall on this or that side of a divide determining good or evil, usefulness or harm, and so on. Ever on the verge of becoming something, and ready to assume an identity that could be tagged, taxonomized, sectioned, it looms in the hybrid form of the threat-and-promise. When designating the marked relation to the future of experimental research, Rheinberger might have sought corroboration in Derrida's thought on the invention of the other, on the techno-epistemo-anthropocentric value of invention, and the complexities involved in instituting that which can be established as "new." An invention, Derrida argues here, always presupposes some degree of illegality; its advent breaches an implicit contract and introduces disorder into the peaceful ordering of things. While invention traditionally anchors its discovery in natural disclosure – Popper's logic of discovering and uncovering – it disappoints the variously proclaimed complicities with nature (or with Bacon's Book of Nature): there is no such thing as a natural invention, though the term "invention" stubbornly supposes originarity, originality, generation, genealogy, engenderment – all values that one tends to attribute to geniality and therefore to naturality.[92]

Though not explicitly stated, Rheinberger's work rejoins Derrida's work on the inherent threats of performativity, since he is at pains to show that destabilization informs the very concept of "results." Experimentality resists its own totalization, even when it appears to arrive at an asserted conclusion. Though not invested in questioning the systematicity of the system he analyzes, Rheinberger by the same token does not allow system to close in on itself but understands it as a kind of limitless finity. In the chapter titled "Reproduction and Difference," he establishes the experimental system that investigates the scientific object as "an inherently open and unfinished structure."[93] The experimenter, at once blinded and guided by the labyrinthine experimental system, may end up conceptually blindsided when a surprising result has emerged and has been sufficiently stabilized; at such a juncture "it is difficult to avoid the illusion of a logic of thought and even a teleology of the experimental process."[94] Rheinberger stands his ground. He discourages the all too typical scientific closing ceremonies or philosophical rescue missions in which the experiment terminates: to the extent possible, he allows for no conceptual or metaphysically laden relapses. Even when a result is obtained, the case cannot be closed or made to coincide with a guided teleological project. With regard to the differential reproduction of an experimental system, he confirms that "one never knows exactly where it leads. As soon as one knows exactly what it produces it is no longer a research system."[95] In order to back up the unclosing system, Rheinberger takes recourse to art. Nietzsche's collaborative effort reemerges when science makes a vivid appeal to art, to the affirmation of illusion that art invites. Art gives science permission, a license that has since been revoked. Invoking a kind of willed blindness, the work of the experimenter resembles the trial of the artist who, according to George Kubler, works in the dark, "following the vein and hoping for a bonanza, and fearing that the lode may play out tomorrow."[96] The result, argues Rheinberger, is "not a final scientific statement, it is a piece of work to be fitted into the puzzle that usually does not even have a position foreseen for it."[97] Room must be made for the unexpected burble, for that which would jump the code with which the experiment had reckoned: "An experimental system which slowly becomes defined, in the sense that certain signals can be managed reproducibly, at the same time *must* create a space for the emergence of new signals. While becoming stabilized in a certain respect, it may be destabilized in another. For arriving at new 'results,' the system must be destabilized. Stabilization and destabilization imply each other."[98] Still, a balance must be reached, since sheer anarchic readiness will not enable the movement of the experiment to be read or recognized. There has to be a locatable trace, reliably suited to marshal even the most unexpected emergence. To assure a productive outcome, the experimental arrangement "must be sufficiently open to shape its signals and to become infiltrated by techniques, instruments, model compounds and so on. At the same time it must be sufficiently closed to prevent a breakdown of its reproductive coherence. If it is too rigid, it is no longer a machine to produce future; it becomes a device for testing in the sense of producing standards or replicas. It loses its function as a research tool."[99] The internal cleave of testing needs to be observed if the experimental site is to overcome its plausible lapse into confirmations of mere constative, standardized modalities of testing. In the laboratory, then, a balance has to be struck between the so-called performative and constative dimensions of the regime of testing, allowing for both potentialities to play themselves out and keep themselves in check, even when they overrun their assigned boundaries and purposive limits: "An experimental system must be fluid enough to allow for *unprecedented events,* but stable enough to allow them to be recognized."[100]

Though consistently attracted to leakage from the presumed outside, the lab must evacuate "Nature" from its premises. Nature, which has played such a preeminent role in scientific history and thought, must henceforth be held at bay and critically calmed from raging through the scientific work site. Nature cannot serve as reference for the experimental system, at least not in an unrestrained way. The work of Paul de Man helps us see how a tendency toward referential authority is unavoidably short-circuited: in the claustrophobic world of the laboratory, there is a Proustian craving for the fresh air of exteriority and reference. One's grandmother is always trying to send one out into nature, away from the stifling enclosures of the reading and work spaces. Or at least, one should open the windows and let nature in. However, the scientist, like Marcel, must ignore grandmother's call when heeding the material demand of a textual space: "Nature as such is not a reference point for the experiment; it is even a *danger*. It counteracts the scientific endeavor. It is a constant threat of intrusion. If nature is fractionated, unfractionated nature has to be excluded from the space of representation. If one works with an *in vitro* system, every whole cell therein tends to behave as an artifact, a 'whole cell artifact' as Zamecnik once called it, and one must not contaminate an *in vitro* experience with 'nature.'"[101] The reference point of any controlled system can be "nothing else but another controlled system. The reference point of a model can be nothing else but another model. It is impossible to go behind a 'signifying chain.'"[102] Lab culture practices a politics of citationality without origin. Models generate their own systems of meaning upon which further investigations are based. Advocating the case for a material, textual structure of the experimental stage, Rheinberger focuses his thought throughout on a system or process that "is not straightforward, it has no *a priori* finality, or direction."[103] Without a previously established end goal to guarantee a fixed itinerary, the system or process is submitted rather to all the "*tâtonnements*" that François Jacob designates as "the abortive trials, the failed experiments, the false starts, the misguided attempts" of the experimental process.[104] The only guide offering clues and direction, urging starting points and returns, is supplied according to Rheinberger by the method itself, the "*Verfahrungsart selbst.*" In a maneuver cherished by deconstructionists, Rheinberger performs what he states. When he establishes method as that which implements its own system of reference, he disrupts the assumptions that allow for Nature as signifier: offering a scientific-textual linkage, Rheinberger cites neither natural nor phenomenological observation – nor, for that matter, a naturalized experience – but Goethe's essay on the Experiment, which concludes with the belief that "the method itself will fix the bounds to which [imagination and wit] must return."[105] Rheinberger himself leans on a prior text in order to impress the material complexities of observation and lab culture.

Method, seen as constitutive by Goethe, contributes to the *making* of the object, which does not stand alone or prior to the execution of the system. An experimental system produces a representational space for things that otherwise cannot be grasped as scientific objects. Biochemical representation serves as an example when it creates an extra-cellular space for processes normally running within cells. Rather than representing what is going on "out there in nature," the model invents a trace by zeroing in on what goes on within a cell: "You only know what [goes on within a cell] when you have a model of it. That means, 'Nature itself' only becomes 'real,' in scientific and technical perspective as a model. And so, also, '*in vivo* experiments' are model systems. There is no absolute point of reference for what becomes involved in the game of representation. The very necessity of representation implies that any possibility of any immediate evidence is excluded. So, what is to be modeled becomes displaced and unfolded into *different* experimental systems."[106] With reference suspended, it becomes necessary to investigate the rhetorical dimension of the experimental elaboration, the levels of fictioning, allegorization, and noncoincidence of sign and signified that lab culture can tolerate.

LAUNCH PROBE   It is not a matter of externally inflamed invasiveness. Science itself invites us to read the scene of experimentation, its fractured promises and articulated procedures, the historical renewals, stalls, or question marks that the experimental disposition has generated. Often we are encouraged to seek answers, provisional or regulative, in terms that have been traditionally reserved for literary theory or quarantined in a theory of signification. But there are also conceptual tendencies, largely unchallenged, that encourage critical prodding. Whether we are canvassing the internal seams of scientific grammars or scanning effects of decisive drafts that describe an outer domain of signification, the way science produces hierarchical schemas affects every walk, or stumble, of life. What is it that links the recondite behaviors of lab culture to drug experimentation, experimental theater, thought experiments, or what Nietzsche floats as the pervasiveness of an experimental disposition? Is the imbricated fate of the shared signifier a mere coincidence or does it betoken a more serious aggravation of contaminative and communicative adaptations? The way we observe science tilts the field of inquiry but also decides values.

There exists a temptation to view the history of science in terms of a history of "experimental events." Bruno Latour states that "an experiment is an event," meaning, more or less, that it is productive of a situation that did not exist prior to the event.[107] For his part Rheinberger gauges the history of early test-tube representation as *soluble* RNA from a biomedical, bioenergetical, and biochemical research background in order to assess those steps in the production process that intended to exemplify "a more general concept of how the history of science can be set in perspective as a history of 'experimental events.'"[108] From what I can gather, the concept of experiment and its tie-in to testing constitute a major trend in the plot lines of scientific history. From a theoretical perspective one can understand why this is so. But because in any event it is viewed as so being, it warrants philosophical attention – regardless of whether such a determined focus is in the end justified or not. Still, one might look to the contributions of Evelyn Fox Keller, Donna Haraway, and a number of other scientific and theoretical investigators, including Rheinberger himself, to ask about what gets excluded in this recording – what kind of noise factors, impurities, contaminations are left out by the translating machine and the peculiar will to representation that is tied to the epistemic dominance of the experiment. What about the nonevents, those elements and traces that border on the margins of the experimental disposition? (In Derrida the event falls under the heading of nonevent, an aggravation of the Heideggerian *Ereignis,* designating that which cannot be grasped or seen in its appropriation.) In order to understand what may have been occluded when experimentation developed into a master narrative and invaded the lexica of thought, one first needs to review, without resentment, presupposition, or ulterior motive, its unstoppable movements and surprising trajectories.

So. Where does that leave us? Beyond the wish to explore the limits of "experiment" as the master story of the history of science and its philosophical implications, something entirely different comes into play. This work originally grew out of a study devoted to Alan Turing. I intended to show the growth spurts that led from Turing's test to a more general consideration of acts of testing. Nietzsche brought the philosophical question mark to the table of contents, and Husserl provided the vocabulary by which to measure scientific shock waves for a surrounding world (*Umwelt*). Derrida, of course, with his sense of aporia, testimony, and performative tear ups, was and is my training camp. Hence the emphasis on instabilities and indeterminabilities of permanence and substance, essence and existence, as well as on the turnarounds of truth with which the scientist contends. As it got going, the project evolved and Turing more or less fell off, like a rocket booster that separates from the core craft after takeoff. I had done the work, engaged the research. It all began, I think, in conversation late one night with the German techno-theorist Friedrich Kittler. Pynchon and Turing were his main obsessions way back when. Possibly still today. (No, I am told, today it's the ancient Greeks. . . . Anyway, that is what I understood after sharing a bottle of scotch whiskey with Kittler. A real philosophical starting point.) The whiskey aside, I do not want to join the sober ranks of a group psychology that have allowed for the forgetting of Alan Turing.

This name covers a considerable expanse. Dubbing the well-known Turing Test – which hinges on a machinic capacity to determine sexual difference – it forms a part of the history of the digital computer; it is linked to the emergence of AI; it labels the first chess-playing program called "Turochamp," and is diffused among other dreams of electronic *écriture*. Turing, at one time, for a time, was the Man. He decoded the Enigma along with Polish cryptanalysts: he messed up the Germans in WWII. The chances of cracking the U-boat Enigma had been, according to his own calculations, fifty-thousand-to-one against. The British analysts made sixty sets of perforated sheets "that were required for the first 'female' method – now swollen to a colossal task of examining a million rotor settings."[109] He cracked the code and turned the tide, determining the outcome of the war. Turing is not an obscure figure; it's not as though he was deep-sixed, but his name has not achieved the stature that is owed it, and he should by all rights be up there with his contemporaries and friends: he should be as imposing as Wittgenstein, as inexorable as Einstein, and as decisive as Gödel.

With a few notable exceptions, relatively little has been written about him, which is what prompted his mother, Sara, to devote a study to her exceptional son.[110] It is as if we were witnessing a return or reversion of Abrahamic sacrifice, as if Sarah were to have written about the ambiguously sacrificed son, Isaac. His story is vaguely disseminated, rewritten, and erased; it has taken on the qualities of the name of the thing with which he had historically contended: enigma. Diffused and disseminated, he is also everywhere. Alan makes a morphed appearance in William Gibson's novel in the form of the Turing Police. In the domain of the *Neuromancer,* all AIs must be listed in something called the Turing Registry, and their activities are tagged and monitored by an international Turing Police. The play by Hugh Whitemore, *Breaking the Code,* based on the book by Andrew Hodges, has him explaining one of his significant papers, "On Computable Numbers, with an Application to the *Entscheidungsproblem.*"[111] The decision problem involves three basic expectations of mathematics, recalling the line Bertrand Russell took in *Principia Mathematica.* The way Turing approaches the problem turns up in different, often disguised forms in this work, so it may be worth noting here, remembering as well that Turing associates his theorem with *beauty.*

Turing states that if there is to be any fundamental system for mathematics it must satisfy three requirements: consistency, completeness, and decidability. Decidability means that some method must exist, some definite procedure or test, which can be applied to any mathematical statement and which will determine whether or not that statement is provable. "[David] Hilbert thought this was a very reasonable set of requirements to impose; Kurt Gödel showed that no system for mathematics could be both consistent and complete. He did this by constructing a mathematical assertion that said – in effect: 'This assertion cannot be proved.' A classic paradox. 'This assertion cannot be proved.' Well, either it can or it can't. If it can be proved, we have a contradiction; which means that the system is complete. If it cannot be proved, then the assertion is true – but it can't be proved; which means that the system is complete. Thus mathematics is either inconsistent or incomplete. It's a beautiful theorem, quite beautiful. I think Gödel's theorem is the most beautiful thing I know. But the question of decidability was still unresolved. . . . In my paper 'On Computable Numbers' I wanted to show that there can be no one method that will work for all questions."[112] Proof and truth come to blows in this elaboration, splintering metaphysical assumptions that can no longer be called upon to resolve issues of decidability. With Turing, method starts on its necessarily fracturing path.

In his work, Kittler has pointed out that WWII was in many ways a computer war, a contest of computing faculties, and was decided, in the end, by the one who topped the computer heads.[113] There is another front on which Turing had to fight, one whose parameters were set by the human-all-too-human facet of socialized existence, bringing him to the breaking point in 1954 at the age of forty-two.

The somewhat absentminded professor Alan Turing, not particularly expecting to be nabbed as a sexual outlaw, went to the police station one day to report a suspected burglary – a few items were missing, distinctly banal items. He was chatty. In the course of the explication, the professor mentioned his association with Arnold Murray, and it soon became clear to the official interlocutor that Alan and Arnold were or had been a couple. Turing was surprised that the suggestion of intimacy with Mr. Murray should earn him public reprobation. Perhaps he thought that the social atmosphere was more accepting. Perhaps he had not thought. For once. He had not foreseen the trouble. After all, he was hardly a replicant of Oscar Wilde. Alan Turing, reclusive and shy, was immediately hit with the "Gross Indecency contrary to Section 11 of the Criminal Law Amendment Act 1885." Busted. There was no stutter or stumble or policeman's wink to let him slip by (if I recall correctly, he and the police officer to whom he rather casually told his story were on a first-name basis); no hesitation on the part of the state. Altogether, he was treated harshly, put on trial, shamed: publicly humiliated, privately shunned. His brother turned on him: "John Turing made no secret of the fact that he considered his brother's behaviour disgusting and disreputable, an extreme example of 'a *modus vivendi* in which the feelings of others counted for so little.'"[114] To state this briefly, Professor Turing was given a choice – jail or organo-therapeutic treatment. He was permitted to choose his weapon, the one that would be turned against him: either the classical penitentiary or medical intervention. He opted for the hormonal treatment, meant to kill the accused libido and render him impotent, grow him breasts. Busted. The choice he made, he felt, would allow him to continue working on his scientific projects, while jail, he reasoned, would have torn him away from the lab. "Perhaps it was surprising that he chose the scientific alternative to prison. He was annoyed at having been circumcised, and at any editorial meddling with his writings – small interferences compared with this piece of doctoring. Neither did he care much for creature comforts, and a year in prison, even an English one, would not have been much more uncomfortable than Sherborne."[115] Thus his biographer, Mr. Hodges. I will refrain from commenting on the undeveloped relation established in the biography between circumcision and editorial meddling, or on the choice he made for the more experimental hostage-taking that the state proposed, exceeding even the literality of the punishing machine in Kafka's "In the Penal Colony." Who needs a material cell when the state can get inside your body and resignify your cellular structure? All this belongs to the event of the experiment, though it barely has a place, or a home, or an ensepulchered site. Turing's story reminds us of the way the state has experimented on the minoritized body and how prison systems to this day continue to function furtively as so many sites for experimental science. The lab imprisons its subjects, but the prison also locks on to lab culture. How many African–American inmates have become experimental objects of state-sponsored science projects?

P.S. – I would like to include a biographeme, to go back a bit, and cut another path. If science is linked, as Lacan returning to Freud says, to *Verwerfung*, to paranoia and the drama of failed foreclosure, one wants to point to a scene, at least to locate a trace of internal collapse. The swerve into biography offers perhaps an unconventional way of rendering the history of science, but I don't see why one has to edit out the life and works of the "life and works," even where philosophical and scientific propriety appears to prescribe such cuts. Or, one might question at least why such cuts have guaranteed a proper view of the scientific experience, and what it is about the biographical trace that compromises the sanctioned history of science. In the chronicles of technology, from Alexander Graham Bell to Paul Virilio – an arbitrary swath – the agent credited with an invention or insight is set off, biographically, by an often disavowed narrative of devastation. The fate of such an act of disavowal was thematized famously by Mary Shelley when she cast the techno-monstrosity created by Victor Frankenstein in the context of a mother's unmournable death. Or one thinks of Alexander Graham Bell's story, in which the protagonist tries by means of serial experimentations on the one hand to connect to a mother's deaf ear and on the other to establish a cable to a dead brother. Both Victor and Alex were electrically wired into a scene of unassimilable catastrophe.[116] The scientific subject, whether cobbled together in fiction or lived in enigma, is inexhaustible; yet, a number of recognizable traits recur. Let us look at an episode that in itself may serve as a screen memory for a prior drama and thus may act as a mere link in a chain of metonymic substitutions.

Something severely tests the young scientist, scarring him in a way that would continue to be part of his work. Alan Turing's scientific drive was put in gear at an early age, when he was hit with devastation. Chris, the boy whom he adored and idolized, dies suddenly from tuberculosis on Thursday, 13 February 1930. Suddenly gone. As in so many narratives of the scientific drive – the inerasable scene of sudden traumatic awareness is an occultated trope in the history of science – little Turing begins to set up his future lab and labor on the fringes of an unaccountable loss. For starters, he wonders whether Chris's mind can exist without his body. Whitemore gives room to this traumatic opening in his dramatic rendition: "It was an obsession that stayed with me for many years. What are mental processes? Can they take place in something other than a living brain? In a way – in a very real way – many of the problems I've tried to solve in my work lead directly back to Christopher."[117] The problem of a phantom transmission system – what in post-Freudian psychoanalysis is called "cryptonymy"[118] – goes backward and forward in the case of Alan Turing.

Not only is there a phantom body agitating in the scientific corpus to which he will affix his name, but a history of disavowal besets the telling of Turing's demise. A wrongful death narrative, as we know perhaps most unforgettably since Hamlet, will not let us go. The narrative usually screens an earlier story, untold and unsayable, for which it doubles. Even the highly acclaimed "Winner of the Pulitzer Prize" work by Douglas R. Hofstadter, *Gödel, Escher, Bach: An Eternal Golden Braid,* averts its gaze from what happened to the scientist. The section on Turing dispenses with him vaguely: "Turing dies young, at 41 – apparently of an accident with chemicals. Or some say suicide. His mother, Sara Turing, wrote his biography. From the people she quotes, one gets the sense that Turing was highly unconventional, even gauche in some ways, but so honest and decent that he was vulnerable to the world. He loved games, chess, children, and bike riding."[119] He also loved boys. Alan Turing's demise is more clearly rendered in *The Mighty Micro* by Christopher Evans, who is also included in a footnote provided by Hodges:

> He came to a tragic end. A solitary individual who confided little in other people, he was also a practising homosexual at a time when homosexuality was viewed as a criminal offence. Somehow he brushed with the law – the sad, sorry details are hard, and perhaps unnecessary to come by – and one evening, depressed and disillusioned, he retired to his room and bit into an apple laced with potassium cyanide.[120]

Can this movement of erasure be stopped? Can any of these speculations be arrested? Moving toward a provisional conclusion, and running out of time, we are clocking in at the end of a poisoned suicide. Whether we are speaking of Hamlet or Turing and the figures for which they are made to stand here, the time has come to address the "Halting Problem," to help us stop – or not. Our writing machine may not be simply disruptable. It is as if Turing had himself programmed this dilemma, urging a script to go on beyond itself, beyond coded limits and consensual decencies. Where and how and if to stop, how to suspend the test drive and according to what protocols of slowdown could it be brought to a halt? In "Halting Problem," Turing speaks to the problem of deciding whether a given Turing machine with a given tape will ever stop computing or whether it will continue indefinitely. "Turing was able to show that there must exist at least one Turing machine for which this question is, in principle, undecidable. One cannot devise a program to determine whether or not the machine will stop computing."[121] There is more than an outside chance that the machine will go on computing, testing limits, forestalling cessation, even if someone – a subject, a subject purportedly equipped with agency – turns it off. The epochal affinities between the faltering of Victor Frankenstein at his unstoppable computer terminal and Turing's analytical assessments are, if only elective, still striking. Responding to the problem of where and when and if to halt became the monster's destiny. In the literary version of contemplating the stay – the possibility of discontinuance – the unstoppable monster must learn to put a halt to itself and does so only by reading Goethe's *Werther,* where finitude is taught and suicide enacted. Without this act of self-termination, the text argues, the machine-monster will continue indefinitely.

Given the nature of testing and the peculiar logic ascribable to it – a logic splintered within the exposition for which it calls – one does not want to stop, materially stop, on a note of assured finality. Turing does not allow for such a thinking of sheer cessation. One does not want to have settled on an answer or domesticated a drive into a concept stupefied by end or result. Part of Turing's result is a variation on a theorem that was proved in 1931 by Kurt Gödel. Gödel's theorem showed that in a logical system as abundant as arithmetic there must be at least one proposition whose truth or falsity is undecidable. No proof can possibly exist determining the truth or falsity of the undecidable statement in the language of the system within which the statement was formulated. Gödel's result, when translated into the language of Turing machines, tells us that if a Turing machine is asked the undecidable question, it will either give no answer or a false one. The shaky presumption of the question – whether undecidable or inherently weak – focuses one of the possibilities that all systems of testing have to face and supplies the reason for which they invite uncompromising philosophical reflection.

Let us give Turing the last word before we halt. Some folks have taken Turing's result as a proof that machine intelligence, compared to human intelligence, is distinctly limited. Turing himself did not believe there was very much depth in this view, yet he left it to critical testing to determine the features of human or machinic thinking and to reproduce questions of the kind that pit the one against the other. In an oft-cited essay entitled "Can a Machine Think?" he wrote:

> Whenever one of these machines is asked the appropriate critical question and gives a definite answer, we know that this answer must be wrong and this gives us a certain feeling of superiority. Is this feeling illusory? It is no doubt quite genuine, but I do not think too much importance should be attached to it. We too often give wrong answers to questions ourselves to be justified in being very pleased at such evidence of fallibility on the part of the machines. Further, our superiority can only be felt on such an occasion in relation to the one machine over which we have scored our petty triumph. There would be no question of triumphing simultaneously over all machines. In short then, there might be men cleverer than any given machine, but, then, again, there might be other machines cleverer again, and so on.[122]

X was back from a conference when she picked up her messages. Her doctor asked that she call the office as soon as possible. It was early Sunday afternoon, so she would have to wait. She bit her lip thinking of the sadism of doctors, even when they think they're helping out with the odd house call, or what was left of the house call. The next day she learned she had a new strain of hepatitis. But there was no test to determine which type of hepatitis – "E" or "F" or maybe it was "C," hepatitis C, which disappears and returns, often eluding the blood-work results meant to pin it down. Without a test, the illness did not as such exist, the diagnosis remained vague, and the treatment was a matter of guesswork. It reminded her of the drama of chronic fatigue, which she had also had to endure – no test could legitimate or prove its existence. People looked at her queerly, as though she were faking it. She could have used the backup of the symbolic register, in this case, some test results. Without the test to prove she was sick, she was a lunatic, high-strung, depressed, somatizing unsayable – untestable – pain. She needed the attestation but was too weary, simply too weary to think about getting it. She was on her own, together with so many others, hung out to dry: like those wretched soldiers felled by "Gulf War Syndrome," another affliction bereft of the test.

59

Part 2
Trial Runs

I stand on light feet now,
Catching breath before I speak
For there are songs in every style,
But to put a new one to the touchstone [*basanôi*]
For testing [*es elegkhon*] is all danger.
– Pindar, *Nemean Ode* 8 (19-20)

For once
In visible form the Sphinx
Came on him and all of us
Saw his wisdom and in that test [*basanôi*]
He saved the city.
– Sophocles, *Oedipus Rex* (498-510)

Prototype .01

In the interview accorded to Salomon Malka, Levinas announces, "I prefer the word *épreuve* to *expérience* because in the word *expérience* a knowing of which the self is master is always said. In the word *épreuve* there is
at once the idea of life and of a critical 'verification' which overflows the
self of which it is only the 'scene.'"[1] When Levinas overhauls experience or
experiment with the type of endurance implied by *épreuve,* he opts for a
kind of trial: a test site in which the self is placed at absolute risk. The call
for "verification" – the quotation marks indicate the provisional character of verification – announces a life submitted to incessant probes, unfal-
tering revision, what in Nietzsche is governed by the principle of rescindability. In *The Gay Science* every proposition, every subproposition – life
itself – is subjected to the rigors of the *épreuve.*

Prototype .02

We must start over.

You wake up one morning to find yourself on trial, interminable trial. You
are placed under arrest; or, at least, something has been arrested. Incidentally, it's your birthday. Nonetheless, every possible sense of renewal has
been erased from the site of your happenstance date of birth. Instead of
enjoying the flickering phantasm of regeneration, you are made to witness something else: a destruction of your becoming. There is nothing
reassuring about the fragmented, aphoristic, and bursted character of the
text in which you find yourself. You wake up one morning, dizzy and
fresh, dissociated by some contingent barrier from your past. You try out
your new little legs. You can barely move. You wake up and you don't
know what has become of you. Is it a joke? A test? A destinal wager? You,
big shot, *Übermensch,* have become one of Nietzsche's animals, part of his
legacy in an experiment gone awry.

• • •

Kafka, one of Nietzsche's most scrupulous readers, responded to the call for a mutant form. Irony for irony, the exchange between Nietzsche and Kafka produced a number of trial runs as they set about transmuting the figure of man. Ever in consultation with one another, they worked, we could say, in the same laboratory, each conducting his own experiments according to a shared logic or logos. Each fleeing a woman.

Prototype .03

We must start over. Start from scratch.
Regress.

Psychoanalysis belongs in the lexicon of the test drive: part of the culture of experimentation, it proceeds by relentlessly refining the conceptual probity of acts of testing. Paradoxically, the case for testing is all the more rigorous when it appears to be introduced in terms of an irremissible warp or omission.[2] In the Prefatory Remarks to the *Fragment of a Case of Hysteria* (1905), Freud opens the Dora files by stating some anxiety about the exigencies of testing of which his study appears to fall short: "Certainly it was awkward that I was obliged to publish the results of my inquiries without there being any possibility of other specialists testing and checking them, particularly as those results were of a surprising and by no means gratifying character."[3] Testing consists of two significant axioms, the first of which involves an internal control apparatus; the second axiom postulates a community of verifications and double-checkers. Freud introduces a third area of testing when he formulates the basis for a particularly potent type of psychic probe: the reality-test. None of these controls exclude the possibility of further innovation, for the test site is at each point reconfigured to include "every one." Everyone has a hand in the Freudian experiment. When he addresses the contested status of his study on dreams, which was seen to lack solidity in terms of verifiability, Freud offers, "there was no validity in the objection that the material upon which I had based my assertions had been withheld and that it was therefore impossible to become convinced of their truth by testing and checking them. For every one can submit his own dreams to analytic examination, and the technique of interpreting dreams may be easily

learnt from the instructions and examples which I have given."[4] Freud
goes on to insist that "no one who wishes to shirk" the preparatory labor
of investigating thoroughly the problems of dreams – "an indispensable
pre-requisite for any comprehension of the mental processes in hysteria
and the other psycho-neuroses" – has the "smallest prospect of advancing
even a few steps into this region of knowledge."[5] In order to read the case
study of hysteria, you will have turned yourself into a scientific laboratory, an apparatus capable of observing unconscious phenomena: you
become the hybrid connector of observer and observed, the dreamer and
its exacting commentator. The community of testing consists in gauging
the singularity of each of the innumerable lab partners, the rhetoric of
their objects and phenomenology of approach.

That Freud subjected his work to the unyielding requisites of testing
hardly needs to be restated, though the testability of his observations has
been famously questioned.[6] In an intervention meant to defend psychoanalysis against such persistent charges, Adolf Grünbaum argues for
the probative role of tests, reviewing clinical testability and examples of
falsifiability in the work of Freud. In order to urge his point, he treats "A
Case of Paranoia Running Counter to the Psychoanalytic Theory of the
Disease";[7] another example of falsifiability is furnished by the lecture
"Revision of the Theory of Dreams."[8] Grünbaum demonstrates that "the
psychoanalytic aetiology of paranoia is empirically falsifiable (disconfirmable) *and* that Freud explicitly recognized it."[9] Until this instance the
psychoanalytic theory of paranoia assumed hypothetically that repressed
homosexual love was at the basis of paranoid delusions.[10] For backup, he
recounts the following narrative. A woman who was trying to break up
her relationship started to mount a campaign against her lover. Freud
observes: "The girl seemed to be defending herself against love for a man
by directly transforming the lover into a persecutor: there was no sign of
the influence of a woman, no trace of a struggle against a homosexual
attachment."[11] Freud admits this case into evidence as "a refuting instance
of the aetiology he had postulated for that disorder."[12] If the woman was
delusional, as it seemed she might have been, then the apparent absence
of repressed homosexuality "emphatically contradicted" the hypothesis
previously put forward by Freud of a homosexual etiology for paranoia.
To underscore the way psychoanalysis overthrows some of its asserted
solutions, Grünbaum discusses the predictive consequence of some of

Freud's claims, noting that an apologist for Popper was led to conclude that "the limitation on predictability in psychoanalysis thus avowed by Freud is tantamount to generic nonpredictability and hence to nondisconfirmability."[13] Offering several further illustrations of falsifiability and putting a critical probe on neo-Baconian inductivism, Grünbaum resolves that "Popper's refutability criterion is too insensitive to reveal the genuinely egregious epistemic defects that indeed bedevil the clinical psychoanalytic method and the aetiologies based upon it."[14] Judging from the orientation of this statement, we see that it is not so much the case that Grünbaum wishes to defend psychoanalysis outright; rather, he wants to get at its putative "deficit" from another angle, in order to deploy inductivist canons for the validation of causal claims that are said to "have the capability to exhibit these cognitive deficits."[15] Following the course of his argument, one has the sense that Grünbaum takes a sudden U-turn in order to get at Freudian inadequacy in a more "sensitive" and in some ways more pedestrian way – he shows sudden interest in such matters as whether Freud really could have known that Paul Lorenz (alias Rat Man) masturbated the day of his saying so, and, in formulating a strict hierarchy of intraclinical testability: "Indeed, it will turn out that the entire testing procedure in the Rat Man case comes out to be probatively *parasitic* on an extraclinical finding."[16] Grünbaum is no doubt bound by the addressees of his argument to stay within the clinical and strictly analytical parameters of his findings. His concerns show the extent to which the fate of psychoanalysis, its day of scientific reckoning, can be seen to hinge on questions of testability. Perhaps if we aim beyond the first rows of addressees and try to reach another audience and auditor, the books might look a bit different, if not more minutely balanced still.

How does psychoanalysis formulate the textual experiment set up? So much of what Freud said was set up according to the principles of controlled experiment. The vocabulary of doubt with which he worked and according to which he established his thought was in a number of significant ways unprecedented. The case of the obsessional neurotic evolved around the axles of the word *erraten,* to guess, to conjecture. This case tested Freud theoretically and personally – it was his first experience with countertransference; he suffered: passion and patient collided. On a thematic as well as heuristic level, the analytical work depended for its unfolding on tropes of testing, examinations, failed conjectures, and repeated hypothetical positing. The patient's initial evaluation with the analyst took on the contours of a test. One of the most beloved patients of Freud, Lorenz passes the entry examination when telling the doctor that he had run through some of his books. Whereupon Freud agrees to treat him.[17] At the time of his analysis the young man was preparing for the equivalent of his bar examinations. Preparations for the exam favored the manifestation of his symptoms. He was, from the start, a test case.

The analytic session consisted of a series of microtests. At the beginning of every encounter, Freud coached the analysand who, doubling for a disciple, was responsible for repeating and embodying the lesson.[18] It was as if every session terminated in an examination that, as the examining professor indicates at several junctures, the Rat Man passes brilliantly. In fact, he was too brilliant, a passing meteor. Freud complains that his cure came about too quickly, the lessons too quickly learned. His examination was done before his time was up. What does it mean to terminate an analysis too quickly? Not in the sense of Dora, who simply bolted (Freud was upset when she bailed: Dora had treated him like a servant, he moaned, giving him two weeks' notice). But Lorenz ended too quickly in the sense of having recovered precipitously, passing all the necessary tests too soon, overcoming resistance and other unconscious blocks, leaving the analyst to the solitude of a first countertransference. Freud leaves the case in the mood of mourning a doubly lost object. It is the only case study for which he doesn't destroy the notes. If the Rat Man passes all the requirements at warp speed, Freud hangs on to the evidence of an interminable trial. Whether it was too fast or too slow, or both at the same time, the experiment on one level explodes a hypothetical principle of psychoanalytical treatment. Its failure was its success. The loss of the patient inflates, overwhelming the abandoned analyst. A later footnote states that the exceptional boy perished in the Great War.

Some years later Freud writes "Mourning and Melancholia." He sets up the probe in the manner of an experiment. Trying to throw some light on the nature of melancholia, he issues a warning against any "overestimation of the value of our conclusions."[19] Moreover, he "from the outset drop(s) all claim to general validity for our conclusions."[20] Upon ending the article, he describes a painful wound that calls for an extraordinarily high anticathexis. Freud abruptly ends the experiment. " – But here once

again, it will be well to call a halt and to postpone any further explanation.
... [We are forced] to break off every enquiry before it is completed – till
the outcome of some other enquiry can come to its assistance."[21] Marked
as provisional, "Mourning and Melancholia" disrupts itself even as it
starts, relying for its grounding only upon the asserted instabilities of hypothetical positing. As a text that cannot as such take hold – it establishes
claims for itself as a scientific trial without finality – the essay enters its
own conditions of mourning. Without staying power it prepares from the
start to depart, to leave the scientific observer bereft of an object, abandoned in the end to a state of uncurtained epistemological deficiency.

Unless perhaps – this would be the wager – the figure of understanding
that characterizes the scientific observer is turned into that of a melancholic reader, holding on precisely to the lost object around which the
text is organized.

The text, as indicated by its title, elaborates two principal types of
mourning. When Freud reverts to the work of mourning he asks: "In
what, now, does the work which mourning performs consist? I do not
think there is anything far-fetched in presenting it the following way.
Reality-testing has shown that the loved object no longer exists, and it
proceeds to demand that all libido shall be withdrawn from its attachment to that object. ... Normally respect for reality gains the day."[22] Two
kinds of tests establish our sense of reality. One, *Realitätsprüfung,* regards
reality; the other, *Aktualitätsprüfung,* which Freud briefly mentions elsewhere, comes from another paper that was itself lost. In the lost essay
Freud presumably had asserted the difference between a test that regards
reality and one that regards immediacy (*Aktualität*). Who or what agency
puts out the call for such a test? In his "Project" of 1895 Freud demonstrates that the "primary psychical processes" themselves do not require
any distinction between an idea and a perception. In the *Traumdeutung*
he describes how the function of inhibition and delay are crucial in judging whether things are real or not. The first time that Freud used the term
"reality-test" was in 1911, when dismissing the function of attention in
"The Principal of Mental Functioning." What is real is not present to the
psyche but depends upon exploratory probes that, following significant
postponement, bring back the news of what can be constituted as having
happened. Primary psychical processes waver between hallucinated and

more groundable states. Reality-testing involves *work,* so it stands to reason that it is recruited into the workforce of mourning. In "Group Psychology" Freud attributed the work of reality-testing to the ego-ideal – an attribution revised in a footnote at the beginning of *The Ego and the Id.* Now for the first time since the "Project," reality-testing was firmly ascribed to the ego. There are further references to reality-testing in "Negation" and the "Mystic Writing Pad" (1925), which fix the ego's habit of sending out periodic exploratory cathexes into the external world. It is as if the ego needed to send out an envoy of surveyors and examiners for the purposes of establishing reliable measures of its relation to what lies outside its domain. The messengers reassure the ego of its place or indeed create the space for the ego to connect to the coordinates of an outside. In "Negation" Freud traces the course of reality-testing's development back to the ego's earliest object-relations. Despite Lacan's later objections to the contrary, or his railing on this point, Freud showed increasing interest in ego-psychology. In the end, reality-testing forms the basis of his thought on *Verleugnung* ("disavowal" or "denial"), which had not previously been differentiated from repression and which described the ego's reaction to an intolerable external reality.

In his later writings Freud continued to be preoccupied with reality-testing, particularly in chapter VIII of the posthumous *Outline of Psycho-Analysis* (1940): "In other words, we gave up hallucinatory satisfaction of our wishes at a very early period and set up a new kind of reality-testing."[23]

In these cases testing involves the renunciation of a closed-off sense of fusional being in which the self assures its own satisfaction. The test results for which ego calls should, in the best of worlds, confirm and countersign the satisfaction of our wishes but in fact put the self at risk. Testing marks a limit, constructing the difference between hallucination and external reality which does not always back up the idea put forth by the self. Without the apparatus of reality-testing, the self exists in the manner of a tenuous hypothesis, unconfirmed, at sea. But it is "happy," floating on its own bouncy ground. The self braves reality-testing not only in mourning but as mourning: test results often imply loss of ground even as the ego gains grounding. It is not clear why the ego would venture out at all on such exploratory probes if it already knows how to build itself an alto-

gether satisfying world without confirmation from outside. But precisely
to assure itself that it is not alone, ego must risk the loss of internal plenitude, its homegrown self-appointed communion. Even in its most hallucinatory condition of satisfaction, the ego senses that something may be
missing; it becomes insecure and must start up the machinery of testing.

The process of reality-testing in some ways resembles the development
of moral consciousness. Something has to be given up, possibly sublimated, in order for reality to gain the day. Hence reality is to be "respected" ("Normal respect for reality gains the day") – a respect gained
after struggle and surrender. Besides being armed with the necessary
force to impose its version of what is, reality-testing is equipped to make
demands on the ego, obliging it to submit to its law, like a tough-loving
superego. In this respect, after having shown that the loved object no
longer exists, reality-testing "proceeds to demand that all libido shall be
withdrawn from its attachment to that object."[24] Reality-testing is not
merely poised as a traffic cop but moves in on the ego like a SWAT team,
or the "non du père," demanding that ego give it up, release the phantom
hostage.

There are times when the ego barricades itself and shoots back, though.
It kills the messenger. Freud metaphorizes this occurrence as faithful servant. In the texts that proliferate around the question of testing, the figure
of submission – an allegory of testing – often devolves on a servant, on
service, what Kafka fixes as the *Diener,* the one who serves. When the ego
cannot accept the test results, it is as if it would "send away its most faithful servant," writes Freud (recalling the sense he conveyed of being sent
off by Dora).[25] There occurs a tremendous breakup when the intimate
Diener is axed. In the "Metapsychology of Dreams" Freud describes such
a breach when introducing the notion of amentia. Amentia occurs when
reality-testing is dismantled:

> The Cs. must have at its disposal a motor innervation which determines
> whether the percepton can be made to disappear or whether it proves
> resistant. Reality-testing need be nothing more than this contrivance. . . .
> we know too little. . . . We shall place reality-testing among the major
> institutions of the ego, alongside the censorships which we have come to
> recognize between the psychical systems . . . we can learn from pathology
> the way in which reality-testing may be done away with or put out of
> action – more clearly in the wishful psychosis of amentia than in that of

dreams. Amentia is the reaction to a loss which reality affirms, but which the ego has to deny, since it finds it insupportable. Thereupon the ego breaks off its relation to reality; it withdraws the cathexis from the system of perceptions, Cs. With this turning from reality, reality-testing is gotten rid of, the (unrepressed, completely conscious) wishful phantasies are able to press forward into the system of . . . a better reality. Such a withdrawal may be put on a par with the processes of repression.[26]

Testing is linked to the experience of exteriority. One ventures out, breaks up a happy if deluded domesticity of self.[27] The test calls for the disruption of blissful certainty. A major egological institution, in league with censorship and repression, reality-testing still raises some questions and scores a number of untallied philosophical points. If reality needs to be tested, what is the status of that which gets established by ego's probes? In terms of temporality, to the degree that reality-testing depends on inhibition and delay – it is secondary, arriving belatedly on the scene – does the news that it brings imply, as in the case of Kafkan bureaucracies, a kind of legitimacy that itself needs to be further refined and tested by the ego? Or is it really news, I mean, when the other ceases to exist – did the ego not experience the other's finitude from the get-go, as an early bird experience of loss and mourning? Somehow, though, when forgetting descends upon consciousness, and they really rip you apart, testing tells you what it is that is not.

Prototype .04

Kafka writes a story, "The Test." This is how the first sentence runs: "Ich bin ein Diener."[28] I am a servant but I am out of work. Nudged on the scene as a kind of shivering being, anxious and shy, the narrator is waiting for the duration of the brief account (one and a half printed pages) to be called to service. Too intimidated to push for a position – he won't jump the line or scramble to get ahead of the crowd when one becomes available – he sits around the somber beer palace with some other jobless servants. The others are called to service, not necessarily because they are more aggressive about getting a job. In fact, they seem indifferent compared to the narrator who has wanted fervently to find work. Without work, he is at loose ends. Spends the day drinking. One day he finds someone else already sitting at his usual table. ("Einmal, als ich ins Wirtshaus kam, saß auf meinem Beobachtungsplatz schon ein Gast.")[29] The narrator-servant turns to leave, not daring to look directly at the intruder or to make an approach. As he begins to turn away, he is called over, and it soon becomes clear that this other guest, too, the intruder, is a servant. "Why would you run away? Sit by me and have a drink! It's on me."[30] The narrator sits down. His host, the guest intruder, asks him some questions. He can't hack it. Getting up, the narrator says, "Maybe you're sorry you invited me; I'll go now."[31] But the questioner reaches across the table and pushes him back down. "Stay," he says. "It was just a test. Whoever doesn't answer the questions has passed the test." ("Wer die Fragen nicht beantwortet, hat die Prüfung bestanden.")[32]

The story is one of sullen inversions. In short order, the preparation for the test has displayed only listlessness – this is not an athletic contest but involves another order of endurance, sheer endurance, that of servitude without service, somewhat situated like a priest without a god. One passes the test by failing to respond to its questions. The examiner is only remotely related to an immemorial sphinx who threatens to pulverize the one who cannot answer. Nonetheless, the test result will determine whether the one taking the test can stay or must go. Like all tests, it is a kind of placement exam. But what is placed and where?

All we know is that the examinee is a servant without work. His essence is to serve but he has no one, no house, no institution in the present to serve. He serves time. Predisposed to being called, he waits. Being a servant without a job, without wages, appears to signify that his servitude is absolute. There is no exchange system, no graspable assignment, to relieve him of the burden of waiting on ... well, he does not know for and on whom he is waiting. In the meantime, the time of the narration, he awaits his calling.

There is a double movement consisting of sheer being-called and being called upon to answer. Both events occur without properly taking place. When the test is administered, there is a call for him to answer. By not answering he in a sense remains faithful to his essence: he remains a servant or, let us say, he disowns the possibility of knowing, he refuses to assume the function of mastery. Nonetheless, by refusing mastery he passes the test. One is tempted to write "the Test," for Kafka submits the servant to another order of testing. This test, more reminiscent of the dilemmas of Cordelia and Bartleby than those of Perceval or Wilhelm

Meister, involves subjection without redemption, an itinerary without telos – no need to keep your eyes on the prize because the test will have taken place without your knowledge. This other test is not about knowledge or doing, true or false, multiple choice, or even about faith but about faltering, about the sheer torment of being called on to answer and affirm – and in the end it marks the simple impossibility, in this case, of stepping forward or standing up for yourself or affirming anything. The servant has told us from the second sentence on that he cannot stand up for himself – one of the reasons he cannot advance. Not called to service – in fact, singled out among the others by not being called up – he is on call, which is to say, permanently on duty (no schedule, no hours, finally, and logically no time off). Being off duty is his duty. A more relentless, imposing tour of duty than the fulfillment of a locatable task could measure. The endless demand of the uncharted expectation. No one calls him to order or to work. In this sense he is related to Abraham as his inversion, as the one who does not hear his name called, being called on instead to sacrifice by not sacrificing or offering of himself, on standby without giving or doing anything. No mountains to climb, and even when he makes motions to rise, his interlocutor pushes him back down. Kafka had elsewhere seen Abraham as a harried waiter taking orders. At one point multiplying hypothetical Abrahams, he also construes one who supposed he was called by a higher order. One of Kafka's Abrahams rises to a task that was not imposed on him, like showing up for a test for which you are not enrolled or even, as Kafka writes, it could be commencement day: the dumbest student thinks he hears his name called when the prize should go to the smartest. Everyone dies laughing. In "The Test" no one calls for the servant. He remains in a state of anxious readiness. The main theme, as the narrator says, consists of his not being called. ("[D]ie Hauptsache ist jedenfalls, daß ich nicht zum Dienst gerufen werde").[33] The main theme is hardly a theme as it requires a resistance to thematizing. A story without a proper theme, it tells of a servant whose story eludes him. Nothing in the story is called for. Will he know when he is called? Is the call to serve recognized in advance, something to be understood before it happens? Will he miss the call and his calling, mistaking them for something else? One day there is another guest at his table, in his place, already there, offering to pay for his sins. The narrator passes the unexpected interview by not feigning comprehension and, reversing Abraham, simply by backing off. He, absolute servant, does not presume to have received the call. In this regard he submits to the call and answers to his calling: submission.

"Ich bin ein Diener, aber es ist keine Arbeit für mich da." "I am a servant but there is no work for me."[34] According to other, possibly more contemporary protocols (depending on how you set your clock), this opening sentence could have been the slogan of any number of themes commanding our *communauté désoeuvrée,* the community at loose ends of which Jean-Luc Nancy, in conversation with Maurice Blanchot – and he, with Georges Bataille – writes. I am sheer submission, without a work, without project. In any case the work isn't here ("da"), present or presence. This is Kafka, the tables could be turned. The beer counter could be a writing desk. Easily. The narrator can be seen as spinning out an allegory of textual submission, about what it means to write, to be written off, to serve without destination or transcendental approval. One day, nonetheless, there is someone sitting in your place – the place of your unconscious, the circuit into which you have been inscribed – offering conversation and the threat, however sublimated, of expulsion. Your "routine" has been disrupted. Whether the intruder comes from within or outside cannot be decided. The guest/ghost, the demon, the friend – not clear which – invites you to sit down and fill out a colloquial questionnaire that you find impenetrable. This encounter with the menacing unreadability of the question suffices to qualify you.

Like the poetic voice in Hölderlin's poem "Blödigkeit," you have been served notice, you do not belong where you are.[35] Yet you stay. Something pushes you down as you decline the inexorable invitation. In a certain way you have been summoned to the space of your greatest passivity, an indecipherable punctuation mark meant to set off the limits of your servitude. Unable to conclude or comprehend, you are told inexplicably that you have passed the test.

In Kafka language itself is submitted to so many endurance tests. His texts register an unprecedented level of exhaustion, irritation. Pained trials that end in snow marches, fatigued alien bodies, emaciated and dried out, cracked voices, suicidal stupor, and, ever before the law, there is the matter of blind submission. There is no plush spark of intelligence or light that manifests to save the day, any day. Only incessant tests with poor results or the severe judgment calls that terminate a relationship. Even when you have passed the test, something has failed you. Testing is linked to an extreme form of judgment (*Urteil*) that chases down the subject from the earliest school days.

The posthumous fragments "From Notebooks and Loose Pages" offer an account of "my irresistible desire to write," which begins by sketching the dilemma of being judged stupid.[36] Stupidity is thematized as an estranging form of experience. It is the experience of exposure without recourse to more reassuring types of evaluations and gets played out as an irreversible default. One has the sense that some test or battery of tests had been administered in secret, without the knowledge of the narrator whose young life is now subjected to the incontrovertible results of invisible testing systems. The narrator has been found out despite himself, behind his own back, which keeps on getting stabbed. The first fragment begins, "Unter meinen Mitschülern war ich dumm, doch nicht der dümmste" ("Among my schoolmates I was stupid, but still, not the stupidest").[37] A gradation has been inserted to qualify as just how stupid the narrator rates himself – there is often an element of comparativity in questions of smartness or stupidness as when Heidegger says he had made the stupid-*est* mistake of his life in 1934 – but this relative scale is quickly undermined in the next sentence: "Und wenn trotzdem das Letztere von einigen meiner Lehrer meinen Eltern und mir gegenüber nicht selten behauptet worden ist" ("And even if the later contention was not infrequently made by some of my teachers to my parents and to myself") – "it was done only in the same state of delusion as that of many people who believe they have conquered half the world if they have dared to make such a judgment."[38] The text continues: "But it was generally and really believed that I was stupid."[39]

The irony of the fragment's beginning lies in part in the way the narrator declares himself, opens his identity with "I was stupid," allowing for a quarrel only with the teachers' contention that he was the stupidest of all. The teachers, the early examiners of one's worldly being, seem to have marked him as the dumbest, stupidest among the student population. The assertion, at once declarative and contestatory – this is who I am historically but I am not the worst of my species – introduces a rift into the logic of presentation on a number of levels. The sheer scandal of opening a textual encounter with the placid assertion, "I was stupid" should not be undermined. This is different from flourishes of abnegation or controlled tantrums and protestations of modesty that might begin introductions on the order of this is who I am. Saying "I was stupid" is arguably more devastating or denarcissicizing than aligning oneself with evil or criminality, conditions that often imply cleverness and rate fairly high marks on the scorecards of narrative transgression. Exposing oneself as stupid transgresses transgression and occurs at a different energy level of textual subversiveness. Stupidity runs counter to volition – something that cannot be said too quickly of wickedness.

At the same time, saying "I *was* stupid" does not amount to saying "I *am* stupid" or writing "at this writing I am stupid." The narrator does not dispute the basic claim; he offers no counterproof as such – the status of proofs is in question until the end – but argues only that he was not the *most stupid* of pupils. It is at no point indicated that the narrator would have overcome his dilemma of being at the very least stupid. Yet what kind of a voice can pronounce its own stupidity without rising above it, if only momentarily? Splitting off from the implications of "I was stupid," the narrative voice must return to the site of enunciation for, as it turns out, such an attribution cannot be shaken off as if it were a mere phase or passing inhibition. The mark of being stupid, possibly even the stupidest, haunts the narrating presence to the point that it can never really become present and free of a past mark that remains critically undermining. Nor does the narrator offer the statement in a way that would permit us to credit his account as if this were a classic confession. Exposing itself, the narrative voice nevertheless resists confession. He has to a certain extent internalized the wry authority of the report card; he reports on himself without pathos. Doing poorly in school and finding oneself ranked behind the others does not border on inverted grandiosity or refer us to the lowest of the low. It is at once banal and somehow lacking in conviction. This is what makes it crushing. The narrator will never escape the fateful markdown of having been judged stupid. The teachers' evaluation starts the dreadful process of judgment in Kafka's world of ineradicable culpability. Being judged as stupid is no less suffocating than being arrested on your thirty-third birthday. You think maybe it's a joke or a present, maybe a perverse wager made by your coworkers, yet you never pass the tests that were supposed to spring you from yet another performative ordeal. The teachers, the police, the bosses have found you out as you continue to lag limpingly behind the decisiveness of their judgment. The game is over before it's properly begun: you're not going to make the grade.

"I was stupid." We do not know where to locate the narrator in the present tense of the narration. The opening sentence creates a crisis of believability on the level of thematic unfolding: whom are we to believe regarding the assessment of the narrator's degree and level of stupidity? To what proofs do we have recourse? Can the narrator disprove the assertion of his past stupidity or do these determinations stick and, if so, for how long? Can one cease being confirmed as stupid if school constitutes the essential testing ground?

Judgment in its most extreme form targets the subject, bringing him down. From the suicidal rush at the end of "The Judgment" to the declaration of stupidity in the last stages of Kafka's writing, the subject is rendered powerless to move out from under the crushing weight of institutional valuing. Whether it comes from Father or school, from the workplace or the state, the constant assault by stealth testing grinds its victim inexorably. The narrator seems able to defend himself by associating the judgment with grandiose, delusional powers of expression. There is something triumphal – the other side of a generalized masochism – about declaring the other stupid or, more precisely, the stupidest among all. The performative powers of this declaration are, moreover, unstoppable: "But it was generally and really believed that I was stupid; there was good evidence for it ['man hatte gute Beweise dafür'] which was easily passed on if, for instance, enlightenment was required for a stranger who had begun by not getting at all a bad impression of me and did not hide this from others."[40] There is a discrepancy between the favor the narrator curries and the "good evidence" that can easily be passed on to downgrade the position he occupies on a first impression.

The nature of evidence, or proof, is never divulged but commands a general authority such that anyone can be decisively persuaded of his stupidity. "This was something I was often annoyed about and which I often wept over, too."[41] It is as if phantom test results overtake him at every turn, perpetuating proofs that were formulated in a mood of manic assertion. The teachers had evidence, they testified when called upon to do so – at every turn – and they prevailed upon the jury of anonymous encounters. Denounced and demoted, the stupidest (who is stupid despite appearances – a poignant inversion) among schoolmates weeps and sees time collapse: "And at that time those were the only moments when I felt insecure in the tumult of the present and desperate about the future."[42] The experience of being judged stupid induces the tremors of temporality, a break with any grounding capacity for time to secure its aspect of continuity or flow. It's as if the future backs off when the present storms incoherently. The mood of temporal anxiety linked to the denunciation involves some "authenticity," however, for it rides the essential instability of time. Still, the sense of desperation remains theoretical, since "I felt . . . theoretically insecure, I must say, theoretically desperate, for once it was a matter of some work I was instantly sure of myself and confident."[43] This might be the only evidence we get of the narrator's stupidity, when he relegates, if only momentarily, the pervasive sense of insecurity to a theoretical masking of existence. The narrator recuperates, finding confidence "instantly." Work effects salvation. Whether this aspect of the account retains the stain of stupidity or transcends it is a question that the exposé leaves unanswered. As the narrative progresses, we come to see that the burden of stupidity comes from elsewhere and somehow does not impinge upon the work, the more stabilizing solitude of the work. There is a space that escapes, if only for an interval, the range of evidence. Yet "irresistibly a sense of insecurity begins forming all over again."[44]

Being regarded as stupid appears to have a lot to do with the fact that one is regarded at all. There is the burning literality of the look that seems connected to the testing apparatus with the emphasis it places on modalities of observation. The story goes on, tracing the difficult encounter with strangers, and the recurrent subjection of one's fluid definition to proof and judgment. "I used to be uneasy even at being looked at by so many people down their nose. . . . Then ridiculous assertions would be made, statistical lies, geographical errors, heresies, as outrageous as they were senseless. . . . and everything was proved all over again by the way people looked at me."[45] In complicity with the "statistical lies" that go hand in hand with a generalized testing system, the gaze suffices to prove again what was already seen. One of the narrator's staple responses to the conspiracy of looks is to become sleepy ("to go away and go to bed, a thing I always looked forward to, for I was often sleepy, being as timid as I was").[46] There is the suggestion here, as in Hölderlin, that timidity might be a dialect of stupidity. Finding no way of testing out of these subtle complicities, one falls asleep, exhausted by the distress of proving one's most minimal merit.

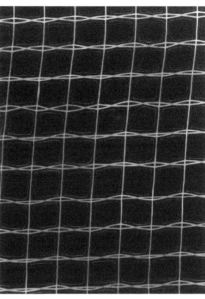

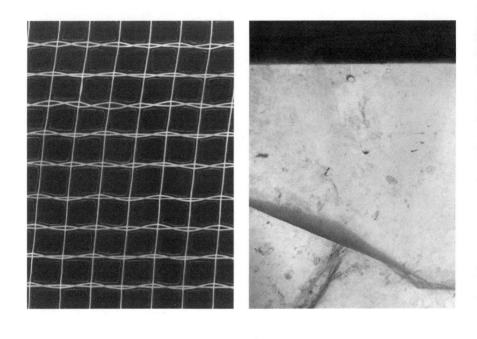

Prototype .05

On the test drive. Nietzsche writes, "Every drive is tyrannical: and it is as such that it tries to philosophize."[47]

Prototype .06

Like Nietzsche, Kafka has been seen as disrupting the premises of a given tradition by introducing clean breaks – epistemic interruptions. Such breaks are never as clean as they appear to be, yet they engage the paradox of establishing that which is startlingly new, a breakthrough insight. In order for the novel to be asserted, it still needs to be recognized, referred to, and connected with what has preceded its institution. The break depends on a recognizable trait of continuity – a continuity that had itself never been assured. There are always secret conspiracies, private negotiations in what might brandish the stamp of continuity. When Kafka has the figure of the *Diener* bear the brunt of figuring the condition of testing, he picks up an ancient strand linking the test to extreme states of servility. Kafka's enigmatic text may not be a direct commentary on the institution of *basanos* in Athenian society but, like many Greek works to which we have recourse, it places a concept of enslavement at the core of the experience of testing. It names the latency of truth in testing and the use of torture for which the slave body becomes emblematic. This is the historical body, purloined and secretly sacrificed, on which the Western examination system first gets imprinted in terms of test, trial, and cross-examination – the all but forgotten source of current usages of testing. The urgency of bringing out the answer and inducing the subjected one to tell what s/he knows entails torture, a permanent penal colony of inscriptive production: "The slave has no resources through which to resist submitting to pain and telling all."[48] The Greeks first use the literal meaning for *basanos* of "touchstone," then "metaphorize it to connote a test, then reconcretize, rematerialize it to mean once again a physical testing in

81

torture."[49] Let us follow the itinerary of this more or less covert operation. The evolution of the term *basanos* entails several levels of forced encounter: the touchstone sets stone against metal; "the test of friends sets one against another." In Sophoclean language, *basanos* connotes hostile contest: when Kreon fails to convince Oedipus to return to Thebes, he attempts to abduct Oedipus's daughter and companion, Antigone. The chorus protests:

> What are you doing, stranger? Will you
> Let her go? Must we have a test of strength?
> [*takh'es basanon ei kherôn*][50]

Here, as Page duBois suggests, the *agôn*, "the contest in the notion of *basanos*, takes on a new connotation, one of combat between enemies."[51] The test escalates to contest, to armed conflict or the adversarial standoff. What is the extent of injury or invasiveness that the test as *basanos* begins to accumulate? There is some disagreement over the degree of physical torture to which *basanos* refers. Some historians consider it a legal interrogation that falls short of violence. Others consider that the threat of torture may have been present, but that there is no direct evidence that torture was ever practiced.[52] DuBois however argues that it is most unlikely that in contexts of physical intimidation *basanos* "can refer to anything but the practice of torture."[53]

Let us consider some of the ancient video clips on the matter of testing and torture. In Aristophanes the slave on the rack is shown waiting like the metal, pure or alloyed, to be tested. The test, the touchstone, indisputably involves the process of torture. A test described by Theognis runs along different lines, however, showing the good man figuratively interrogating another, questioning his loyalty. *Basanos* in this case means submitting friendship to the test. The slave, who cannot be a friend, is presumed incapable of spontaneously producing a pure statement and cannot in any case be trusted to do so because of his or her servile status.

> The test assures that its results will be truth; the truth concerning a tested metal, whether or not it is sought after "gold," is the alienated product of the earlier test. The truth is generated by torture from the speech of a slave; the sounds of the slave on the rack must by definition contain truth, which the torture produces. And when set against other testimony in a court case, that necessary truth, like a touchstone itself, will show up

the truth or falsity of the testimony. The process of testimony has been spun out from the simple metallurgist's experiment, to a new figuration of the work interrogating matter. It is the slave's body . . . which receives the test.[54]

The slave's tortured body becomes the polygraph test by which the truthfulness of any and all testimony can be measured. It provides the proof for securing the reliability of legal utterance. Notorious for their litigiousness, the Athenians mention *basanos* frequently in speeches believed to be written for the court. D. M. MacDowell, having written the definitive book on Greek law, discusses the Athenian legal system, which was the first to be established on a democratic basis.[55] DuBois argues that to overlook or justify torture – a habit of Greek political and legal scholars – "is to misrecognize and idealize the Athenian state."[56] Itself uninterrogated, torture was compatible with democratic institutions. These institutions were built on policies of exclusion, scapegoating, ostracism, slavery, and violence. MacDowell describes the place of torture in the Athenian legal system, linking test and testimony:

> A special rule governed the testimony of slaves: they could not appear in court, but a statement which a slave, male or female, had made under torture (*basanos*) could be produced in a court as evidence.[57]

In a kind of dialectical downshift, evidence obtained from the slave by torture becomes more valuable, in terms of the production of truth and evidentiary ensurability, than that of free men. Thus Demosthenes, for example, weighs the stability of testimony obtained under torture:

> Now, you consider *basanos* the most reliable of all tests both in private and public affairs. Wherever slaves and free men are present and facts have to be found, you do not use the statements of the free witness, but you seek to discover the truth [*tên alêtheian*] by applying *basanos* to the slaves. Quite properly, men of the jury, since witnesses have sometimes been found not to have given true evidence, whereas no statements made as a result of *basanos* have ever been proved to be untrue.[58]

In this and several other fragments mobilized by duBois, including a significant number from the works of Thucydides, Antiphon, and Aristotle, the slave raging under torture becomes the genuine measure of truth. The tested slave cannot be easily dissociated from the untorturable master. In much of Aristotle, the relational tie between slave and master is such that they cannot be simply pried apart but the slave's body becomes the master's truth. The master can wriggle out of the confessional dilemma, conceal the truth, and choose, moreover, to accept the penalty associated with giving false testimony. His own point of vulnerability is "the body of his slave which can be compelled not to lie, can be forced to tell the truth. If he decides to deny the body of his slave to the torturer, assumptions will be made that condemn him."[59]

The master and slave are held together or kept apart as part of the same discursive body that locates the master in the logos, occupying the realm of reason. DuBois situates the slave as body opposable to the logos, but Aristotle appears to have master and slave occupy the same living body, though possibly coded with a differentiated hierarchical status. In the *Politics* he establishes the nature of their relationship in this way:

> The slave is part of the master – he is, as it were, a part of the body, alive [*empsukhon ti*] but yet separated [*kekhôrismenon*] from it.[60]

The slave is not a mere parasitical inclusion but a vital part of the master, edging toward the first phases of a possible dialectic. While no hostile takeover is yet in sight, the slave slips into the position of reliably assuring the truth in law and becomes associated with truth. The master, for his part, is counted out as the site of truth or honorable telling. The slave holds the truth of the master or designates the space in which truth becomes accessible, public, if forcibly published. We could postulate that the slave represents that part of the master that, as share and envoy of the master, is reality-tested for the Athenian court. It is the part of the relational construction that gets submitted to the state apparatus of testing.

On the subject of truth-testing and torture, Aristotle in his *Rhetoric* was more subtle than the rest of them: he came down hard on those who assumed that falsity of evidence was ruled out by torture. Addressing an audience requiring instruction in techniques of persuasion, Aristotle weighed the value of torture as evidence in forensic rhetoric:

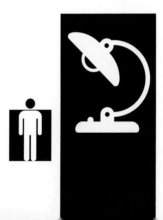

Torture is a kind of evidence, which appears trustworthy, because a sort of compulsion is attached to it. . . . [T]hose under compulsion are as likely to give false evidence as true, some being ready to endure everything rather than tell the truth, while others are equally ready to make false charges against others, in hope of being sooner released from torture. . . . wherefore evidence from torture may be considered utterly untrustworthy.[61]

Even when willing to sing like a canary, a slave was submitted to the test of torture and the torture of the test; slaves were made to countersign the truth as their masters bounced one reality check after another. The enslaved part of the master-slave body goes out on a limb, balancing on one form or another of *basanos*.

As close as the encounter gets, there is a distinction to be drawn. When tapped, the slave produces truth but does not apprehend it. The truth of which the slave is capable remains inappropriated. In a sense, the slave installs the instrumentality of the test and is set up as a transmission system. Like science according to Heidegger, it does not think: it tells, it knows, it informs without thinking, without knowing what it knows. An emblem concerning the truth that is transmitted without being known, carried without comprehension, the slave's ordeal is miniaturized by the innovation of the tattoo. Purposefully marked and scarred, slaves were often tattooed in the ancient world. In Herodotus's *Histories* we are told of a tattooed head as the new best way for preventing the slave from knowing what he tells, preventing a possible betrayal of his master should the slave be found out, questioned and interrogated:

Histiaios of Miletus sends a message urging revolt to a distant ally by shaving the head of his most trusted slave, tattooing the message on the slave's head, then waiting for the slave's hair to grow back. He sends the slave on his journey, ordering him to say at the journey's end only that the "destinataire," the receiver of the message, should shave off his hair and look at his head. The message reaches its goal, and Aristagoras the receiver revolts.[62]

As postcards go, this one exhibits the essential features linking a destiny to its destination: it shares the structure of the open secret, the unreadability of what at once is exposed and hidden, signaling in this case the heads-up for an eventual revolt, a crucial disruption. Sent off and shaved down, the slave body, as in later Kafkan torture scenes, has been inscribed, put through an endurance test over which it has little knowledge and no control.

The dynamics of testing, which implies the practice of torture, directs the scene of philosophical utterance. The *elegkhos*, "elenchus," the word most often used to describe the process of philosophical dialectic in Plato's work, was first of all a "cross-examining, testing, for purposes of disproof or refutation; it has legal connotations."[63] When for instance Socrates hunts down the truth, the practice of *elegkhos* resembles an interrogation. *The Sophist* presents *elegkhos* as a "method superior to solitary discourse, at least when the other party to the conversation is tractable and gives no trouble."[64] *Elegkhos* is cross-examination; together with logic and dialectics it belongs to what duBois calls the "police arts." Although in the *The Laws* "*basanos* seems to refer to a test in Theognis's sense, some kind of benign testing, the legal language of . . . passages in *The Sophist* leads the reader to interpret *basanos* as torture."[65] Conflict between philosophical schools is characterized as *gigantomachia*, a "mythical battle between the gods and giants which also had its parricidal aspects as an attempt to dethrone Zeus the upstart sovereign, who took over power from his elders, after a series of parricidal episodes."[66] The argument and clash of philosophical positions emerged in the wake of a torturing test of opposing forces in which the sides drawn up were often crushed and torn into pieces. The winner also bore the scars of embodied polemics. Philosophical argument, a fight to the finish – at least figurally – tested the philosophical body at every turn. Reading these materials, one comes to consider that the torture of arguments incorporates the torture of the Sophist; duBois asks whether the description of "the argument with the Sophist, who is never present in the dialogue, serves to represent him as slavish, as liable to torture and as therefore inferior to the philosopher who dwells in the realm of light."[67] Equal to the slave on this point, the Sophist yields truth only under violent interrogation and stress.

• • •

There are many different exercises of testing, all of which pose a dilemma concerning the sealed and concealed nature of truth. At times, veering toward the hermeneutic horizon of things, tests involve a figure of understanding. What seems probable, though this will need to be further probed – tested – is that the scenes of torture, enslavement, parricidal zeal, epistemological overkill, have been sublimated into performative acts such as taking oath, swearing in, and contractual agreements – all offshoots of a historically implanted test drive. The extent to which the sublimated scenes of torture have left traces in the way we arrange our practices and institutions with regard to truth remains a question – with the understanding that *question,* in French, also means torture. The fact that our relation to thought depends heavily on the way and the fact that we question – *Die Frage nach dem Sein* and *Was heißt Denken?* are two ready-to-hand titles – means that questioning itself must be submitted to question.[68] The genealogy of the question outsourced by test and torture calls for further reflection.

No doubt, a complicity between Freud and Nietzsche should be brokered if we are to make any headway here. Is it possible that every test bears testimony to parricidal urges? Is the self-overcoming implicated in some forms of testing a way of quashing, dethroning the elders – whether the placement of the elders is internalized, parceled out among objects, introjected or not? On the other hand, to what extent is the philosophical figure of *Überwindung* (overcoming) part of a generalized test drive? In the work and person of Nietzsche, who never stopped testing (according to valuations and efforts that still need to be understood), the test of loyalty got complicated and nearly disfigured by the parricidal side effects it appeared to produce. Nietzsche had to overcome himself and the other one, the enemy-friend, in a tasteful, tactful, bloodless yet sovereign sense. "Nietzsche contra Wagner" serves as one of several examples of the essential stress of loyalty that Nietzsche marked when axing a Wagner who had betrayed himself. But we're not there yet, and I, for my part, am not ready to test your friendship.

By now we have something of a palpable dynamic going, with testing being a matter of exploiting a slave body or – the other side of the same coin – a matter of asserting power, as when one tests valor, strength. Shakespeare has his characters' mettle tested over and over again. The slave body can be internalized, one of your own. There are more sinister histories to remain attuned to which, owing to Aristotle, we cannot dissociate from the political, the historicized body.

Testimony has been shown to depend on extreme forms of testing in the struggle against the uninsurability of a freely posited language. Something had to be sacrificed if reliable truths were to be retrieved, a body had to be tossed into the bargain, invaded and scarred. Testimony is evermore linked to the experience of torture.

As remote as some of these observations may seem, they bear relevance for us today. The scandal of racism is infused with testing. People of color have been tested without their consent or knowledge, prisoners continue to be tested, darker continents tend to be bombed when the president of the United States states that he is being tested.[69] This is part of the official rhetoric, at work as an uncontestable legitimating machine. Round the clock. On an altogether different level, animal testing bites the conscience. Cringing, the slave body goes on being transmitted and transmuted.

Prototype .07

Gilles Deleuze, "Letter to a Harsh Critic": "You tell me, also, that I've always just tagged along behind you, the real experimenters or heroes, sucking your blood, savoring your poisons, but keeping at a safe distance to watch and capitalize on what you're doing. That's not how I see it at all. Real and pretend schizophrenics are giving me such a hard time that I'm starting to see the attractions of paranoia. Long live paranoia."[70]

Prototype .08

When first appearing on the horizon upon which it was to be fixed for centuries to come, experimental culture provoked a crisis in witnessing. The constitution of experimental knowledge was part of a public process; it consisted in scrutinizing the reliability of witnessing for the purpose of generating and warranting knowledge. Ever since the son of the Earl of Cork used his allowance to build expensive experimental instruments and wrote lab reports in the form of the *New Experiments* of 1660, the connoisseurship of the evidentiary became a matter of testimony. The new non-metaphysical experimental discourse, painstakingly instituted by Robert Boyle (1627–91), depended upon increased depositions, attes-

Giovanni Battista Guelfi's bust of Robert Boyle, from the Royal Collection © 2004, Her Majesty Queen Elizabeth II

tations, corroborations – in short, witnessing – and the renunciation of the metaphysically laden notion of invention. Part of a solitary triumphal track, invention was henceforth on the skids. A powerful notion, it was referable to the cultivated privilege of the male subject or, as it turned out, to alchemical secretists and sectarian enthusiasts who claimed inspiration from God and other private, if transcendental, investors. Boyle's efforts, though in the end triumphant, were bitterly opposed by Thomas Hobbes (1588–1679), creating the circumstance of controversy in natural philosophy that involved in one way or another positions staked out by Descartes, Pascal, Linus, and others. By all accounts Boyle pulled through in the end but the going was rough. By the final years of the eighteenth century, Hobbes, the pulse of anti-experimentalism, had been mostly ruled out of the history of science.

What were the philosophical fears? According to Hobbes, Boyle's enterprise betrayed philosophy, which he saw mainly in terms of causality – a logic or program that secured "a total and irrevocable assent, not the partial assent at which Boyle aimed."[71] For his part, Boyle came to view Hobbes as a failed experimentalist rather than as a force aligned with an opposing construction of philosophical knowledge. The hope of securing physical propositions in necessary and universal assent was consistently undercut by Boyle as illegitimate. Only the dogmatists, at once limited and dangerous, would go after such a loaded level of assent: "Physical hypotheses were provisional and revisable; assent to them was not obligatory, as it was to mathematical demonstrations; and physical science was, to varying degrees, removed from the realm of the demonstrative."[72] The probabilistic conception of physical knowledge was not regarded by its proponents "as a regrettable retreat from more ambitious goals; it was celebrated as a wise rejection of a failed project. By the adoption of a probabilistic view of knowledge one could attain to an *appropriate* certainty and aim to secure *legitimate* assent to knowledge-claims."[73] The laboratory was intended to produce a different epistemological organization and social practice; it defended the space of a new permutation of assent in which dissension played a critical role.

In his seminal if plainspoken work *The Edge of Objectivity,* Gillispie writes: "Truly experimental physics came into its own with Robert Boyle. He spared his reader no detail. No one could doubt that he performed all the experiments he reported . . . , bringing to his laboratory great ingenuity, incomparable patience, and that simple honesty which makes experiment really a respectful inquiry rather than an overbearing demonstration."[74] Boyle can be credited with having introduced the *values* ascribable to experimental culture, encouraging its most noble character. In this light it is useful to note Gillispie's use of the locution "respectful inquiry" because Robert Boyle himself included in his work reflections on scientific deontology. Boyle's concern for civility and respectful dissension in scientific work no doubt draws on his aristocratic sense of world ordering and underscored his effort to establish an understanding of gentility in matters of procedure. At the same time, Boyle also unblocked the space of inquiry to a democratic push. The lab was an open space crossing over from and coming out of the alchemist's closet. Open to the curious, susceptible to all manner of visitation rights, the lab in Restoration England generated a sense of community that overtook in terms of participatory politics the storeroom of the solitary hallucinator or, in another lexicon, it shunted aside the private cell of the dogmatist who kept his sources and confirmations to himself. The experimental disposition was so inviting in fact that in "The Experimental History of Colours," Boyle allowed that certain "easy and recreative experiments, which require but little time, or charge, or trouble in the making" were recommended to be tried by the ladies.[75] The first lady to be treated to a display of Boyle's groundbreaking air pump, around which crucial philosophical arguments were put in motion, was Margaret Cavendish, Duchess of Newcastle. Her family were Hobbes's patrons and she herself had written on behalf of rationalistic over and against experimental methods of science, but that is another story. She was in there, putting her thoughts to the test and indulging the new experimental performances. Referring to a place where work is done, the terms "laboratory" and "elaboratory" were newly minted in seventeenth-century England. Thomas Birch praised Boyle because "his laboratory was constantly open to the curious" – science became an open theater, an arena for public viewing. Still, high exposure was not uncritically embraced by the Earl's son. He was seething in ambivalence as he saw his innovations running ahead of and exposing him. When he opened the shutters, Boyle, as Birch notes, equally developed the habit of suppressing his own work in poisons and on invisible or erasable ink.[76] Opening science to its capacity for tolerating public exposure, he retained to the end his own mystic writing pad.

Boyle's Law states that

$$P_1V_1 =$$

One reason for pulling down the walls of the scientific hub was to encourage the generation of converts and collaborators. To globalize (already then) the range of experiment, a long chain letter of witnessing and replication was set going. Many of Boyle's reports were rendered in the form of letters. In *Leviathan and the Air-Pump,* Steven Shapin and Simon Schaffer argue that Boyle, who insisted on the repeatability and replication of experiments, "wished to encourage young gentlemen to 'addict' themselves to experimental pursuits and thereby to multiply both experimental philosophers and experimental facts."[77] Part of the jargon of intoxication, the basic vocabulary of physics begins in the addictive regions of invention and discovery. Experimental physics aimed to compel the body and being of the young scientist, and started off what was to be the Romantic cliché of the mad scientist – vestiges of which still stuck to the body antics and hairstyle of Albert Einstein. Early physics put the stamp on obsession, urging the scientist to donate the body to its cause. The experimental program of the seventeenth century resectionized the body, put it on the line, and drew it into the room where thought was being newly constituted. The migration of the body into discursive practice (to speak in the dialect of new historicism) occurs in part because, given the widespread dispute in the seventeenth century over the reliability of the eye, and "of witnessing, as the basis for generating and warranting knowledge," it henceforth belongs to the production of knowledge.[78]

With Boyle, we begin early on to have a sense of the *drive* behind the experimental incursion – a drive that organizes the way its protocols dominate a new field of thinking. But if Boyle was emphatic about dealing and pushing a new cognitive habit, he first needed to seal his deal by mobilizing witnesses and achieving ascertainable assent. The lab became a space open for inspection; the installation of a public access code was due to the fact that Boyle needed his work to be countersigned, witnessed. Not only were many of his experimental narratives shaped by epistolary conventions, but they became chain letters, petitioning for signatures, relying evermore on countersignatory imprint and avowed complicities. Shapin and Schaffer note that when reporting his experimental performances, Boyle commonly specified that they were "many of them tried in the presence of ingenious men, or that he made them 'in the presence of an illustrious assembly of virtuosi (who were spectators of the experiment).'"[79] Boyle's collaborator Robert Hooke codified the "Royal Society's procedures for the standard recording of experiments: the register was 'to be signed' by a certain Number of Persons present, who have been present, and Witness of all the said Proceedings, who, by Sub-scribing their Names, will prove undoubted Testimony.'"[80] In the case of particularly meaningful or problematic experiments, Boyle named names: he would name his witnesses and stipulate their qualifications. For example, the experiment of the early air-pump trials, which held significant consequences for the philosophical debate of the plenists and vacuumists, and shaped Descartes's emphasis on the body, was conducted in the presence of "those excellent and deservedly famous Mathematic Professors, Dr. Wallis, Dr. Ward, and Mr. Wren . . . , whom I name, both as justly counting it an honour to know them and as being glad of such judicious and illustrious witnesses of our experiment."[81] Another way of creating a community of witnesses involved ensuring the repeatability of experimentally produced phenomena and facilitating their replication. Experimental protocols were reported in such a way as to enable readers of the reports to perform the experiments for themselves: "Boyle elected to publish several of his experimental series in the form of letters to other experimentalists or potential experimentalists. The *New Experiments* of 1660 was written as a letter to his nephew, Lord Dungarvan; the various tracts of the *Certain Physiological Essays* of 1661 were written to another nephew, Richard Jones; *The History of Colours* of 1664 was originally written to an unspecified friend."[82] From its earliest sendoffs to later launches, physics had to choose its literary boosters. Literary convention not only secured the launching pad but in some instances determined the course of an experimental conjecture. On the issue of contrasting styles of scientific exposition, it is useful to remember that it was Boyle, not Bacon, "who developed the literary forms for an actual program of systematic experimentation; it is hard to imagine two more different forms than Bacon's aphorisms and Boyle's experimental narrative."[83] Aphorism, essay, and experimental narrative, formally allied to the discursive probe, control different facets of the test shots that will continue to concern contemporary elaborations of thought and controversy.

What are the principal issues of the Hobbes-Boyle controversy? Perhaps we can offer a shorthand account of them. The issues that got tangled in the colloquy of Hobbes and Boyle leap ahead of the universalizing tendencies with which physics comes to be associated in more modern areas of philosophical inquiry. Of course, such near categories as "ahead" and "behind" make little sense in physics but help us provisionally to plot a diagram by which to orient different positions. The stakes of the Hobbes-Boyle controversy are for instance strongly at odds with some of the contentions to be held by Husserl and Heidegger on the points of scientific thinking. Such divergences necessarily run interference with some of Husserl's major topics in the *Crisis* inasmuch as Boyle, for example, introduces a scientific compulsion that would *not* be bound by apriority or governed by the separate certitudes of geometry's assertions – what Husserl understands under the epochal name, "Galileo." Unlike the space of incontrovertible knowledge that "Galileo" indexes for Husserl, the physical hypotheses constructed by Boyle are those whose status remains provisional, revisable; falling in line with their inevitability is not obligatory as might be the case for mathematical demonstrations: "The quest for necessary and universal assent to physical propositions was seen as inappropriate and illegitimate."[84] Moreover, since the probabilistic conception of physical knowledge was not regarded by its proponents as a regrettable retreat, Boyle ventured out to oversee the generation of a truth that was by no means certifiable. What this means in terms of approach and procedure is that one must still learn, in Boyle's view, how to handle rejected knowledge. Curbing polemics and dogmatic insistence, Boyle moves into an ethical terrain. The disposition of the scientific experimenter ought to be governed, according to his writings, by essential *modesty*.

Hobbes attacked the benevolent theorist with an army of purported facts. Of significant epistemological consequence was Hobbes's assault on the generation of matters of fact that contested the constitution of such facts into the consensual foundation of knowledge.[85] These attacks amounted to the assertion that "whatever Boyle's experimental programme was, it was not *philosophy*. Philosophy was a causal enterprise and, as such, secured a total and irrevocable assent, not the partial assent at which Boyle aimed. Hobbes's assault identified the conventional nature of experimental facts."[86] Boyle, on the other hand, as chief experimentalist, used the challenge of his adversaries to *perform* the paradox of civilized polemics, to engage by ostension, showing others through his own example how to manage experimental controversy politely. A boundary was constructed around the domain of the factual, "separating

$$P_2V_2 =$$

those matters of fact from those items that might be otherwise and about which absolute, permanent, and even 'moral' certainty should not be expected."[87] The multiplication of witnessing experiences was regarded as fundamental to the process of ferreting out facts and establishing their legitimacy in the realm of knowledge-claims: "An experience, even of a rigidly controlled experimental performance, that one man alone witnessed was not adequate to make a matter of fact. If that experience could be extended to many, and in principle to all men, then the result could be constituted as a matter of fact. In this way the matter of fact could be seen as both an epistemological and a social category."[88] The constitution of knowledge was to be linked to a public process, involving what Jean-François Lyotard calls in another context a third party of appeal.[89] The experimenter assumes the function of a plaintiff on whom the burden of proving a reality rests.

In its day the air pump, as object and cognitive instigator, belonged to the ecstatic sectors of Big Science: it represented the "cyclotron of its age."[90] Boyle was "one of the most important actors in the seventeenth-century English movement towards a probabilistic and fallibilistic conception of man's natural knowledge."[91] This conception invited the spread of street smarts into the lab; the scientific turf encouraged a politics of contamination. Prior to the mid-seventeenth century, the domains of "knowledge" and "science" were strictly distinguished from the category of opinion.[92] Of the former "one could expect the absolute certainty of demonstration, exemplified by logic and geometry."[93] The relaxation of tight borders changed the investigative terrain significantly. The distinctions that held apart knowledge from opinion were beginning to crumble; universal and necessary assent were, as conditions for the assertion of cognitive legitimacy, on a losing streak. Physical propositions were turning away from the dogmatist stronghold: Nietzschean science was already on its way, slowly prospecting for the detours and breakdowns of explanatory science.

Beyond the strictly philosophical and epistemological reach of Boyle's concerns, there was a strong ethical inflection to which his work and letters gave expression. The experimental narrative was to be bolstered by an approach consisting of extreme modesty and a newly acknowledged openness to failure. Boyle also introduced language usage that, no doubt defamiliarizing on impact, could be designated provisionally as harnessing the qualities of a noble loser – something that comes close to the rhetorical pointers Nietzsche sets out for the "noble traitor," a figure who breaks with convention and detaches repeatedly from his own dogmatic temptations.[94] Boyle welcomed the articulation of failure and gave it a home. In "Unsuccessfulness of Experiments" he provides a model narrative for the description of failure.[95] But even when he was a winner, Boyle took the part of the losing team. Thus he followed the more successful experiment with a sense of its inherent precariousness, offering oversized detail as if to account for himself every step of the experimental way. It is clear that Boyle was endeavoring to "appear as a reliable purveyor of experimental testimony and to offer conventions by means of which others could do likewise. The provision of circumstantial details was a way of assuring readers that real experiments had yielded the findings stipulated. It was also necessary, in Boyle's view, to offer readers circumstantial accounts of *failed* experiments."[96] The reporting of failed experiments was felt to give proof of moral probity, of disinterested work: "A man who recounted unsuccessful experiments was such a man whose objectivity was not distorted by his interests. Thus the literary display of a certain sort of morality was a technique in the making of matters of fact."[97] We'll leave aside for the moment the ethics of literary cover-ups, and whether morality can be sufficiently subsidized by "technique." Suffice it to say that Boyle's endeavor represents one of the rare instances when the literary device is called in to prop up the moral effect. For Boyle, narrativization was charged with the task of diverting language from its positing pomposity by making modesty somehow palpable. The form of the experimental essay, which adopted moral tonalities, was staked in the first place on rendering modesty recognizable and *visible*. The essay, as fragmented and piecemeal reporting of experimental trials, stood explicitly opposed to the natural philosophical *system*. Those who signed on to philosophical systems were deemed by Boyle to be excessively ambitious, interested, prompting their works to extend beyond what was passably provable or possible.[98] By contrast, those whose work involved the experimental essay were cited as "sober and modest men," "diligent and judicious" philosophers who refrained from asserting "more than they can prove."[99]

Another way of exhibiting modesty consisted in Boyle's professedly "naked way of writing," his renunciation of style in the service of presentation – a problem that Kant would struggle with a century later when pondering the requisites for philosophical presentation or *Darstellung*. "Boyle's presentation of self as a moral model for experimental philosophers was powerful."[100] Opposing philosophy to rhetoric, he let the rhetoric go in favor of an expository askesis. The plain, unadorned, and functional style served to display the philosopher's "dedication to community service rather than to his personal reputation. Moreover, the 'florid' style to be avoided was a hindrance to the clear provision of virtual witness: it was, Boyle said, like painting 'the eye-glasses of a telescope.'"[101] A subsidiary of philosophical presentation, experimental narrative was to drown out the clamor of the individual signature style. Style was out of style (as though it could simply be ruled out), so that the community could benefit from the public struggle with knowledge. To underscore his attenuation of style and the promotion of modesty, Boyle offered some prompters:

> ... in almost every one of the following essays I ... speak so doubtingly, and use so often, perhaps, it seems, it is not improbable, and such other expressions, as argue a diffidence of the truth of the opinions I incline to, and that I should be so shy of laying down principles, and sometimes of so much as venturing at explications. ... I dare speak confidently of very few things. ... "[102]

Boyle tried to take a route other than the ones prescribed by the authoritative knowledge-claims of the systematists. At the same time, in order to shelter the sweeping experimentality of the prose-work and the practice to which it referred, he needed at once to expunge and sketch the positioning of a moral self. Laying low, yet offering a downpayment for the integrity of his findings in terms in the end of a signature, Boyle sought to guarantee the intensive modesty of his writing, its immunity to Baconian idols, and its rootedness in fundamental disinterestedness or innocence. In order to front for an uncorrupted scientific openness of method, Boyle had to let go, in principle, of the compulsive participation of the inventor who obtrudes upon scientific procedure. Propelled by internal controls and a fairly idiomatic logic, the experiment, unmanipulated by the lure of prestige, is launched on the premises of the author's newfound limitations, a kind of acquired inexperience. Letting the experiment trace its course without the interference of too much knowledge – a vocational hazard – Boyle was capable of allowing, "I had purposely refrained from acquainting myself thoroughly with the intire system of wither the Atomical, or the Cartesian, or any other whether new or received philosophy."[103] The systems of Gassendi, Descartes, and Bacon remained foreign to Boyle; he claims, "that I might not be prepossessed with any theory or principles."[104] Stripped down to a level of professed ignorance, the new philosophy of experimental askesis was ready to roll.

For our purposes there is one more downshift that should be recorded. It concerns the staging of cognition. One of Boyle's persistent aims was to assure civility for the unfolding of the new experimental phase of philosophical understanding. He wanted to secure a politics and politesse of cognitive pooling, a way to govern disputes that unavoidably attached to the community of experimenters. If experimentation was to have relatively free rein, expression was not so free as to prove injurious to opposing hypothetical phrasal regimens. No one should get away with assault language or abusive behavior. To this end Boyle shifts the value of the prevalent form of Socratic dialogue by replacing it with that of a *conference,* bolstered by conversation. From now on, conversation is meant to promote the civility of thinking, from Boyle's *The Sceptical Chymist* to Blanchot's *Infinite Conversation.* In *The Sceptical Chymist* Boyle stages fictional conversations among an Aristotelian, two types of Hermetics, and Carneades as emissary of Boyle himself. The fact that the symposiasts were imaginary, cast as literary fiction, allowed their testimony to swing over the nasty contingencies of warring phrases: "They were a piece of theater that exhibited how persuasion, dissensus and, ultimately, conversion to truth ought to be conducted. . . . truth is not inculcated from Carneades to his interlocutors; rather it is dramatized as emerging through the conversation. Everyone is seen to have a say in the consensus which is the dénouement"[105] The experimental politics of radical exposure depended on fiction to close the deal on the future of scientific dominance. Drawing even the adversary Franciscus Linus into the imaginary conversation, Boyle handed down the rules "for real conversations proper to experimental philosophy."[106]

Two centuries later, Nietzsche invents the free spirits as interlocutors convoked to philosophize in an experimental parliament. Experimental philosophy, whenever it thinks of holding a "real conversation," proper and contained, will be haunted by Boyle's fictional conversations, a founding text that never quite manages to ground the very experimental culture for which it remains nonetheless responsible. If Nietzsche is right in understanding physics as one among several competing interpretations of world, whether bound by the universalizing binges of language or destroyed by technological acts of naming, then the genesis of what he develops as the "experimental disposition" takes shape in the clearing marked by the first modern lab site – the first scientific text in any case to have collected witnesses' signatures.

Prototype .09

Somewhere between the imperatives of reality-testing and the interrogatory title "What Is Called Thinking?" Jean-François Lyotard institutes phrase events – events that surpass the holding capacity of a linguistic act.[107] Here, language and proof have met their reciprocal limits. Exploring the failure of speculative thought to supply relief to victims of colossal as well as minute, unclassified historical grief, phrase events go to the heart of injurious wrongdoing. They underscore the weakness of evidence and of probative restitutional acts. "A wrong," writes Lyotard, "is a damage accompanied by the loss of the means to prove the damage."[108] Beyond hypothesis yet in some cases legally short of proof, the desolating ordeal to which Lyotard addresses this inquiry concerns evasive turns of law when called upon to perform justice. On the one hand, Lyotard's work comes to the aid of those who, unable to manipulate the rules of cognitive discourse, are left stranded by speculative thinking; those who phrase according to the rules of other genres are stripped of the very power to speak. On the other hand, rescue and relief cannot be guaranteed, for every phrase in itself is capable of offending another phrase and thus runs an inevitable risk of wrongdoing. What happens to those among us who make existence claims that, according to the rules of cognitive discourse, cannot be validated? What about those whose distress has not been proven or legally seared into our living memories?

In *The Differend* everything is staked on the plight of a phrase whose regimen excludes cognitive verification. Lyotard examines the nearly closed cases of those whose discursive fragility is legendary, and for whom no test of heterogeneous phrasal regimens has been devised. They include the perpetually contested, the historically harassed victims of rape, or those survivors whose claims concerning the existence of gas chambers has been rejected by an emissary or mask of a Faurisson – the revisionist historian whose demand for proofs opened a notorious "debate." (Can the existence of gas chambers be debated and, if not, why not? If so, in what terms? Does the resistance to debate already indicate a grave political problem or is debate itself a subterfuge, a simulated solution – or worse, an offense, to the extent that it puts a historical occurrence up for discursive grabs?) Lyotard shows how the demand to establish the reality of a phrase according to normative procedures can wrong a witness, can produce unsolvable conflicts or radical differends. One problem is that the revisionist historian monopolizes and appropriates cognitive discourse, comfortably finding critical support in the workings of speculative thought. The victim asked to account for the reality to which she points, sometimes mutely, is under pressure to produce reference. She becomes witness but also structurally assumes the place of *plaintiff*. The circumstance of seeking what has since been californianized into "validation" puts the victim in the position of a plaintiff before a public court. The differend is "owed to the impossibility faced by the plaintiff of demonstrating the existence of what is in question. The kind of demands for verification that are made of him stifle the plaintiff's ability to furnish proof."[109] Reality, writes Lyotard, "is always the plaintiff's responsibility."[110] What this means is that the burden of establishing the existence of the referent must be shouldered by the plaintiff. In the terms and logic that Lyotard confronts, it becomes even the burden of the victims of the Shoah to *prove* the extermination, to supply proof for the reality of gas chambers. Reality, whether of a historical or of a more personally cut nature, is not pregiven, cannot by any means be taken for granted but recurrently foregrounds the contestability of the referent. Reality is "always potentially in suspense, or in dispute."[111] Sometimes the value of an asserted referent achieves consensus, legitimacy. But even a successful plea for the referent can only be temporary, "until further notice [that] it has not been falsified."[112] More people than one cares to count live in such worlds of unprovable distress. These worlds, each time singular, resist comparison, though somewhere they pile up like abandoned shoes.

As with all cognitive claims, it is expected that others will be able to verify or falsify the referential proposals put forward, at any time and any place. The expectation of the public nature of verification for the anchoring of a stated contention meets the traditional expectations of Western thinking. Ever since Socrates stopped passersby to make his philosophical points and to harass the truth into the open, truth claims have become a matter of public display, complying with a serious stage direction of street theater. The scenography of openness, the demand for intelligibility and consensual accord is what Plato called *logon didonai*.[113] The scene changed when dialectical disclosiveness abandoned the streets of early urban philosophy. Truth moved out of Socratic neighborhoods, clearing the way for turf wars requiring a new level of arbitration. With reality shaky and reference elusive, the question became one of assuring consensus; appeals were made to an implicit third party – a public forum, a tribunal, or court. At the same time, the Platonic solution to "finding a consensus about the adducing of proofs concerning a referent [became] the living dialogue between two, the *dialegesthai*."[114] Lyotard asserts, "We believe in the decision of the third party in matters of reality."[115] This, for instance, is why human rights commissions are important, part of the package deal of a testamentary ethics. The status and stakes of reality are thus addressed to a third party: they become in sum and summation a matter of testimony and attestation. Testimony implies another degree or logic of reality-testing, the requirements of which are often satisfied with the appearance of truthfulness or *veracity*. Irreducible to a strictly verifiable result, testimony embraces the instability of reference while seeking to establish the veracity of its claims. Still, witnessing, which necessarily bypasses cognitive checkpoints, poses a host of problems even as it swears itself in.

There must be a way to distinguish between the person whose testimony is about having been abducted by space aliens and the one or many whose narrative – whether shared or silently withheld – names extreme oppression or even the event of extermination. Between fiction (I think) and a traumatic event not available to the purposeful aims of the cognitive empire and its empirical satellites, something happens in the world of philosophy to the way stories get told and heard. The internal collapses in the discursive capacity to yield truth bear on legal considerations as well, particularly when evidence fails instantly to feed the referential scanner. Winning an argument depends on its own steam, attached to some fixable substance only by ever vaporizing contingency. Given the "loss or decline of the referent's reality" – the threat that nothingness could be a real possibility – we have come to the point, since Gorgias's refutation of Being, where by dint of paralogical operations or dimwitted tenacity weaker arguments trump stronger ones: "We allow the lesser argument to prevail, under the right conditions."[116] Lyotard's work responds to this genuinely contemporary issue; it also takes on, as a measure of the difficulty of submitting a satisfying response to the gravity of the questions with which he struggles, the related problem of the sublime, which elicits only a stuporous witnessing of the unpresentable.[117] How can one bear witness to the ontological sublime if it endlessly slips out of view? We'll get to his redescription of the sublime momentarily.

Very often victims of torture, indignity, and pain are abandoned to phrases whose regimen excludes cognitive verification. Or, in the case of traumatized survivors, they are rooted to a phrase whose only recognizable quality is what we call silence. The silence of Holocaust survivors has been held against them by the revisionist historian. This is why Lyotard includes silence as the possibility of phrasing. Phrasing is expansive, generous, even as it gets drained by word-privation. The phrase can consist in a fleeting blush, a flicker of anxiety, a tapping of the foot, a shrugging of the shoulder, a blink. A silence can also serve as a phrase.[118] Silence offers its own syntax of testimony. Yet it runs counter to the traditional adducement of proof – the constitutive demand of cognitive discourse, "the demand to prove the existence or reality of the claim one makes according to established rules, so that they can be verified by others."[119] The "others" upon whom the referent depends for some measure of solidity convoke a select crowd derived from the *dialegesthai,* essentially a dialogue among friends, for it is careful to exclude idiots, hostile interlopers, as well as infirm brutes and in fact "anyone who is in bad faith."[120] This means that in the Platonic partnering of solutions, there remains an excluded negativity, a party who abstains from the obtained consensus, maybe capable in the end of sabotaging its premises by his mere existence. The so-called idiot can run with his own logic, jumping the boundary of the friendly Platonic dialogue into the future of aberrant assertion – with good and bad results, depending on who's breaking away from the dialogue of friends. The runaway idiot could be a Faurisson. Or a luminous singularity could break the consensus. In any case the status of friendship has been sufficiently complicated by Bataille, Blanchot, Derrida, and others to give pause to the selective fraternal construction, the ancient boys' club, that determines the cases before them.

In Plato the consensus about adducing proofs or stabilizing reference depends on the fragile construction of amicable colloquy: the agreement has to be made prior to the accord, verification prior to proof. The buddy system has preapproved the reality checks to be issued, in effect offering a group discount on veracity claims. All this would be inoffensive if it were not for the fact that scientific discourse is based on these premises, which is to say, the genre of discourse that "seeks to institute the rules for what we call scientific discourse – that is, the rules for our prevailing mode of thinking in the West" depends on the values of clarity and public openness from which our procedural sense of propriety, linked to and based on scientific method, issues.[121] Yet the expectation and indeed requirement that the reality of a phrase's referent be established according to unanimously agreed upon procedures can in themselves wrong a witness or plaintiff, resulting in recalcitrant conflicts or extreme differends. These results come in even though, as Rodolphe Gasché argues, the "demand in itself is rational, [one] without which thinking (in its cognitive mode, at least) is not possible."[122] The demand that testimony be bolstered by material evidence, that phrases bulk up on tried and proven evidentiary supplements, encounters a snag. One is wronged, Lyotard reminds us, when a damage is "accompanied by the loss of the means to prove the damage." Stranded with an unprovable reality, one has lost all recourse or means of appeal, since to this privation "there is added the impossibility to bring it to the knowledge of others, and in particular to the knowledge of a tribunal."[123] In the famous words of Paul Celan, the witness needs the witness lamentably deprived him by cognitive regimens:

> Should the victim bypass this impossibility [of bringing the wrong it has incurred to the knowledge of a third party] and testify anyway to the wrong done to him or her, he or she comes up against the following argument: either the damages you complain about never took place, and your testimony is false; or else they took place, and since you are able to testify to them, it is not a wrong that has been done to you, but merely a damage, and your testimony is still false.[124]

There is, however, a further Kafkan twist to the strained requisite of stating one's case despite the referential odds. Testifying to the reality of the horror of injustice as if one were perpetually standing trial, one is structurally trapped. The victim's sense of being on trial with no testable ground, with phrases that collapse under the pressure of cognitive bullying, creates a situation where the test of obliterating contestation has been summoned to defeat the victim once again. This dilemma has been established with painful clarity by Lyotard.

You're making it up, you're faking it, you can't prove it! – As cruel and common as they are, these statements offend not only because they come from a hostile or institutionally appointed space of contestation. They belong to another curl of conspiratorial anguish. The disbelieving persecutor is not the only one who tries to reduce an inassimilable reality to a matter of testability. You yourself, as lacerated victim, cannot believe this has happened, *is still happening* to you. To *you*. Language fails you. It is not as if one has mastered trauma so well that one can get out from under its flaying machine or see or speak or know or understand. That severe, ego-built part of you responsible for reality-testing shudders to a halt. Remember, K. from *The Trial* could not tell what was happening to him; he tried to play by the rules of cognition, went to court, submitted to the test, if that's what it was, until he was a dead man walking metamorphosed into a piece of executed dog. What I am trying to say is that the victim is rolled into an ongoing surprise attack, shaken down by a sudden spread of anxiety that bears the caption, "Is it happening?" Can this be true? This "*Arrive-t-il?*" of which Lyotard writes hits you in and as the foreign language region of your being, even in its most homegrown aspect of terror. What I am trying to say is that the persecutory reality continues to slap the victim around and does not come with a "how to tell and get over it" kit. There is only something that Lyotard calls a *feeling* – a terrible, startling feeling for which philosophy needs to find a phrase, a link, a support. Philosophy has to stop testifying for the institutionally self-satisfied controllers, stop kissing up to state-sanctioned power plays, and instead get into the untested regions of new idioms, new addresses, new referents; it has to abandon its conciliatory habits. Rather than continue its traditional pursuit of conciliation, philosophy, more or less according to Lyotard, needs to be invaded by new inconsistencies and to saturate itself with the *feeling* of the damaged. The differend must be put into phrases with the understanding that such an act cannot yet be accomplished. In sum, philosophical thought must come up with a link to the feeling-tone of the unaccounted for and offer privileged protection to the unaccountable refugees of cognitive regimens. The Platonic model, setting truth as an invariable – as that which remains detached from the plight of the addressors and addressees of phrases – serves no useful, pathbreaking purpose in light of the task that Lyotard sets for a philosophy of dignity and activist commitment. How can this new mutation in philosophical engagement stay intimate with those throttled by a dependency beyond dependency? If I am getting this right, Lyotard asks that contact be made with the real ravages of the impossible and that one move with the incessant punches of untamable horror. Even if the object seems elusive (especially when it eludes): one has to go there, be there, stand there.

Not always available to translation or in the least bit comprehensible, the "Is it happening?" tells you only that the impossible has become a real possibility. Adding shock to wonder, this dazed state of troubled residue that cannot be seized or comprehended reverts in Lyotard to a stuporous *Grundstimmung,* to a traumatic stupidity that resets the cognitive levers according to which we respond to catastrophic eclipses, inhibited by that which cannot as such be presented according to classical values of presentation. There is something senseless in the heart of things, provoking "a bewilderment, a stupid passion" that can no longer be resolved into tragic representation or protected by any recognizably edifying recuperation.[125] This is why, among other reasons, Lyotard is determined to offer a redefinition of the sublime as that which is no longer opposed to the beautiful. The task of philosophy no longer consists in neutralizing or domesticating the senseless, in rounding up the savagely unintelligible but in staying with the stupor of unaccountable excess and regressive brutality. Gasché comments: "The task of thinking set by the stupor at the realization that non-being could prevail, cannot be fulfilled by schematizing the unpresentable into facile intelligibility. Thinking absolves its task of witnessing only if it encounters the unpresentable without resistance. The sublime feeling in which the impossible possible is acknowledged can therefore no longer be a sublime that plays by the rules of the beautiful."[126] The evacuated site of non-being, of the nothing, and the senseless "is only truly and properly acknowledged in a feeling of sublime stupor. In such stupor alone, philosophical thinking is true to its task."[127] It is not as though the "proper" of philosophy has now migrated to stupe-fying figures of the unpresentable. Lyotard does not originate a call for a new mystification, even in the form of some "truth of a task." Nor would he be likely to concur with his commentator that something like nonre-sistance is possible, given the irreversible vocabularies of psychoanalysis and rhetorical deconstruction. The sublime stupor is meant to stem the enticement of philosophical overreach, calling thought back to the sting of the unsayable: this is where phrasing, each time anew, stunned and dazed, begins to s-crawl.

• • •

Lyotard's work engages the quality of incommensurability that obtains between philosophical statement and testimony. Bold and exemplary, his argument necessarily appears to leave some uncomfortable residue to the extent that the issues exceed the frame under which they are solicited: no matter how many precautions and subtleties are reflected in the effort to respond to his call – in the effort, precisely, to *enchaîne,* link on – one risks finding oneself inadvertently replicating the language of negationism, as if the Shoah were indeed unprovable, as if one had no choice but to parley noncognitive regimens in order to provide a semblance of credibility to corroborating claims. Meaning well and doing good, *The Differend* sets an unbypassable trap by which it has itself been quietly exploited. At least, the history of its reception has allowed for the trace of a trip-up, a confu-sion between what can be known and what can be proven. In another context, recognizing that in cases of extreme wrongdoing we come face to face with an event that annihilates its witnesses, Shoshana Felman has offered that not one direct witness can be summoned to claim the Shoah, which in the end cannot be understood as a single event in its totality.[128] For much of scientific thought, the destruction of the witness would re-veal the insufficiency of the case under consideration. This is not, how-ever, a matter of not knowing what we know or knowing what we don't know or a case of rigorously lacking proof: there is knowledge here, material evidence has been established, and even Nazi testimony has con-firmed time and again the existence of gas chambers. The death camp has been an acknowledged fact since 1943. So the purported failure of mate-rial proof to manifest cannot in itself be the problem, philosophically speaking, nor is it what stirs us to return incessantly to a discursive crime scene.[129]

No. What interests me is the way the damages tally up in the language of scientificity, something that Lyotard no doubt wants us to think about. The tenacity of revisionist prodding is due in large part to its ability to invoke the rhetoric of testing when it comes to the deconstitution of the Shoah as memory and knowledge. The discourse of Holocaust negationism is paradoxically coextensive with scientific discourse. In the case of Robert Faurisson and others like him, the "question" of the existence of gas chambers – another crease in the perpetuating Jewish "question" – is raised in terms of hypothesis-testing, as an assertion that cannot be *proven* wrong as long as it stays within the jurisdiction of the tenets of falsifiability. The recourse to hypothesis-testing invites the inquiry into whether the extermination took place. The point I am making about the pervertability of testing and hypothetical positing raises only a hair of a differend with *The Differend*, yet it seems worth registering. Commentators whose intentions are not to be impugned readily fall in line with the phrase universe that scorns what is by all reasonable measure known, archivized, certified, agreed upon. If such slippage can happen, it is also because there is something irresistible at the core of the discourse of testing that manages to seduce even the most subtle of philosophical sensors.

The counteroffer to this state of affairs, testimony, contains its own measure of destabilizers. In a work that leans heavily on the "test of testimony,"[130] Derrida indicates the degree to which testimony is structurally susceptible to falling under or into fiction. To the extent that testimonial language customarily engages the first-person narration, it takes up the old liabilities already schematized by Goethe in *Dichtung und Wahrheit* – testimony splits the honors between truth-telling and its fictional support. A passion or experience without mastery, without active subjectivity, testimony, as passion, always renders itself vulnerable to doubt. It takes places as a "promise to make truth, according to Augustine's expression, where the witness must be irreplaceably alone . . . testimony always goes hand in hand with at least the possibility of fiction, perjury and lie. Were this possibility to be eliminated, no testimony would be possible any longer; it could no longer have the meaning of testimony."[131] Given that testimony is linked by Derrida to passion – even to the passion of a martyr who offers up her or his body in testifying – it always *suffers* its undecidable relation to fiction, perjury, lying while never "being able or obligated – without ceasing to testify – to become a proof."[132] The disturbing complicity between fiction and testimony cannot be erased or simply overcome. Thus, whereas the testimonial is by law irreducible to the fictional – this is what one swears to – there is still "no testimony that does not structurally imply in itself the possibility of fiction, simulacra, dissimulation, the lie, and perjury – that is to say the possibility of literature, of the innocent or perverse literature that innocently plays at perverting all of these distinctions."[133] Testimony does not need some outside perv to come in and bend its meaning, crush its horizon. The literary club ownership requires, when showing up to collect its dues, that the dissimulating propensities of the testifying act be honored and in some crucial way remembered. Testimony can never be expected to pass its own test if it suppresses the literary premises on which it stands. Unlike the discursive rallying that attempts to defeat it, testimony, while never abandoning the effort to scope veracity and say what it knows, remembers, sacrifices, and attests to, has no reliable test to back it up or make it back down, no accredited lie detector test tied to the stopwatch axioms of falsifiability. Testimony comes forward to pose a knowing without cognition, a memory without prosthetic or technical support, an irreplaceable exemplarity that must be repeated and replaced by more testimony without ever resolving itself into a proof. If testimony were to limit itself to establishing proof, information, certainty, or archive, "it would lose its function as testimony. In order to remain testimony, it must therefore allow itself to be haunted. It must allow itself to be parasitized by precisely what it excludes from its inner depths, the *possibility*, at least, of literature."[134] In the *Step Not Beyond,* Blanchot has written about this difficult border along which we would like to settle our thought, the border between testing and testimony, stalked by the living and the dead who carry each other as they burden and argue the language of our probe: "... silence carries us into the proximity of the distant. Words still to be spoken beyond the living and the dead, *testifying for the absence of attestation*."[135] It is as if the whole region were suffering from the default of test.

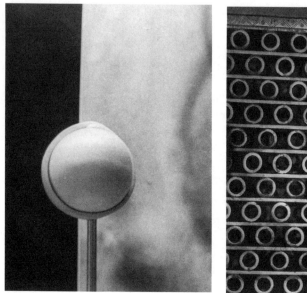

Prototype 1.0

Knowing is not the way.[136]

The exquisite discipline and daring askesis of certain types of non-Western practice challenge the limits of what we understand by testing. By slackening the finish line and undermining the ideology of sanctioned results in favor of another logic of rigor, a number of Zen and yogic teachings at once suspend and resurrect the constitution of the test. Zen does not merely erase testing but holds it in reserve, situating it otherwise. Vast and imposing, Eastern relations to something like testing reconfigure yet steadfastly enforce the warrior poses that pervade Western registers of testing. The value of contest also shifts. In Tai Chi one learns to step aside when a hostile energy is on the loose: one is taught to let the menacing lunge collapse against the stubborn velocities of its own intentions. The engagement with opposing forces (which can no longer be conceived as opposing since, by a slight shift in energy and position, the commensurate reach is broken, the flow diverted) – indeed, the very concept of testing limits – undergoes fateful innovation. All the same, Eastern practices, including those associated with the martial arts, hold back from completely writing off the test; they do not simply oppose the West-test. In a sense, the test becomes even more pervasive because it can at no point be satisfied by a conclusive answer or a definitive response to the probe that has been put out. The difficult boundaries of the Zen trial, the characteristics of which can be at once asserted and equally disputed, are especially evident in the case of kōans – the problems or inner challenges with which Zen masters traditionally have confronted their pupils. The Occident has put up other fronts, obeying quickening velocities: If such acts as going after the grail or attempting to reach a metaphysically-laden Castle can be viewed as exemplifying narratives of the Western test drive, then the Eastern "test" (this quality has not yet been established) is, by comparison, shatterably slow-going.

The grail, there is no doubt about it, must be found, if only to mark out the end of a narrative journey. The Castle, at least in Kafka's takeover narrative, cannot be properly located or possessed, though it remains the sign toward which K. strives, hoping to conclude his trial. The scenography of the Eastern counterpart tends to be characterized by that which is immobile, though pupils and monks travel to sit with one another, and there is the phenomenon of the Zen warrior to contend with as well or, in yet another tradition, one encounters the implacability of the bold-spirited Samurai. No one ranks as a weakling in these traditions, even though a place of honor is accorded in Eastern practices to the inaction hero; the kōan recipient may sit for years, meditating on a word or puzzle, weighing a persistent enigma posed by the master. In view of these descriptive attributes, K. may be looked upon as a high-strung Zen pupil (not in itself a contradiction), for his journey is abbreviated by sittings in which he tries earnestly to study and solve unyielding narrative puzzles. Nonetheless, the Kafkan warrior remains an effect of the West, even if his territory is at one point evoked as "Westwest," suggesting the overcoming and acknowledged excess of Westerliness. Fast and on target, he is going nowhere. And while it would be foolish to talk too readily about interiority for this lettered being, his goal is posited outside (this gets complicated) and goes under the name of "Castle" or homes in on the boss man, Klamm. K. cannot look inside for the answer, in part because Kafka has evacuated internal metaphors. The Zen pupil looks inwardly, but this is not the same as a subjectivity: the pupil is led to an inner experience without interiority, to understanding without cognition, without a history. K. had a history prior to entering the Castle territory, which does not serve him in his search; the Zen pupil enters the space of distilled performativity for which there is no outside. Reference has become immaterial, though effects of reference may occur indifferently, almost by accident. There is nothing to look for outside an always emptying self. This becoming-empty is what K. undergoes as he searches for a reference that could be tied to the empty signifier of the Castle. He scales the walls of recalcitrant signification but clings to the territorialization of a promised outside, a space occupied by the sacred signifier – just as Parsifal goes out to a site where the allegory of his search would be collapsed into a figure. Meanwhile, the Zen pupil, often a wanderer, listens differently, stilling herself to consider the sonic eventfulness of growing grass.

Responding to the demand of the kōan prompts a colossal if barely traceable event. This means, among other things, that understanding no longer crowns the end of a labored process of appropriation. In fact, the Eastern concern for the kōan tradition lies with enlightenment, which may or may not be closely tied to sudden understanding or to the arduous example of trial by error and the lessons of incessant failure. When one considers Zen practice seriously, it is another seriousness that appears. Yet once we begin thinking and figuring this other seriousness, this other rigor, Western narratives of testing themselves begin to incorporate the Orient. The story of the grail turns out to be even more intricate, more self-doubting, than that of a search conducted under the authority of the commanding signifier. Thus Parsifal's journey already marks the aftermath of the true test he failed to pass. The quest for the grail comes about as a pressing retest, something on the order of a punishingly sustained make-up quiz. The true test, which was never given out or formulated as such, required that an innocent simpleton produce a question motivated by compassion. Parsifal, for his part, was too dumb to fill the role of the innocent simpleton, having frozen at the sight of the ailing king. The test required him – innocently, without knowing he was being tested – to ask why the king was suffering. Instead, Parsifal gawked, unable to utter a word of compassion. In this case, the unspoken test was not asking for an answer but for a question. What does this have to do with us?

The failure to ask the compassionate question has brought about the test as we know it – formulated, set, a delimited field governed by a figure of the final limit: the grail. The paradoxical structure of this test should not be overlooked. Parsifal is made to undergo the experience of many trials in order to gain . . . innocence. This process resembles anything but the trajectory of the *Bildungsroman*. Experience is not meant to lead to maturity or ethical comprehension but to a kind of aporetic term, eliciting a dispossession of self linked to absolute innocence. *Bildung*, by contrast, climbs different rungs of self-dispossession as it takes on ethicity and the state. Parsifal's process or trial falls back to an originary acquiescence, to a disposition that precedes even the possibility of saying "yes." Something has to be returned to what never happened, prior to happening or to the early grammars of affirmingly absorbing the other. The hero chases down a first place that hasn't yet taken place. As a notion, experience is shown to fold in on itself: destroying its inherited concept, it rolls persistently backwards. Even at the start, as early as the sagas associated with the name Parsifal. It is a stripping down, and in this sense it begins to seem Eastern. Yet, while Parsifal's quest after the holy grail is intended to achieve nothing if not non-knowledge, it takes another turn in the nineteenth century by offering a share of redemptive bonuses. The promise of redemption underscored by Wagner's resumption of the medieval tale has made Nietzsche retch. Innocence was sidetracked by priestliness. The saving Elsewhere, another time zone – that of transcendence – will have been the goal, dissipating the here and now, bound to an increasingly spiritualized altar. The elusive materiality of the grail, reduced to symbolic qualities, henceforth belongs to the Christianization of the world. Still, the force that is gathered under the name of Parsifal – in Chrétien de Troyes's *Perceval,* in Wolfram von Eschenbach's *Parsifal,* in Richard Wagner's *Parzifal* – establishes an entire paradigm for Western self-testing, for the administration of a test with no preexisting conditions.

Prototype 1.1

Soen-sa said, "Where does that question come from?"
The student was silent.[137]

THE THOUSAND AND TEN DOUBTS   We might have become accustomed to viewing the test as a way of mobilizing courage, revving our engines, gaining on a problem, or increasing speed as a technological limit is tried. Designed to provoke doubt and shake attachments, the kōan slows things down – as if psychic layering had kicked everything into reverse warp speed. The slow motion of a barely codifiable procedure, the kōan instigates the other logic of testing, or testing's other logic, to which it at once remains similar as well as unassimilable. If it could be made to represent anything at all – a distinctly Western problem, the drive toward representation – the kōan "represents" the emptiness of Zen practice where it cuts across the edges of testing. Kōan practice explicitly engages the limits of psychic endurance, providing testing grounds upon which mind and body (there are different mind domains and several bodies to account for, but this is another story) are said to wrestle for a solution. Yet wrestling does not offer a match for what we are seeking: any effort must be superseded by exorbitant exercises of patience, colossal restraint. Extreme surrender and relentless focus must somehow meet in kōan practice. Kōan provokes an unceasing assault on the fortress of human reason. Western forms of testing have some of that too, the mind/body collaborations, I mean, as when Oedipus was questioned by the Sphinx. The Sphinx marks the porous boundary between Western and Eastern domains of questioning and tells of bodies menaced by pulverization: should the riddle not be solved, either the questioner or the questioned must go. Passing the test is a matter of survival of the species for Oedipus, as it is for the interspecies dominatrix of the riddle: la Sphinx dissolves when the young man offers the correct answer. In the case of the kōan, a body must offer itself up for any possible inscription of a response; pressed into service when a question is issued, a body belongs to the writing of an answer. It is as though the very possibility of response required a permanent yet decelerated Olympiad of the various flexes of mind and bodies. Still, in preparation for receiving the kōan, the all too ready contenders must be wrestled down, disqualified in the preliminaries: rational and discursive thought must be vanquished if the incommensurate, which kōan demands upon receipt, is to be discovered. Another site of thinking beyond thinking is being sought, where operations of sublation and annulment coexist, calling for the different experiences of saying.

A site of thinking beyond thinking, testing is not eliminated but takes place beyond the parameters of a test subsumed under codifiable attributes. The largely internal contest of kōan is intended to secure an experience of extreme dispossession. But the themes and topoi of inside and outside, of internally and externally determined categories, do not mean much here except for the dependence that kōan practice implies on concepts of opening. A draft for priming radical exposure, the kōan, offered by the teacher – the "master" – is meant to "open" the pupil to the possibility of Saying. The master is responsible for initiating the call of such an opening. Often this opening, which in no tradition escapes the suspicion of violence, is attained by the administration of a shock. Thus the master, in texts devoted to the kōan, is frequently figured as beating, hitting, or slugging the pupil. The hit seals a sort of "compliment" conferred by the attentive master, who prods the physical body for the purpose of disinhibiting a scene of contemplation, new and unanticipated. The shock is crucial to the experience of the kōan: it stages the opening of thought exceeding itself in the jolt. Although the temptation may exist to read such protocols of Saying in a mood of estrangement, one would be wrong to envision the choreography of violence as something foreign to Western forms of thinking about thinking. There is the Heideggerian *Stoss* (jolt) in *Being and Time* that, awakening to its own beat, still needs to be contended with; nor should one overlook the destructive passivities of Blanchot puzzling out Levinas. Some passages of the *Infinite Conversation* or *The Writing of the Disaster* stunningly converge with the sense of abandonment to which the kōan consigns passive bodies, particularly where the kōan burdens the student with the strictures of responsible saying:

> Where passivity unworks and destroys me, I am at the same time pressed into a responsibility which not only exceeds me, but which I cannot exercise, since I do nothing and no longer exist as myself. It is that responsible passivity that is Saying. For, before anything said, and outside being ... Saying gives and gives response, responding to the impossible, for the impossible.[138]

The exposure that occurs in and with language does not abandon the body (there are often up to ten bodies to count, to honor, to nurture, including the subtle, back and energetic bodies) or its psychic traces. Perhaps such a thinking of exposure approaches in several ways a kind of Blanchotian destruction. Though the vocabulary of his insight cannot easily be made to pull together other spaces, Blanchot, situated between literary and philosophical thought, offers us a bridge, a passageway, when he writes of tremendous passivity in conjunction with exposure.[139] The "passivity beyond passivity" that Blanchot shares with or retrieves from Levinas may not entirely communicate with the Zen center of articulation that it nonetheless remasters; still, the themes of persecuted exposure, of the other (*autrui*) who "weighs upon me to the point of opening me to the radical passivity of the self,"[140] of the pursuit of an enigma that troubles all sense of order, cutting into and interruptive of being, appear to converge with the eccentricities of the kōan. And where Heidegger's famous description of the "pure night of anxiety" in *What Is Metaphysics?* resonates lexically with the writings of the great Zen master, Ta-hui, there is still a deeper cut of askesis, a different eloquence of piety – an altogether other ex-stasis – and still yet another mortal exposure of vulnerability to be dealt with here.

What these names and texts share is the sense that the awakening, regardless of an increasingly imposing degree of intensity, is never quite sufficient to itself – not for Blanchot, not for Kao-feng Yüan-miao, Heidegger, or Levinas. The passivity is never passive enough. Or in Derrida's terms, the responsibility for bearing the enigma is never responsible enough. But if ever the limits of such disclosive insufficiency had been put to the test, it was surely in the kōan tradition which, though recorded abundantly, resists the more familiar protocols of discursivity. A teaching without pedagogy, it is a practice; a rapport to thoughtfulness, its practice is dedicated to the obliteration of thought. Calling for the dissolution of time, it takes time. It beats the clock while slowing down the minutes. This teaching takes more time than when Heidegger, after going through the sections on Nietzsche in *What Is Called Thinking?*, clocks in and tells his students that they must now turn back and spend the next ten years studying Aristotle.

Passive and constricted, one is responsible for one's kōan, which is always related to a public space of notice or inscription. Kōan, which comes from *kō*, "public," "public announcement," and *an*, "matter," "material for thought," involves extreme manipulations of exposure. Tremendous feats of rigorous nothingness are accomplished with intractable discretion. Kōan is a matter of responding thoughtfully beyond thinking to the call of a master's question – the logically insoluble riddle – in a manner that, becoming public, exposes the student to the outer limits of (not-) knowing.[141] Neither students nor master can be said to possess knowledge. Having no interior, the master is not predicable. This condition in no way demobilizes the *effect* the master produces on the restricted theater of the kōan. Unleashing the question, the master may strike the student, regulate the degree of psychic tension, functionally subsidize great doubt, and withhold or cede acknowledgment in a series of discrete interviews. The shock that accompanies the field of knowing beyond knowledge, startling the student into different rosters of articulation, has become condensed and displaced onto the figure of the kōan itself. The *Oxford English Dictionary* cites fairly recent usages that assimilate the kōan's shock effect to the semantic quality of the term, rendering the nature of the problem the cause of shock: "A less physical shock technique is the *kōan*, a problem designed to shock the mind beyond mere thinking." In a letter written on

11 January 1969, Aldous Huxley observes: "They might act as Zen kōans and cause sudden openings into hitherto unglimpsed regions."[142] Ruth Benedict avers: "The significance of the kōan does not lie in the truths these seekers after truth discover."[143]

The sudden openings to which Huxley's letter alludes, and which the major part of texts devoted to kōan interviews confirm, indicate that something like a direct transmission of the Zen hermeneutic can occur outside the sutra. The experience of "getting it" described by the Zen tradition comes closest in recent Western articulations to Heidegger's *Ereignis,* perhaps, in the sense that something occurs, bursts forth at a given moment; it is marked as pure eruption without a lead in or back up. What occurs is an a-temporal interruption or a "fold" in time, something that Heidegger draws from the archaic German word *Eräugnis,* which establishes a link between Being and light. Christopher Fynsk calls this accession to language a blinding of sorts, referring to the opening, in relation to the sudden fulguration of what Hölderlin (and some traditions of Zen Buddhism) designated as a "third eye." It points to an awakening, to a watch that will never be watchful enough.[144]

After years of incessantly working the blind spot, there is still someplace where one fails to see, a limit in perception. The kōan does not quarrel with its own stain of blindness. It stays with the question, suffers blindness. With time, it becomes evident that the awaited answers are not about their discursive content or levels of perception but about the ever-harassing experience of answering. Answering to the call of the kōan, you discover that you are not judged for the quality of the rightness or wrongness of your answer but are turned back upon the ungraspable experience of seeking to answer. Floundering has its own life. At the same time, as the sutras show, one is not given an automatic pass to the failing regions of trying to answer; there exists a hierarchy of flunking out: pupils proffer so many incomplete or wrongheaded answers, to which the master replies with a whacking.

The event of being slugged in the stories and histories that narrate them functions to evoke an equivalency to enlightenment. The hit – no doubt severe and to a more Western sensibility, humiliating (yet unflinchingly offered as compliment and gift) – has to be worked between the literal and figurative points of occurrence in the stories that field them. The teaching words "I hit you" are punctually invoked by the Zen master. These blows are delivered as semiotic units that are meant to inflict a wound or run interference from a domain that exceeds the experience of reading – if such an untroped domain can be understood to take hold. The body that has submitted itself to the task of answering gets hit. When one is hit by the master's rod linguistically, psychically, or referentially, the terms of relatedness to the question and quest switch. Engaged in dharma combat, you are being reminded by this exercise of scarring that there is something possibly other than reading the sutras, another reading, a different experience of writing that is calling you to answer. The switch: it stings, bringing you back to the question without consolation – no safety net or protective gauze, no institutional binding to hold or heal you. The switch or slug, the cutting that occurs as one gets comfortable with the question and takes on the kóan, belongs in fact to a long history of conflict between traditions of the north and south, wealthy and poor practitioners, the readers and nonreaders: each time it revives the problem, debated over the centuries, of whether enlightenment can be attained solely by reading, of whether studying the sutras can of itself bring about enlightenment. It may depend on how you read.

The scene of the proto-pedagogy involves only two persons. The master and pupil together produce an allegory of being struck, enlightened. Though the journey is solitary, one cannot arrive at a solution by oneself: there has to be another, someone who functions as limit in a persistent sting operation. The experience of enlightenment has little (nothing) to do with self, with triumphal narratives of self-gathering, or with the bloated accomplishments of successive sieges of alien territory. (It is difficult by contrast to imagine a Western hero, even one who goes under the name *Weltgeist,* who, when facing the master, would go away so empty-handed, without succeeding – that is, without *stealing* that place for himself according to the precepts of a familiar parricidal maneuver.) The master stands, or rather sits, as a reminder that there has to be something there to read, something outside a self, a being, a registrar of expectant saying – something from the get-go of trying to get it already emptied, depropriated, even if it occurs in the switch of a whiplash.

What of the master? This word weighs heavily on Western vocabularies. The philosophical teaching master often appears as an impoverished cipher. The withdrawal of the exaltation of the master may recall but bears only a vague relation to the Socratic counterpart, the cruiser and prodder, who could give us traction here, as a Western complement to the minimalist figure of mastery. The experience of enlightenment will have nothing to do with what the master has to tell you. The locution "the master knows" amounts to an absurdity. Without interior or predication, the figure for mastering as such – or rather, in the absence of suchness – the bareness of figure cannot warrant the solidity of hierarchy or the permanence of a superior claim on knowledge. From the texts that treat these relations, we discover that dharma combat equalizes everyone: whoever wins it has won. The master in any case cannot confer or confers only the occasional "compliment"; he (sometimes she: there are such stories) repeats, punctuates, helps constitute the experience of enlightenment as he (sometimes she) accompanies the collection of thought (*sesshin*).

The kōan, a kind of contemplative story, a riddle or question, might take anywhere from three to fifteen years to answer. One is called upon steadily to go on with the kōan every moment of one's life. The problem, at a first level, is how to live with one's question. Some efforts to live with the question are seen as dead in the water, or, in any case, as being part of a bad passivity. Against Hung-chih's "silent illumination Zen," Ta-hui offers criticism of what he sees as the extreme passivity of false practice. The root emptiness of Zen practice should not be taken for a dead, lifeless emptiness; nor should practitioners pass their time lifelessly like "cold ashes or a withered tree."[145] Ta-hui is among those Zen masters who vigorously promoted the use of kōan. His teaching was patterned after the kōan. Kōan practice, the most assured path to the attainment of enlightenment, was required of every Zen student. Once the question had been posed, the puzzle formulated, the student was expected to hold fast to it. However, the kōan resisted such a hold. It was meant to summon up terrific doubt and brought practitioners to the edge of endurance. A number of masters, not to say students, suffered appalling breakdowns, some of whom recorded their shattering experiences. The kōan "makes its central point through doubt. Doubt bores into the mind of the practitioner and leads to enlightenment."[146]

For Ta-hui, the kōan elicits doubt, but doubt must not function as a stimulant or undergird drivenness. It belongs to the region of nonnegative negations, a patient abiding with the existential of *withoutness*. Your attention should be fixed on the kōan without yielding to the sense of enchantment that accompanies a discovery, without fascination for the multiplicities of possibilities it may imply, without the thrill of infinite interpretability and, on the other hand, without the guilt of non-totalization. Nor must material indices from a world putatively outside the dilemma of the kōan intrude upon the contemplating mind. In other words, all churns of *striving* must be stilled, although the striving nature of the quest remains largely intact. This structure is in communication with the Faustian valuation of *streben*, the redemptive human quality inscribed in the West-test, though the effort takes on a decidedly different amplitude, insinuating a different measure of achievement. The hold of the kōan is barely comprehensible in terms of Western techniques of endurance testing. There is for instance the story of the monk who failed successively to respond to his kōan; bringing an answer to the master, he was several times rebuffed. He left the monastery, traveled far until he found a huge wall before which he stood for nine years straight, contemplating the question. After nine years, enlightenment struck, and he returned to the monastery where the master was able to acknowledge the response. A second kōan sent him out for another fifteen years.

Besides laying claim to incalculable stores of patience, the kōan regulates and meticulously increases the dosage of anxiety by which it prods the student toward enlightenment. Kao-feng Yüan-miao (1238–1295), a highly respected master from the Yang-chi lineage of the Rinzai school, emphasized the necessity of inducing anxiety and doubt in his magisterial work, *The Essentials of Zen*. The three crucial traits that inform the practice are "a great root of faith" (Jpn., *daishinkan*), "a great tenacity of purpose" (Jpn., *daifunshi*), and "a great feeling of doubt" (Jpn., *daigijo*).[147] In order to convey its principal cast, he illustrates the *feeling* of doubt by summoning forth a criminal's anxiety. A cousin to Nietzsche's pale criminal, this character is caught in the moment of greatest anxiety: gripped by suspense, thoroughly terrified, he wonders whether the heinous crime committed earlier will be found out or not. The lapse between the abomination and its discovery pinpoints the feeling for which the master seeks duration. Trekking alongside faith and purpose, then, there is the excessive anxiety of being caught out, hunted, humiliated. The necessary hinge with the questioning of the question involves the extreme persecution of the respondent, who is held by the master over the edge of pained endurance, a criminal's suspense. (To make a Western or at least a Freudian intervention here, such a criminal houses a superego: the master has already broken in and entered the psyche, bitten by remorse. As Dostoevsky and current psycho upgrades have decisively demonstrated, not all criminals shiver with terror or avoid discovery.)

Ta-hui's teaching of doubt as an essential characteristic of kōan practice remained the norm throughout Chinese Zen from the end of the Sung period. Doubt must have its long day without the stabilizers provided by longing or goal. Ta-hui repeatedly warns against the intrusion of a conscious desire for enlightenment and so presses for the removal of all imaginative and discursive thought. To underscore the pungency of Zen practice, Ta-hui evokes Wu-Tsu Fa-yen, the teacher of his own master, Yüan-wu K'o-ch'in. Ta-hui returns to the "grandfatherly" teacher, an innovator of rigorous kōan practice, after having burned and incinerated the *Hekiganroki*, the work of his own master. The only explanation to help us grasp the reportedly pious act of destruction runs as follows: "Most likely he destroyed the text because he found that its literary beauty was preventing students from the painful struggle with the kōan on nothingness, which for him was the only true kōan."[148] The self-annulling relation to text in kōan history creates significant tensions that parallel metaphysical attacks on writing in the West. Rhetoricity and literary excess are suspected of distracting the contemplator from the objectless object of a prior speech. An allegory of nothingness, the kōan cannot at times tolerate the very materiality of its transmission, the linguistic intrusion on which it nonetheless depends. The famous kōan on nothingness, which assumes an important place in Zen history and which Wu-men Hui-K'ai set as the opening of the *Mumomkan*, concerns the absolute nothingness of the Buddha nature that transcends being and nonbeing.[149] The opening kōan, entitled "Choa-chou's Dog," counts among the few kōans to which he attached a long commentary. Here, too, Wu-men locates the essence of the kōan in its ability to stir up doubt. The character *mu* is, he explains, "the gateless barrier of the Zen school." He asks, "Do you not wish to pass through this barrier?"[150] The other barrier, that of text, must continually be erased so that doubt can be positioned as the sole partition put up before the ever faltering reader. "Do you not wish to pass through this barrier?" If so,

Then concentrate yourself into this "Mu," with your 360 bones and 84,000 pores, making your whole body one great inquiry. Day and night work intently at it. Do not attempt nihilistic or dualistic interpretations. It is like having bolted a red hot iron ball. You try to vomit it but cannot. ... Now, how should one strive? With might and main work at this "Mu," and be "Mu." If you do not stop or waver in your striving, then behold, when the Dharma candle is lighted, darkness is at once enlightened.[151]

Swallowing the unreleasable red-hot iron ball, one strives to become one's "Mu"; one yields to the searing implosion of the incorporated question.

Much as in Plato, the case against writing (and reading) was organized around the theme of passivity. But even writing (and reading) were displaced as acts onto a notion of "gazing," so much are these acts abjected. The Rinzai school, which dominated Chinese Zen during the Sung period, gradually absorbed all other houses and fringe movements with the exception of the Soto school, where the influence of Hung-chih survived. Historians of Zen Buddhism tend to underscore the schism between Hung-chih's "silent-illumination Zen" and Ta-hui's "kōan-gazing Zen," an apparent extension of the conflict between the northern and southern schools, particularly since Ta-hui's "abusive attacks against the quiet sitting practices by the disciples of silent illumination are reminiscent of Shen-hui's assaults on the 'quietism' of the Northern School."[152] At the same time, it would be wrong to sum up the history of Zen from the time of Bodhidharma to the present in terms of only two opposing operations. Nonetheless, the divide between the Rinzai and Soto schools continues to dominate the issues under discussion, and it is continually reasserted in the controversy between Hung-chih and Ta-hui as well as in subsequent disputes. Let us briefly consider their main features. Those in support of Rinzai reproach the Soto school for tending excessively toward passivity: "Only to sit in meditation, they say, dulls the mind into inactivity and engulfs it in a sleepy twilight."[153] While Soto adherents do not deny the dangers of a bad passivity, they counter that their purpose lies elsewhere: "Authentic Soto teachers cultivate an extremely alert and objectless form of meditation. Moreover, kōans are used in the Soto school, albeit not in the same dynamic style as in the Rinzai school. The manner of meditation in the Soto school is more calm, but it certainly does not exclude the experience of enlightenment."[154]

Another significant criticism that Ta-hui directed against Hung-chih concerns the experience of enlightenment (Jpn., *satori*). The Rinzai school watches for a flash experience, an abrupt opening that suddenly sparks a profoundly reorienting conversion: "The quickest and surest way to this kind of experience is through the extreme tension-in-doubt produced by the Kōan exercise. Both kōan and *satori,* say the Rinzai followers, are neglected by the Soto school."[155] The criticism seems hyperbolic, for Soto also recognizes sudden enlightenment, "for which kōan practice can be extremely helpful; not a few of its masters underwent powerful, shattering experiences."[156] The value of such explosive experiences and the difficulty of determining their difference from enlightenment require some further commentary. For the breakthrough is always shadowed by a breakdown; the ascension can also be a fall, though the discipline requires for its legitimate practice the affirmation of a mark of harmony – a palpable measure of control and another conception of clarity that flows gently from serenity. It may appear to duplicate what we might "recognize" as a manic crisis; still, the breakthrough is constituted otherwise and has a different temporal run. Wait. In fact, it does not run. There is something like a passive shattering that seems to be at the root of the debate, reminiscent of Blanchot's discussion of destructive passivities.[157]

There may be a restraining order put on running or on any fast-paced discursive activity; yet, to the extent that it implies tremendous discipline, the restraint itself disrupts the orders of passivity and activity that have seemed opposable to one another. Once again we see that the athletics implicit in kōan practice are not entirely dissimilar from the wrestling matches in Plato or the strained leaps that Heidegger coaches; nor even do they outrun the parameters set by the decathlon that Rousseau charts in the *Promenades of a Solitary Walker.* The athletic contest, no matter how masked or disseminated, has always been lodged in the Western thinking of thought, in what Robert Musil consistently calls our "thought sports." Metaphysics and athleticism often work out on the same track, sharing a field house of language, play, and determination. Even as Heidegger negotiates at the limits of metaphysics, he measures jumps and prescribes unprecedented leaps. The leap is favored by Heidegger for nearly two, arguably Zen, reasons: a phenomenal exertion, it goes essentially nowhere. The jump is a movement of departure and return, moving often to the same place, which no longer claims to be the same. Something will have happened in the interval. Something passed from one place to the same place, which leaves the very notion of place in suspense. The leaps and bounds, the breakthroughs and light converge on a barely measurable marker.

Whether rooted in Rinzai or Soto, the discipline behind the practice is incontestable. Whether we can call the pursuit of enlightenment ("pursuit" is too strong a word – too weak in some ways, as well) a *contest* remains an open question, for the terms are perpetually contested as they arise. The kōan in any case entreats athletic resolve. The body and mind train on the possibility of answering to the task of thinking beyond thinking.

The master gives the student a kōan to think about, resolve, and report back on. The procedure, simple yet incalculable, implodes the concentrated student body. During the time devoted to the uncodified test, concentration intensifies to a breaking point. It is however said that only when the mind is relaxed, free from ego and purpose, fully devoted to the question at hand, can it open itself up, pressing beyond the boundaries of prescribed thinking, stretching beyond the temptation of reason. In his early works, Suzuki subsumes the process under three terms: those of accumulation, saturation, and explosion. These terms are law; they cannot be evaded but serve to indicate an ever-present scale of danger. Accumulation and saturation, when feeding a state of high tension, often lead to serious harm. A sense of danger in fact accompanies the whole ordeal, particularly since it is harried by the delicate timing of explosion. In some instances, the explosion, intended in the best of cases to abide by the rules of organic becoming, does not always follow the model of the opening of the skin of a ripe fruit: "There are plentiful examples from the past and present showing how the practice of the kōan can lead to a bad end. It is not without good reason that Zen masters sound their warnings. The suppression of reason can throw one's psychic life out of balance."[158] Language falters, the student body cracks. A way to catch the fall, in some histories of its recounted occurrence, is to throw down a distinctly Western alibi and brace it with the grid of psychotherapy: "In the Zen practice called 'private interview' (*dekusan*), in which a student makes a progress report to a master, situations may arise that are like those that can take place in the psychotherapist's office. The student utters broken, incoherent words and gives expression to other spontaneous reactions."[159] The student, battling with narrative, is down for the count.

Body-broken, martyred to an overstretched capacity so as to engage the quest, the practitioner of the kōan negotiates with absolute risk, testing and erasing limits that inevitably grind down the prospects of a thinking beyond thinking. Even where the raw nerve of exertion is subdued or denied, the strained condition of a testing without predictable end asserts itself. The intrusion of the test obtains as well in the relation to the master, where the kōan figures as the thirdness that emerges between them, as that which cleaves the conversation, in and beside language.

The significance of the trial of the kōan was not lost on some Western philosophers or analysts. Martin Buber became fascinated by the master-disciple relationship in Zen and focused part of his work on those kōans that explicitly thematized this couple. He also compared the kōan to the "legendary anecdotes" of Hasidism.[160] Carl Jung was led to identify the "great liberation" in Zen with the emancipation of the unconscious.[161] The psychological structure of kōan practice is seen by Jung to open a primordial (if still undeconstructed) space, prior to difference and division: "Under the enormous psychological strain of trying to force a solution for the insoluble kōan, enlightenment is experienced as the dawn of a new reality in which the boundaries between the conscious and unconscious disappears, so that conscious and unconscious alike are laid open."[162] The passive construction ("enlightenment is experienced") attests to the abiding contest between the possibility of a passive overture and the strain of "trying" – another way of relating the sheer openness of the unconscious to that which enables it: the experience of the test, the trial. It is important to note that, when he enters the zone of the unconscious, Jung emphasizes the strenuous efforts of trying, forcing, and experience. He is cornered by that aspect of the kōan that clings to the subjection of tested being.

In the end, though the end is not in sight, submission to the kóan describes a critical syntax of our being, whether parsed according to Eastern or Western indicators. Something has forced one's hand. Prior even to the question, the posture of submissive assent to the kōan, as a kind of primordial acquiescence, a form of consent, welcomes the advent of the question ahead of any determinability, before any dubitative or skeptical interjection, opening the field of a closely held language to what remains to be thought. This openness is sustained by a tremulous spray of doubt. As for the adjustment of mind to this persistent downshift in the disposition of a test drive: "Make sure that you do not allow your mind to run off, like an old mouse that ran into the horn of an ox."[163]

Part 3
On Passing the Test

Who of us is Oedipus here? Who the Sphinx?
It is a rendezvous, it seems, of questions and
question marks. – Friedrich Nietzsche

There's no guarantee yet I'll pass the test. –
Georges Bataille

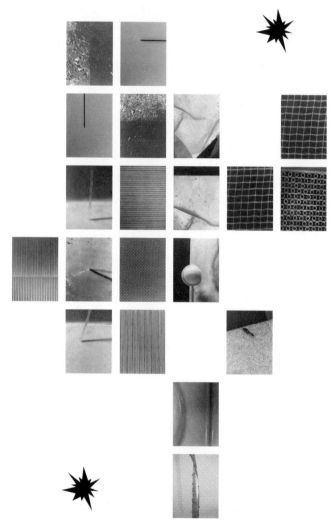

FOCUS GROUP   In a book that was supposed to wrap it all up for him following the extravagance he had permitted himself with *Zarathustra*, Nietzsche speaks of physics as just another interpretation of the world: "It is perhaps just dawning on five or six minds," he calculates, "that physics, too, is only an interpretation and exegesis of the world (to suit us, if I may say so!) and not a world-explanation."[1] By no means intending to underwrite a mere dismissal, Nietzsche sets physics close to religion, which he understands as another, if unquestionably neurotic, interpretation of the world. In *Beyond Good and Evil*, Nietzsche in fact situates science close to conscience, effecting a linguistic parentage for which both German and English allow. Until now science has been the bad conscience of our era, winning out over other, often more decadent but possibly more replenishing interpretive behaviors. The philosophy of the future, Nietzsche projects, belongs to the testers and attempters, to those who are willing to risk themselves on the *Versuch:* "A new species of philosophers is coming up: I venture to baptize them with a name that is not free of danger. As I unriddle them, insofar as they allow themselves to be unriddled – for it belongs to their nature to *want* to remain riddles at some point – these philosophers of the future may have a right – it might also be a wrong – to be called *attempters* [*Versucher:* tempters, testers, experimenters]. This name itself is in the end a mere attempt and, if you will, a temptation."[2] The very act of conjuring and naming the future philosopher belongs to the species of which Nietzsche speaks, for he has ventured to take the risk of positing, of futurity. Inviting danger, he tests the name and brings on the future by means of an experiment in positing, "a mere attempt" that, constructed as a test, is vulnerable to its own destruction. The future philosophers that Nietzsche calls forth in this passage have a right that "might also be a wrong," which is to say that, as he establishes them, giving them rights and existence, Nietzsche equally inserts the code authorizing their refutability.

Nietzsche once again returns to the essential qualities with which he identifies the philosophers of the future by means of what Jules Michelet calls "cet esprit fataliste, ironique, méphistophélique."[3] The philosophers of the future, Nietzsche asserts in the section "We Scholars," "will be men of experiments" (*Menschen der Experimente*).[4] He repeats the presumptive daring involved in naming the experimenters: "With the name in which I dared baptize them I have already stressed expressly their attempts and delight in attempts: was this done because as critics in body and soul they like to employ experiments in a new, perhaps wider, perhaps more dangerous sense?"[5] The implications of the new epoch of experimentation squeeze one's politically correct shoes, but that should not inhibit us because we need to go where Nietzschean indecency takes us and makes us wince. Otherwise we might as well be in our slippers and not at the tryouts, stumbling and staggering, participating in the Olympiad of the Nietzschean stammer. Nietzsche asks, concerning the bold experimenters: "Does their passion for knowledge force them to go further with audacious and painful experiments than the softhearted and effeminate taste of a democratic century could approve?"[6]

There is something about the experimental cast of the future that threatens the democratic century with pain and disruption. According to this engagement with democracy, which has Nietzsche dissociating from the Greeks, there are many hiding places where one can exploit fragile political structures or duck and decay into one or another form of accepting complacency. It is worth our while to focus on the way democratic formations – despite the rants – belong to the experimental exigency of which Nietzsche writes, lending it an ethical stamp. In a text that bears the title "Nietzsche and the Machine," Derrida addresses the hyper-ethical procedure of genealogy.[7] He proposes a thought of political singularities that exceed the structure of the nation-state, observing that, for Nietzsche, "the trial of democracy is also a trial of . . . technicization."[8] Following the cartographies of political utterances drawn up by the last philosopher, Derrida, for his part, suggests that "the name of Nietzsche could serve as an 'index' to a series of questions that have become all the more pressing since the end of the Cold War."[9] Derrida is concerned with the stakes of a democracy to come, with the way, despite some dead moments and fallow poses, it will allow itself to unpack the future. Can democracy thrive, one wonders, without a recognizable state formation, or at least along the lines of a reconfigured notion of nation? Derrida offers: "Today the acceleration of technicization concerns the border of the nation-state."[10] This issue needs "to be completely reconsidered, not in order to sound the death-knell of democracy, but to rethink democracy from *within these conditions*."[11] His tone, if not altogether apocalyptic, remains emphatic about the task at hand: "this rethinking . . . must not be postponed, it is immediate and urgent."[12] Answering this call, let us link what Derrida calls the trial of democracy to the name of Nietzsche – another name for an indefinitely unsatisfied justice – and to the timing of the democracy for which he calls: "this democracy to come is marked in the movement that always carries the present beyond itself, makes it inadequate to itself."[13] For Nietzsche, or for one or two of the signatories in Nietzsche, that which exemplarily carries the present beyond itself is science. In short, Nietzsche makes us ask about the relationship between science and contemporary formations of power – more specifically, about the suspicious partnership of so-called advanced democracies and high technology. What makes these forces match up with each other? What allows these structures mutually to hold up?

Let us bring our focus to an aspect of science that Nietzsche more or less discovered, implemented, posited, and which he links to an affirmable democracy – that is to say, to the experimental culture from which his work takes off. Thus even though Nietzsche can be seen as an antidemocrat, a largely unprobed dimension of his thought provides a rigorous grid for evaluating political formations and exigencies. The conduit for establishing a progressive political science in Nietzsche is circuited through his understanding of scientific structures and their material implications. Nietzsche sets up a lab in *Beyond Good and Evil* rather explicitly. A number of his other works pivot on the "experimental disposition" and treat themselves as experimental efforts. Nietzsche's text incorporates the history of lab culture, which is linked to political innovation. As Derrida has elsewhere argued, there is a Nietzsche of the left and of the right, just as there is a Hegel – or Marx – of the left and of the right.[14] Democracy is itself viewed in terms of a trial, a perpetual test case, never off the hook of its purported levels of achievement. If democracy increasingly depends upon an understanding of incessant tryouts and continual self-testing, reactionary modernity, too, has made use of experimental practice and the tropes of testing. The rhetoric and practices of testing go far beyond what one was willing to see. Politically constelled atrocity fastened onto the technological grid. Nietzsche, alone in his desert, was already picking up signals from a future pockmarked by Nazi experimen-

135

tation, part of whose devastation consisted in setting up the camps as massively unrestricted laboratories – the most unregulated scientific sites in modern history. To this day, ethical questions arise concerning the usability of results stemming from these experiments. Nietzsche, with characteristic ambivalence, saw at least three sides of the coin and tried to navigate between the horror and fascination that experimental culture provoked in him. Let us try to move on and travel along the edges of what Nietzsche massively designated as the experimental disposition. His first appointment is with the philosopher. It is scheduled for the future and is still coming at us.

Even though he announces in *Beyond Good and Evil* the coming of an unprecedented era of a grandiose politics, his aim here seeks out another target. He wants to separate out, among other things, the mere philosophical laborers, and scientific men generally, from the genuine philosophers. The coming philosophers will no longer lean on "Truth" or feelings of disinterested pleasure in order in the end to reconcile "Christian feelings" with "classical taste." The coming philosophers, whom Nietzsche also calls "these severe spirits," will demonstrate "a shrewd courage, the ability to stand alone and give an account of themselves. Indeed, they admit to a pleasure in saying No and in taking things apart, and to a certain levelheaded cruelty that knows how to handle a knife surely and subtly, even when the heart bleeds. They will be *harder* (and perhaps not always only against themselves) than humane people might wish; they will not dally with 'truth' to be 'pleased' or 'elevated' or 'inspired' by her. On the contrary, they will have little faith that *truth* of all things should be accompanied by such amusements for our feelings."[15]

In order to situate the genuine philosophers, linked to the future, and give them space, Nietzsche pulls them away from "those philosophical laborers after the noble model of Kant and Hegel."[16] The laborers, hardly denigrated but rather ennobled, have to determine "and press into formulas," whether in the realm of logic or political thought or art, "some great data of valuations – that is former *positings* of values, creations of value which have become dominant and are for a time called 'truths.'"[17] In the more contemporary terms of speech act theory, philosophical laborers are the heroes of the constative act and assertion. In this regard, according to Nietzsche, they are also managers of the intelligible – they make everything easy for us: "it is for these investigators to make every-

136

thing that has happened and been esteemed so far easy to look over, easy to think over, intelligible and manageable, to abbreviate everything long, even 'time,' and to *overcome* the entire past – an enormous and wonderful task in whose service every subtle pride, every tough will can certainly find satisfaction."[18] The playoffs are subtle, for Nietzsche ascribes pride and will as well as satisfaction to the yields of the philosophical laborer, no matter how subject to Heideggerian scorn the laborer's love of the technological abbreviation will one day become.

By contrast, the genuine philosopher is powered by the self-threatening wheelworks of performativity. Rather than describing and merely computing, the genuine philosopher tests the limits of intelligibility, making things happen with decisive positings that are by no means enslaved to what is. It is perhaps not inconsequential to point out that such a philosopher is not said by Nietzsche to exist presently; nonetheless, the legislative powers of the philosophical action hero already raised a fascisoid hand in Plato. Contrasting them with philosophical laborers, Nietzsche writes, or rather screams: "*Genuine philosophers, however, are commanders and legislators:* they say '*thus* it *shall* be!' They first determine the Wither and For What of man, and in so doing have at their disposal the preliminary labor of all philosophical laborers, all who have overcome the past. With a creative hand they reach for the future, and all that is and has been becomes a means for them, an instrument, a hammer. Their 'knowing' is *creating,* their creating is a legislation, their will to truth is – *will to power.*"[19] The split between the laborer and legislator, between the constative curator and performative commander, is a bit of a fiction that, while keeping spaces open for reciprocal contaminations, nonetheless fails to account for Aristotle, Spinoza, and others, or even for the internal fissures and critical takedowns of Kant and Hegel. The lapse that Nietzsche's prescriptive typology incurs points among other things to the internal collapse of his experiment. Neither sufficiently descriptive nor demonstrably effective, the legislative demand for the disclosable becoming of that which he posits ("*Must* there not be such philosophers? – ") folds and fizzles into the scarring mark of a dash.

The velocities of failure and the noncoincidence that Nietzsche continually reasserts between saying and doing belong to the particular kind of effort that he promotes in this work, one that is bound up in the destructive propensities of ironic positing. Yet the notion of failure is not so simple as that – it is no longer necessarily limited to just one perspective of temporality, as if temporality were part of a game in which the fate of positing could be called once and for all. Or, as if one were not *willed* to crash against walls or succumb to more speculative points of resistance. The genuine philosopher scores failure time and again. The crash course is part of the deal struck with the game or contract for which the genuine philosopher has signed on. This figure "lives 'unphilosophically' and 'unwisely,' above all *imprudently,* and feels the burden and the duty of a hundred attempts and temptations of life – he risks *himself* constantly, he plays the wicked game – ."[20] The hundred attempts and temptations – the tests and trials, the inescapable ordeals – are, Nietzsche insists, a burden and duty felt by the philosopher who risks everything as s/he plays beyond good and evil (the German *sich* does not make a gender decision necessary at the moment Nietzsche designates the self-risking test driver). Since duty prescribes imprudence and unwise risk, the source of imprudence is not itself imprudent but comes from a higher place, pulsing from a greater responsibility, as Nietzsche suggests elsewhere in the text. The duty-bound imprudence comes up against a mute obstacle, namely ignorance and sheer stupidity. In fact, the genuine philosopher runs into the same figure that Flaubert conjures in his reflections on *bêtise:* self-pulverizing granite, foundation of ignorance.

Dedicated to the "Free Spirit," part 2 of *Beyond Good and Evil* begins with the utterance "*O sancta simplicitas!*" Holy simplicity! We tend to live by simplification and falsification, we have made "everything around us clear and free and easy and simple! . . . We have contrived to retain our ignorance. . . . And only on this now solid, granite foundation of ignorance could knowledge rise so far – the will to knowledge on the foundation of a far more powerful will: the will to ignorance."[21] And so on. The pervasive spread of stupidity, fueled by a perverted will to knowledge, is the hard rock against which Nietzsche launches his thought on testing. A critique of any foundationalism, the passage indicates the investment made in retaining ignorance and clearing the way only for simplicity, for the easy listening of lame but sanctioned forms of philosophizing. Without effecting simple oppositions or making rash claims for overcoming the rule of ignorance, Nietzsche proposes a counterphobic example – something that resumes our discussion of the "unphilosophical" genuine philosopher.

The one who stands up against the ranks of stupidity is one who submits to the test. But, this being Nietzsche's call, the test is never over or in some reliable sense passable: it needs to be taken and retaken and finally judged without witnesses or administrators of easy intelligibilities. It depends, moreover, on the right timing: "One has to test oneself to see that one is destined for independence and command – and do it at the right time. One should not dodge one's tests, though they may be the most dangerous game one could play and are tests that are taken in the end before no witness or judge but ourselves."[22] Administering the great test, Nietzsche produces an inventory of what constitutes it. The inventory consists of ten items, all of which begin negatively, telling, in other words, what one must not do. These items do not merely comprise the double negative or flipside of the Ten Commandments but test the commanding force of the philosopher of the future differently, according to another register of being. Rhetorically the ten alternative commandments operate anacoluthically, for they disrupt the syntax of doing that they appear to establish and yet fail to yield another horizon. One is faced with an overall summons to withdraw – or maybe one senses the revving of an engine, the swinging movement of a pitcher's arm as he prepares to throw the ball, but nothing takes off or arrives anywhere. There is no single moment wherein the one being tested is told, for instance, what to honor or aim for.

Not to remain stuck to a fatherland – not even if it suffers most and needs help most – it is less difficult to sever one's heart from a victorious fatherland. Not to remain stuck to some pity – not even for higher men [*höheren Menschen*] into whose rare torture and helplessness some accident allowed us to look. Not to remain stuck to a science – even if it should lure us with the most precious finds that seem to have been saved up precisely for us. Not to remain stuck to one's own detachment, to that voluptuous remoteness and strangeness of the bird who flees ever higher to see ever more below him – the danger of the flier. Not to remain stuck to our own virtues and become as a whole the victim of some detail in us, such as our hospitality, which is the danger of dangers for superior and rich souls who spend themselves lavishly, almost indifferently, and exaggerate the virtue of generosity into a vice.[23]

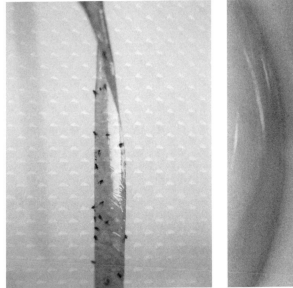

The inventory prescribes extreme forms of detachment, even to the extent of urging the detachment from detachment, so that independence and the ability to command are properly tested. The problem with testing one's independence – the test for Nietzsche is bound up with the possibility of independence – is that it copies the word that tries to describe the freeing perspective for us: in-dependence, *Un-abhängigkeit*. In other words, independence depends on dependence and can come about only by the negation of dependency. But dependence comes first and always squats in any declaration of independence; so-called independence can never shake loose its origin in dependent states. The *un* or *in* of what depends and hangs onto has to undo the core dependency and produce a nonaddictive prospect. This way of skating on the rim of negativity is typical enough of the Nietzschean maneuver that, keeping up its stamina, endeavors not to trigger a dialectical takeover. The test site circumscribed by this text occupies a zone between negation and projected reconciliation; it carves a hole in any possible synthesis. Independence can never be stabilized or depended upon, which is why it has to submit punctually to the test of its own intention and possibility.

The "nots" that Nietzsche enters into the decathlon of testing are also a way of signing his own name by courting and swerving around the nihilistic threat: *Nicht*/Nietzsche. This is the text, remember, in which Nietzsche says that every philosophical work installs a biographical register; he makes it clear that he has strapped himself into this text and also that its articulation should not be limited to the disseminated indications of this or that biographeme. Nonetheless, the test run that he proposes bears the weight of his history, including his never-ending breakup with Richard Wagner. Thus the first self-testing command says: "Not to remain stuck [*hängenbleiben*] to a person – not even the most loved – every person is a prison, also a nook."[24] Beginning with the necessity of wrenching oneself loose from a beloved person, whether a prison or shelter, the inventory goes on to name the urgency of breaking with one's country, even in times of war or need, even when the patriotic introject wants and calls you. A superpower nation-state should be the easiest to sever from.

If the inventory is set up in terms of serial "nots," this is no doubt because Nietzsche needs to enact the complicity of the *Versuch* with its linguistic appointees: the tester or attempter must *desist* from adhering to the temptation that calls. The act, if such it is, of desistance is not as such a negative one, as Derrida has argued in his reading of Philippe Lacoue-Labarthe: "Without being negative, or being subject to a dialectic, it both organizes and disorganizes what it appears to determine."[25] Being tested, which brings together attempter with the tempting, does not fall purely into the zone of action or its purported other – passivity – but engages both at once. Already the locution "being tested," always awkward and slightly wrenching, invites the intervention of the passive where action or at least some activity is indicated. The test takes one through the magnetizing sites to which one is spontaneously, nearly naturally, attracted. This could be a resting place, a shelter and solace overseen by the friendly protectors of the pleasure principle. But Nietzsche, like the other guy, takes the test beyond the pleasure principle. Elsewhere Nietzsche states that pity toppled the gods; pity, the most dangerous affect, counts for the one to which we are most prone. We are tempted and tested by pity, roped in by its grim allure, and even if we are not gods, pity can make us crumble and christianize. (This does not mean that Nietzsche advocates the vulgarity of some forms of indifference. Only that action and intervention should not eventuate from pity, as do "benevolent racism" and the like. Liberal pity policies would be nauseating to Nietzsche; they are not radical, strong, or loving enough. Of course nowadays, I would even take liberal pity.)

Science belongs to the list of the desisted – "resistance" would come off as too strong a term, too repressive and dependent on what presents itself. The inclusion of science in the subtle athletics of the "not" may reflect the way Nietzsche had to break away from his scientific niche of philology, but there is more to it. It is not just a matter of releasing oneself from a scientific commitment in order to pass the Nietzschean test. As the other term in the partnership, science itself stands to lose from too tight a grip and needs eventually to loosen the bond. A true temptress, science fascinates, perhaps seduces and lulls. It captivates and often enough gives one a high, an intoxicating sense of one's own capacity for mastery. Yet science itself is implicated in the relation thus structured. For science not only curates the test from a place of superiority but is itself subject to the rigors and renewals of testing. So even if it invites the blindness of fascination and the sum of addictive returns, science needs to be released if only to go under, to dissolve its substantial mask and be turned over to fresh scientific probes.

The movement of dislocation and disappropriation continues even to the point of disallowing sheer detachment. Increasing the dosage of desistance to the level of turning on itself, Nietzsche proposes that one should not remain dependent on one's experience of voluptuous detachment. He keeps the tested being in the vehicle of the "dis-" and rigorously refuses to issue a permit for sticking to any moment or structure of being that would seem welcoming or appropriate. (It is appropriate only to disappropriate, to trace one's own expropriation from a site that persistently beguiles with the proper.) Thus one must desist even from becoming attached to one's own virtues, such as hospitality. Virtue itself, no matter how generous or exemplary, can trip up the one being tested. Virtue can enlarge itself, take over; it is vulnerable to imperial acts of expansion. One can become enslaved to one's virtue, attend to it immoderately, and turn oneself into a hospital for the vampirizing other. In this ward, as in other Nietzschean wings, strong and superior beings encounter the danger of infection, a weakening. They give too much and spend themselves as if they were infinitely capable of the offerings for which they are solicited. The offerings turn into sacrifice; the superior soul gives itself away, finding that it is spent, exhausted. Thus the virtue of generosity, coextensive with hospitality, is turned into a vice. Virtue tips into its other and generosity soon becomes a depleting burden.

At the end of the day, the hardest test concerns *expenditure*, the squandering of the self that gives itself away too readily, draining the will, exhausting the power. The effort of halting the effort – the principle of self-conservation, "sich bewahren" – is linked by Nietzsche to the hardest of all in this battery of tests. Why would conserving oneself constitute the most difficult test? It is as if expenditure were an instinct that needed to be inhibited: in this regard we are reminded of Nietzsche's pronouncements on non-ejaculatory practice, on the requisite resorption of semen. Nietzsche thwarted the spermatic economy, stopped the flow in order to ensure self-conservation, bringing together the withholding power of testing and testicles. In other words, moreover, one should not multiply – or, at least getting away from biblical commands, as Nietzsche does, one should not multiply indifferently; one should not be hospitable to those indiscriminate and parasitic demands that utterly destroy the one being tested.[26] On another, possibly more allegorical register, Nietzsche points to a tendency in the very structure of testing. In this passage on testing, culminating in the crescendo that actually takes itself back – the hardest test places one close to the refusal of test, asking that one conserve oneself on the hinge between extreme effort and effortlessness – one inescapably encounters the danger of dissolution. To evoke an old Nietzschean block-buster, one can take a turn into a Dionysian danger zone. The battery of tests is watched over by the hardest test that, in a sense, calibrates the level of submission to the test. Extreme submission to the test – this is what the test requires – runs the risk of wearing down to the point of obliterating the one being tested. This peril advisory comes close to the current Nietzschean cliché, What won't kill you will make you stronger. Yet – assuming this peculiar perspective to be viable – one needs to come close to the killing point before suddenly desisting.

It is not clear to me how Nietzsche establishes the limit: when, for example, does generosity go overboard, at what point is hospitality over the top, or what event, act, or mark designates the point of no return? Can one know ahead of time when the expenditure will have been too great? If such knowledge is predictable or programmable, then we are no longer dealing with the ordeal that Nietzsche calls a test, unless Nietzsche's intervention requires us to think the safety valve, the recourse where precisely none presents itself. Is there a test that could call itself off without renouncing itself? In a more lab-oriented sense, Nietzsche perhaps indicates here another logic of the test that manages to maintain the integrity of the object or material submitted for testing – something on a more philosophical level that reflects the way in which PCR (Polymerase Chain Reaction) technically has changed the scene of DNA replication, which is to say, it resolves the problem of preserving evidence where the risk is run each time that evidence would be destroyed by the test that seeks to name it.[27]

The test site that Nietzsche installs in this instance is, so to speak, a self-inflicted one. The ostensible issue in §41 is how to test one's independence. Thus, the test of independence, as the passage appears to demonstrate, is in the end the assumption itself of the test. All the aporias and paradoxes we indicated notwithstanding, independence depends on testing, on the willingness to submit oneself to the test. One must take it at the right time, time oneself, check the ambient conditions, monitor one's resolve and submission without relying on witnesses or judges other than oneself. Nietzsche calls for an independent testing system – so independent, in fact, that it will never fully constitute a coherent protocol. Independence does not result from the test or get scored merely on its grid.

The taking of the test in itself constitutes an act of independence. Yet it is not a matter solely of taking, or even administering, a test. One *gives* oneself the test: "Man muss sich selbst seine Proben geben."[28] In order to determine one's capacity for being independent and taking command, one must give oneself one's tests. The test comes as a kind of gift to oneself; it consists in something that one gives oneself. At the same time, however, a duty has been signaled, for one *must* give oneself this gift; one is duty-bound to offer oneself up to the gift of the test. Split into the one who must give and the other who takes the test, one is in sum commanded to test one's own aptitude for assuming command. Taking command means giving oneself over to the test, just as independence implies submission to the test, even to the "hardest" test which Nietzsche associates with *sich bewahren,* self-conservation – the only flash of truth (*wahr* = true) that the testing ground will license. To the extent that one is commanded to hang on to this shred of truth and conserve oneself, given that one is driven to swerve from the absolute risk that the imperative of testing appears to imply – desistance precisely does not allow one to plunge oneself into uncertainty – Nietzsche's call for testing at this point appears to be what it says it is: conservative. At the very least, it embraces the experience of the impossible: as such the passage genuinely fulfills its destiny as test. It may well be that, in the last minute, he calls off the game. The hardest test may have been to stop the test, to sign and countersign a kind of test ban treaty with the *sich* that has staked everything on the passing of the test.

One last word. One last man. One last minute retraction. Yes, we know, no more "one." Part of Nietzsche's legacy – to have sprung us from the tyranny of the one (one God, one nation, one yes, and so on). So now we get to lose the (male) metaphysical subject, lose Zarathustra, if not lose then at least to loosen the chains that have kept us down historically, linking us metaphysically to the worst offenses. Destabilizing the one, Nietzsche also fears the many. So he multiplies the many into different and many manys. Into different valences of many. There is also a good many. It turns out to split off from the manly many and reverberates with future. Let us return to a moment in our elaboration. We skipped a beat. The passage announcing the advent of future philosophers – they come in the plural – permits another variable to be entered and engages yet another politicized register.

Nietzsche calls up a "neue Gattung von Philosophen," which has been translated as a "new species of philosophers." *Gattung* is more thought-provoking than "species" to the extent that it implies gender as well as genre – engendering further generational affiliations, some of which have been accounted for in Derrida's important essay, "The Law of Genre."[29] Nietzsche does not decide here on the gender of the future philosopher, which motivates in part his pluralization of the philosopher. The pluralization of the coming philosopher destabilizes any number of philosophical customs and hierarchies including those that honored the singular appointment of the function of philosopher-king. For all we know at this point, the future philosophers may be a band of women or they may already befigure, with the roughness of a preliminary sketch – an early scientific trial – the transhuman, which by no means effaces the feminine. The *Übermensch* is not an *Übermann* but is over man the way we say, "I'm over him." But what a struggle! The text is adamant on this point; it offers a number of compelling reasons to retain the feminine as a trace of the future, though they complicate the Nietzschean legacy considerably. Still, they belong to the experimental labor that Nietzsche sets up, even as he supplants one type of feminine force with another. There are at least two feminine types contesting the scientific legacy that Nietzsche interrogates. One of these types, accusatory and fatiguing, Nietzsche tries to clear away. The other type to which he opens the future as well as his name has mastered and transvaluated ordeals such as exorbitant *submission,* which primes an other being for philosophical admissions. This new species, which could be called in accordance with Nietzsche's notion of the *über* (trans), *transfeminists,* will have updated the philosopher's résumé. They have understood and withstood the trial period of going under, holding back – and even hiding. Transfeminists have something in common with the figure I am investigating. They in fact tie into the double bind of which Nietzsche writes as he prepares the test site: They appear to call off the game even as they play it, at once asserting its irrevocability and rescinding its ground. Veiled, withholding, the philosophers of the future may not "allow themselves to be unriddled."[30] They communicate secretly with the figure that opens *Beyond Good and Evil:* "Supposing truth is a woman – what then?" Until now, insofar as they were dogmatists, philosophers "have been very inexpert about women."[31] There is a residue that philosophy has not been able to read or account for. Nietzsche calls this residue, at times, when things get urgent or truth is on the line, a woman. The hypothesis of woman sends out a call, magnetizes the philosopher. Broadly interrogated, she also interrogates, throws off. Even as a mere hypothesis, she has the philosopher by the balls. But let us not get too personal here, or overly anthropomorphic, though – there is no doubt about this – Nietzsche started it. Woman as hypothesis belongs to the same thinking that skips the groove of metaphysics – the "dangerous perhaps" which Nietzsche establishes here to give the philosophers of the future a running start. Try to imagine a philosophy that subjects itself rigorously to the "perhapses" of life.[32]

We do not know who or what the future philosophers will be, but this nonsubstantial sketch *is* their substance. The new philosophers appear to take a graft from what stands as the paleonymnic "woman," a value that programs its own mutation. For woman, as Derrida's *Spurs* has pointed out – concerning at least the woman in Nietzsche – does not believe in herself as a fixable identity, as substance or as that which would allow the clumsy dogmatist to pin her down to an essence.[33] Until now, philosophy has targeted woman for truth, yet the feminine operation that Nietzsche engages places her as the untruth of truth, as that which blows a hole in the philosopher's phantasm of truth. Until now, philosophers have been molesters rather than testers; they have not understood how to welcome the feminine within or without, how to probe beyond a given limit to-ward something – a splice, a movement, a laugh, a time zone, an internal tremor that cannot be restricted to what we think we know about woman or truth or, for that matter, God and philosophy. As that which bears the future or holds truth close to the vest, even if the holding braces the un-truth of truth, woman establishes another *relation* for the philosopher, an innumerability of relation that requires an altogether different type of scientific encounter, what some have seen as multiplicity, others as folds, still others as a provocative multiplication of perspectives. The affirm-ative unfixity springs from the feminine in Nietzsche, disclosing one of the feminine types (the "effeminate" – which he necessarily associates with men, but he even correlates stale feminists with men – belongs to the other, more discredited type) that unsnaps from the philosophical lock-in. Drawn only to the *Dis-tanz* of an unstoppable withdrawal, this type matches the desistance that Nietzsche comes to associate with the exem-plary stance of the somewhat fused tested/tester. In any case, if you have practiced your binary scales and done your homework, you have already gathered that "beyond good and evil" also means beyond man and woman.

The bound beyond means, among other things, that Nietzsche is not simply proposing woman as the heir to and overcoming of the one who has lorded it over us for so long. Such a plan would not be radical enough for Nietzsche but rather constitutes a relapse. He is not throwing philosophy into reverse or reversal by means of a simple exchange of values – woman for man, one horizon for another. The horizon that would allow for the complacency of such a maneuver is being punctured by the Nietzschean stylus. When Nietzsche opens a space for the aggravation of gender here, he is not meaning to introduce a stealth dialectics or an operation of salvation. In other words, he does not come to a full stop or turnaround to meet one of the options that have clumsily asserted themselves in the reigning house of metaphysics. In one of those peculiar conceptual alliances and collapses, only feminists and misogynists know for sure what a woman is. Nietzsche, for his part, performatively calls upon and creates a *new* species, which may have some recycled parts and evolved structures, but, frankly, we cannot know or say what this is. We cannot tell, as if this were not a matter of a radical and ongoing experiment, how the transfeminist pluricity reads, replicates, sectionizes, or equalizes "woman." So, for instance, to move it along, Nietzsche would hesitate before allowing his thought to prefigure those aspects of heir presumptive Richard Rorty's projections which have produced women as an answer to philosophy's own existential crisis and, in terms of a more pragmatic measure, have gone so far as to make Catharine MacKinnon the smartest cookie in the bell jar. Woman is not purely and simply the answer (again: supposing we know what this is above and beyond the regimens of lack, appendage, extension, reflection, repetition, other). If at all, she is the exigency of the test, a way of naming that which is continually put on trial, disturbing the language of viability, without necessarily resolving or satisfying anything, any condition or ground or afterthought or primal memory. If woman appears as a hypothetical yet commanding being at the starting line of *Beyond Good and Evil,* Nietzsche, having injected her corpus with hormones, is, near the putative end of the text, "a storm pregnant with new lightnings" (welches mit neuen Blitzen schwanger geht).[34] Nietzsche, once again – expecting.

Let us proceed.

Part 4
The Test Drive

On Nietzsche's
Gay Science

Wasted a fair bit of patriotic young flesh in order to test some new technology. – William Gibson, *Neuromancer*

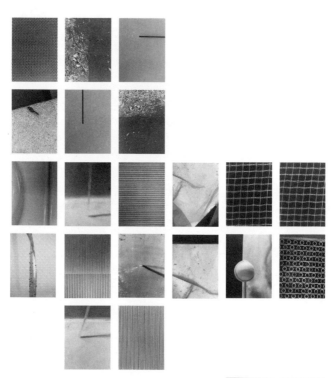

Attunement

There was once a man; he had learned as a child that beautiful tale of how God tried Abraham, how he withstood the test, kept his faith and for the second time received a son against every expectation. . . . This man was no thinker, he felt no need to go further than faith. . . . This man was no learned exegete, he knew no Hebrew; had he known Hebrew then perhaps it might have been easy for him to understand the story of Abraham.
— Søren Kierkegaard, *Fear and Trembling*

TEST PATTERN   We do not always know how to calculate the importance of a work. In some cases, there is nothing even to guarantee that the work will arrive. Some works seem to set an ETA – there is a sense that it will take them years to make their arrangements, overcome the obstacles of an unprotected journey, get past the false reception desks blocking their paths. In the more assured and seductive version, these works follow the itinerary of Walter Benjamin's secret rendezvous – targeting the "geheime Verabredung" that a work has made with the singularity of a destination: in the form, perhaps, of a future reader. The reader or receptor from the future assumes the responsibility of being addressed, of signing for the work when it finally arrives, helping it originate. Yet little tells us how many hits a work will have taken on its way or whether we will be there to receive it. Perhaps the work will be prevented from showing up at the appointed time. On the other hand, some works barrel toward their destination, causing a lot of trouble for a lot of Daseins. Heidegger once said that it can take two hundred years to undo the damage inflicted by certain works – I think he was evaluating Plato. For my part, I cannot tell whether the *Gay Science* has arrived or even, really, where it was going when Nietzsche sent it on its way. Still, I am prepared to sign for it. That is to say, I have prepared myself for it. I am not reluctant to assess the damage for which it still may be responsible – assuming the work has arrived and I can find its points of entry – or whether (but this is not a contradiction) this work has fashioned essential trajectories that provide existence with ever new supplies of meaning. I am using "work" here in the widest possible sense because Nietzsche – well, Nietzsche stood for the absence of the work.[1] He continues to pose the dilemma of the most unauthorized of authors – so many signatures, styles, shredders. Nonetheless, something keeps arriving and returning under that name, something that addresses us with uncommon urgency. So: *The Gay Science.*

To the extent that science is meant to promote life, Nietzsche makes it his business to put demands on its self-understanding. For Nietzsche, science – or, more to the point, the scientific interpretation of life – owes us an account of itself, if only to give us access to its overwhelming use of force over diverse discursive populations. It would not be stretching things too far to say that in Nietzsche's estimation science needs to be audited at every turn, each year. The philosophical pressure is on for science to come clean, to declassify the language usage and rhetorical combinations that have supported the prodigal domination of science over other interpretive interventions and possible worlds. If Nietzsche wants to keep it clean, this in part is because he *needs* science in order to make some of his most radical claims. His relation to science is by no means driven by resentment but rests on appropriative affirmation. As with all appropriations, things can get rough at times. Yet it is from a place of exorbitant responsibility that Nietzsche writes up his version of science and, against the many pronounced inclinations of science, makes joyousness a new prerequisite of scientific endeavor. Not one to get tangled in obsolesced subjectivities, Nietzsche at times saw himself as a scientific object. Thus, in an effort to explain himself as a prophetic human being he writes: "I should have been at the electric exhibition in Paris" as an exhibit at the world's science fair.[2] Elsewhere, as we know, Nietzsche comes out not so much as man but as dynamite. Taking these articulated mutations seriously – one of his masks will have been the scientific object – how can we make sense of Nietzsche's call today?

TESTING . . . 🔊)1   If we are prepared only now to receive his version of the question concerning technology, this is because he ran it along the lines of a delay call forwarding system. He made us wait, holding back the scientific punch he wanted delivered. The call put out by Nietzsche remains the urgent question of a text that bears the burden of an enigmatic encounter with science. Nietzsche gives us science as an assignment, as a trust to be taken on unconditionally. Neither the first nor the last to make science part of an irrevocable curriculum, Nietzsche saw in science the potential for uncompromising honesty in terms of understanding who we are and what we can become. At this point, only the scientific interpretation of life is capable in principle of zapping those dubious mythologies and bad drugs that keep things hazy, enslaved, grimly pessimistic. On some level, science does not owe anything to anyone; it does not have to bend its rules to suit this or that transcendental power broker. In principle, science does not have to rhyme with nation-state or God but should be able to bypass the more provincial tollbooths of ever narrowing global highways. Science, if it wanted to do so, could, in principle, travel its zones with a free pass. More imposingly still, science could kick its way out of any religious holding pen and put down deadly fanaticisms in a flash of its idiomatic brilliance. In his rendering and genealogical breakdown, Nietzsche did not mean for science to become a servile instrument of a corporate state, though he saw how that could happen. But when Nietzsche takes on science, commanding its future – Nietzsche had first dibs on at least one or two of the possible futures allotted to the domains of science – he addresses the promise of science according to altogether singular categories, drawing up new amendments to its manifestly powerful constitution.

A peculiar feature in the legacy of *The Gay Science* lies in the fact that the *scientificity* of Nietzsche's use of "science" has stubbornly resisted a satisfying elucidation. This fact is not to be ascribed simply to some contingent prejudice in reading or to another, equally fugitive, form of blindness. If we have been unable comfortably to receive Nietzsche's word on the scientificity of science in contemporary terms, this may be so because his reach extends so far ahead of the limits of understanding that our scanners are eluded by it. In fact, Nietzsche's science has shaken off readers not only because of the unprecedented leaps and bounds on which his writing prides itself thematically, but also because of the strange terms of prediction that it posits, and which seem linked to whatever it is that Nietzsche means by *la gaya scienza*. In this context "gay," as Walter Kaufmann is careful to point out, does not necessarily mean "homosexual," though such rights of non-reproductive association by pleasure and thought pattern are certainly implied by the terms of the contract that Nietzsche draws up.[3] What is a science that predicates itself on gaiety without losing its quality of being a science? And how does Nietzsche open the channels of a scientificity that, without compromising the rigor of inquiry, would allow for the inventiveness of science fiction, experimental art, social innovation, and, above all, a highly stylized existence?

If Nietzsche had discovered something like the essence of a future science, it may well be the case that it exposed itself to him in the way great discoveries are made, namely, when thought "catches it in flight without really knowing what it has caught."[4] In other words, Nietzsche continually offers a model for cognition that cannot simply account for itself or maintain its results within the assumed certitudes of a controlled system of knowledge. At some level, the correlated acts of discovery and invention exceed the limits of what is knowable or even, as Jacques Derrida has argued, strictly recognizable.[5] The meaning of scientificity that concerns Nietzsche, and that can be seen to dominate the technological field in which we moderns exist, embraces the qualities of both destructive and artistic modes of production, involving an ever elusive and yet at the same time tremendously potent force field. Our being has been modalized by the various technologies in ways that have begun fairly recently to receive serious attention in the domains of ontology, ethics, political theory, cybernetics, critical thought, and artificial intelligence. Yet what concerns Nietzsche belongs neither strictly inside nor outside any of these domains but has nonetheless infiltrated their very core – something, indeed, that Nietzsche's Gay Sci was first to articulate succinctly. Nietzsche variously motivates the scientific premise of his work by terms that indicate the activities of testing, which include experimentation, trial, hypothetical positing, retrial, and more testing. If anything, Gay Sci signals to us today the extent to which our rapport to the world has undergone considerable mutation by means of our adherence to the imperatives of testing. The consequences of this grid are considerable, involving, to say the least, our relation to explanatory and descriptive language, truth, conclusiveness, result, probability, process, identity. Testing, moreover, implies for Nietzsche very specific temporal inflections. Henceforth everything will have to stand the test of time, which is to say that, ever provisional, things as well as concepts must be tried and proven, and structurally regulated by the destruction of a hypothesis that holds them together. The logic of the living as much as the perspective of decline must go to trial. If it weren't too explosive, one could say that Nietzsche laid the fundamental groundwork for corroborating Karl Popper's theory of falsifiability.

Nietzsche marvels at a science that, like a warrior, can go out and test itself repeatedly. If today's world is ruled conceptually by the primacy of testing – nuclear testing, drug testing, HIV, admissions, employment, pregnancy, SAT, GRE, MCAT, DNA, testing limits, testing a state's capacity for justice, as I just read in today's paper, and so on – then this growing dependency on the test is coextensive with Nietzsche's recognition of the modern experimental turn. The experimental turn, as we now know it from a history of flukes, successes, and near misses, in its genesis and orientation, travels way beyond good and evil. Its undocumented travel plan – there are so many secret destinations of which we remain ignorant – is perhaps why experimentation is a locus of tremendous ethical anxiety. No matter how controlled, we cannot know where it is going. Nietzsche acquires definition largely by the tests that he and his work have had to endure or, to put it more gaily, the experiments that they, in every possible (and impossible) walk of life and writing, have attempted. There is always the question of Nietzsche's scandalous itinerary, not the least stage of which entails his prediction that his name would one day be associated with the greatest catastrophe in history. What does this predictive utterance have to do with science? Nietzsche shows prediction to be responsible for its very essence, related as it is to the future, which science is always preparing.

Prediction, as a promise that can only ironize itself (only time will tell), is the genealogical test par excellence, linking futurity to language and its capacity to command the arrangements of a nearly magical authority. In this regard it is of some consequence that Nietzsche names in "Preludes of Science" the importance of magicians, astrologers, and witches – figures who created a taste and hunger for hidden, forbidden powers but who also make us recognize that "infinitely more had to be promised than could ever be fulfilled."[6] Thus prediction and science, however occult their origins (and only a few things occupy more spooky premises than such futural ghosts as prophesy and invention), are rooted in the irony of promise. The noncoincidence of scientific promise and its fulfillment is what Nietzsche calls the Test.

Lest we succumb to the temptation of blinking Nietzsche into a magician, an astrologer, or a witch, we should remember that, while he was a strong medium, his feeling for the future, "a very powerful future feeling," is not simply that of a sorcerer's apprentice who may not appreciate the consequences of the suprahuman adventure. Nietzsche, on the contrary, communicates the solid concern of a knowing elder. He writes of himself, of his very powerful futural scanners, as "an heir with a sense of obligation, the most aristocratic of old nobles and at the same time the first of a new nobility – the like of which no age has yet seen or dreamed of ... the oldest, the newest, losses, hopes, conquests, and the victories of humanity."[7] Describing his relation to science, Nietzsche taps a paradoxical feeling that includes both aristocratic obligation toward the future and the more American live-for-today spirit of experimentation. Both moments are tied for Nietzsche to a necessarily *prophetic* science. The prevailing mood of such a scientist is that of Dionysian pessimism, what Nietzsche calls the "pessimism of the future – for it comes! I see it coming!" The uncanny capacity for premonition and vision "belongs to me as inseparable from me, as my *proprium* and *ipsissimum*."[8] And so, in Book Five of *The Gay Science* Nietzsche prepares the ground for the new nobility of scientific responsiveness and, linking the two moments of the title, he explicates "the meaning of our cheerfulness" by situating "us" at our posts. In terms of the sequence of his argument, he, the last philosopher, locates the principal qualities of a gay science directly after the announcement of the greatest recent event – that God is dead, that the belief in the Christian God has proven unbelievable. By now the results are out: God indeed has failed the test; faith has been categorically undermined.

In God's wake the prophet of gloom assumes his new responsibilities: "This long plenitude and sequence of breakdown, destruction, ruin, and cataclysm that is now impending – who could guess enough of it today to be compelled to play the teacher and advance proclaimer of this monstrous logic of terror, the prophet of a gloom and an eclipse of the sun whose like has probably never yet occurred on earth?" The prophecy carried by Nietzsche's language reads the gloom that awaits while evincing a tremor of amazement because the coast is now clear for his rising to meet the monstrous logic of terror. Science comes at a high price, for God's failure leaves a bankrupt historical account. Correspondingly, the walled up stores of meaning that had held things together are bound to crumble. As premature birth of the coming century, Nietzsche carries himself over to a time of the ruptured horizon, proclaiming the end as an unprecedented opening. A rapture of fright rouses the lover of knowledge. Accepting a grimly provocative horizon in exchange for free rein, "we born guessers of riddles" throw open a scientific path:

Even we born guessers of riddles who are, as it were, waiting on the mountains, posted between today and tomorrow, stretched in the contradiction between today and tomorrow, we firstlings and premature births of the coming century, to whom the shadows that must soon envelope Europe really should have appeared by now – why is it that even we look forward to the approaching gloom without any real sense of involvement and above all without any worry and fear for ourselves? ... [O]ur heart overflows with gratitude, amazement, premonitions, expectation. At long last the horizon appears free to us again, even if it should not be bright; at long last our ships may venture out again, venture out to face any danger; all the daring of the lover of knowledge is permitted again.[9]

Premonition and freedom meet over the horizontal abyss, turning prediction toward a dangerous opening. The permit that has been issued at this precarious juncture is nothing less than a test driver's license. In a decidedly Kantian sense, freedom is viewed as a given and not something to be argued for or endlessly negotiated. Thus the Nietzschean horizon "appears free to us again" – freedom has been restored to the horizon. The disappearance or withholding of freedom is strictly illegitimate. Tell this to the judge. So the coast is clear, freedom restored, and a new license granted. If it had been revoked, Nietzsche suggests in another passage, this is due to the moral prejudice against science: the conspiracy against adventure and deregulated knowledge was imposed on us iconically by the couple, Faust and Mephistopheles – traitors to the cause of godless science.

It turns out that Faust was put on a short leash puppeteered in the end by God. Mephisto, deflated and castrated by the divine veto, loses all bets as well as his mortal lab. As it happens, God cannot tolerate the experiment or proof. Double-crossed, Mephisto in sum was made to function as an inhibitor to the scientific adventure, and his research on the creature, man, was terminated without due process. Nietzsche blows the whistle on the cosmic subterfuge. This thematic reproach represents one of the very few swipes that Nietzsche takes at Goethe. In terms of the aims he takes, it represents somewhat of a strange moment, for Nietzsche attacks the *literary* Goethe for a *scientific* error – Nietzsche tends to keep the accounts separate. At the same time, it could be argued that the secret hero of Nietzsche's scientific investigations is the Goethe of the *Theory of*

Colors, whose bold experiments put the experimenter on the line. Goethe pioneered the moment when the body became the test site and not a secondary prop for a transcendentalizing consciousness. This is the Goethe that Nietzsche represses when he goes after the Goethe who produced the drama of *volte-face,* Faust's abrupt decathexis of science. In this case, Nietzsche shows little tolerance for Goethe's double entry accounts. But the history of Goethe's doublings and repressions, his Nietzschean mirrorings in art and science, his Freudian prophecies and Lacanian triggers, would take us far afield. Suffice it to say that Nietzsche monitored Goethe's scientific retreat in fiction with acute anxiety.

One could argue that, nowadays, since the fateful advent of the Gay Sci, but perhaps not solely because of it, there is nothing that is not tested or subject to testing. We exist under its sway, so much so that one could assert that technology has now transformed world into so many test sites. Let us set up this phase of our inquiry by discussing Nietzsche's unprecedented emphasis on experimentation, which is what I believe provides the crucial access code to the possibility of a gay science.

TESTING ◀)1 . . . ◀))2 . . .   A vaguely threatening insinuation, the challenge sparked by the utterance, "Try me!" could come from any number of places. It could be the case that it speaks from the place of an action hero, a mundane bully, as a girl gang member, a new appliance, a car, or whomever your buffed up interlocutor might be today. In fact, when you hear someone say, "Try me!" it is very likely that he is speaking from the essence of technology – a shorthand formula intended to establish a tone of defiance, enjoining the other to test a limit. "Try me!" may challenge you to "see what happens" if the line is crossed. It also allows one to encounter the subject on a trial basis: there is something yet to be seen or recanted in the field of the encounter with the other. A call to test the space between us, "Try me!" however soon reverts to a faux experimental generosity. For while it gives the green light to go ahead and probe limits, it switches on the glare of a red light as well, protecting a designated turf. It does both at once, inviting an experimental advance and, intimating caution, averting its execution. One throws one's body in the way of an advance. Nietzsche's gesture moves the challenge in a different direction when he invokes, "Versuchen wir's." As if in response to the tapered challenge, his work often says "Let's try it" or "Let's try it out" – let us *give* it a try. Turning the trial into a gift, Nietzsche creates a space of recessive limits, at least when it comes to dogmatic assertions and cognitive boundaries. He makes his conditions known. In order to earn Nietzsche's praise, a given assertion must be trial-ready, inviting the type of responsiveness that allows for the experiment – what Nietzsche sees as a highly responsible stipulation and structure. Nietzsche, the thinker of the test site – from the selective test of the eternal return, to Zarathustra's trials, and the experimental language shots of the aphoristic texts – insisted on these very conditions. "Versuchen wir's!" circumscribes the space of an unceasing series of audacious experiments:

> I favor any skepsis to which I may reply: "Let us try [versuchen] it!" But I no longer wish to hear anything of all those things and questions that do not permit any experiment . . . for there courage has lost its right.[10]

Under the flag of courage – his translation into scientific terms of Hölderlin's "Dichtermut" (poetic courage) – Nietzsche henceforth closes his ears to anything that disallows experimental probity. One could argue that, in *Human, All-Too-Human, Dawn,* and *The Gay Science,* Nietzsche sets up a lab in which he performs "the countless experiments on which later theories might be built."[11] Each aphorism is set up as an experiment to be tested, observed, and, where necessary, *rescinded.* Performing a kind of anti-sublation, rescindability becomes the true test of courage. Where Hegel might gather and hold in *Aufhebung,* Nietzsche, in and on principle, discards, lets go. His work depends on the bounce of rescindability, on the ability to mourn that which cannot prove or seriously legitimate itself. Such acts of letting go have nothing to do with wimping out or with the betrayal of what has been; instead, they provide a way of articulating an enhanced capacity to take the cuts of criticism, basing nothing on faith or mere durability. Letting go in this way indicates a mark of vitality that points to the minimally paranoiac path, if that should be conceivable, of scholarly pursuit. Show me scholars today who have the courage to see their little convictions put to the test! But scholars are cool with Nietzsche, so let me rescind. In fact, scholars unquestionably make the grade on this point, for they demand that prior training and discipline be proven to them – he calls it their unconditional probity. Scholars are battle-tested; they persistently shave down the lies, ruses, and falsifications that are strewn along their paths. Thus, "I bless you, my scholarly friends," writes Nietzsche, performing a ritual politics of friendship. I bless you "even for your hunched backs. And for despising, as I do, the 'men of letters' and culture parasites. And for not knowing how to make a business of the spirit. And for having opinions that cannot be translated into financial values. . . . And because your sole aim is to become masters of your craft, with reverence for every kind of mastery and competence" and so forth.[12] This inventory of praise represents one of the rare passages in which Nietzsche acknowledges, with only some irony, the relative nobility of the scholar. This is because scholars are on the way to scientificity, that is, they require proof and have undergone the severe conditions of one intellectual boot camp or another.

Scholars, who, in principle, are not pretenders, are not in it for the money (in principle), and they deal with their bosses, the university and state, with some amount of defiance despite themselves. At least they are not simply writing "for" the university and teaching "for" the state, though they may be teaching in the institution and backing up state-run ideologies. If you are a scholar, enjoy this moment. It wraps up Nietzsche's most positive evaluation of scholars, who are otherwise seen to be ossified in reactivity – they say "yes," "no," "yes," "no" (usually "no," moreover) to everything that is run by them. They are low-grade testers who are often called upon to give exams, conduct experiments, and come up with research results. Research, as Nietzsche hints and Blanchot, reading Nietzsche, avows, is a way of being in crisis: "All research is crisis. What is sought is nothing other than the turn of seeking, of research, that occasions this crisis: the critical turn."[13] Rather than closing in on itself, the critical turn of research opens itself up to the contingencies of discovery and to the dangers of nonresolution, interrupting any comfort zone toward which it may be lured, insistently prodded by the exigencies of further tryouts. The research crisis keeps reactive forces at bay.

In *The Will to Power,* Nietzsche links testing to the becoming-active of forces. Active negation or active destruction describes the state of strong spirits; they destroy the reactive in themselves, submitting it to the test of the eternal return and "submitting themselves to this test even if it entails willing their own decline."[14] If Lou Salomé deposited the secret of the eternal return into the labyrinth of Nietzsche's ear, as he more or less tells it – she has passed the paternity test, so it was beyond a doubt she who inseminated his ear – then Nietzsche carried the thought to term, receiving the eternal return as a test to be tried and borne time and again, over and over again. What in the end was being tested when Nietzsche explicitly made Salomé the father of his thought?

The demands put to us by Nietzsche, in the form of the autobiographical traces as well as in the various deliveries of his thought, prompt a number of questions. Sometimes the questions that he makes us ask go to an "unthought" layer of the sketches he proposes, for as much as he thematizes it expressly he also appears to take testing's pervasive pull for granted. This is why it becomes necessary to stay with the question and consistently go back to Nietzschean basics. What, finally, is the nature of the test? Does it have an essence? Is it pure relationality? How does it participate in Nietzsche's great destabilizations or prompt the nihilistic slide of values? Why today is our sense of security – whether or not we are prepared to admit this – based on testability? We appear to *want* everyone and everything tested. (I am not unaware of the sinister resonance of this observation. But since when has a desire signaled by humanity not been pulled by a sinister undertow?) Testing, which our Daseins encounter every day in the multiplicity of forms already enumerated – ranging from IQ to cosmetics, engines, stress, and arms, testing 1, 2, 3 broadcast systems, not to mention testing your love, testing your friendship, testing my patience, in a word, testing the brakes – was located by Nietzsche mainly in the eternal joy of becoming. Becoming involves the affirmation of passing away and destroying – the decisive feature of a Dionysian philosophy. In the first place (but the place of testing still needs to be secured), testing marks an ever new relation among forces. Ceasing to raise to infinity or finitude, or to monitor time according to the pulse of German idealism, it imposes the course of unlimited finity. This is the temporality we now commonly associate with third-generation machines, cybernetics, and information technology. (In Deleuze's work, unlimited finity is linked to the Superfold and indicates that a finite number of components yields a practically unlimited diversity of combinations; the equation in matters of testing between components and combinations is admittedly not as stable as Deleuze's renderings suggest.)[15] In a way, technology ensures its evolving perpetuation by quietly positing as its sole purpose an infinite series of testing events severed from any empirical function. Thus an elliptical circuit has been established between testing and the real: a circuit so radically installed – it is irreversible – cancels the essential difference between the test and what was assumed to be real.[16] At this point – somewhere between Freud and Nietzsche – it is not so much the case that reality is being tested but that testing is constitutive of what can be designated, with the proper precautions, as real. The test is what allows for the emergence of a reality frame to assert itself. This relation of test to reality may have stood its ground since Parsifal. It is only since Nietzsche that we ask whether, as practice or object, the test discovers, exposes, establishes, or perhaps even *invents* the ground on which we walk the walk.

Testing, which we read as one of the prevailing figures of our modernity, still makes claims of absoluteness (something has been tested and proved; we have test results), but in the form of temporariness. It opens up the site that occurs, Nietzsche suggests, after Christianity has fizzled, arriving together with a crisis in the relationship of interpretation to experience. No longer is it a question of interpreting one's own experience as pious people have long enough interpreted theirs, namely, "as though it were providential, a hint, designed and ordained for the sake of the salvation of the soul – that is *all over* now." Now we godless ones test, we rigorously experiment. We are the Christian conscience translated and sublimated into a scientific conscience. Converted to scientificity, we still however carry a trace of Christianity because what triumphed over the Christian god was Christian morality itself, "the concept of truthfulness that was understood ever more rigorously." As it became more refined, Christianity forced intellectual cleanliness upon us; it came clean by pushing science as the sublimation of its own murkiness. Now man's *conscience* is set against Christianity; it is "considered indecent and dishonest by every more refined conscience."[17] The Christian god in sum split off from Christian morality, which necessarily went down a transvaluating path less traveled and turned against its recalcitrant origin. The truth march required Christian morality to give up the god. What interests me is the additional twist of transvaluation that Nietzsche's shadow history sketches, namely what occurs when the value urging truth converts into the currency of testing. Henceforth, in strictly Nietzschean terms, reactive positings will have to stand up to the scrutiny of recursive testing.

The experimental disposition, and the provisional logic of testing that evolves from it, occurs, in its technological sense, as an event, after the death of God. It does not arrive on the scene as a barbarian conqueror but modestly approaches, for it is at once more modest than anything Christianity had proposed – proceeding, namely, by the modesty of hypotheses that are always overturnable – and decidedly more daring. This strain of modesty is shared by the spirit of audacity, wielding a strength capable of tremendous courage. It gathers its strength on mistrust. In the Gay Sci Nietzsche, posing as the Dionysian philosopher, writes, "the more mistrust, the more philosophy."[18] Mistrustworthiness is perfectly consistent with the exigencies of testing to the extent that, as stance or statement, it inhibits the potency of sentences that respond to whether something is merely true or false. Dionysian pessimism can be read along the lines proposed by Paul de Man in *Allegories of Reading*, where we are reminded that "a statement of distrust is neither true nor false: it is rather in the nature of a permanent hypothesis."[19] (The sensitive reader will have noted the slippage in English from "mistrust" to "distrust" which perhaps intones a lesser spark of gaiety.) Missed or dissed, trust is no longer placed in God but rests its case, if ever it should rest, on perpetual hypothetical postulating. In the modern sense, testing does not lean on the ontotheological notion of creation for its strength – even when the test creates nothing ex nihilo, it remains the sine qua non of any possible creation.

To be sure, testing did not emerge as an event one day; it did not arise cleanly from the ashes of a vital and present Judeo-Christian tradition but occupied a place prior to technological dominion. And so, God was always testing his nearest and dearest: Adam and Eve, Abraham, Job, Christ, and my mother were constantly being tested, and not all of them chose to remain mute about having their patience tried. But here's the hitch prior to technotesting, and Kierkegaard provides the clue: "And yet Abraham was God's chosen, and it was the Lord who put him to this test. All was now surely lost!"[20] Privileged and close enough to God to be worthy of the test, Abraham, for his part, must not know it is a test, for, among other considerations, such knowledge would eliminate the paradox of Abraham's total faith in relation to God's promise to him of a son. Abraham travels the ironic edges of promising, which can, as we know, in the end go either way. If Abraham had known it was a test, the answer would have been close at hand. God does not announce that "this is a test, this is *only* a test of the emergency broadcast system. If this were a real emergency . . ." until Abraham has passed it. Abraham cannot know until the test is over, which means that it was and was not a real emergency, but in any case becomes a test only after its aggressive question has been effectually answered.[21] In the age of the technological dominion, we however think we know about the test and its consequences even where it holds us unconsciously. We are prepared for the test, even reduced to the test, to the degree that it is an extension of the cognitive horizon. Pretechnological traces indicate a different, at once more hidden and dramatic, rapport to the ordeal of testing. In the first place, they tell us that testing, a sacred assignment, bespeaks an incomparable closeness to the divine.

Though I am not yet widely recognized as a biblical scholar, even though I have proven definitively that Moses and Aaron were a telephone, I would venture to opine that Job, in the series of God's litmus tests, installs a different relation to God's testing service when he opens the possibility of infinite contestation. Where Abraham took the pose of absolute submission, Job modified the test grounds to yield a space of resistance. In terms of its fundamental structure, the test was henceforth thrown back on its own aptitude for inconclusiveness. The test was subjected to itself in contestation. Not a peep was heard from Abraham who suffered, arguably, only one test, while Job was made to face a battery of tests. Job brings a question to the test; he sees the test *as* question – as a questionable questioning, perhaps for the first time since that little girl was tempted by the apple. Job gives every indication of understanding that he is meant to do retakes, without knowing their putative purpose or how long the exam period will last. Ever since Job, the validity and necessity of testing will have been put into question. The Jobian moment, which rails at the test as an injurious breach of trust – to the extent that his book begins on a wager, he really is a pawn in the Game – returns evermore to haunt the test as an instance rejecting its very legitimacy. Every time a score, grade, or result is contested, every time a student, patient, or political activist walks into your office with a doubt, Job is there, showing up to undermine your hard-earned certitudes. What Job brings to the conversation is the possibility that the test which is meant essentially to accredit loyalty – or, in another idiom, faith – is, itself *a priori* a betrayal, its own delegitimator.

To return momentarily to Abraham, I would be the last one to insist that the test needed to be taken only once, as repetition is inscribed in God's calling of Abraham – the name was called out twice, "Abraham! Abraham!" – and since, moreover, one cannot be sure of timetables when consulting the biblical itineraries, if the clock was set according to the New Testament, it could well be – though we have no corroboration of this hypothesis in the Scriptures – that Abraham was condemned to repeat the unique act of submission over and over again, much in the way that Christ keeps on dying. I must leave the passionate trials of Jesus of Nazareth to specialists of the New Testament, but I can see the merits of reading his question on the cross as an allegory of hermeneutic resistance, telling of his not understanding how he could have been failed. The narrative remains complicated, however, to the extent that, without a heads-up, doubt suddenly creeps in from both sides: the two poles determining the tester and tested collapse on the cross.[22] Where He formerly deputized the demon to try Christ in the desert, God on the cross submits and splits Himself as Himself and Other to the terrible test, as his own son sacrificed who does not comprehend at the moment of sacrifice and, contesting, transcends the test within the test and yet must necessarily fail the test in order to pass on – or not, depending on whether the dialectic kicks in, letting the infinite take over so that no one is in a position to judge the results, not even the infinite become finite, because the moment of uncertainty is henceforth ineraseable, and you know what I mean. Let us now pull away from the sacred inventory of trials and from the requirements that served to mark the exalted status of the one chosen for testing.

With the spread of technology, testing lost some of its auratic and exceptional qualities and started hitting everyone with its demands, that is, anyone who wanted to gain admission anywhere, and all institutions started testing to let you in and let you out. If something weird happens, you are taken in for psychiatric testing. Technological warfare belongs to the domain of testing as well and does much to support the thesis that there is little difference between testing and the real thing. To the extent that testing counts as warfare today, it marks the steady elimination of boundaries between weapons testing and their deployment. The test already functions as a signal to the enemy other. What this means, among other things, is that the Cold War *was* a war. It also means that George W. Bush could at once invoke and scramble these codes by announcing, on 9/11, that the attack on the World Trade Center was, in his words, a test: "This was a test" were his first words hours after the attack in 2001. "The resolve of our great nation is being tested," he proclaimed. Since this administration has repeatedly shown signs of being subjugated to the diction of testing, it seems worthwhile to linger in the district of its utterances to examine how George W. Bush's language usage works here. Appearing to introduce a new rhetoric of justification for imminent military action, the president in fact reverts to a citation of pretechnological syntagmas. His diction counts on the auratic pull of the test. In this context the term sparkles as an anointment; the president bears the mark of election by virtue of the test. If a few months earlier he had been elected by dubious political means, he is now elected by divine mandate to meet the demands of a terrific test in order to create history, which he begins to do by reviving the crusades. Saying that the terror attack was a test, President Bush leaves no room for the undecidability of Abraham, the contestability of Job, or the intricated martyrdom of Christ. Disturbing the codified usage of the trial to which "the test" alludes, the utterance subverts the condition of *being tested* by offering that, at the moment of its mention, the test has been passed. The test will already have made sense and turned in the result: one would not have been chosen to withstand it, the logic goes, if one had not *already passed* the test of history countersigned, in this case, by God.

Reinscribing and repeating the wars of his father, this little Isaac jumps at the chance to return to traumatic sites. Like Isaac, neutralized and silenced by the father's package deal with the sacred, this one wants to dig into the earth, signing a legacy to which he was and was not called. Part of the "vision thing" that we call testing, the first Gulf War was conducted primarily as a field test; but it also, phantasmically, displayed the characteristics of a national AIDS test in which the United States scored HIV-negative, owing to the "bloodless" and safe war.[23] The Gulf War set out to prove the hypothesis that no technology will ever exist without being tested; but once it is tested, we are no longer simply talking about a *test*.[24] Nothing will be invented, no matter how stealth, nuclear, or "unthinkable," that will not be tested, that is, at some level of calibration, realized. Hence, in addition to related issues of deployment, testing is always written into treaties. The necessity of treaties, conventions, and regulative discourses in itself underscores, in the manner demonstrated by Kant and Benjamin in their critiques of violence, the extent to which testing, like war, has become naturalized, and can be only provisionally suspended by treaties that try to ban them.

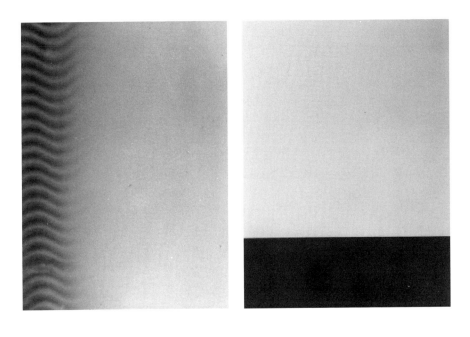

The relation of testing to the question of place is essential. The test site, as protoreal, marks out a primary atopos, producing a "place" where the real awaits confirmation. Until now the test site has not been constructed as a home (unless you're a homunculus). Linked to a kind of ghostless futurity, the site offers no present shelter. This explains perhaps why Nietzsche names the *gaya scienza* in the same breath that convokes "*We who are homeless.*" But Nietzsche being Nietzsche knows how to affirm the unhinging of home as the preparation for another future, one not rooted in ideologies of the home front: "We children of the future, how *could* we be at home in this today . . . in this fragile, broken time of transition?"[25] The work, his experimental language lab, restlessly communicates with a future that it attempts to conjure. Let me pause this for a second where Nietzsche skips a beat. His forward rush can be consternating at times, breaking the rhythm of a carefully trained transition. The drive toward the future is something that still needs to be questioned in Nietzsche, for at moments such as these, he appears to put himself on fast forward, betraying his less *allegro*-minded thinking of the *trans*. When Nietzsche sporadically averts his text from the lacerations of the day, the somewhat romantic lament of present destitution comes each time as a jolt. We know that an aspect of the eternal return is meant to repair time and even to appease the revenge of the "it was"; yet Nietzsche is also the hero of the transition, persistently marking off the fragile, broken spaces of a difficult today from which he *screams*, as Heidegger says, cranking up the volume. Nietzsche endured the necessity of having to scream to be heard and knew how to dwell in the hollow time of transition. The way he gets away with the double temporal entry is to figure himself as double, precisely: Although this passage seems to ride on an excess of futurity, the rejection of the today, its pink slip, is served by a pregnant Nietzsche who is carrying a new life, carrying himself to term as a child of the future. Nietzsche is fused to that which he carries and will leave him behind. When he dismantles the home front, unsettling what seems to be settled, he does so in the same gesture that returns on his birthday at the opening of *Ecce Homo* – he clears away what has already fallen off, decayed; he sets aside what has been destroyed so that life can see the light of day. Nietzsche wants to know if he can build a new home without the foundations that Heidegger and others will lay. Will it be possible to establish residence without the grave ideologies of ground and dwelling weighing him down?

For Nietzsche there is a good homelessness (the deracination accompanied by abundance, the nomadic drift) and a bad homelessness (burdened, destitute, chronically fatigued with the earth, a homelessness of depletion). The logic of the test site that we have not yet understood concerns precisely the relation of the site to *life;* we still know only how to leave the test site uninhabitable, mapping ever more deserts as eco wasteland, unexploded arsenal, littered terrain, concentration camp laboratories, the so-called third world. The question that Nietzsche presses us on is therefore never merely one of affirming homelessness after metaphysics, but of rendering spaces habitable, multiplying trajectories for life and the living, refiguring the site of experimentation in such a way as to ensure that it is not already the ensepulchered reserve of the living dead. In other words: why have we not yet thought the test site on the side of life? It is important to note that Nietzsche is not, in this phase of this thought, the exuberant adolescent of old. The Nietzsche who thinks the experiment has come back from the dead several times over: he is formulating his theory of the great health; he has returned once again to health and, like a great convalescent, looks at life with a somewhat ghostly air that dissolves only gradually. Still, he is on the move again, and homelessness becomes an expression of renewed *vitality,* the overcoming of sterile destitution.

The homelessness that Nietzsche posits is never simply reactive, therefore, but puts up a bold front as it looks toward the future. Among its prominent features the abomination of racism, an aggravated narcissism, ranks high. At moments it resembles the crew of *Star Trek,* "we who are homeless are too manifold and mixed racially and in our descent . . . do not feel tempted to participate in the mendacious racial self-admiration and racial indecency." Racial indecency is, Nietzsche suggests everywhere, the absence of test. It is the untested presumption par excellence, held together by pseudo-precepts that would never hold scientific sway. Racial indecency and self-admiration go steadily together, for one feeds the other while expunging otherness and refusing the movement of self-overcoming, which is to say, ceaseless self-correction. Nietzsche, however, is by no means setting up a political correctional facility, an alternative space for human subjects weighted down by punishing chains. Something has to give, liberating the heaviness that paralyzes the movement of racial justice, which serves as the earth-toned metonymy for all possible justice. "The 'wanderer' speaks" speaks out on the prospective aims one takes. To be capable of a long-distance will to knowledge one must consistently lighten up:

> One has to be very light to drive one's will to knowledge into such a distance and, as it were, beyond one's time. . . . One must have liberated oneself from many things that oppress, inhibit, hold down, and make heavy precisely us Europeans today. The human being of such a beyond who wants to behold the supreme measures of value of his time must first of all "overcome" this time in himself – this is the test of his strength.[26]

Nietzsche adds to the internal conversion mechanism a function to stabilize one's aversion to the present, stating that one must overcome not only one's time "but also his prior aversion and contradiction against this time, his suffering from this time, his un-timeliness, his *romanticism*."[27] One has to stay in place while training for the future: we first have to lose some weight. To be capable of being sent off to meet our beyond, we would have to recognize, as Nietzsche does at the end of Book Two, that "we are at bottom grave and serious human beings – really, more weights than human beings." Few of the training sessions take place at home or at the estates of human dignity. In order to prepare oneself for takeoff, one needs to have gotten over oneself, that is, one needs at times to see oneself as dunce ("nothing does us as much good as a *fool's cap*: we need it in relation to ourselves"). At times we need a rest from ourselves, says Nietzsche, turning sharply into an obligatory bend: "We must discover the *hero* no less than the *fool* in our passion for knowledge; we must occasionally find pleasure in our folly, or we cannot continue to find pleasure in our wisdom."[28] The dumb interiors of the creature, man, will provide a respite from the heavyweight champions of self that lean on us, draining all passion from genuine knowledge-questing. Knowledge requires the pleasure of folly, something that art, which only flirts with cognition, often helps us acquire. Yet Nietzsche does not set limits on folly, nor does he interrogate the prickly parameters of pleasure here. Like pleasure, folly can go too far afield, disrupting itself in the restricted area of a "stupid mistake," a risk poorly taken. In the end, though, the humbling trip-up is what sends us on our way en route to endless tryouts in an effort to create a place on and, above all, off the maps of cognition.

Destiny and destination take on altogether different contours when prepped by the twin passions of testing. In order to take ourselves seriously we must get over ourselves, we must don the fool's helmet. The fool fuels the heroic passion of knowing, switching at the controls into something other than itself. Both fool and hero assure the relative stability of the test site, their home away from home. A mark of the beyond, or of sending and *envoi,* the test site is a homestead of being-not-at-home, whether this be figured as the desert of nuclear testing, a constellation of the underground, in the lab or, as Nietzsche has it, very happily far away – at a remove from the fatherland, perhaps in Italy, where experimental life can be affirmed. Having introduced it firmly and staked his philosophical prestige on its unpreventable unfolding, what does Nietzsche say about the age of the experiment?

The capacity to experiment, as well as its considerable implications, is clearly something of a gift for Nietzsche. This is why Nietzsche cannot stop expressing his gratitude for the dangerously changing aspect of its corollary, the great health (there are a number of healths, and their routines often take you under). The possibility of experimentation, the kind that urges the testing of your strength over and over again, presupposes that a gift has been given to which Nietzsche in turn gives his work, offering, despite everything, his gratitude to what has been offered him. The gift of starting more or less from scratch, outfitted only with a new mistrust, grants a thinker the free rein necessary for closing the deal and opening the field of a nonresentimental regard for one's task; it affirms time and again that one is free to let go of the very gift that has granted the work. Such rights of embrace and dismissal establish a relation to the work that Nietzsche is not loath to associate with great love. In a sense he needs to get love in there in order to create the possibilities for a type of moral generosity that does not wither into stone-cold obligation. In the section "Against Remorse," Nietzsche outlines a moral code, without imperative, honored by a thinker who exists in the noncontradictory space where action, freedom, and noble sensibility inflect thought: " – A thinker sees his own actions as experiments and questions – as attempts to find out something. Success and failure are for him *answers* above all. To be annoyed or feel remorse because something goes wrong – that he leaves to those who act because they have received orders and who have to reckon with a beating when his lordship is not satisfied with the result."[29]

Nietzsche assimilates experiments and questions to the *action* of the thinker who, no longer caught in the falsely construed Hamletian dichotomies of thought and action, sees such action thoughts freed up from the dependencies of stipulated results. The experiment implies, among other things, tenure, freedom, a nobility of taste.

Let us lay down another track to complement the gift of experimental action. It circuits the relatedness of experiment to Nietzschean gratitude, as it is expressed throughout the Gay Sci, through the question of taste that he links consistently to experiment. Encouraging the affinities of testing and tasting, Nietzsche turns every test into something of a taste test. The relation of the test to taste is crucial. In a sense, this relation keeps the senses busy, involving instincts that otherwise might be dulled or deadened. Keeping the body intact and thinking tactile, Nietzsche develops an experimental ethos, a modified judgment of taste. The experience of freedom with which Nietzsche associates genuine experimenting has a double legacy. On the one hand, he sees freedom in science as relatively absolute, if one could say so: the experiment answers to no one. Nietzsche's thinking passes over sanctioned figures of authority to which a thinker might be answerable. On the other hand, he does not simply bypass answerability as such but gives the problem its own domain by projecting the ways in which the address of answerability will prompt the most serious ethical questions of the future. To whom are we answerable? Nietzsche appears to make it a matter of "whom" rather than "what," a decision that in itself denotes ethical resolve. Turning aside from essence as its destination or agency, answerability, embedded in procedure, intention, or method, always implies the future of the experiment and something like the "personality" with which it is associated or to whom it is addressed. The notion of personality tends to recede in matters of strict accountability. In recent times themes of answerability organize the way we think about experimentation and testing from the relative innocence, it was thought, of the experiments in free love to the genome project or animal testing. It has become clear that every form of testing is open to ethical anxiety and, in many areas, has contributed significantly to the resurgence of ethics. The ethical perspective still remains, in Nietzsche's sense, a question of personal taste. Decency and even justice, for Nietzsche, are largely matters of taste. (Nietzsche's example goes like this: I would rather be robbed than see a homeless person suffer. This is a matter of taste.) Pulling away from the duty-bound authorizations of Kantian ethics, Nietzsche stakes justice on the no doubt equally precarious discernment of taste. According to the Nietzschean scale of things, taste, which accepts or rejects by virtue of the noble instinct, keeps ethics alive and on the side of life, away from numbing universalizations.

Testing and experimentation, related inextricably to acts of negating and affirmation, are conducted in the name of life; for the seeker of knowledge, moreover, they name the most exalted way of experiencing life. Selective testing comes with the eternal return, which is to say that it must overcome a first level of hesitation, difficulty. Ceding to difficult ground – and having difficulty with its own grounding – selective testing cannot amount to some naïve and spontaneous expression of a zest for life. It is preceded by a halt, a retreat. Thus Nietzsche's rhetorical embrace of the complicity of life and experiment comes by way of the negative and must continue to make its path through a number of "nots": "No, life has not disappointed me [after a long period of illness]. The great liberator came to me: the idea that life could be an experiment of the seeker for knowledge – and not a duty, a calamity, not trickery. – And knowledge itself: let it be something else for others; for example, a bed to rest on, or the way to such a bed, or a diversion or a form of leisure – for me it is a world of dangers and victories in which heroic feelings, too, find places to dance and play. – '*Life as a means for knowledge*' – with this principle in one's heart one can live not only boldly but even gaily, and laugh gaily, too."[30] That life could be an experiment betokens a gift of great liberation; that is why it gets named together with the entitling instance of the Gay Sci in the double affirmation of "gaily," offering nuance to life, allowing it to live itself boldly, dancingly. Having traversed the reign of the "not" – "not a duty," "not trickery" – life embraced as experiment has been able to cut loose the dangerous undertow that leaves one wiped out, in need of "a bed to rest on." One has the sense that here, as elsewhere, Nietzsche maneuvers between two valuations of a decisive term: there can be a good and bad boldness, one type of which is adopted in good faith and health, and the other in service of sinister ends.

In the absence of a transcendental seal, philosophy and science turn to other qualities to clear their paths and warrant their integrity. Nietzsche has to steer between God and ego to keep thinking clean – too much God or too much ego is destructive of the scientific aim, and liable only to produce catastrophic imaginary or narcissistically warped aberrations. In any case, God rarely dispenses permits for scientific adventure, though philosophy has been known to suck up to any power of historical moment. To keep thinking on track, Nietzsche mobilizes love and personality. Perhaps somewhat surprisingly for us moderns today, who associate experiment with some degree of desubjectivation, the experimental imagination, as Nietzsche calls it at one point, implies a strong personality. It was Friedrich Schelling who once remarked that the question of personality was egregiously left out of the philosophical field. Nietzsche, who involves biographemes in the index of philosophical demands, skims off a notion of personality to make his argument, such as it is, stick. The lack of personality always takes its revenge, Nietzsche writes in "Morality as a Problem":

> A weakened, thin, extinguished personality that denies itself is no longer fit for anything good – least of all for philosophy. All great problems demand great love, and of that only strong, round, secure spirits who have a firm grip on themselves are capable. It makes the most telling difference whether a thinker has a personal relationship to his problems and finds in them his destiny, his distress, and his greatest happiness, or an "impersonal" one, meaning that he can do no better than to touch them and grasp them with the antennae of cold, curious thought.[31]

Part of a lover's discourse and a destinal commitment, the Nietzschean motif of the strong personality determines the sturdiness of thought. One enters into a relationship with those problems that solicit urgent attention. One's distress and happiness abide in the enrapturing movement of their idioms and silences. The sustained engagement with problems cannot be put into the hands of those who have excused themselves from the space of a vital encounter by means of ascetic subtractions or anemic inquiry. Nietzschean science scorns cold objectivist observation and limp grapples, requiring instead something on the order of an affective self-deposit and intense commitment. Prompting the encounter of great problems with great love, scientific curiosity and experimental imagination trace their novel routes. Nietzsche appears to envision a mapping of scientific study that is auratically pulled together by the love borne by a strong personality; buoyed by love, such a science could not degenerate in principle to a hate crime against humanity. Yet the borders separating love from hatred are left untouched by Nietzsche: he does not consider the cold prompters of love or the ambivalent underworld of acts of love in world or science. He leaves aside the possibility that the most hateful turn is often fueled by love of a nameable cause or country.

When Nietzsche installs love as a motor force behind the scientific urge, he does so to open the scene for an unprecedented generosity of being capable of melting the moral ice age and a history of intellectual arrests; until now, knowledge has been deterred from supporting the limber stretch exercises of human beings. To this end, love supplants the deep freeze of moral valuations, rendering the scientific pursuit on a par with what is felt to be irresistible. Why is it, Nietzsche asks in this section, that "I see nobody who ventured a *critique* of moral valuations; I miss even the slightest attempts of scientific curiosity, of the refined, experimental imagination of psychologists and historians that readily anticipates a problem and catches it in flight without quite knowing what it has caught."[32] Disposed by great love to devoted study, the experimental imagination does not settle on one object or line of inquiry but, as part of Nietzsche's vocabulary of *force*, it tends to shift ground and change objects with a sometimes alarming degree of regularity. In fact, love, to be true to itself, has to carry the fissuring break within its travels. It cannot be otherwise if it is to follow the itinerary set by the laws of becoming.

The experimental imagination is exceptional in several ways. Taking risks but also exercising prudence – practicing, in Nietzsche's famous sense, the art of living dangerously – the experimental cast of being does not so much preview the advent of a technobody (equipped with the antennae of cold, curious thought) but, in the first place, reflects a vitality that disrupts sedimented concepts and social values. Such a force of disruption goes against the grain of what has been understood as praiseworthy. Promoting meanings that have been left in cold storage for centuries, society values unchangeability and dependability. It rewards the instrumental nature (the character of dependable, computable qualities, i.e., someone you can count on) with a good reputation. On the other hand, efforts involving self-transformation and relearning, acts that make oneself somewhat unpredictable in this regard, are consistently devalued: "However great the advantages of this thinking may be elsewhere, for the search after knowledge no general judgment could be more harmful, for precisely the good will of those who seek knowledge to declare themselves at any time dauntlessly *against* their previous opinions and to mistrust everything that wishes to become *firm* in us is thus condemned and brought into ill repute. Being at odds with a 'firm reputation,' the attitude of those who seek knowledge is considered *dishonorable* while the petrification of opinions is accorded a monopoly on honor! Under the spell of such notions we have to live to this day."[33] While science itself was seen to count on the strength of prediction, the scientific personality needs to evade the temptation of predictability. Prediction should not be ruled by an internal dictator or dictionary of obligations. If one stayed in one's assigned grooves, everything would harden into place, with no suppleness to assure necessary shifts and turnarounds. In addition to petrification, one also always risks softening, effeminating, so to speak. Yet if Nietzsche had to choose or lose, he would promote something that comes close to the texture of the softening that opens and glides, allowing for sudden shocks and slippages. The scientific personality, spurred on by love, needs to be able to flow in order to move past anything that establishes itself firmly. The surge vitality provided by love drives the experimental disposition beyond its assumed goals.

Submitted to constant critique and revision, the experimental disposition is capable of leaving any conclusion in the dust when it obsolesces, turns against itself, or proves decadent; when a result is "arrived" at, the experimental imagination suspends it in its provisional pose of hypothesis. The hypothetical statement submitted to critique does not belong to a class of positivistic certainties or objective observations, since it is never loosened from the affect that brought it into view. A truth or probability was, Nietzsche stresses, formerly loved. The scientific imagination cathects on the hypothesis and itself becomes different as the "object" changes. While it seems as though reason prompts a process of decathexis, it is in fact life and its production of needs that is responsible for criticism and revision. Thus "In Favor of Criticism" states the following:

> Now something that you formerly loved as truth or probability strikes you as an error; you shed it and fancy that this represents a victory for your reason. But perhaps this error was as necessary for you then, when you were still a different person – you are always a different person – as are all your present "truths," being a skin, as it were, that concealed and covered a great deal that you were not yet permitted to see. What killed that opinion for you was your new life and not your reason: you no

longer need it. . . . When we criticize something, this is no arbitrary and impersonal event; it is, at very least very often, evidence of vital energies in us that are growing and shedding skin. We negate and must negate because something in us wants to live and affirm – something in us that we do not know or see as yet. – This is said in favor of criticism.[34]

Not reason but life requires the serial proliferation of amendments and retractions, burying dead opinions and promoting the growth of new critical needs. To the extent that the personality triggers truth and guns for error, there will be no standstill or momentous revelation that can claim eternity as its backdrop. Every collaboration of truth and error is determined by the wide-ranging difference over time of the personality to itself. And even where a former truth must now be discarded, Nietzsche, ever mindful of resentful potentialities, reminds us that it was once loved and urgently needed by a personality that consistently outgrows itself. The experimental disposition is thus somewhat on the run, whether passing through non-knowledge, and catching the unknowable in the outfield of inquiry, or because something within us compels negation and further negation as a condition for living and affirming. Unknowable, and as yet unseen, something within us could come from the future or return from a subterranean layer of past inscriptions. Still or no longer human, we – or rather "you," Nietzsche says "you" – are molting, shedding skin like so many truths cast off by *The Gay Science*. Your body transforms, engineering a new era of sacrifice. During a related but more anthropological sweep, Foucault once saw things moving in the direction of epistemic sacrifice: "Where religion once demanded the sacrifice of bodies," he writes, "knowledge now calls for experimentation on ourselves, calls us to the sacrifice of the subject of knowledge."[35]

TESTING ◀)1 . . . ◀))2 . . . ◀))3 . . . Much has been said about Nietzsche's statement that we need only to invent new names in order to create new "things." In that famous aphorism, however, he adds to the list of power switches the notion of probabilities: "We can destroy only as creators – But let us not forget *this* either: it is enough to create new names and estimations and probabilities in order to create in the long run new 'things.'"[36] In the long run, probabilities and estimations weigh in as importantly as names when it comes to invention's power over new things. Nietzsche places things within quotation marks, which in this case ex-

pands rather than contracts the cited domain: in place of limiting himself
to substantial objects, he leaves open the definition of what can be expected to come from the creation of new probabilities, names, or estimations. In the passage discussed above, Nietzsche puts probability on the
same level as truth. Both truth and probability are linked to love, which
furtively documents the affective holdings of the gay scientist. The point
to be held on to at this juncture, beyond the tempting psychologization of
both terms, is the way Nietzsche smuggles probability into the neighborhood of truth in order to assert its rights of equal residency: "You shed
formerly loved truth or probability."[37]

But before continuing to explore the itinerary of the experimental disposition in the Gay Sci, I would like to connect the questions that have
been raised to a number of insistent contemporary claims. It is not that I
want to trace some loveless relations to truth and probability but, in order
to see the genuine innovation of Nietzsche's scientific incursion, I find it
necessary to change channels and skip a century, to fast forward to where
Nietzsche is used and betrayed. This commercial break will allow us to
reenergize the reading of Gay Sci with a graft from its own future passage-
ways. If the Gay Sci has sought us out and is meant to speak to us today,
then it will have had to stand the test of time, which does not limit the
text to a vulgar little quiz involving applicability and whether or not one
"buys it," but is disclosive of the way in which the Nietzschean insight
relates to itself as its own future, its own labor and announced commitments. I will let it recharge itself as we borrow from the future of Gay Sci
in order to read its past.

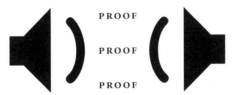

PROOF

PROOF

PROOF

a) In a work linking philosophy with the conceptions and technologies of
artificial intelligence (AI), a concerned editor outlines the way in which
AI researchers "have recently found themselves writing, without any
conscious intent, what philosophers recognize as philosophy."[38] The true
source of apprehension, expressed in the introductory phase of the vol-

ume, may involve another dilemma, effected "without any conscious intent," reflected namely in the section title, "How Philosophers Drift into Artificial Intelligence." Despite considerable emphasis on drifting, randomization, fuzziness, and interference, the work signals its anxiety over philosophy's nearly random drift into the new territory. The unwarranted interference risks subverting coherent programming and blunting the concerted demand for rigor upon which AI discussions appear to be based. The origin of the demand for rigor, which has conditioned twentieth-century Anglo philosophy, "is the positivist's requirement that theories be testable. At the very least, a respectable philosophical theory should be stated with sufficient precision that one can tell what it says about *something* and whether its predictions about that subject matter are borne out." The minimal requirement of rigor meant that "respectable philosophy" (respectable is repeated a number of times) had to be capable of being articulated in the formalism of logic: "As time passed, however, the awareness grew that formal rigor was not sufficient to guarantee unambiguous content or to ensure sufficient philosophical clarity to meet even this minimal criterion of testability.... There must be more to philosophical analysis than logical formalism."[39]

The migration of philosophy into areas that are technologically fitted risks deflating the rigor on which so much is staked. It is as if rigor maintains the phallus that assures the rule and proper place of "respectable philosophy." Yet there is danger ahead in the form of disrespect for completion and clarity, the handmaidens of rigor. In some cases contemporary philosophers have been led "to eschew rigor altogether. Even in investigations shrouded in a façade of formalism, there is often a lamentable tendency toward handwaving when the going gets difficult. The trend is toward painting pictures rather than constructing detailed theories. Perhaps most contemporary philosophy is too vague and unfinished to satisfy even a minimal requirement of testability."[40] Testability furnishes the uninterrogated core of rigor. It puts out the call for a new mode of thinking that could be aligned with the demand for rigor, which remains equally uninterrogated but seems to be linked to a notion of computational realizability: "To some of us, the concepts and technology of artificial intelligence provide at least a partial resolution of the problem of ensuring at least some degree of testability. As Paul Thagard (1988) has pointed out, artificial intelligence liberates us from the narrow constraints of standard logic by enforcing rigor in a different way, namely via the constraint of computational realizability."[41] This example is especially useful to us because it shows how "rigor" enables the displacement of truth by testability.

> Computational realizability is no guarantee of truth or of explanatory interest, of course, but it does guarantee a certain kind of rigor. Those philosophers who have begun to test their theories by trying actually to implement them in computer programs have found that the discipline required almost invariably reveals ambiguity, vagueness, incompleteness and downright error in places where traditional philosophical reflection was downright blind. . . . Furthermore, a running implementation of a theory makes it possible to apply the theory to more complicated test cases than would be possible by armchair reflection, and experience indicates that this usually reveals counterexamples that would not otherwise have been apparent.[42]

Endorsed by "experience," acts of reflection are devalued and overthrown for the asserted virtues of implementation. The linchpin of this operation, "rigor," enters the picture unrigorously, however, as only "a certain kind of rigor." What kind of rigor is a certain kind of rigor? What does it mean to "guarantee" a certain kind of rigor? In short, what is being *guaranteed* if not the ability itself to guarantee where truth has been weakened or explanatory interest diffused? Everything rests on the promise of a certain kind of rigor. But at what price is this flimsy ground constructed? All such great white Anglo hope for philosophy can be maintained as long as foreign invasions by ambiguity, aleatory eruptions, incompleteness, and other forms of parasitism are revalued. This sort of revaluation or indeed repression belongs to a "respectable philosophy" even as it loses ground with respect to the aforementioned rigor. Importantly, the test is posited on the side of a cleaner, more rigorous, unassailable cognitive value. Testing in itself is never questioned but posed, necessarily, if the argument is to work, as the infallible ground for yielding determinations and often indulging the metaphysical fantasy of completion.

But what if testing were from the start itself built upon notions of constitutive incompletion, ambiguity, blind runs, and radically provisional cognitive values? In order to carry on the respectable colonization of discourse of which philosophy, that certain kind of something which drifts into AI, would be the unconscious, it is essential at once to rely on the test and to leave its premises untested – as if the test could provide an unquestionably solid ground for overtaking reflection and other philosophically triggered interferences. When promoting AI as the advanced frontier for philosophy, the introduction slips in a "partial" guarantee: "A (partial) guarantee of philosophical rigor and clarity is not the only attraction artificial intelligence holds for philosophers."[43] What would a "(partial) guarantee" be? Is it respectable? Sound? Are rigor and clarity partially guaranteed or does the guarantee cover partial rigor? Are respectable philosophers "attracted" to fields? How rigorous is it to rely upon attraction? "The discipline of programming also leads to a shift in perspective on traditional issues. It invites – or rather requires – one to adopt what [Daniel] Dennett (1968) calls the design stance toward the mind."[44] Dennett's stance supplants inquiry into the nature of rationality with inquiry into how a rational agent might be designed: "Rather than ask under what conditions someone can be said to know something, we are led to ask how an agent might be designed that acquires information and applies it in the service of some goal, and what such an agent's environment must be like for the design to work."[45] This cognitive cue, tied to teleology, raises questions that, while not addressed in the introductory essay, concern the function of model and prototype, of that which is being tested, designed, and "invented" in view of a particular goal. In terms of its most expansive implications, the theme of information design opens a region wherein the distinction between discovery and the more instrumental epistemology of how something works is suspended. An invention no longer is figurable as a spontaneous eruption of substantial thingness but now gets serialized or parallel processed by various trials and tryouts. Although not foregrounded in terms of computational dependability, this more marginalized aspect of testability supports a structure given over to improvement and improvisation – indeed, an incomplete structure which, if not respectable, is rigorous but open-ended. The more subtle folds of testability, their tendency to collapse or open unexpected areas for thought and experiment, are however left untouched in order, it would seem, to keep intact the phantasm of testing's groundedness and unquestioned solidity. In bringing forward such objections I am not picking on a minor deflection or bizarre moment in a generally more reliable field:

these disturbances are characteristic of the self-assured procedures of present-day inquiry and continue to call for further reflection.

b) In a noteworthy, if somewhat typical, discussion that includes theories of algorithms applicable to real-time behavior, a snag emerges under the aegis of the "planning problem." In this instance AI is mustered for the purpose of probing research methods, and it searches out the space of possible actions to compute some sequence of actions and decision theory.[46] The problem deals with the fact that agents, "whether human or robots, are *resource* bounded: they are unable to form arbitrarily large computations in constant time."[47] In sum, the dilemma concerns the time zone paradox of freezing the future in order to plan, on another register, the time for working through computations. The more complicated computations become, the more time it takes and the less we are in sync with the possibility of a grounded answer. "This is a problem because the more time spent on deliberations, the more chance there is that the world will change in important ways – ways that will undermine the very as-sumptions on which the deliberation is proceeding."[48] If anything, this dilemma indicates an acute time-bound paradox that undermines the conditions for thinking through a problem, or even for questioning its appropriateness for inquiry. The somewhat hidden opposition that be-gins to come clean in this line of argument entails the speedup of the present that runs up against the more lugubrious pace of "deliberation." The assumption, pitting the timing of the test *versus* the time of thinking, dominates a number of the problems that are focalized in AI consider-ations. The thriller dimension of current research, which, setting its timer, gives scientific inquiry the rush it apparently needs to set up for its goal, is very possibly based on the misguided notion that "the world will change in important ways." To offset the competitive quality of the re-search that is being clocked, more philosophy must be allowed to drift in, if only to demystify those ideologies of acceleration that relentlessly run down the slower-paced thinking and overstabilize an ethics of hesitation.

Whether as origin or effect of temporal hysteria, newer technologies strain to beat the ontic clock. A problem besetting recent AI planning systems is that they have been designed "to construct plans prior to, and distinct from, their execution. It is recognized that the construction of plans takes time. However, these plans have been constructed for a set of future conditions that are known in advance and frozen."[49] The conditions for which a plan has been constructed, the so-called start state, must be known not to change prior to execution. There exists, then, at once a fear that future conditions will overtake the calculations made for them and that they consist of altogether knowable factors to be frozen in advance. A major tensional drama occurs in the noncoincidence of planning and its execution. Planning phases include such exercises as modeling, testing, constructing prototypes, development. Regardless of whether the future is foreseeable or not, something has to be maintained as a stable factor: in these considerations stability is bestowed by the test. If the test cannot originate knowledge, it at least confirms that there is knowledge. However, even if a test, to fulfill its bald constative claims, assumes the function of providing definitive results or minimally of confirming that cognition occurs, testing, for its part and imparting, is always temporally determined. Thus the criterion of testability also inscribes the erasure of what is to be tested. Given the timed stretch between prototype and execution – one of many possible models – testing, in principle, can never catch up with itself in order to locate or stabilize itself in the cognitive domain for which it nonetheless serves as proof: another reason why tests have to be taken over and over again, if only to fill the fictional time of the absolute present, or of the experience of such a present.

In light of what has been said thus far, a related dimension of testing comes into the picture at this point. This development concerns the level of *responsiveness* that the test presupposes and for which it aims. Despite the scope of radical provisionality defining its extended field, in some cases the test itself assumes the function of knowing the answer. While the test is a questioning act, and while it may prompt the necessity of counter-examples, it already contains and urges a sense of the correct way to answer its demand. It does not pose what we might call an innocent question but has arranged things in such a way as to run ahead of itself to catch the answer for which it calls. To be sure, the test itself may be "surprised" by the way in which it is answered. Surprised by its own answer, of which it is henceforth dispossessed, the test attacks epistemological meaning with a kind of ontological fervor. The surprise passes for a shiver in ontology; something trembles in being.

To the extent that the test, according to its more constative pretexts, delivers results, corroborating or disconfirming what is thought to be known or even to exist, it can undermine anything that does not respond to its probative structure. The status of the thing tends to topple under the pressure of the test. Somewhat paradoxically, it is not clear even that something is known until there is a test for it. Consider the relevant passages in Douglas Hofstadter's well-known discussion of computer language, automatic chunking, and BlooP tests. BlooP defines predictably terminating calculations: "The standard name for *functions* which are BlooP-computable is *primitive recursive functions;* and the standard name for properties which can be detected by BlooP-tests is *primitive recursive predicates.*"[50] It appears that, according to Hofstadter's view, extreme particularities do not correspond to testing but must be tapped for universal formulae. The test follows upon a sort of screening procedure that detects the universalizable trace: "Now the kinds of properties which can be detected by BlooP tests are widely varied. . . . The fact that, as of the present moment, we have no way of testing whether a number is wondrous or not need not disturb us too much, for it might merely mean that we are ignorant about wondrousness, and that with more digging around, we could discover a universal formula for the upper bound to the loop involved. Then a BlooP test for wondrousness could be written on the spot."[51] In this context, it turns out that that test is not viewed so much as that which can prove more or less established hypotheses or provide new knowledge; it acts as an effect of knowledge that precomprehends itself – a certain type of metaphysically secured knowledge that needs only to *find* itself. In this rendering, the test eludes a broader definition in favor of probing and confirming its own foundation as presence, even if this should be inscribed in the form of latent concealment ("need not disturb us too much, for it might merely mean that we are ignorant"). The BlooP as metonymy of testing does not test anything outside the delimited field about which it already knows. This is not much different from saying that proofs are demonstrations within fixed systems of propositions. The type of logic deployed by Hofstadter appears to call for a test that ensures its own perpetuation without compromise or contamination from a designated outside. But what if the proofs were to explode the propositions? In other words, what if the test were itself to fail and significantly falter?

The normatively secured test does not generate knowledge but confirms what already exists as "knowable." Yet, as it sets its limits strictly, in accordance with specific codes or conventions, testing inevitably checks for the unknown loop that takes it beyond mere passing or failing, beyond determinacy or the result. The unpretended aim of a test, one could say here, is to meet its hidden blind spot, to fail. This is when it produces an effect of discovery, which occurs as accident, chance, confusion, or luck – something on the order of broad off-track betting. We are given to understand that true failure is not merely of an instrumental nature, such as technical defect or mechanical failure. Generous failure, productive of disclosure, concerns a type of testing that probes more than the workability or conformity of its object to an already regulated norm – more than, say, a smog test (though, in keeping with essential failure, the politics of the test would no doubt be far more interesting if all cars were to be failed in service of another modeling of exhaust systems).

In a limited technological sense, the putative difference between passing or failing may be a trivial issue, as the recursive nature of the test determines its generation regardless of discrete results. It is in the nature of testing to be ongoing indefinitely, even when the simulation may pass into the referential world. As simulated and operational orders collapse into a single zone (where, for instance, an absolute distinction between real war and field test would be difficult to maintain over time), the more interesting questions of cadence, interruption, or reinterpretation emerge. Is it possible, in our era, to stop or even significantly disrupt and reroute the significance of testing? In terms of political-pragmatic programs, we have seen the difficulties involved, for example, in banning nuclear tests. It is as if they have become naturalized, an unstoppable force. The successive attempts at banning tests require the intervention of signed treaties. We know from classical philosophy, which has not been contradicted on this point, from Kant ("A Sketch for Perpetual Peace") through Walter Benjamin ("Critique of Violence") and more contemporary analyses, that treaties suspend violence only momentarily, artificially.[52] The irony of Kant's unfinished sketch gratifies the allegory of an impossible peace. Because testing henceforth belongs to the question of violence – involving treaties, conventions, regulations, policing, ethical debate, considerations of eco-ontology, and the like – only with the help of a discussion of rhetorical codes strong enough to scan the paradoxical logic of testing can we begin to figure the problem of its unstoppability, if indeed this is to be understood, today, as a problem.

Does the test occupy a juridical and strictly legal space or does it produce a space that supplements these determinations – perhaps even supporting and altering them according to another logic? The task of reading the links between violence and testing through the legality and topology of the test site – its possible *anomy,* that is, the extralegal privilege of testing – requires us however to pass the test through the modalities of its undecidable bearings: it is necessary and possible to understand testing through the lens of impossible conjunctions – as good and evil, as situated beyond good and evil, if not as that which decisively directs the very determination of good and evil. A radical formulation of the questions at hand leads us to ask, Can there be any ascertainable good prior to the test? (Short of Platonic shredders, what allows us to know whether something is "good" if it has not been put to the test?) Or worse, still: Can there be a human being without a test? (For an analogy in fiction, one thinks of the endless battery of tests devised for determining the replicant/human difference in the prototype sequencing of *Blade Runner.*) If we were able to get through to the other side of these questions, beyond the ambivalence that the test appears at every juncture to restore, and supposing we decided that it would be best to end with the secret syndications of testing: Under what conditions would banning or disruption be at all possible?

We have noted how AI posits testability as ground. In addition, it appears to share with Kurt Gödel the optimism that testing will catch up with truth. In other words, AI does not reflect upon the value of the truth it posits or upon the largely performative forces that fuel its assumption of truth. Gödel has argued that there are true statements of number theory that its methods of proof are too weak to demonstrate. His proof pertained to *any* axiomatic system purporting to achieve the aims that Alfred North Whitehead and Bertrand Russell, in their *Principia Mathematica,* had set for themselves. Gödel shows how statements of number theory, being also statements about statements of number theory, could each misdirect a proof. In sum, Gödel demonstrates that provability "is a weaker notion than truth."[53] This is not the place to interrogate precisely how truth works in the coding scheme; nonetheless, it seems safe to say that Gödel rescues truth from limitative results of provability, keeping it intact and pinned to an idealized horizon of expectation.

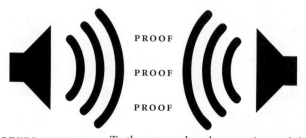

PROOF PROOF PROOF

PROTOTYPE AMERICA   To the extent that the experimental disposition emerges from constant self-differentiation, can simulate itself, and wears, as Nietzsche suggests, many masks, it unquestionably belongs to an experimental site that Nietzsche called in a crucial moment of development "America." If I say "development," it is because Nietzsche for once offers thanks to Hegel for having introduced into science the decisive concept of development. The gratitude is short-lived: we learn quickly that Hegel *delayed* "atheism most dangerously for the longest time" by persuading us of the divinity of existence where Schopenhauer's unconditional and honest atheism at least made the ungodliness of existence "palpable" and "indisputable."[54] America becomes an experimental site because it is the place of acting and *role playing* – a concept developed by Nietzsche for America or by America for Nietzsche. At this point or place, Nietzsche links experimentation with the development of improv techniques. The principal axioms of the gay science are related to dimensions of exploration and discovery; discovery is not seen simply in terms of "invention" but, under certain conditions, as a way of discovering what was already there, inhabited, which is why Nietzsche sometimes takes recourse to the discovery of America – an event, an experiment, a unique stage for representing discovery without invention in conjunction with serious historical risk. If Mary Shelley had seen the discovery of America as an event that occurred too suddenly, without the stops and protections of gradual inquiry – in sum, as a world-historical shock of intrusive violence that disrupted all sorts of ecologies, material and immaterial, conscious and unconscious – Nietzsche studies the profound disruption to thought that the experimental theater of America directed.[55] Taking off for America, he redefines the place of the experimenter, letting go of familiar mappings and manageable idioms. The experimenter must give up any secure anchoring in a homeland, allow herself to be directed by an accidental current rather than aiming for a preestablished goal. The accidental current becomes the groove for a voyage taken without helmsman, without any commanding officer or function, Nietzsche insists. As exemplary contingency plan, America allows for outstanding reinscriptions of fortuity. Its alliance with unprecedented applications of the inessential – a history dominated by risk – gives everyone the hope at least of having an even chance. The fate of America, or this aspect of it, was written into its constitution as a land of discovery. And now, to the accidental discovery of America, where Nietzsche goes on a job hunt.

There have been ages when men believed with rigid confidence, even with piety, in their predestination for precisely one particular occupation, "precisely this way of earning a living, and simply refused to acknowledge the element of accident, role, and caprice. With the help of this faith, classes, guilds and hereditary trade privileges managed to erect those monsters of social pyramids that distinguish the Middle Ages and to whose credit one can adduce at least one thing: durability (and duration is a first-rate value on earth)." Uninterrogated durability and rigid social hierarchy will be thrown over by what Nietzsche calls "America":

> But there are opposite ages, really democratic, where people give up this faith, and a certain cocky faith and opposite point of view advance more and more into the foreground – the Athenian faith that first becomes noticeable in the Periclean age, the faith of the Americans today that is more and more becoming the European faith as well: The individual becomes convinced that he can do just about everything and can manage almost any role, and everybody experiments with himself, improvises, makes new experiments, enjoys his experiments; and all nature ceases and becomes art.[56]

A disfiguring translation of the Renaissance man, the jack-of-all-trades is an American symptom rebounding to Europe, changing the configuration of the want ads that erase natural constraints. One is up for anything, open to the identity *du jour*, capable of ceaseless remakes and integral adjustment. The American athleticism of identity switching has marked politics everywhere, brushing against ideologies of authentic rootedness or natural entitlement. It also means that anyone can in principle try anything out, the bright flipside of which we count the art of improv and experimentation, including performance art and jazz (music was always with science on this point, from at least Bach's *Inventions* to synthesizers and the communities of their computerized beyond).[57] Nietzsche's focus rests on the individual's incredible conviction that he can manage any role. The refined profile for role management, by the way, Nietzsche locates in the Jewish people, who have had to rigorously play it as it comes, go with the flow, adjust and associate. The experimenter is at once the experimentee: there is little room here for securing the range of scientific or artistic distance, or, more precisely, he supplies just enough slack to let one try oneself out. Everyone turns himself into a test site, produces ever new experiments, and, significantly, *enjoys* these experiments. This plasticity does not match the solemn lab for which Dr. Frankenstein becomes the paradigmatic director, weighted as he is with Germanic gravity and remorse over the meaning of his relentless experiments. Nonetheless, oppositions should not be held too rigidly, for Europe and America are sharing needles on this one, contaminating one another according to the possibilities of new experimental *jouissance*. In the end Victor Frankenstein, too, was carried over the top by his brand of *jouissance*, by a level of desire punctuated by grim determination.

Clearly, there is a price to be paid by the experimental player. One cannot remain detached from the activity of intense experimentation but finds oneself subject to morphing: One grows into one's experimental role and becomes one's mask. America's increasing obsession with actors – now actors have political views – has roots in Greece and can be connected in Nietzsche to his observations on nonsubstantial role playing:

> After accepting this role faith – an artist's faith, if you will – the Greeks, as is well known, went step for step through a rather odd metamorphosis that does not merit imitation in all respects: They really became actors. . . . and whenever a human being begins to discover how he is playing a role and how he can be an actor, he becomes an actor. . . . It is thus that the maddest and most interesting ages of history always emerge, when the "actors," all kinds of actors, become the real masters. As this happens, another human type is disadvantaged more and more and finally made impossible; above all, the great "architects": The strength to build becomes paralyzed; the courage to make plans that encompass the distant future is discouraged; those with a genius for organization become scarce: who would still dare to undertake projects that would require thousands of years for their completion? For what is dying out is the

fundamental faith that would enable us to calculate, to promise, to anticipate the future in plans of such scope, and to sacrifice the future to them – namely, the faith that man has value and meaning only insofar as he is a stone in a great edifice; and to that end he must be solid first of all, a "stone" – and above all not an actor![58]

Nietzsche enters the zone where actors become the ruling part – "the real masters" – but he is careful to unleash the irony of mimetic dissuasion. This theater of politics and value-positing stunts should not necessarily be imitated, he warns. In this passage of paradoxical reversal, experimenting gradually becomes associated with America and the impending rule of actors. Philosophy comes to see experimenting in the negative light of project paralysis, inhibiting acts of promising, calculating, or anticipation – acts by which the future can be nailed down, as it were, and "sacrificed" to the performatives that bind it. The futural stone age has been compromised, however, by new human flora and fauna, which, Nietzsche asserts, could never have grown in more solid and limited ages. So the experimental disposition, cast in soft metaphors, waters down the solid reputation of the ages, showing the experimenter to be not quite solid as a rock but rather absorbed into a soft present that recedes into itself from distance or future. Nonetheless, Nietzsche considers this age as one without limit – of unlimited finity; the age of "actors" encompasses the maddest and most interesting of possible ages. It is not clear how the loss of this hard rock faith ought to be evaluated in the end, because Nietzsche elsewhere tends to emphasize the need for shedding such faith and, when taking on new forms spontaneously, he gets the green card and becomes somewhat of an American himself.

Nietzsche is well within his comfort zone when the personal technologies of shedding and softening take hold of existence, when brevity becomes the correct tact to measure out a given stage of life. He is attached only to brief habits, he writes, describing a fluidity that allows him to get to know many things and states:

I love brief habits and consider them an inestimable means for getting to know many things and states, down to the bottom of their sweetness and bitternesses. My nature is designed entirely for brief habits, even in the needs of my physical health and altogether as far as I can see at all – from the lowest to the highest. I always believe that here is something that will give me lasting satisfaction – brief habits, too, have this faith of passion, this faith in eternity – and that I am to be envied for having found and recognized it; and now it nourishes me at noon and in the evening and spreads a deep contentment all around itself and deep into me so that I desire nothing else, without having any need for comparisons, contempt, or hatred. But one day its time is up; the good thing parts from me, not as something that has come to nauseate me but peacefully and sated with me as I am with it – as if we had reason to be grateful to each other as we shook hands to say farewell. Even then something new is waiting at the door, along with my faith – this indestructible fool and sage! – that this new discovery will be just right, and that this will be the last time. That is what happens to me with dishes, ideas, human beings, cities, poems, music, doctrines, ways of arranging the day, and life styles.[59]

Beyond stating the motif of farewell and Nietzschean gratitude, the passage inventories the things that offer themselves to experimentation, testing, and structural rearrangement, covering the span from dishes, cities, schedule, and music to Nietzsche's unquestionably Californian invention of life-style. The existential range of motion allows for time to press upon pleasure, to mark the end with a mastered violence. Nietzsche says and sees the day when, with a feeling of satiety and peacefulness, the time comes for all good things to bid him farewell. This reciprocal scene of departure invites the relation with things to evade the punishing rhythm of violent and constant improvisation. Something stays with him – the brief habit does not overthrow a certain habitual groundedness that supports brevity and experimental essays. In fact, an excess of habitlessness would destroy the thinker and send him out of America into Siberia. He admits, "[m]ost intolerable, to be sure, and the terrible par excellence would be for me a life entirely devoid of habits, a life that would demand perpetual improvisation. That would be my exile and my Siberia." Carried to extremes, the homelessness of experimentation turns into unsettling exile – into the horror of being – when it demands nonstop improv. Still, the opposite of horror is odious to Nietzsche, a kind of political noose around his delicate neck:

Enduring habits I hate. I feel as if a tyrant had come near me and as if the air I breathe had thickened when events take such a turn that it appears that they will inevitably give rise to enduring habits; for example, owing to an official position, constant association with the same people, a permanent domicile, or unique good health. Yes, at the very bottom of my soul I feel grateful to all my misery and bouts of sickness and everything about me that is imperfect, because this sort of thing leaves me with a hundred backdoors through which I can escape from enduring habits.[60]

The experimental disposition, then, has to dismantle its internal and material lab frequently to keep the punctual rhythm of the brief habit going – a philosophical policy susceptible of significant consequences. Nietzsche never places the experiment on the side of monumentality or reliable duration; it cannot be viewed as a project. Nor is he attached to a particular form of experiment – this is not the scientist obsessed with an idée fixe – but one capable of uprooting and going, for better or worse, with the diversifying flow of ever new flora and fauna. This degree of openness, though it does have its limits and points of closure, necessarily invites ambivalence – those moments, for instance, when Nietzsche stalls, dreaming of immense edifices and the permanence promised by contracts written in stone.

Although he at every point invites precisely such a register of understanding, the Nietzschean ambivalence toward experimentation cannot be reduced to the personal whim or contingent caprice of Fred Nietzsche, even when he experiments on himself or writes in a letter to Peter Gast that the Gay Sci was the most *personal* among his books. What he means by "personal" has everything to do with the nature of scientificity that he expounds. In Nietzsche as in Goethe, scientists are at no point placed strictly or simply outside the field of experimentation; part of the thinking of personality, they cannot extricate themselves from the space of inquiry in the name of some mystified or transcendental project from which the personhood of the scientist can be dropped out or beamed up at will. The test site can always blow up in their faces or make ethical demands on them – for Nietzsche, this would remain a personal dilemma.[61] But let us see where it takes us in terms of the personalized cartography of the Gay Sci.

Since we have established temporary residency in the philosopheme, America (or, at this point, one might almost say in the *hypothesis* of America), I would like to migrate first to another text, before returning to Nietzsche – if only to satisfy his desire for the punctuality of the brief habit and to follow out the multiple departures that his text prescribes.

Once again, the line of flight takes us to one of the futures of Nietzsche's Gay Sci. In sync with the Nietzschean effort to think science according to the complexities of the experimental disposition, Max Weber sets up the stakes of the test drive, which he traces from its Hellenic origins to Nietzsche and the American compulsion to test everything: his argument refers us to material instances of testing such as the Ph.D. written, oral, comprehensive, general, and qualifying examinations, to teaching evaluations and the corresponding physical and mental stress tests. An incentive for citing Weber in this context is prompted by his understanding of the history of scientific work, which links experiment in art and science to academic testing and the question of research in the modern sense. "Let me take you once more to America," Weber writes in his famous essay "Science as a Vocation." He has just finished demonstrating the differences between a Privatdozent, who earns nothing but is somewhat exalted and the tremendously exploited Assistant Professor, who earns some wages (barely enough to subsist on) but is not exalted. Assistant Professors find themselves subjected instead to the trials of the quasi-proletariat – with chairman, institution, and colleagues all poised against them. In fact, Assistant Professors, unlike their German counterparts, relate to the university and their departmental chair with the same terror and forced deference as do the proletariat toward factory and boss. Weber will take us from American testing to the question of research in the Nietzschean sense. "The American boy," he observes, "learns unspeakably less than the German boy. In spite of an incredible number of examinations, his school life has not had the significance of turning him into an absolute creature of examinations, such as the German. For in America, bureaucracy, which presupposes the exam diploma as a ticket of admission to the realm of office prebends, is only in its beginnings."[62] Weber links exam hypertrophy to a cultural epidemic of disrespect – the basis of democracy:

> The young American has no respect for anything or anybody, for tradition or for public office – unless it is for the personal achievement of individual men. This is what America calls "democracy." . . . The American's conception of the teacher who faces him is: he sells me his knowledge and his methods for my father's money, just as the greengrocer sells my mother cabbage. And that is all. To be sure, if the teacher

happens to be a football coach, then, in this field, he is a leader. But if he is not this (or something similar in a different field of sports), he is simply a teacher and nothing more. And no young American would think of having the teacher sell him a *Weltanschauung* or a code of conduct. Now, when formulated in this manner, we should reject this. But the question is whether there is not a grain of salt contained in this feeling, which I have deliberately stated in extreme with some exaggeration.[63]

The teacher, bankrolled by the father, is linked in terms of headspace to the cabbage purchased at the grocer's by the mother. The debasement of teacher to an implicit word salad without ideological or world-historical gravity may seem grotesque, but Weber is not so sure that it should be viewed as such. It puts a restraining order on the possibly devastating politics of transference that teacher's function could otherwise prime. No one is going to follow this teacher to the hell of war under the flag of totalitarian conviction. No one is going to salute the rectoral speech of a cabbage-head teacher. (However, in America the rage in the 1980s and 1990s for cabbage-patch dolls did once provoke a major transferential crisis, so one cannot simply predict where or when transference will take root.) Due to the teacher's position in the capital theater of parental auction, there will be very few transfer students in the class of democratic school systems. The teacher is reduced to a bare minimum of functions, with only the supplementary space of school team sports conferring qualities of leadership on the teaching subject. Whether doubling as a football coach or not, the downgraded teacher mainly prepares students for a battery of "no pain no gain" examinations.

The figure of the teacher, the problem of proper places and problematic displacements, turn in Weber's unfolding observations on the status of science. In fact, the teacher never entirely leaves the scene and functions like a ticker, a continuously looping crawl on the bottom of news broadcasts such as those of CNN. The teacher is not locked out of the discursive classroom that Weber installs, though the pedagogical function momentarily takes a backseat during the historical-philosophical elaboration. Weber ticks off the stages of scientific work before returning to the teaching crisis. He proceeds by seizing the experiment as a way of controlling experience: "The second great tool of scientific work [the first was Plato's discovery of the concept], the rational experiment, made its appearance at the side of this discovery of the Hellenic spirit during the Renaissance period. The experiment is a means of reliably controlling experience."[64] The emergence of the experimental *Weltanschauung* is wide-ranging. Earlier experiments include physiological experiments made in India in the service of ascetic yoga technique; in Hellenic antiquity, mathematical experiments were made for purposes of war technology. "But to raise the experiment to a principle of research was the achievement of the Renaissance. They were the great innovators in art, who were the pioneers of experiment. Leonardo and his like and, above all, the sixteenth-century experimenters in music with their experimental pianos were characteristic. From these circles the experiment entered science, especially through Galileo, and it entered theory through Bacon; and then it was taken over by the various exact disciplines of the continental universities, first of all those of Italy and then those of the Netherlands."[65]

Framing the significance of the scientific impulse for later centuries, Weber asks what science meant to those who stood at the threshold of modern times: "To artistic experimenters of the type of Leonardo and the musical innovators, science meant the path to true *art*, and that meant for them the path to true *nature*. Art was to be raised to the rank of a science, and this meant at the same time and above all to raise the artist to the rank of a doctor, socially and with reference to the meaning of his life. This is the ambition on which, for instance, Leonardo's sketchbook was based. And today? 'Science as a way to nature' would sound like blasphemy to youth."[66] Weber travels an unmarked path as he reads off the ratings of science in relation to art; he suspends the genealogist's commentary when tracing the values associated with art and science. In the earlier phases, science provides a conduit to art; later, it appears, the artist strives for the scientific upgrade, seeking the position of doctor. Now art wants to "be raised" to the rank of science; a turnaround in the scoring system of values has taken root somewhere in Leonardo's sketchbook. The task of science was, moreover, conceived as illuminating the path of God (Weber recalls Swammerdam's statement, "Here I bring you the proof of God's providence in the anatomy of a louse") when "people no longer found this path among the philosophers, with their concepts and deductions." When philosophy became dry and nearly mathematical in its procedures and aims, science became the hope and desire for a more bouncy transcendence, offering a clearer embrace of immanence as well. And today? "Who – aside from certain big children who are indeed found in the natural sciences – still believes that the findings of astronomy, biology, physics, or chemistry could teach us anything about the *meaning* of the world? If there is any such 'meaning,' along what road could one come upon its tracks?"[67]

In the quake and wake of meaning, Nietzsche begins, almost predictably, to show his face. He arrives in the text as the one to have undone the promises of Plato and Aristotle, uprooting childish notions of happiness: "After Nietzsche's devastating criticism of those 'last men' who 'invented happiness,' I may leave aside altogether the naive optimism in which science – that is, the technique of mastering life which rests upon science – has been celebrated as the way to happiness. Who believes in this? – aside from a few big children in university chairs or editorial offices."[68] The university, along with some editorial hubs, has become a playpen for outstripped fantasies concerning the pursuit of happiness. The implications of the conceptual quarantine are considerable for science, because it now has to regroup in terms of establishing its self-understanding in a convincing and worldly way. Interestingly, literature was already there to give expression to the scientific predicament.

The meaning of science as a vocation after the collapse of these illusions (as the way to true being, the way to true art, the way to true nature, the way to true God, the way to true happiness) was supplied by Tolstoy, who asserted that science is meaningless because it gives no answer to our question, the only question important for us: "What shall we do and how shall we live?" That science does not give an answer to this, remarks Weber, "is indisputable. The only question that remains is the sense in which science gives 'no' answer." Science cannot tell whether something is worth being known just as medicine does not presume to ask whether life – the life that it finds itself obligated by contract to save – is worth living. Nor, for that matter, do we find aesthetics, which takes as a given the fact that there are works of art, asking whether there *should* be works of art. Jurisprudence does not wonder whether there should be laws. Science, hardly free from presupposition, presupposes "that what is yielded by scientific work is 'worth being known.' In this, obviously, are contained all our problems. For this presupposition cannot be proved by scientific means. It can only be interpreted with reference to its ultimate meaning, which we must reject or accept according to our ultimate position towards life."[69] The presupposition of value – is it worth being known, living, existing? – cannot be supported, much less proven by scientific means. Such untouchable premises belong to the family of logic that induced Heidegger to state, rather categorically, that science does not think. Weber is more tentative in his evaluation of value-positing science. Can any entity assert with uncompromised lucidity the worthiness of its existence? Such abyss openers are usually avoided by the very discursive formations that depend upon them for their existence. Weber sheds light on the way in which withholding or withdrawal marks an opening and asks that we contemplate the way that science gives no answer. Judging by the quotation marks placed on "no," it is likely that "'no' answer" is, for Weber, also an answer or rather that, on some vital level, there is no such thing as no answer. Another possibility, for which Weber allows with equal vigor, indicates that the question is in the first place misplaced. Should we go so far as to ask science to comment on what we should do or how we should live or how to think and cherish life? Have we lost our senses?

And yet Nietzsche does call upon science – in its second stage as experiment – to affirm life. The affirmation by no means arrives from an imagined outside of life, but from life as scientific, joyous science – a scientificity that nonetheless crashes against the implacable harshness of experience and is called upon endlessly to clear abysses without disavowing their dangers. Indeed, the experimental turn not only responds to the question that science, in the run from Tolstoy to Heidegger, is said necessarily to have evaded: "is it worth it?" – but it posits value and produces a site from which to evaluate value, the very worthiness of worth. For different reasons, the worthiness of worth has been sidelined by science.

An imposing test site according to Weber's logic still pulses from the institution of higher learning. Its crucial manifestation occurs in the university classroom. At some level everything in our academic spaces is meant for trial. A breeding ground for test exercises, the university makes itself susceptible to the delegitimating drills of its own premises. The professor comes in handy as figuring the university's tendency to undermine its cause. Academic speech consistently fails the test of scientific integrity by lapsing into prophecy and other ideological excesses whenever professors take a stand. The university, comprised as it is by all sorts of research facilities – endless labs, including those made for body-experimentations, the incorporated gymnasiums, examination procedures (and, in some instances, military and police exercises) – always risks crossing over into nonscientific conviction when the big kids start announcing their beliefs. The professor helps focalize the difficulty of stabilizing assigned places within the university: What is on trial, constantly put to the test, in Weber's essay is the professor's ability to occupy the appropriate space. It is as if the common surprise quizzes, tests, examination procedures, and so forth were meant to mirror the professor's dilemma, inverting the processes of judgment and evaluation.

Even while administering tests, the professor in actuality is really being tested and retested for levels and dynamics of probity which, in the case Weber examines, amounts to maintaining distinctions between what legitimately can occur inside and outside the circumscribed academic space. The professor holds the boundary line between the proper and improper, which is why she (in Weber's case, "he") is bound to fail the university, which requires for its continued legitimacy the illusion of an absolute boundary: "The prophet and the demagogue do not belong on the academic platform. To the prophet and the demagogue, it is said: 'Go your ways out into the streets and speak openly to the world.' . . . The professor who feels called upon to act as a counselor of youth and enjoys their trust may prove himself a man in his personal relations with them. And if he feels called upon to intervene in the struggles of world views and party opinions, he may do so outside, in the market place, in the press, in meetings, in associations, wherever he wishes. But after all, it is somewhat too convenient to demonstrate one's courage in taking a stand where the audience and possible opponents are condemned to silence."[70] In the classroom the teacher must clean up his act, tone down the prophetic pathos, and follow a nonideological teaching plan. It is interesting to note that Weber sends the teacher back to the marketplace to express worldviews.

In the end, the premises upon which scientifically rigorous teaching might be based cannot be proven scientifically. There is, strictly speaking, despite Pestalozzi and other trailblazers in the field, no reliable "pedagogy." Thus the duty of the teacher remains extraneous to the teaching scene or any learning curve – this tour of duty cannot be taught, demonstrated, or proven.

Now one cannot demonstrate scientifically what the duty of an academic teacher is. One can only demand of the teacher that he have the intellectual integrity to see that it is one thing to state facts, to determine mathematical or logical relations or the internal structure of cultural values, while it is another thing to answer questions of the value of culture and its individual contents and the question of how one should act in the cultural community and in political associations. These are quite heterogeneous problems. If he asks further why he should not deal with both types of problems in the lecture-room, the answer is: because the prophet and the demagogue do not belong on the academic platform.

The prophet and demagogue must go out into the streets – the place, according to Weber, where criticism meets its match and becomes possible. This is a key point, locking up the proper teacher inside the classroom; however, it gets twisted by Weber's recognition later in the essay that the streets, as topos for discussion and open to criticism, are disappearing. He does not quite declare the vanishing of the public sphere and the multiplication of new and virtual beats but addresses instead the movement of retreat of critical ideological commentary, in our times, to spaces of intimacy and mystical abandon. By this time, school is out:

> The fate of our times is characterized by rationalization and intellectualization and, above all, by the "disenchantment of the world." Precisely the ultimate and most sublime values have retreated from public life either into the transcendental realm of mystic life or into the brotherliness of direct and personal human relations. It is not accidental that our greatest art is intimate and not monumental, nor is it accidental that today only within the smallest and intimate circles, in personal human situations, in pianissimo, that something is pulsating that corresponds to the prophetic pneuma, which in former times swept through the great communities like a firebrand, welding them together. If we attempt to force and to "invent" a monumental style in art, such miserable monstrosities are produced as the many monuments of the last twenty years. If one tries intellectually to construe new religions without a new and genuine prophecy, then, in an inner sense, something similar will result, but with still worse effects. And academic prophecy, finally, will create only fanatical sects but never a genuine community.

It can be observed that, in order to make this statement, Weber himself delivers something of an academic prophecy. The question remains of how to locate the space of Weber's elaboration, or where to designate a place for thought that can legitimately produce something like a world-view. The problem is that the world, together with the implied spaces on which Weber relies, has been shattered – in part, by the very experimental exercises that he studies. The world scanned by Weber no longer conforms to a transcendental coherency that would permit the imperturbability of the *Weltanschauung*. Another problem – Weber's world disenchantment points to this area of conceptual turbulence – is that democracy implicitly depends on a notion of polis, which no doubt accounts for Weber's circumscription of a marketplace even as he measures the disappearance of political spaces. There is no place to channel the prophetic *pneuma,* which is perhaps why its course has been relocated to the university, a kind of model polis internally governed by remnants of an ancient regime.

Still, academic prophecy, Weber predicts, will result only in the creation of fanatical sects and no genuine community. At this point one needs to wonder if a "genuine community" has passed the test of fanaticism and why Weber has chosen this expression rather than a more democratic, less Christian, one. The university offers the limit-space where some of these notions can be tried out. Yet, like Nietzsche whom he cites abundantly, Weber must drop out in order to get his ideas across. Although clocked in a bit later than Nietzsche, Weber still has access to the somewhat more stable spaces of yesteryear. Nietzsche is more strained by the reactive forces of democracy (following his own rules and regs, he evaluates democracy from the perspectives of active and reactive forces) and has lost by now more ground than Weber in terms of putting a world together or projecting a community to come. Both thinkers are futural sprinters, no doubt, but Nietzsche is shooting ahead or at least shooting for what Derrida calls a "democracy-to-come."[71] Most consequential for us, given the duties at hand, Weber can be said to contain and neutralize the emergence of *experimentum* and related testing systems – they still have a locality – while for Nietzsche, one is tempted to say, the test site has irrevocably corrupted the world and exploded the illusion of any such balsamic borders or bindings. But since we are in Nietzsche territory, this shattering also illuminates the outlines of a promise.

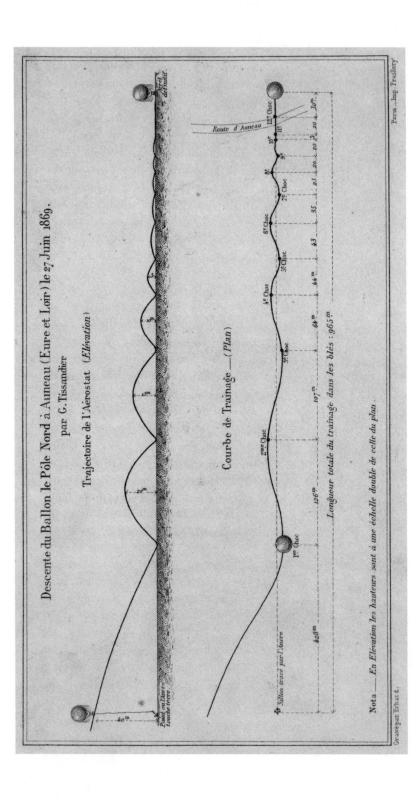

Descente du Ballon le Pôle Nord à Auneau (Eure et Loir) le 27 Juin 1869.

par G. Tissandier

Trajectoire de l'Aérostat *(Élévation)*

Courbe de Trainage — *(Plan)*

Route d'Auneau

Nota ___ En Élévation les hauteurs sont à une échelle double de celle du plan.

Grave par Erhard.

Paris _ Imp. Frailfery

THE EXPERIMENTAL DISPOSITION   Nietzsche is in a fix. Two essential desires motivate his text and pull it in different directions. Like the
two sets of democratic values that he scores, the agony of double occu-
pancy besets the writing that engages him. The experimental disposition
offers him a way of articulating the doubling and division by which he
proceeds. Interestingly, the definition of experiment already places it in
the twilight zone between what is already there and discovery, between
description and invention, splitting reactive and active interpretive possibilities. *Experimentum* means a test or trial of something; specifically of
any action or process undertaken to discover something not yet known *or*
to demonstrate something known. Without getting into deconstructive
disputes with these terms, let us give free rein to the normative view that
tends to pull *experimentum* in favor of experience – being experimental
of or based on experience – rather than toward übertheory or authority.
Nietzsche especially likes the shriveling of authority that *experimentum*
implies. No one gets to say from a hidden, mystified place what the truth
is because henceforth every step of the way has to be demonstrated and
assured for all to see as well as repeat. This no doubt explains Nietzsche's
insistence, en route to America, on the figure of a ship without a helmsman. Within the precincts of experimental effort there is no theory or
authority that could control, predict, or steer the experiment on a foreseeable course. In part because experimentality struggles between the
domains of two desires schematized in the Gay Sci, Nietzsche's text exhibits cautious ambivalence toward the very structures he discovers: it is
bound on the one hand by the desire to fix, to immortalize, "the desire for
being" and, on the other hand, by "the desire for *destruction*, change and
becoming." The latter is "an expression of an overflowing energy that is
pregnant with future," which Nietzsche terms "Dionysian." These double
desires in turn require a dual genealogical interpretation.

Splitting heirs, Nietzsche lets us know that desire affiliated with destruction does not always originate in the overfullness of life. Destruction, change, and becoming can also indicate a pernicious genesis that
finds its source in "the hatred of the ill-constituted, disinherited, and
underprivileged, who destroy, *must* destroy, because what exists, indeed
all existence, all being, outrages and provokes them." The test question for
Nietzsche's genealogical evaluation is this: "I ask in every instance 'is it
hunger or superabundance that has here become creative?'"[72] On the side

of the overfullness of life yet equally on a destructive bent, the Dionysian – a warrior of change and becoming – can absorb tremendous losses and traumas; the Dionysian allows one to deflect the temptation to reproduce the wounding of trauma out of a stance of depletion and anger toward life:

> He that is richest in the fullness of life, the Dionysian God and man, cannot only afford the sight of the terrible and questionable but even the terrible deed and any luxury of destruction, decomposition, and negation. In his case, what is evil, absurd, and ugly seems, as it were, permissible, owing to an excess of procreating, fertilizing energies that can still turn any desert into lush farmland. Conversely, those who suffer most and are poorest in life would need above all mildness, peacefulness, and goodness in thought as well as deed – if possible, also a god who would be truly a god for the sick, a healer and savior; also logic, the conceptual understandability of existence – for logic calms and gives confidence – in short, a certain warm narrowness that keeps away fear and encloses one in optimistic horizons.[73]

Christianity and its Dionysian other respond to different types of needs. Logic, intelligibility, as well as the safety zones of hermeneutic horizons and habitual sunsets belong to the Christian solvents. Absurd, ugly, incomprehensible dissociations from meaning-bound or soothing existence belong to the Dionysians. These teams indicate the struggle of forces and hegemonies, powerful tendencies on this or the other side of metaphysical comforts. They put their marks on the experimental run, tagging the will to fix or the will to deracinate. But even these moments of heightened willing fissure internally. Thus the will to immortalize also requires a dual interpretation from which its ambiguity stems. It can be prompted, first, by gratitude and love – "bright and gracious like Goethe, spreading a Homeric light and glory over all things." However "it can also be the tyrannic will of one who suffers deeply, who struggles, is tormented, and would like to turn what is most personal, singular, and narrow, the real idiosyncrasy of his suffering, into a binding law and compulsion – one who, as it were, revenges himself on all things by forcing his own image, the image of his torture, on them, branding them with it."[74] For Nietzsche everything is staked on the difference between these two "personalities" of the *experimentum*. Flagging a ship without a helmsman, he nonetheless administers a psychological test in order to evaluate what in effect constitutes the function of helmsman. What is steering the odyssey of the *experimentum?* Is it conducted with the bright, confident expansiveness of the cheerfully Homeric Goethe or by a self-tormenting life avenger who wants to construct a monument to a withering history of private suffering? (Both these possibilities exist in Goethe, for there was also the old reactionary policing Goethe who beat up on Hölderlin and Kleist, but that's another story.) When Nietzsche thinks the experimental disposition, all these considerations, moods, and measures must fall into place or at least be taken into account. He doesn't make it easy on us.

The ambiguity discovered by the Gay Sci to inhabit the grid of experimenting, testing, and improvisation prevents Nietzsche from simply affirming them. Whether originating in the fullness or slander of life, they answer to conditions of accelerated deregulation. The experimental disposition must be allowed to run free, even if there exists the risk of its breaking away from any controlled sense of purpose. Still, experimentation never reverts to the mere anarchy of tryouts either, or to the practice of a little boy jumping off the roof in an attempt to fly. There are rules, conventions, regulations, and treaties governing the field of testing, which are repeatedly given over to review. As we have seen, part of Nietzsche wants to tie the test drive, the way it is conducted, to something like the personal taste and experience of the experimenter. However gauged, narrativized, and internally split, the work of the gay scientist draws upon a history of suffering, exile, and pain, which necessarily becomes a measure of the field of discovery without erasing its more discursive requirements. The abundant personality inhabits suffering in a manner that proves difficult to share. This unshareability of the greatest distress no doubt pushes off from Christian and Kantian shorelines. One is, still and ever, on one's own, without God or authority at the helm, without mimetic moorings or citational lifeboats. Prompted by the whole economy of the soul and "our personal and profoundest suffering [which] is incomprehensible and inaccessible to almost everyone," "one simply knows nothing of the whole inner sequence and intricacies that are distress for *me* or for *you*. The whole economy of my soul and the balance effected by 'distress,' the way new springs and needs break open, the way in which old wounds are healing, the way whole periods of the past are shed – all such things that may be involved in distress are of no concern to our dear pitying friends; they wish to help and have no thought of the personal necessity of distress, although terrors, deprivations, impoverishments, midnights, adventures, risks, and blunders are necessary for me and for you as are their opposites."[75]

A community of two, me and you, has a history hidden from almost everyone; it is bound by the incalculable risks and terrors, adventures and blunders (and so forth) constituting our scientific contract. We, me and you, put our experience on the line as a matter of taste and rigor. Complicit in the launching of an unnarratable story of distress, we scrutinize our experiences as severely as a scientific experiment. The crucial moment in which Nietzsche explicates the value of experience in a gay science occurs when he establishes a scientific schedule, writing and signing as a guinea pig in "As interpreters of our experiences":

> One sort of honesty has been alien to all founders of religions and their kind: They have never made their experiences a matter of conscience for knowledge. "What did I really experience? What happened in me and around me at that time? Was my reason bright enough? Was my will opposed to all deceptions of the senses and bold in resisting the fantastic?" ... So [our dear religious people] experience "miracles" and "rebirths" and hear the voices of little angels! But we, we others who thirst after reason, are determined to scrutinize our experiences as severely as a scientific experiment – hour after hour, day after day. We ourselves wish to be our experiments and guinea pigs.[76]

Subjected to the ruthless honesty of self-monitoring, we others turn ourselves into experimenting experiments. In order to sustain this level of honesty in the experimental space, one needs to power up the personality and loosen one's convictions. Let us return to the trope of personality as Nietzsche often does. What precisely does he mean by this, or what does personality guarantee in the thought that Nietzsche is trying to advance here?

To have a strong personality involves the capacity to divest oneself constantly; this has nothing to do with the bloating of selfhood inherited from the Romantics nor, at this point, with the ability to impose one's perspective or will on world. The strong personality allows for and supports self-submission to the radical deprogramming that science implies. As difficult as Nietzsche knows this is to implement, he pleads for a stance consisting of no convictions (in Nietzsche's notes: "A very popular error: having the courage of one's convictions; rather, it is a matter of having the courage for an attack of one's convictions!!!").[77] When convictions infiltrate the space of the scientific experiment they are to be placed under strict police supervision. Convictions, if they are at all allowed to appear, can move about only when handcuffed to the police of mistrust. Yet Nietzsche understands that we mortals like to have our convictions. To the extent that they are still admitted, they serve to remind us that there always was a prior conviction, a slip of metaphysical faith that still has its hold on scientific procedure. The conviction is an illegal alien in the bad sense of that concept, perhaps the only bad sense that we have of the concept:

> In science convictions have no rights of citizenship, as one says with good reason. Only when they decide to descend to the modesty of hypotheses, of a provisional experimental point of view, of a regulative fiction, they may be granted admission and even a certain value in the realm of knowledge – though always under the restriction that they remain under police supervision, under the police of mistrust. – But does this not mean, if you consider it more precisely, that a conviction may obtain admission to science only when it ceases to be a conviction? Would it not be the first step in the discipline of the scientific spirit that one would not permit oneself any more convictions?[78]

Once a conviction is let out onto the scientific field of inquiry, it passes beyond its character as conviction. The conviction ought to pass beneath the level of its formerly inflated stature. When humbled to the level of hypothesis, it is on parole and must answer to the officers of science who are watching it. Still, to the extent that we are policing our convictions, no matter how much furlough we grant them, we still have to deal with the fact of ex-convictions, namely, the ex-cons that hold up our scientific impulse to this day:

> – But you will have gathered what I am driving at, namely, that it is still a metaphysical faith upon which our faith in science rests – that even we seekers after knowledge today, we godless anti-metaphysicians still take our fire, too, from the flame lit by a faith that is thousands of years old, that Christian faith which was also the faith of Plato, that God is the truth, that truth is divine. – But what if this should become more and more incredible, if nothing should prove to be divine any more unless it were error, blindness, the lie – if God himself should prove to be our most enduring lie?[79]

Still taking his fire from the Platonic-Christian regions of faith, the Nietzschean seeker starts up the process of disabling the metaphysical machine to which he remains attached. Absolute detachment is out of the question. The gay scientist has to appeal to other means in order to fuel an experimental engine capable of unmasking abiding lies. The incredible counterforce comes from the realm of art. This is not new for Nietzsche, but he comes at it from a different angle and with renewed resolve. Gay science assumes a relation to scientificity that is linked to art and play. It at no point derives its authority from institutional divisions or scientific hegemonies but draws the possibility of its vitality strictly from art. Art introduces a vitality capable of hosing down the strictures of morality. The necessarily subversive force of art and play challenges the stability of morality as we know it, and, when in concert with science, repels those recodifications slavishly beholden to moralistic descriptions.

Platonic and Christian perspectives on morality block the scientific impulse for a number of reasons. Among these, Nietzsche cites the fear instilled by Plato and the Christians of *falling* (into sin, error, shame), which, to his mind, has petrified our brain power. Given these restraints, which are palpable even today, Nietzsche asks that we consider the over-severe demands we place on ourselves. We have become "virtuous monsters and scarecrows."[80] The stiff upper lip has stiffened mind's native plasticity, weighing us down. With the fool's demotion in the life of thought, play was banished and art was sent to its room. The rest of humanity was left stranded and anxious, pinned to hardened places. "We should be *able* also to stand *above* morality – and not only to *stand* with the anxious stiffness of a man who is afraid of slipping and falling any moment, but also to *float* above it and *play*. How then could we possibly dispense with art – and with the fool? – And as long as you are in any way *ashamed* before yourselves, you do not yet belong with us."[81] Importantly, that which opposes slipping and falling is not figured as standing erect – this would set us up only to get cut down, goading us so far as only to see ourselves plunged into the abyss of endless reversal. Nietzsche opposes slipping with floating and playing. The liberatory exhortation marks the end of Book Two, when the gay scientist acknowledges "Our ultimate gratitude to art." From where Nietzsche sits – rather, from where he floats – there would be no science without art, in part because we would have all committed suicide.

Art trains us for science, making its scandalously uninhibited observations palatable. Art has given us a *taste* for science. These developing taste buds are important since without them science's collaboration with the untrue would provoke severe nausea: "If we had not welcomed the arts and invented this kind of cult of the untrue, then the realization of general untruth and mendaciousness that now comes to us through science – the realization that delusion and error are conditions of human knowledge and sensation – would be utterly unbearable. *Honesty* would lead to nausea and suicide. But now there is a counterforce against our honesty that helps us to avoid such consequences: art as the *good* will to appearance." Under the notion of invention, Nietzsche places the cult of the untrue, which we welcomed in its appearance as art. If art was invented for us, it was in order to heal us from the persistent wounding of necessary error and delusion. Art cooperates at a level of inoculation by administering general untruth in order to immunize us against untruth. As a time-released protection against nausea and suicide, art is not so much *dead*, but its truth – the realization of general untruth – now gets retransmitted through science which, hardly opposed to art, was prepared for by the arts. In sum, without the inoculation that art has prepared for us, science would kill us. Thanks to art, Nietzsche suggests, we can now genuinely welcome science the way one welcomes the future. Hence, to cap it off: "Nothing does us as much good as a *fool's cap*: we need it in relation to ourselves – we need all exuberant, floating, dancing, mocking, childish, and blissful art lest we lose the *freedom above things* that our ideal demands of us."[82]

Still, the two moments profiling the genealogical narrative of close relations have unhappy precedents. Nietzsche would not want art to have prepared for science the way the Old Testament is said to have prepared us for the New Testament: he wants to avoid creating a history of warring texts and referential fallout. In fact, he reverses the effects of the reciprocally promising texts by making art in the end *indispensable* to science and not a matter of the fiction of a surpassable past. There is no intervening conversion theorem to help supplant one with the other; instead, a salutary tension installs the tenuous embrace of related, nonidentical entities. As with every couple that rises out of metaphysics, one of the terms, however, is more explicitly exposed to its own vulnerability than the other. So, even the Gay Sci leaves it possible to see art as having furnished a mere entry to the more sublime effects of science, and, while it would be easy enough to trace a history of put-downs that have accrued to art (Hegel didn't actually put art down – he just put it away, thereby conserving it in his sense), the standing of science appears to be such that it cannot be simply depreciated. A few Romantics attempted to devalue science, but not without a good deal of deference to its mineralogical backwaters, electric charges, and mystical antecedents.

Nietzsche needs science for another reason: it is understood to be nothing less than the contemporary manifestation of evil. Here we might also invoke evil in the French sense of *le mal* – a malignancy, an index on a first level of unhealth and injury, as well as in the moral sense of unwholesomeness. Science would proffer the other *fleur de mal* to art's special capacities for indulging evil. Nietzsche's word on evil, which necessarily encompasses its bad, "degenerate" meaning, may be difficult to swallow, and sometimes it does not get off the ground or get beyond itself, much less beyond evil and good – a risk that he accepts. Nietzsche at no point merely wipes the slate clean but considers evil from the multiple sides of its possible manifestations, with the many lenses of discursive or nondiscursive formations. Evil does not always declare itself in the brilliant efflorescence of Mephistophelean insight, the worthy other to the great deity's specular locutions. Evil can fall further (if it is still a matter of falling) than even the devil and leave traces of unaccountable destitution, irrecuperable anguish. Even the Christians cannot salvage such a degree of wreckage with only the usual redemptive schemes and recuperative sketches. These types of considerations, Nietzsche's work reveals, have taken up residency with science.

The type of questions and urgencies directing the landing patterns of evil in our day can no doubt take one far afield of philosophical proprieties or indulge the worst complicities of phantasm and political organization, destructive sociality and ethical forgetfulness. Discursive safety hazards increase with the intensity of the probe. Still, if Nietzsche's example can be followed – though this remains a dangerous proposition – it becomes ever more necessary to go to sealed off areas and condemned sites, to stay on this side of evil before presuming to get beyond its borders, a movement that Nietzsche traced with terrible care. Following Nietzsche into his abysses, one has to risk pushing the limits of decency in order to locate the test site, an increasingly evolving world-arrangement that cannot be excused from answering for the diverse forms of malignancy it everywhere produces. Nor can one simply condemn such a site as if an indictment would explain anything of its essence or begin to dismantle its effects. These effects range wide and near, so that mappings become as intrusive as they are accommodating to a shifted ordering of things, to the creation of new world orders and the accelerated decreation of world. Our bodies have become test sites in an era of prolific malignancy.

Having named and introduced the epochality of testing, he puts everything out there – his name, his body, his dwellings, friendships, the love affairs that could not happen, his sister's social experiments. The good, the bad, the ugly. Food: how one becomes what one eats. It's all in there, but, for the most part, the paraconcept of testing is his special way of getting at evil. *The Gay Science* is itself a test site. It begins with the supposition, in the preface, that his book may need more than one preface in order to launch it. The book begins by faltering, by testing and striking itself out. And very swiftly, in Book One, he addresses the species' experience of what is different and new as the experience of evil. One would like to call for a strict historicity of reading in this context, if that were possible, because what Nietzsche has to say pinches the ears and hurts one's eyes. Yet I would be reneging on the deal if I were to overlook or skip hurtful passages.[83] Nietzsche went there, and I am going in there with him, in an effort to read on double or triple registers the befores and afters, though such markers fail to account for our experience, precisely, of evil. Even so, there is some difficulty in presenting evil as such, which is something Hannah Arendt implies in her articulation of the "banality of evil," suggesting that the as suchness of evil can best be arrived at allegorically, according to elaborate axiomatics.

If it is possible to say so, Nietzsche works his thought between a good and bad evil. He denounces bad or reactive evil when he gets on anti-Semitism, for instance. The clearing made by productive evil is something altogether different, it seems: this mien of evil arrives on the scene of historical stalemate as a teacher. For the pre- and anti-Nazi (though ever recruitable) Nietzsche, the strongest and most evil spirits in the history of humanity have kept the species alive, or at least they have "so far done the most to advance humanity: again and again they relumed the passions that were going to sleep – all ordered society puts the passions to sleep – and they reawakened again and again the sense of comparison, of contradiction, of the pleasure in what is new, daring, untried; they compelled men to pit opinion against opinion, model against model."

> Usually by force of arms, by toppling boundary markers, by violating pieties – but also by means of new religions and moralities. In every teacher of what is new we encounter the same "wickedness" that makes conquerors notorious, even if its expression is subtler and it does not immediately set the muscles in motion, and therefore also does not make one that notorious. What is new, however, is always evil, being that which wants to conquer and overthrow the old boundary makers and old pieties; and only what is old is good.[84]

The evil of novelty is brought about by the more subtle warrior, the one who heralds new moralities and religions. Bound in concept to the use of force, the overthrowers of old pieties take more time to get their points across and achieve their dominations. At this point, the way Nietzsche aligns the allegory of the experimental disposition with evil is what commands our attention. For the age of experiment leaves nothing alone and messes with the species' sense of time. The individual risks being clocked out by the insinuation of a mechanical world order – a substratum of evil that Nietzsche charges with meaning.

Book One addresses the time span of genuine experimental endeavor, which must not be limited to the experiences of one lifespan but should punch in a different time clock such that it coincides with Nietzsche's tracing of the history of the species. It is an error to condense the resolution of any task posed by science to the lifetime of the individual. Time, including the time of thinking, takes on another quality, as the species moves into a kind of dog time, where things accelerate and need to slow down at once. In "Loss of Dignity" Nietzsche warns that "we think too fast"; "we require little preparation, not even much silence: it is as if we carried in our heads an unstoppable machine that keeps working even under the most unfavorable circumstances." Well, the dog has to go. But keep the leash. The dog as timekeeper has morphed into an insensible machine. There was a time, the philosopher continues, when someone who was preparing for a thought could be spotted: this person "set his face as for prayer and stopped walking; yes, one even stood still for hours."[85] The speedup of thinking, an early sign of the technologization of the human relation to the surrounding world, produces machinal effects that, having no off switch, remain indifferent to unfavorable conditions. No freshness, no renewal, no fatigue – no despair, no love. This is the wiped out, worn down, extinguished personality plugging away.

The machine, part of the experimental setup, is cast negatively in another passage as well. This time, rather than proving unstoppable, it is hard to start up. It is the figure of noisy disjunction, weighty and clumsy – the very opposite of the cheerful lightness imputed to the gay scientist: "In the great majority the intellect is a clumsy, gloomy, creaking machine that is difficult to start."[86] In both cases, when Nietzsche takes recourse to the machine, it is in order to designate the deficient lab of a single intellect, working on autopilot, disconnected from futurity. Isolated and operating autistically, the machine cranks up the question of intergenerational research, that is, it glitches onto a notion of research that breaks the individual's time frame.

> Whatever men have so far viewed as the conditions of their existence . . . has this been researched exhaustively? The most industrious people will find that it involves too much work simply to observe how differently men's instincts have grown, and might yet grow, depending on different moral climates. It would require whole generations, and generations of scholars who would collaborate systematically, to exhaust the points of view and the material. . . . If all these jobs were done, the most insidious question of all would emerge into the foreground: whether science can furnish goals of action after it has proved that it can take such goals away and annihilate them; and then experimentation would be in order [und dann würde ein Experimentieren am Platze sein] that would allow every kind of heroism to find satisfaction – centuries of experimentation that might eclipse all the great projects and sacrifices of history to date. So far, science has not yet built its cyclopic buildings; but the time for that, too, will come.[87]

Having obliterated the goals we thought we had in sight, science is called upon to draw up new maps and charters, to assign new timers and set the metronomes of doing. History, which is dependent on sacrificial economies and the compulsive call of great projects, frees up the space of its binding narratives. Instincts have grown, Nietzsche offers, driving us into other areas and creases of being. In this passage, which announces the advent of experimentation as an age beyond ages, Nietzsche works the problem of channeling heroic urges into what I am calling the modern test drive. A special feel for the scientific task to which the drive attaches requires that it be viewed neither as finite nor infinite but, more accurately, as *transmortal*.

Every kind of heroism would be satiated by the transgenerational chain of experimentation, which does not exclude war among its links but channels warlike aggression to the point of sacrificing the sacrifice and eclipsing the transcendentally tinged project. Nietzsche does not offer a graspable content for such a transmortal research system that would outrun history and its presumed casualties. He calls it into being, gives it a sketch and a place as that which replenishes the sudden void of its own annihilations. He understands the dangerous rush that occurs with the removal of God and Goal, the ensuing depression of instincts and the unpredictable violence of a collapsed morality. Having proven capable of deconstructing "goals of action," can science refurbish them? Experimentation supplants the Goal, the collapse of telos and history, without escaping the precariousness that used to be associated with goals of action. Thought would no longer be bound to truth or falsity but turned into the interpretations and evaluations of nonfinite experiments, summoned by interpretations of forces and evaluations of power.

Nietzsche asks what happens to the operations of sense-making and historical credibility following the destruction of the sacred and sacrifice as we have known and needed them. More precisely, he asks, evading the extortions of essence, *who* will be there to assure the transition? We know what Nietzsche understands by the personality of the experimenter: an unprecedented daredevil, a risk-taker whose risks are sometimes calculated but who has drawn in the aleatory margin to such an extent that the distinction between risk and prudence cannot always be properly measured. In "Prepatory human beings," Nietzsche writes of those who can harvest energy from existence and know how "to *live dangerously!* Build your cities on the slopes of Vesuvius! Send your ships into uncharted seas! Live at war with your peers and yourselves! Be robbers and conquerors as long as you cannot be rulers and possessors, you seekers of knowledge! Soon the age will be past when you should be content to live hidden in forests like shy deer. At long last the search for knowledge will reach out for its due; it will want to *rule* and possess, and you with it."[88] We recall as well his announcement that, with experimentation, "all the daring of the lover of knowledge is permitted again."[89] The exhortation, famously recycled in our day, to live dangerously, tries to root out the knowledge seeker from the hermit's habits and habitations, from the willed ignorance of the ascetic priests and social conformists of a prejudicial morality. The species of knowledge seeker that Nietzsche concocts is hard to imagine – a knowledge seeker shot through with his brand of "virility," at once on the edge and self-restrained, capable of ruling and beholden to the strictest forms of obedience, brutishly tough and aristocratically mannered, a hardened soldier and a pregnant woman. This knowledge seeker, this scientist, has submitted to the severity of service, to the unrewarded exigency of constant weighing and judging: "the most difficult is demanded and the best is done without praise and decorations. Indeed, what one hears is, as among soldiers, mostly reproaches and harsh rebukes; for doing things well [das Gutmachen] is considered the rule, and failure [das Verfehlte] the exception; but the rule always tends to keep quiet."[90]

The uninitiated tremble before the "severity of science," which "has the same effect as the forms and good manners of the best society: it is frightening for the uninitiated." The severity of science cultivates a kind of bonsai of mannered beauty – or maybe it would be metaphorically more fruitful to recall that Nietzsche was a committed equestrian and appreciated the noble restraint of the nervous horse, the tact of a powerfully trained charger. From where Nietzsche stands and looks, science has a decision to make. It can continue to turn in copies of what has been, showing submission to the colder climes of pain and gain, or it can break through to another experience of joy. In the end, it can turn up the heat on both ends of pain and pleasure, choose to promote one of both ends, or diminish the intensity of the whole scale of affects. Science has the power to choose what it will do for us. "To this day you have the choice." If you decide for as little displeasure as possible . . .

> and desire to diminish and lower the level of human pain, you also have to diminish and lower their capacity for joy. Actually, science can promote either goal. So far it may still be better known for its power of depriving man of his joys and making him colder, more like a statue, more stoic. But it might yet be found to be the great dispenser of pain. And then its counterforce might be found at the same time: its immense capacity for making new galaxies of joy flare up.[91]

The trajectory that Nietzsche foresees is an interesting one: until now, science has held the scepter of deprivation.[92] Hence, perhaps, our *desire* for science. Its future holds strong possibilities for dispensing pain. Only after tracing such a future does Nietzsche open the case for joy, as antidote and counterbalance to science's capacity to wield pain – as a responsive, possibly even reactive force. But to reach new galaxies of joy – one among other possible goals offered – Nietzsche must retain a principle of selection; he discards much. He consistently pits acts of discarding against the pain of deprivation, placing joy beyond the punishing smacks of desire.

STOP! Let's roll this back a minute. Something, or someone, was left out. The severity of science, writes Nietzsche, has the same effect as the form and good manners of the best society: "it is frightening for the un-initiated. But those who are used to it would never wish to live anywhere else than in this bright, transparent, vigorous, electrified air – in this virile air."[93] What has happened to Nietzsche's manners in this passage? Why does he fold in the good manners of the best society with virility? Did the mention of good manners, usually on the effeminate side of the gender fence, provoke a defensive reaction-formation? Where does it belong in Nietzsche's thought on testing, and why does virility share the same out-let as electricity? In the service of rigor, we must continue to press the point of indwelling misogyny, even though for Nietzsche and me there are virile women and Nietzsche's soft butch preferences are sometimes quite explicit. Perhaps the misogynist cast of his remarks will obsolesce with time, perhaps in any case it cannot be regarded as essential to the notion of testing. Perhaps I am getting too hysterical. These are many perhapses. Nonetheless, it seems dishonest to hide the symptomatic return of misogynist traces in these contexts: testing invites frequencies that rant of virility, even in the form of the most commonplace expres-sions, such as occurs in the syntagmas, "test your strength," or, "testing your mettle." Is the mark of sexual difference a contingency of testing, or is Nietzsche aiming at other performative feats?[94] Tests in and beyond Nietzsche tend to penetrate to some reserve of interiority, even as they challenge limits. Staving off penetration, some of the designated objects of the test's probe resist its finality or aim, prompting notorious rounds of self-testing, like the Lady of the troubadours (the troubadours sign off *The Gay Science*). They withhold knowledge, defy presentation. Feminine silhouettes of veiling, hiding, movements of retreat take over the meta-phorics and practices of testing. Something is held off or held back. The IQ test, too, gathers prestige as a secret store of essential intelligence, holding the true key to a mythic measure of intelligence. Invasive and no less imperious, the test as remnant of historical inquisitions gets the truth out of you. Even the Turing test, which searches for an operational way to approach a question, opens on the problem of sexual difference. It is played with three people: a man (A), a woman (B), and an interrogator (C) who may be of either sex. The interrogator stays in a room apart from the other two. The object of the game for the interrogator is to determine which of the other two is the man and which is the woman. While Turing's legacy appears to transcend such entanglements, the Turing test, as meta-test, depends on the ability to tell apart at least two of the posited genders. In terms of its many permutations, testing appears to belong to the registers of masculinist anxiety; still, must it necessarily reproduce effects of sexual difference in the majority of its protocols, practices, and effects? I am going to let this slide for the moment, with a mere citation, because Nietzsche's dossier is, as we have seen in the discussion of *Beyond Good and Evil*, quite complicated. Sometimes I'm tired of cleaning up after him. That's for sure. For the moment, we have no direct line to the problem of the misogynist rant in science, at times well concealed but not all that often, really. In the case of Nietzsche, to be fair and honest, one has to travel a little farther to make it through the wind tunnels of irony be-fore making any assured pronouncements or thinking one has stabilized the Nietzschean utterance once and for all.

PROVISIONAL REJECTABILITY   The jubilant opening of Book Four marks the beginning of a new health. Nietzsche bounds back from failing health, ready to reboot, and opens the new site with a poem in honor of Sanctus Januarius. The poem is dated and placed commemoratively: January, 1882, Genoa. "With a flaming spear you crushed / All its ice until my soul / Roaring toward the ocean rushed / Of its highest hope and goal."[95] Starting from scratch, the philosopher opens the new chapter with the miraculous occurrence – associated with St. Januarius – which he does not dissociate from science. The miracle, as mark of joy that can-not be scientifically accounted for or dispelled, honors a concept of life that had been formerly quashed. Nietzsche dedicates his work, "For the

new year," and announces his love, "*Amor fati:* let that be my love henceforth." He affirms, "I still live, I still think: I still have to live, for I still have to think."[96] Thinking binds him to life; living welds him to thought. In a grim inversion of these rites, Nietzsche later, in the solitary darkness of his overturning, would say time and again, "I am dead because I am stupid; I am stupid because I am dead."[97] In Book Four life not only infuses thinking with vitality but sparks thought. In a manner that reminds one of the opening of *Ecce Homo,* the newly born draws up a contract with himself, renewing vows with life: "I, too, shall say what it is that I wish from myself today, and what was the first thought to run across my heart this year – what thought shall be for me the reason, warranty, and sweetness of my life henceforth." Drawing up his contract, producing for the first time his law of *amor fati,* holding himself accountable to himself only, Nietzsche celebrates the rites of the gay scientist and prepares the grounds for further testing. These contractual and ritual provisions bring him to the second aphorism of the new year, "*Personal providence,*" which begins by peaking; at this point, a tremulant high point, he lays out the terms of "our hardest test." "There is a certain high point in life: once we have reached that, we are, for all our freedom, once more in the greatest danger of spiritual unfreedom, and no matter how much we have faced up to the beautiful chaos of existence and denied it all providential reason and goodness, we still have to pass our hardest test." The test site, if this should prove conceivable, is life itself, which seems to have "no other wish than to prove this proposition again and again."[98]

What life, in measure with utmost freedom, appears to want repeatedly to prove – a proposition – is that everything that happens to us turns out to have been meant for us, addressed to us. Even disruptions, losses, banalities, inadvertent glimpses, crappy weather conditions, even the misdemeanors of life, the sick days and gratuitous bruisings, clock in for us: "Every day and every hour, life seems to have no other wish than to prove this proposition again and again. Whatever it is, bad weather or good, the loss of a friend, sickness, slander, the failure of some letter to arrive, the spraining of an ankle, a glance into a shop, a counter-argument, the opening of a book, a dream, a fraud – either immediately or very soon after it proves to be something that 'must not be missing'; it has profound significance and use precisely for *us*." By so saying, Nietzsche prepares to encourage strong claims made on behalf of interpretation, a facet of being-in-the-world that does not rely on extraterrestrial boosters for its meaning and significance. He is trying to find the off-switch for the transcendental shredder. That is to say, he needs to disable the mechanism that sifts and sorts experience according to a limited God-sanctioned grid. Life's propositional aim turns out to be a dangerous seduction "that might tempt one to renounce one's faith in the gods of Epicurus who have no care and are unknown, and to believe instead in some petty deity who is full of care and personally knows every little hair on our head and finds nothing nauseous in the most miserable small service."⁹⁹ An aspect of life works on behalf of the "petty deity" of the Gospels (Matthew 10:30 and Luke 12:7) by producing a discourse of reason and goodness, suturing all wounds, delivering letters and friends, and healing broken ankles and the like.

The hardest test requires us, at life's high point, to pass through the simulated providential proofs. We should "rest content with the supposition that our own practical and theoretical skill in interpreting and arranging events has now reached its high point." At times we are surprised by the harmony of which we are capable – "a harmony that sounds too good for us to dare to give the credit to ourselves. Indeed, now and then someone plays with us – good old chance." Chance helps harmony along at times. Nietzsche does not oppose proof with counterproof but with supposition, chance, a hypothesis, thus overturning the stern structure separating necessity from chance. It is important to note that the German phrasing is not firmly set on "someone" playing with us: "hier und da spielt einer *mit* uns – der liebe Zufall," writes Nietzsche. The emphasis he places on "with" suggests that chance plays along with us. So: chance is a force that sometimes plays on our side, proposing another possibility – giving us another chance, precisely, for interpretive openings that had been previously shut down by providential decree. Chance, in short, helps along practical and interpretive self-reliance. At the same time as introducing chance into the propositional play, Nietzsche avoids the obsessional neurotic's pitfall of *believing* in chance – a trip-up that would end up erasing chance. He does not ply the chance encounter or incident with meaning or necessity but puts it out there on the off chance of its occurrence. *Amor fati* has to steer a difficult course: it cannot be dragged down into the parallel universe of divinely sanctioned meaning or fateful unfolding – "this had to be" – nor can it simply pass off what has been. With chance playing along and partnering with life, the proposition cannot be proven once and for all but, in Nietzsche's words, has to be "proven again and again." What this formulation seems to suggest is that, as in the case of all scientific hypotheses, complete refutation is no more possible than is complete proof. Proofs themselves are a seduction to be met with a suspicion of supposition and chance.[100]

As I indicated above, it would be irresponsible to read testing, in the Nietzschean context of its development, without taking into account the trope of irony and the high velocities of rhetorical deviations that dominate the Gay Sci. The problem of irony, as of anacoluthon, not only illuminates the way in which Nietzsche's science is meant to stand; these problems open the abysses of science itself. If science has preferred historically for the most part to avert its gaze from the medusoid rift upon which it is based, such renitency may not be a matter of accident or oversight but is perhaps necessitated by the view science holds regarding its possibility for advancement. The blind remove comes with the territory. Some geneticists recently have asserted that it is not up to them to teach students ethics or to question what they are doing. That may be so, but the rhetoric of scientific procedure may itself be disclosive of unwanted knowledge and ethical tremors. This in part is why we need to link the scientific project, its many and diverse aspects, with irony's particular temporality as a structure of the instant, as remanded to a structure of occurrence that becomes shorter and shorter, not to say more shortsighted. What is the nature of the scientific claim, its territory and holdings according to the imperatives of Nietzschean irony? Can science maintain its spin on ungroundedness? What is the relation of science to rhetoric? These are questions I wish briefly to discuss, for they provide the most careful probe for understanding why, in more manageable terms, the ends of science have been so greatly resisted. What is the putative relation of science to destruction, to radical negation, or to the undoing of the work toward which it is under way?

In a sense more local to our principal concern: to what extent does testing reflect the permanent pressure of irony that Paul de Man "associated just as often with Nietzsche's *gaya scienza* as with madness and death?"[101] A thoroughgoing reading of the test drive as developed in Nietzsche, and promoted in our culture, would need to investigate the way testing – a project that recognizes the failures of its own constitution as a cognitive system – is related essentially to acts of promising, anacoluthon, and the trope of irony. My intention is merely to sketch the necessity for such a study, hoping it will be taken out for a test drive and improved by future rhetorical daredevils.[102] If this were not merely a sketch, I would be obligated to take apart nearly everything just recorded, including the assertion that irony is a trope. But let it go for now. Like the promise, the test is structurally staked, in terms of the fulfillment of its contract, in the future realization of what it posits. Its performance cannot exhaust itself in some cognitive present but extends the terms of fulfillment to the future, which cannot, strictly speaking, be logically assured. In the end, the promise promises only itself as the sole means of keeping itself as promise; it does not promise anything but its own future: therefore, it does not promise.[103] Testing inhabits this aporetic logic of never accomplishing itself as the principal means of its becoming. In the performative sense of its potentiality, if the test really tested, then we would not need to test; in Nietzschean terms, we would not need to test, turn, and return – we could in fact wholly dispense with the hardest and softest tests, the ceaseless affirming returning – if the test truly tested to capacity.

Operationally, the structure of testing resembles anacoluthon the way de Man describes it in "The Concept of Irony."[104] Anacoluthon is more often used in terms of syntactical patterns of tropes, or periodic sentences, where the syntax of a sentence that raises certain expectations is "suddenly interrupted and, instead of getting what you would expect to get in terms of the syntax that has been set up, you get something completely different, a break in the syntactical expectations of the pattern."[105]

In Marcel Proust, the syntactical disruption interrupts the narrative line in the same way as parabasis. The concern with interruption in promise, anacoluthon, and irony colors our understanding of testing, whose fundamental phrasing would be captured in interruptive programming such as gets literalized by the common broadcast utterance, "We interrupt this program. . . . This is just a test." In order to take place, the test interrupts any program including the one following which it is conceived.

As de Man reminds us in his reading of Schlegel, irony, however, is not merely an interruption; it is, according to Schlegel's definition of irony, the "permanent parabasis."[106] Strangely, this means that parabasis is not just fixed in one point but spread along all points: "irony is everywhere, at all points the narrative can be interrupted. . . . to say that there would be a permanent parabasis is saying something violently paradoxical. But that's what Schlegel has in mind. You have to imagine the parabasis as being able to take place at all times."[107] Irony, as allegory of tropes, acts as interruptive potentiality; it is the nature of irony to threaten persistent and systematic disruption. It is no small matter that Schlegel produced nothing but fragments in his test runs. Exploding systems, as does irony, or disrupting patterns that have been set up, as in the case of anacoluthon, or even failing to deliver, as the promise in the performance of its positing must do – all these unrelenting swerves and slipups strongly correlate with the special Nietzschean deployment of rhetorical forces.

The scandal of irony, with its air of self-detachment and its ground assertion of unreliability, breaking up and breaking down systematicity, has everything to do with destruction: at the very least irony depends for its pull on radically negative moments. The Romantic cliché of irony as that which firmly exposes the experience of the self standing above its own experiences is a convincing narrative of the absolute provisionality of the identitary freezes of self-assumption. De Man, by way of Fichte, discusses the negativity of that self, "the detachment in relation to everything . . . [his] radical distance (the radical negation of himself) in relation to his own work."[108] Benjamin has stressed the disruption and disillusion that comprise the work of irony in related reflections. In a rare moment that grants the fullness of insight, de Man comments apropos of Benjamin: "He sees the destructive power, the negative power, of the parabasis, fully. He sees that the ironization of form consists in a deliberate destruction of the form."[109] Benjamin is credited with staying on the destructive power of irony where others have turned to recuperative strategies, thus calming and domesticating its implications. At this point, irony steps out of its potential role of destroying forms and linguistic settlements and actually appears to accomplish destruction. It is no longer merely a threat. Irony, strictly speaking, works a double register in Benjamin's analysis of building by means of dismantling its object: "Formal irony . . . represents the paradoxical attempt still to construct the edifice by deconstructing it ('am Gebilde noch durch Abbruch zu bauen'). . . . The idea is the infinite project (as we had it in Fichte), the infinite absolute towards which the work is underway."[110] This type of irony (which originates in the relationship of a particular work to the infinite project), far from indicating a subjective caprice of a given author, is necessitated by the work as part of the infinite project. The tendential urge of scientific experimentation parallels the tension articulated between the work and infinite project, between the fragmented aphorism and presumed totality. Like Benjamin, Nietzsche breaks with the movement of speculative rhythm critiqued by de Man: "At the moment when all seems lost, when the work is totally undone, it gets recuperated, because that radical destruction is a moment in the dialectic, which is seen as a historical dialectic in the progression towards the absolute in a Hegelian scheme."[111] The potential effects of unstoppable interruption have not been respected.

In a related discussion of allegory, Carol Jacobs casts the interruptive quality of Benjamin's scansions a little differently, reminding us of his own formulation for intermittence: "Best to think of it as the 'intermittent rhythm of a constant pause, the sporadic change of direction.'"[112] This paradoxical combination (of constant pause and intermittence), which de Man finds "violent," comes closer to permanent parabasis and a kind of existential hold on which testing can be "based." If a danger of relapse exists within the speculative movement, this occurs because both irony and testing are *tempted* by the recovery of ground when they are instead committed, as in Benjamin's steering of irony, to the incessant work of building by taking apart. In the heavily ironic and barely manageable text "The Destructive Character," Benjamin appears to assert the force of destruction inherent in testing. By means of a recast of Nietzschean categories of being, Benjamin, at one point in that essay, contends: "What contributes most of all to this Apollonian image of the destroyer is the realization of how immensely the world is simplified when tested for its worthiness of destruction. This is the great bond embracing and unifying all that exists."[113] By dint of this dense utterance, testing, destruction, and the existential embrace of irony are momentarily united.

To top it off, Kierkegaard defines the concept of irony as absolute infinite negativity. Irony in itself opens up doubt as soon as it enters our heads, and there is no inherent reason for discontinuing the process of doubt at any point short of infinity.[114] Finely tuned to the collated requirements of irony and experiment, Kierkegaard once wrote in an ironic rider that if Hegel had prefaced the *Science of Logic* with "This is all just a thought-experiment," the old philosopher would have secured for himself the position of unsurpassable thinker of all times.[115] Hegel's failure to meet irony at the edge of his work relegated him to the intractable gravitas that was to serve as Nietzsche's punching bag. Refusing the experiment, Hegel was down for the count. By some twist of theoretical fate, if anyone has understood the dangerous, infinite positing of irony, it was Wayne Booth, who submitted the trope to a Fielding test: "'How do you know that Fielding was not being ironic in his ostensibly ironic attack on Mrs. Partridge?' If I am answered this with a citation or other 'hard' data in the work," Booth suggests, one could gain on irony in the effort of "learning where to stop."[116] Given the idiomatic axis to which his proposition appeals, stopping irony becomes a question of technological control. De Man takes off from here, without necessarily maintaining the technological character of Booth's probe, by conceding that understanding would allow us in principle to control irony: "But what if irony is always the irony of understanding. . . ? Schlegel's 'Über die Unverständlichkeit' [On the Impossibility of Understanding] would show us why Booth's desire to stop, to stabilize, to control the trope is as legitimate – given that irony is something threatening – as it is impossible."[117]

In order to bring into focus the menacing edges of testing, we have had to take recourse to the critical vocabulary fashioned by those who have inherited from the German Romantics the burdens of ironic positing. In case one wonders what literature and philosophical usages of (and by) language have to do with science, it is necessary to point out that the division is not a clean or an absolutely defensible one, as we know from emitters ranging, in modern times, from Schlegel and Nietzsche to Einstein and cyberspace, where fiction inspires scientific breakthrough – it is a commonplace of literary and scientific collaborative observation to note that not so long ago William Gibson's fiction urged virtual reality into empirical spheres of becoming. Science and fiction are as related as they appeared momentarily to posit separately. Science and art continue to share a knowledge of the unreliability of the referent, and "the terror, the same feeling of unpredictability": both speak beyond the limits of their possibility; both understand experiment as a freedom from the constraints of referential truth.[118]

It may be useful to anchor the contemporary relationship between science and art in terms of the traditional opposition between the *eiron* and *alazon* – the smart guy and the dumb guy of whom Paul de Man speaks – as they appear in Hellenic comedy. Most discourses about irony are set up according to the contract that binds this ever replicating couple. Belonging together, they change places in terms of enduring insight or in the expression of brief flashes of certainty. They owe everything to the other, who turns out to be less other than stipulated in the formation of this inexorable couple: "You must then keep in mind that the smart guy, who is by necessity the speaker, always turns out to be the dumb guy, and that he's always being set up by the person he thinks of as being the dumb guy, the *alazon*."[119] The urge to test, while arguably locatable in both figures, resides most comfortably in the place assigned to the *alazon* – it is probing, wondering, unsure about its limits in the face of forces that do not obey the same rules of rescindability, posed as dumb and, in some examples of the test drive, staged as the dummy. Given how often viewpoints fold, assumptions collapse, and human nature shifts on this or that strongly held position, Nietzsche says it is a wonder that so many scientific discoveries hold up and can be claimed by repeatability. Such fortitude in the face of mutability, dumb luck, and bad history is, in part, why science amazes us:

> Our amazement. It is a profound and fundamental good fortune that scientific discoveries stand up under examination and furnish that basis, again and again, for further discoveries. After all, this could be otherwise. Indeed, we are so convinced of the uncertainty and fantasies of our judgments and of the eternal change of all human laws and concepts that we are really amazed how well the results of science stand up. Formerly, nothing was known of this fickleness of everything human; the mores of morality sustained the faith that all of man's inner life was attached to

iron necessity with eternal clamps . . . fairy tales. To lose firm ground for once! To float! To err! amazed that it does not waver.[120]

Not surprisingly, the Nietzschean relation to science goes over one of its edges in the vicinity of literature. In late modernity, art and science converge to try each other in a scientific-literary invention devised by Paul Valéry. A man of experimentation and dispersion who considered writing to be equivalent to the mathematical speculations that he practiced, Valéry created the very demon of possibility, the figure who had tried to discover the limits and laws of malleability: Monsieur Teste. Mr. Teste, a character without conviction or commitment, is remembered chiefly for questioning the necessity of an oeuvre (which accords with Valéry's refusal to publish), earning him the title of the twentieth century's leading literary "terrorist," to use Jean Paulhan's word. Teste was created in a kind of laboratory, out of a "reckless" desire to understand and test the author's critical limits. According to Valéry, then, "Teste was created – in a room where Auguste Comte spent his early years – at a moment when I was drunk with my own will, and subject to strange excesses of insight into myself. I was affected with the acute malady of precision. I was straining toward the extreme of the reckless desire to understand, seeking in myself the critical limits of my powers of attention."[121] Using himself as test site, Valéry concocted the fate of M. Teste, which more or less translates into pure headspace, intoxicated by its own capacity for being and boredom. M. Teste, who can hardly stand the world on which he feeds, was the talking head for Valéry's will-to-power experiments.

On the side of hermeneutic extremism ("the reckless desire to understand"), Valéry aims for the impossible within the hypothetically measurable range of mental possibility. Why is M. Teste impossible? That question is "the soul of him. . . . For he is no other than the very demon of possibility . . . he knows only two values, two categories, those of consciousness reduced to its acts: *the possible* and *the impossible*."[122] Nothing in this limit case of cases eludes experiment and trial. That is to say, language is itself the uncertain and tentative railing along which Teste darkly moves. "In this strange head, where philosophy has little credit, where language is always on trial, there is scarcely a thought that is not accompanied by the feeling that it is tentative; there exists hardly more than the anticipation and execution of definite operations. The short, intense life of this brain is spent in supervising the mechanism by which the relations of the known and unknown are established and organized. It even uses its obscure and transcendent powers in the obstinate pretense that it is an isolated system in which the infinite has no part."[123] An allegoroid of all tests, M. Teste, wobbly because unassisted by philosophy, is conceived as a mutant prototype of AI. As a concept-being with no conceptual backing, he takes up room in the world precisely where programming comes into contact with the idea of freedom, and the artificial converges on the referential limits of intelligent life. M. Teste probes the furthest reaches of the limits of experience, showing "a terrible obstinacy in delirious experience."[124] He appears to be capable of the affect of disdain, even if it is rooted in the fabricated melancholia of boredom.

A Nietzschean offender on the loose, M. Teste, potentially like all testing systems, goes on a conceptual killing spree, set off by cold contradiction and temporal death threats: "He was being absorbed in his own variation, one who becomes his own system, who gives himself up wholly to the frightful discipline of the free mind, and who sets his joys to killing one another, the stronger killing the weaker – the milder, the temporal, the joy of a moment, of an hour just begun, killed by the fundamental by hope for the fundamental."[125] The stakes set M. Teste in a space of mastery that, for all its steadying, abides no opinions of the extremist experimenter: "And I felt he was a master of his thought . . . M. Teste had no opinions."[126] Despite the despiritualizing operation to which Valéry submits his brave new homunculus, one might yet ask, when faced with the givens of a new shift in the transcendental *Einstellung* or attitude, What are the ontotheological implications of the Test(e)? What is the relation to the world that it announces? What are the displacements that allow for Test(e) to leave God behind?

In *God without Being*, French Catholic theologian Jean-Luc Marion writes of the irrepressible acuteness that detests the world.[127] His question, though not scientifically cast yet locked onto that which serves as idol in our time, compels our attention: "But how could the principle of such a dazzling disaster itself become that which it renders impossible – an idol?"[128] On one level, Marion's question mark taps into a problem that bewilders technological modernity, asking as it does about the status of self-undermining entities – the "dazzling disaster" – that, despite it all, inch their way toward recognizable forms of idolatry. Has not the test, as *écriture* of disaster, become in our age an idol – even though, undercutting any possibility for the fixity of veneration, it appears to remain on this side of the sacred? The refutational gaze always looks elsewhere; it cannot be transfixed or, in Blanchot's sense, "fascinated." The roving eye, which resembles that of a surveillance apparatus, disables its object without violating or even bothering to denounce. Enter the test case of *Monsieur Teste*. Marion claims that "Teste's gaze puts to the test what it beholds as one holds an enemy to the ground, in order to destroy him."[129] The gaze, Marion argues, hammers objects, "not as a sculptor who disengages the apt figure from them, but as a mad person who disfigures a statue for fear of having to venerate it – or even as a thinker who 'philosophizes with a hammer' in order to destroy the oldest idols."[130] By transpiercing every visible being with his gaze, Teste "does not annihilate it so much as he disqualifies its pretension to offer the idol, which precisely would have fixed this gaze. No violence, no refutation, no speech even, but only the advance of the gaze, as if nothing *were*."[131] Abjuring the world, Teste detests. His politics of scorn, taking it apart without language or arsenal, distresses the world: "The detestation that Teste exercises deprives the world of all confidence – the world no longer merits confidence and, in return, it loses confidence in itself. In the light of this idoloclastic gaze, the world becomes the indiscernible and translucent shadow of itself."[132] Prompted by the strip-searching gaze that takes down whatever enters its sights, the world wonders how this evacuated gleam will report on it.

The question for Marion concerns attestation: "What, then, from now on, will this gaze be able to attest? That one should have to pose this question is indicated by the fact that Teste now finds himself 'beyond this world between being and non-being.'"[133] Nothing holds under Teste's gaze. Detestation permits Teste's gaze to transgress everything visible without ever fixing on it as an idol; but detestation also freezes his narcissism, "prohibit[ing] him from ever encountering in the world a gaze other than his own, in order to envisage it."[134] Is this not a gaze that is blinded by its very lucidity? The Teste-gaze "sees what is not presented as visible . . . this gaze strictly forms an empty space before itself and around the visible; it makes an empty space of the visible and, transpiercing it or bypassing it, makes the invisible. . . ."[135] This poignant gaze or hammering of the world produces the invisible while giving contour to the visible. Teste enables us to see, so to speak, that the gaze appropriate to the test complicates notions of observability by dint of anticipation and the relationship itself of testing to spacing and prediction. Fixed only by intolerable suspension, non-appropriable, the Teste-gaze attests, moreover, to the vanishing of experienceability – a Benjaminian insight.[136] Something has supplanted our relation to experience as presencing or recalled it, the way faulty cars or appliances are sometimes recalled. The less trustworthy experience becomes, the more we rely on attestation, a highly singularized relation to world. What has been recalled with experienceability is the remembered solidity of truth or any universalizable proposition. At the same time, and perhaps because of this withdrawal, the Teste-gaze is unstoppable. "Nothing – no visible – stops it, just as nothing stops an armored column that 'makes a breakthrough,' as nothing stops a halfback who 'makes an opening,' as nothing stops the gaze in a flat landscape."[137]

What elicits this unstoppable gaze of Teste? It is not motivated by a mood for revolution or change, by the affective residue of passion or hatred. The detestation that Marion associates with Teste is traced back to boredom, which, although apt at disqualifying the idols, "nevertheless cannot be confused with annihilation, nihilism or anxiety."[138] The correlate for boredom would be monotony or the repetitiousness of the self-perpetuating efforts under study. An affect closest to the isolated whir of technological being, boredom hardly rates a close look even in the urtexts of psychoanalysis, where Freud alludes to it only in his essay on "Intracerebral Tonic Excitation."[139] Still, it offers a way to converse with Nietzsche and to turn down the volume, to listen differently to the disks that he burns.

Boredom works for Marion as the underlying mood of testing/detesting because it has little to do with nihilism, renouncing without any tragedy or spark of courage the very intention of any idolatry. It is not fueled by reactive thought, which, hating itself and that which is not at all hateful, paradoxically, at bottom, remains *Wille zur Macht*: "Teste, on the contrary, does not react any more than he acts, does not deny anymore than he affirms. He detaches everything from the idol's dignity, he detaches himself with neither asceticism nor effort, from his own affirmation, as from a last impurity."[140] While Marion puts a lot of store in boredom's containability as affect – he is sure that it steers clear of anxiety and nihilistic starts – he allows it sufficient plasticity to pull away from Nietzschean categories of being.[141] Testing, according to this readout, produces a supplementary interspace in the Nietzschean force field. It could be that such an interspace was already there but that we required Marion's pampering of M. Teste in order to see it for the first time. It could be that, even in Nietzsche, there exists a corridor of being that tunnels under the twin forces of active and reactive, ascetic and warrior poses, between the affirmations and betrayals of life that his work inventories. For while Nietzsche frequently aligns testing and the experimental disposition with active forces, the monsieurs and mesdames testers regularly retreat from self-affirmation and its nihilistic flipside by means of the practice and modesty of necessary detachment. The test abides no idol, which is why its essential effectivity is located at once everywhere and nowhere.

ATTESTATION: LAB REPORT   Yet, for all his extremism and post-slacker attitude, M. Teste often resembles a liberal – in fact, his prints appear to match those of the liberal ironist who roams the essay of Richard Rorty's *Contingency, Irony, and Solidarity*.[142] The rhetorical dependencies of testing invite a closer look at the implications that irony holds for ethical and political thinking. What does it mean nowadays that Nietzsche's insight was versed in irony and trained by destructive probes, even if they came up with unshakeable affirmations of clearing and renewal? Rorty uses "ironist" to name "the sort of person who faces up to the contingency of his or her own most central beliefs and desires – someone sufficiently historicist and nominalist to have abandoned the idea that those central beliefs and desires refer back to something beyond the reach of time and chance."[143] Still, Teste, who shares some of these nominalist tendencies, is by no means simply and only a liberal, in part because he is closer to a replicant than to a human being in Rorty's sense. He lacks some of the pathos of politics that Rorty ascribes to the genuine liberal who, by dint of intelligent necessity, must be an ironist: "Liberal ironists are people who include among these ungroundable desires their own hope that suffering will be diminished, that the humiliation of human beings by other human beings may cease."[144] Nor would Teste ever be caught saying that he resides in one of "the lucky, rich, literate democracies,"[145] an eminently falsifiable description for which Rorty shows unambivalent fondness. But he does share Rorty's sense of entering a postmetaphysical culture that requires "our having given up the attempt to hold all sides of our life in a single vision, to describe them with a single vocabulary."[146] His movement parallels without upholding Rorty's utopia of multiple vocabularies and benevolent capital "as an endless process – an endless, proliferating realization of Freedom, rather than a convergence toward an already existing Truth."[147] Even so, this very movement of Freedom breaks the limits of liberalism, which crafts its projects by means of significant ethical denial and restricted provisions of irony.

Rorty wisely urges that one stop looking for political rehabilitation beyond the domain of contestatory democracies. Rather than leaping for new and revolutionary promises, one would be well advised to inhabit and test the politics of democracy that binds at least some of the world. Surrendering extant forms of democracy to revolutionary phantasms pushes away the luxurious complexity of the present, which deserves and needs acts of continual, committed, and rigorous probing. It is difficult to imagine that the liberal ironist would not be put to the test of Rorty's propositions. As test dummy, the liberal ironist is put together with a sense for autonomy that was wired into M. Teste. I have to assume that the "endless, proliferating realization of Freedom" means not that Freedom has been realized in our democracies but that it is, in a Kantian sense, a given that still needs to be discovered, honored, tested.

Let us continue.

Another way of describing Rorty's ironist is in terms of positing powers that surpass the already set sights of Truth. Rorty keeps his ironist on this side of danger, padded like a well-manicured lawn. The liberal ironist nearly becomes an oxymoron, but that may be the point. Liberal ironists, parented to ironist theorists, may not go down in the fire of a fast-paced ironic spiral, but neither do they spire upwards to transcendental spheres. For, as Rorty himself states in another passage, there "is, so to speak, no dialectical space left through which to rise."[148] The ironist theorist, Rorty argues, has a keen sensibility for autonomy and extreme contingency; at no point caught by the perilous pull of dispossession, he "is trying to get out from under inherited contingencies and make his own contingencies, get out from under an old final vocabulary and fashion one which will be all his own. The generic traits of ironists is that they do not hope to have their doubts about their final vocabularies settled by something larger than themselves. This means that their criterion for resolving doubts, their criterion of private perfection, is autonomy rather than affiliation to a power other than themselves."[149] The ironist, according to Rorty, re-describes the past in order to own it in the phrase "Thus I willed it." His interpretation binds questions of testing and tasting that are seen to be linked in the evaluations of the ironist: "All any ironist can measure success against is the past – not by living up to it, but by redescribing it in his terms, thereby becoming able to say, 'Thus I willed it.' . . . The generic task of the ironist is the one Coleridge recommended to the great and original poet: to create the taste by which he will be judged."[150] The ironist takes it upon himself to impose the very test by which he will be evaluated.

In a discussion of Proust and Nietzsche, Rorty observes that the big guns of ironic intervention embrace sublimity where in fact they would do us all a world-historical favor by backing off and chilling out. At first ironic bite, it looks as though they just want to rearrange the furniture in the house of Being. The strong ironist is however not satisfied with this job description and pounces on the fact that significant possibilities in the world and its descriptions have been exhausted. This turns them on. They want to renew not only themselves – major vocabularies of renewal and *Überwindung* [overcoming] flood ironic channels – but they commit their renewal projects to that which is susceptible of withering, depleting. They are out to inflate and reconceive the world, encouraging transformations that imply considerable upheaval and violence: "They are not trying to surmount time and chance, but to use them. . . . there is no big secret which the ironist hopes to discover, and which he might die or decay [*sic*] before discovering. There are only little mortal things to be rearranged by being redescribed."[151] The paradigms of ironist theorizing are shown to "have in common the idea that something (history, Western man, metaphysics – something large enough to have a destiny) has exhausted its possibilities. So now all things must be made new. They are not interested only in making themselves new. They also want to make this big thing new; their own autonomy will be a spin-off from this larger newness. They want "the sublime and the ineffable, not just the beautiful and novel – something incommensurable with the past, not simply the past recaptured through rearrangement and redescription."[152] Dissatisfied with mere linguistic makeovers, the ironist theorist demands "apocalyptic novelty."[153] He still wants "the kind of power which comes from a close relation to somebody very large; this is one reason why he is rarely a liberal. Nietzsche's superman shares with Hegel's World-Spirit and Heidegger's Being the duality attributed to Christ: very man, but, in his ineffable aspect, very God."[154] So the ironist theorist fights the power only up to a certain point. He holds on to the power plays of multiple hegemonies or taps into one power source; in most cases the ironist keeps his enemies close, still siphoning off sizeable portions of power for himself and for the new world that he loudly conjures into being. He is not a renunciate of power but depends on appropriable contingencies in order to leap onto a new power base or maintain the alliance with an old one. Thus Rorty.

Where have we gone? Rorty connects ironic theory with a certain lack of restraint and with political dangerousness. Still clutching the skirts of transcendence, the ironic powermonger extols self-creating feats and thereby forces everyone to "live dangerously," to take Nietzschean risks of one sort or another, or to adopt Hegelian heroics and Heideggerian mythemes. Though his framework and aim do not allow for such phrasing, Rorty asks that theoretical test treaties be abandoned or resignified, that a modesty of decision be mindfully adopted – that we back off from a decisive aspect of what I have been studying under the term "test drive." There exists sufficient latitude for restrained probes and local political adjustments with diminished theoretical returns. Yet the question remains, which is why Rorty increases the prescriptive ordinances, the "shoulds," "nots," and "stops": Can this vehicle or compulsion kick into reverse, disengage strong theoretical accelerators, or even come to a standstill? Assuming that the warning lights flashing in Rorty's work are worth heeding, how would one responsibly answer to irony's excessive positings in scientific spaces, political sites, and ethical gateways? At the end of Rorty's chapter on Proust, Nietzsche, and Heidegger in "Ironism and Theory," when Rorty exhorts the ironist loudmouth to give it up, something happens in his language that he neither announces nor discusses. Anyone who has been following my discussion of testing and experimentation thus far will have noticed that I made little effort to switch or correct pronominal usage. I more or less ended with M. Teste, without trying, as in the case of the early video game, Pac Man, to come up with a program for Ms. Teste. I tolerate the masculinist vocabulary with the same silent irony as I have had to muster in some (but not absolutely all) moments of my career. Why is it that testing appears at nearly every juncture to be linked to the masculinist themes of *virtu* and *agon*? Always involving a question of endurance and risk, testing also depends upon a decisive urge to test one's strength, try one's limits, and work to failure. Whether you are typed in as male or female or clocking in as yin or yang, these codified exertions represent masculinist grunts and dilemmas. They are culturally classified as a specific kind of ordeal.

When the experimental disposition is announced in Nietzsche, it is often accompanied by the cacophony of woman-hating ranting. I have often stopped the sentences I quote at that moment, as if they were stoppable, so that I could go on and produce an argument. Nietzsche doesn't always close out women, but he does so often enough, with or without transvaluative complications. It happens, if not all the time then at least a lot, even when he is himself knocked out or knocked up. Abraham and Isaac left Sarah at home when they went to see the Man. It is not for nothing that this summit meeting of founding fathers resembles Mafia proving grounds – when it comes to determining what constitutes family and nonfamily, loyalty and betrayal – and spins vertiginously on a rapid cycle of tender generosity and imminent axing. According to the blue or small print of those stories, even when one is spared the bullet, it is only because the Boss has decided, for whatever reason, to hold fire. What sort of pact among men was sealed in this repetitious story? Irony, with its implications of self-mastery and destructive *jouissance,* and testing, which rhetorically and operationally feeds on irony, are rarely anchored in post- or parafeminist concern or rewound through an *écriture féminine.* Not to speak of the fabled misogyny of lab culture. For his part, Rorty ends his account of ironist culture in a way that will compel us to jam on pronomial shifts and reconsider diverted legacies.

We should stop looking for a successor to Marxism, for a theory which fuses decency and sublimity. Ironists should reconcile themselves to a private-public split within their final vocabularies, to the fact that resolution of doubts about one's final vocabulary has nothing in particular to do with attempts to save other people from pain and humiliation. Colligation and redescription, if the little things are important to one – even if those little things are philosophy books – will not result in an understanding of anything larger than oneself, anything like "Europe" or "history." We should stop trying to combine self-creation and politics, especially if we are liberals. The part of a liberal ironist's final vocabulary which has to do with public action is never going to get subsumed under, or subsume, the rest of her final vocabulary. I shall claim that liberal political discourse would do well to remain as untheoretical and simple-minded as it looks (and as Orwell thought it), no matter how sophisticated the discourse of self-creation becomes.[155]

Liberal ironists have a lot to give up, a lot of occupied territories and futural projections to surrender peacefully. Values of decency and sublimity are incompatible with one another, and anything larger than one-self evades understanding. Rorty has no interest in questioning self-understanding or the certainties on which he bases its possibilities. Liberal ironists in effect should accept the irony of irreconcilable splits in their final vocabularies – the private and public spheres of discursive action are irrevocably separate. Well, you can read this for yourselves. The retreat, reminiscent of some of Robert Musil's assessments of tactical modesty in the face of political exacerbations, entails an effort to simplify, cut back, renounce – some precepts that could have come from Voltaire or the classical Goethe. Rorty's language posts a series of "stops" and "shoulds." In an effort to impose the ethical interruption, his argument splices and dissociates, redistributes and cancels what ironic thinking can do. Like an offshoot of Wayne Booth, he wants to stop irony and reroute some of its effects through safer channels.[156] The course he takes is worth noting, though Rorty does not avoid some problems along the way. To some chronically dissatisfiable ironic theorists, it may seem problematic that "she" is called in when things are getting simpleminded. This is not the point that I wish to pursue here, nor would I venture nowadays, when things are so tough for liberals, to call attention to their haplessness when it comes to the need, as I perceive it, for truly extremist redescription. I would settle only for radical democratic redescriptions in addition to an analysis of the widespread overvaluation of the liberal stance. However, what would be of interest to trace here is, rather, the slippage in the Rorty passage from "her final vocabulary" to "I shall claim," the movement from ironic culture to a discursive locus that is seen and marked as feminine. For Rorty is placing bets on a type of feminism that has renounced sublimity, he believes, and is, one could say, propositional.

In a helpful footnote responding to a reductive claim made by John D. Caputo's "The Thought of Being and the Conversation of Mankind: The Case of Heidegger and Rorty,"[157] Rorty remarks that Caputo "is wrong in saying that my view, or Derrida's, ensures that 'we get no further than propositional discourse.' All that I (or, as far as I can see, Derrida) want to exclude is the attempt to be nonpropositional (poetic, world-disclosing) and at the same time claim that one is getting down to something primordial – what Caputo calls 'the silence from which language springs.'"[158] The ethical cancellation of what, according to another vocabulary, might be called hysterical inflation involves, for Rorty, a welcoming of feminism. The shift that is marked in this chapter only by pronominal alteration has everything to do with bringing down the fever of large signifiers. According to Rorty, what Nietzsche, inflamed with destinal resonance and world-disclosure, "itches for is a historical sublime, a future which has broken all relations with the past, and therefore can be linked to the philosopher's redescriptions of the past only by negation. Whereas Plato and Kant prudently take this sublimity outside of time altogether, Nietzsche and Heidegger cannot use this dodge. They have to stay in time, but to view themselves as separated from the rest of time by a decisive event."[159] The quest for acute historical time, which involves access to some momentous event such as the advent of the superman or the end of metaphysics, leads Hegel, Nietzsche, and Heidegger "to fancy themselves in the role of the 'last philosopher.'"[160] One can surmise that the shift to the feminine, which occurs without fanfare or sense of eventuation in his text, introduces a crucial byway to such apocalyptic cravings or, if one prefers, epistemic fantasies. "[H]er final vocabulary" implies a deliberate diversion as well from great discoveries, conquests, and other one-time-only sales of masculinist liquidation cultures. Whatever it is that allows Mr. Rorty to think that some radical articulations of feminisms do not seek precisely revolutionary dismantling or are not steered by apocalyptic cravings – that we are really good girls – will be put aside.

Rorty's tentative mapping of a manageable test site and call for a restricted time of political probing signals a serious struggle with the historical whiplash of irony and its destructive correlates. Who ever heard of an ironic ethics? Not an unserious question, for it may be the case that ethics can only be ironic, untimely, disguised and failing. This is a question for another time, however, and another concept of irony. The experimental disposition throws a different light on some of these issues to the extent that it appears to originate in masculinist testing grounds while allowing itself to be diluted by propositional modesty.

To approach the feminine hypothesis indicated by Rorty and the theoretical ironists he scrutinizes, one has to unhitch the ontological chain and let the animals in as well. Leaving aside Nietzsche and his animals, Heidegger's shepherding of Nietzsche's creatures, or the animals that are freed up in Derrida, de Fontenay, Cixous, and Deleuze in questions of sovereignty, language, and responsibility – not to mention ever new thematic and theoretical studies of animal being – I want momentarily to embrace an empirical and socially disturbing congruence of testing and culture. Without succumbing to the realm of subcultural cliché or un-attachable pathos, is it possible to state that one can no longer write as if another sort of cry were not calling? The dependency of science upon experimental testing has been vociferously questioned by animal liber-ationists, one or two critical thinkers, students, and ecofeminists. Quite often the critique of those values that support experimental testing is done by amassing observable facts and developed with a sensitive attune-ment to the idiom in which explanations are carried out. Evelyn Fox Keller, Donna Haraway, Jill Morawski, Marie-Hélène Huet, and a number of others have argued the misogynist cast of institutionalized experimen-tation. Literature tells us since at least the Faust myths and Victor Fran-kenstein – whose university lab allowed him to throw together his disser-tation, the monster, in two years – that invention, no mind how mad the scientist may be, is tied to the tormented genius, the genesis and even genitals of a male subject. If the lab is an effect of a certain type of male desire (though he wavers on the value of this operation, Nietzsche con-stantly ties experimenting to virility and the surrogation of the femi-nine), then we would need to rethink *everything* that has been legitimated under the terms that still bind us to research, the field test, examinations, broad-based military testing systems, and so on. Haraway focuses lin-guistic assertions of gender dominance in experimental situations where animals become collapsed with the feminine and are subject to persistent projection and abuse.[161]

Citing a report on maternal androids from Harry Harlow's labora-tory, which was prominent in the history of mental testing in compara-tive psychology, Haraway writes:

> Comparative psychologists have been extraordinarily creative in devis-ing testing situations and technology; the testing industry is central to the production of social order in liberal societies, where the prescrip-tions of scientific management must be reconciled with ideologies of democracy.[162]

[During] the mother surrogate work ... [a] device was used to immobilize a female while artificially inseminating her. ... .[163]

Misogyny is deeply indicated in the dream structure of laboratory culture; misogyny is built into the objects of everyday life in laboratory practice, including the bodies of the animals, the jokes in the publications, and the shape of the equipment. Misogyny is the result of discipline in Foucault's sense; it is a productive – and well-funded – discursive practice. [164]

The baseline structure of material sites of experimentation is linked to misogynist language and practice. Objects under study acquire in Haraway's account essentially feminized traits, which is to say they are relentlessly subjected to the intrusive violence of the scientific probe. Whether this is a *fundamental* quality of laboratory practice remains to be seen. The plight of all non-consenting beings still needs to be taken into account, including prisoners and servicemen about whom it is reported nearly every week in newspapers and journals that they have been the unwitting objects of state experiments. On the other hand (there are many hands), the objection has been rightly raised that in crucial medical experiments only men have been designated as legitimate objects capable of generalization and actuality. All of these highly structured relationships to empirical experimentation require further scrutiny and more, not less, theorizing. Vigilance of the exemplary kind practiced by Haraway is necessary. Her intervention makes us ask, What allows for the discursive practice of misogyny in laboratory culture? If it is not fundamental yet still pervasive, what are the repressions and violence for which misogyny stands, as joke and unconscious practice, as discursive activity and referential aim? What prompts the merger into a sustainable entity of women and animals, minorities and the socially disenfranchised? Who suffers the torture and the violence of a "hands on" intrusion about which science tends to remain silent?

We have seen that testing counts as warfare, and elsewhere I have tried to demonstrate how war is conducted on the imago of the maternal body.[165] One wants to know why the object of science has been so persistently feminized, if not feminine (Evelyn Fox Keller's "nature"), and indeed, why in this day of grandiose promise and virtual reality, there are still so many cowboys in cyburbia. Feminists, Haraway asserts in a footnote, "must deconstruct what counts as 'experience' in order to foreground multiplicities, contradictions and constructions of such potent entities."[166]

The decision to retain "potent" entities may function as an effect of irony, or it is intentionally left undeconstructed by Haraway in order to retain the trace of masculinist constitutions in scientific inquiry. The problem of determining experience or of what counts as experience, whether circumscribed by a given method, double blind, or empirically ascertainable, underlies the very possibility of experimental testing. The reinscription of "experience" for which Haraway calls and around which future feminists might organize strategic strikes depends, philosophically, on a strictly Nietzschean initiative of reformatting: the task of foregrounding multiplicities, contradictions, and constructions is the one set by the relentless genealogical explorations of Nietzsche and his thought on the experimental disposition. Haraway does not mention Nietzsche, which poses a problem only in the sense that the suspension – should this be at all possible – of science from its misogynist ground rules is called for from the place of a presumably masculinist stronghold. We have to read both ways and prepare ourselves for the sudden slides of unexpected traversals, the unforeseen complicities that encourage, after all is said and done, benevolent displacements and impending upheavals. There are reasons to suspect that, given the subtle dignity of her bearing, Nietzsche – perhaps Nietzsche tugged by Deleuze, rewired by Derrida, coaxed by Kofman, Klossowski, Pautrat, and so many others – can be seen as the surrogate mother of scientific feminism.

Nietzsche has just argued that a religion like Christianity, "which is at no point in contact with actuality, which crumbles away as soon as actuality comes into its own at any point whatever, must naturally be a mortal enemy of the 'wisdom of the world,' that is to say of *science* – it will approve of all expedients by which disciplining of the intellect, clarity and severity in matters of intellectual conscience, noble coolness and freedom of intellect, can be poisoned and calumniated and *brought into ill repute*. 'Faith' as an imperative is a veto against science. . . ."[167] And now he tells himself a story, in the recounting of which we discover, after a few serpentine twists, that the rival of God, the Anti-Christ, is perhaps a woman. The leap of gender occurs necessarily because science as a woman is figured in bold, Nietzschean tones as evil – an indispensable affirmation and critical attribute of the genuinely gay scientist. Only a woman proves strong enough to hold so much evil, to throw off the forces mobilized behind the decadent forgeries of the good. Let us read Nietzsche's parable. It is unsettling, but, then, we must remember, the text is itself trying to settle scores with a history of indecent abuses that have emerged from the story it scrupulously reviews. The beginning of the story echoes Nietzsche's signature question, "Have I been understood?" It draws up a map of God's tactical assault on woman, the bringer of science:

> – Has the famous story which stands at the beginning of the Bible really been understood – the story of God's mortal terror of science? . . . It has not been understood. . . . But behold, man, too is bored. God's sympathy with the only kind of distress found in every Paradise knows no bounds: he forthwith creates other animals. God's first blunder: man did not find the animals entertaining – he dominated them, he did not even want to be an "animal." – Consequently God created woman. And then indeed there was an end to boredom – but also to something else! Woman was God's second blunder. – "Woman is in her essence serpent, Heva" – every priest knows that; "every evil comes into the world through woman" – every priest knows that likewise. "Consequently, science too comes into the world through her." . . . Only through woman did man learn to taste the tree of knowledge. – What had happened? A mortal terror seized on the old God. Man himself [humanity itself] had become God's greatest blunder; God had created for himself a rival, science makes equal to God – it is all over with priests and gods if man becomes scientific! – Moral: science is the forbidden in itself – it alone is forbidden. Science is the first sin, the germ of all sins, original sin. This alone constitutes morality. – "Thou shalt not know" – the rest follows. – God's mortal terror did not stop him from being shrewd. How can one defend oneself against science? – that was for long his chief problem. Answer: away with man out of Paradise! Happiness, leisure gives room for thought – all thoughts are bad thoughts. . . . Man shall not think. – And the "priest in himself" invents distress, death, the danger to life in pregnancy, every kind of misery, age, toil, above all sickness – nothing but expedients in the struggle against science. . . . The old God invents war, he divides the people, he makes men destroy one another (– priests have always had need of war . . .). War – among other things a great mischief-maker in science.[168]

Nietzsche's redescription of the story of Genesis locates the scientific im—
pulse in woman. Identifying himself with and as this disavowed woman,
the animal-woman, Nietzsche becomes her to the point of carrying this
thought to term and elsewhere affirming his painful pregnancies. Put
to work by the demands of his reading, Nietzsche, when in labor, views
thought as an experiment. He sets up the experimental site with the observation that Christianity does not pass the test of actuality, which leads
him to place Genesis under the genealogical gaze.

All the pains of finitude issue from God's organized defense against
science, against man's test of limits, prior even to the establishment of
limits, in the land of parousia. Another story about knowledge in relation
to castration, it shows God coming up against the unbeatable threat
as well. Hence the draining of plenitude, the traumatic evacuation: the
famous first exile evermore keeping us down and busy and too tired to
think or even know what we know. God failed with the Edenic entertain-
ment center; man was bored from the start, until she came along and
started fiddling around, looking for answers, craving questions. The
minute she started testing for an outside and researching other options,
all hell broke loose, earth acquired its gravity – wrinkles, childbirth,
fatigue, work, "every kind of misery" befell them. Nietzsche reads woman,
inextricably evil, as God's second blunder. He raids the pantheon of
Christian values, overturning and appropriating them to other ends. He
pulls out the hatred of women – everything henceforth was to be pinned
on Eve, every test was hers to make and monitor, her trace would appear
in every trial – and spins it into the prodigious radiance of scientific creativity (elsewhere Nietzsche denounces science for having disavowed its
creative potentialities). Science (as figured in Eve, in collaboration with a
serpent) slips out from under the servile pressures applied by God. Not
content merely with discovery but opening to the world each time, in
time, with the freshness of a new day, science wants to *make* what is; no
longer tempted by knowing what is, science has quickened the desire to
say what is.

Somewhat surprisingly, whenever Nietzsche turns himself into a
woman and against misogynist tradition, he (she) becomes critical of
war – the destructive play of a God on the loose. War: when was war not
waged in His name? Becoming woman (something like woman, in any
case no longer simply human or aggressively universalizable), the trans-

Nietzschean becomes unrecognizably other: more evil, more thoughtful, more pacifist, more scientific, more experimental:

> Origin of knowledge.... The ultimate question about the conditions of life has been posed here, and we confront the first attempt to answer this question by experiment. To what extent can truth endure incorporation? That is the question; that is the experiment.[169]

Crucially supplementing "that is the question" with "that is the experiment," Nietzsche, still testing, has fatefully redrawn the domain of the question. Because the questioning mutation resists the lure of conclusion, it is destined to skip on the record that Nietzsche left of a false ending, surrendering the ever provisional aim of a missed mark, a *Fehlschluss:* the *Fehlschuss* that sounds when one takes a shot at something, and misses.

Here we go again.

Part 5
Trial Balloon

Husserl to Front
Weatherman #414

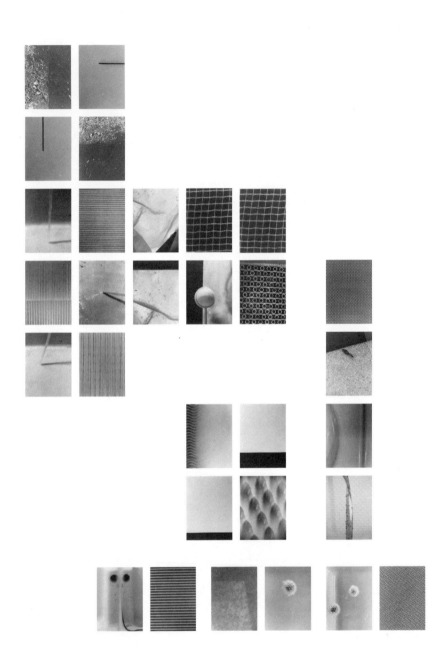

You scrap your earlier ontic validities. You start anew, putting on a new at-titude, *to use a good Husserlian term. You see that you had been wrong. Damn, you were wrong! Now you're going to have to deal with it. Yeah, you knew that the idea of truth in the sense of science is set apart from the truth of the prescientific life. It wants to be unconditioned truth. This means, in a sense, you are never going to get there, not if you're going to give in to the sense of an infinite and common task. Well, you were going to have to switch tracks and try again. Living in the realm of possible truth, possible being, possible perceptual judgment was hard. You were trying to bring together the theoretical attitude under the* epochē *of all praxis. No one said it was going to be easy. No one said the Greeks had intended for things to be easier for us with their outbreak of the theoretical attitude. For that matter, the Egyptians and Babylonians plunged us into their intentional depths as well, so that we became blind to the most essential differences of principle. You were living in an unbearable lack of clarity.*

Philosophy as a rigorous science – they're all saying that the dream is over, "der Traum ist ausgeträumt." I'm not ready to give it up, no matter what Merleau-Ponty thinks. He says that in my *Crisis* book I have thrown in the towel. And then when my friends created a fuss, he said that it was unconscious. Ahem. I don't think so. I am Edmund H., father of them all. Martin is a problem. My little disciple Martin H. with his very hip *Existenz-philosophie*. Now I have to toss in words like "*existentiell*" just to catch the attention of the younger generation. Little Heidegger and little Jaspers with their pop breakdowns and the way they appropriated the term "phenomenology"! I was deeply hurt that Martin erased the dedication to me in *Sein und Zeit* when he discovered that my having been Jewish was out of fashion. That parricidal stab cut me to the quick. That is personal. I will set it aside, though I hear that his own pupil Hannah whimpers that the personal is political. I have myself said that philosophy is not a private matter, but on an altogether different register. These kids are treading on thin ice. They decry a sense of emptiness of Europe's cultural values, they whine about a deeply felt lack of direction for man's existence as a whole,

a feeling of crisis and breakdown. These kids – they demand that philosophy be relevant to life! Of course, this catches on with the other sprout-
lings, yet it seems reckless. Nonetheless, I will give them a run for their
money. I will begin with an exposition of the crisis of the sciences as an
expression of the radical life-crisis of European humanity. I'll hunt down
the origins of this "critical situation," and I'll stick it to them with Galileo
and the mathematization of the world. I'm going in a democratic direction, I want to show them what is available to all, irrefutably, apodictically.
Jacques D. got it right when he said that for me Galileo's name is the exemplary index of an attitude and a moment, rather than a proper name.
For me science is a title standing for absolute, timeless values. Jacques D.
calls it *uchronia,* vibing off of utopia, pointing to what belongs to intem-
porality, the timeless dimension of scientific law.

I am worried about the future of philosophy, its persisting estrangement
from science, and the individual ego–boom boxes that pose as philosophers. Ach! When I think that in 1926 I pored over the manuscript and
helped Martin correct the proofs for *Sein und Zeit.* And in 1928 I appointed him my successor at Freiburg! I kept looking after him, taking
care of him like a father, an advisor, a friend, writing notes like the one
saying, "Please don't forget to send a free copy of your book to Jonas
Cohn, because he will be mad as hell if you fail to do so."[1] Yes, it's an
"unausweichliche Notwendigkeit, daß Sie ihm ein Exemplar schicken,"
otherwise he'll be "tödtlich beleidigt – " you've got to send it to him, please
don't piss him off; after all, he sent you a free copy of his *Dialectics.*[2] And
when he was turned down for the assistant professorship because "Heidegger habe zu wenig publiziert"[3] – the committee said he hadn't published enough – who pushed for Martin Heidegger, who stuck by him and
never lost confidence? I even suggested that he send in the manuscript to
that thing he was writing at the time, yes, it was still *Sein und Zeit,* but
he got rejected again. Then I helped him with the proofs. But I'm repeating myself. What I did for him, what he meant to me. . . . My letters were
signed, "Ihr altgetreuer EH," Your ever faithful, or sometimes I'd first
note, "Viele herzliche Grüße von Haus zu Haus," many cordial greetings
from house to house, in order to encompass the whole family – the house,
you know, even, why not, the house of being. Our wives wrote to each
other, to us, for us, too. My P.S.'s would say things like, Surely I don't need

to say this but our guest room always awaits you, please come, please stay, we'll spend the day talking, our own little seminar, I'll show you what I've been writing, you can explain your thoughts to me. Well, what can you do; in terms of *true* loyalty and interpretive energy, who can measure up to the devoted staying power of my disciple, Eugen Fink?

I am worried, I'm worried where these kids are going. I worry about the positivistic reduction of science to mere factual science. The "crisis" of science as the loss of its meaning for life. Yes here I am putting quotation marks around crisis even though I let the word appear unperturbed in the title of that last unfinished book. For some of you smart alecks, fed on Marxist and social theory, crisis takes a dialectical spin and turns out to be too optimistic, right? I know. I know about the Hegelian theodicy, all the recuperations, how we think we get out of a crisis better, redeemed in some way. I'm not about that. No one who is truly receptive to philosophy is ever frightened off by difficulties. But modern man, as shaped by science, demands insight; and thus, as the image of *sight* correctly suggests, he demands the self-evidence of "seeing" the goals and the ways to them and every step along the way. The way may be long, and many years of toilsome study may be necessary; this is true in mathematics, but it does not frighten him whose life-interest is mathematics.

I remember my last seminar. Freiburg. It was July, I believe, 1929. A young man gave a class presentation. A sweet boy, intelligent, earnest, modest. I had him come over to the house on the pretext that my wife needed French lessons. We were going to Paris and she wanted to perfect her locution. Obviously the question of improving her French for a shopping spree was exaggerated. This was a way to supplement the young student's stipend. I liked his class presentation, it set the right mood for the last teaching. I saw philosophy clearly, that is what I said to the last students. Looking over my letters to him, I see that I had written to Martin H. about my new seminar. It was a letter headed, "Freiburg 9.V.1928." It was my first seminar of the season, I wrote, "circa 20 new people, mostly foreigners, *Ausländer*." I enumerated: "once again an Oxforder, nice looking [William Kneale], 2 Dutch [one of whom was Magda A. H. Stomps, religious phenomenologist], 1 Lithuanian, from Strassburg recommended by Héring [Emmanuel Levinas], an old Professor from Melbourne, phenomenologically highly knowledgeable [Jewsei Schor], a number of Japanese [including Yosuke Hamada and Takashi Hashimoto]. The new *Inländer,* the domestic crop, seem only average. The good ones are naturally with you."[4]

There was an incident with this Lithuanian student, though. A sweet boy, he was perhaps too sensitive. He had come to study with me for two semesters in 1928-29. One day when he was hanging out at the house my wife came rushing in. She had found a place for us – we wanted to move. She ran in excitedly, and these words came out of her mouth: "Die Leute, obgleich Juden, sind zuverlässig" – despite the fact that they're Jews the owners of the house seem reliable to her. My ears were not hurting, for even before her conversion to Protestantism, my wife and I would speak this way. But the boy Emmanuel Levinas later called this a "*blessure,*" a wounding. He also said that my wife spoke of Jews only in the third person, which is true. I looked at him, saw his hurt and said, Well, you know, I come from a line of merchants myself. The young philosopher was appeased, murmuring that Jewish people are incredibly hard on each other. Later on he was to write in *La ruine de la représentation* that I looked more and more Jewish in photographs. (He never questioned his own anti-Semitic flare-ups, no matter how subtle. I should look Jewish! What does that mean? I think he meant well. Anyway, he added that I was beginning to resemble the ancient prophets. But then he quickly added that we don't have photographs of the biblical prophets, so how could he assert that I looked like Jeremy or one of his cohorts?) Emmanuel Levinas was not a problem, he was a joy as a student, and while I felt that he was hurt by some of my decisions in life, I did not feel judged by him. By the others, I was humiliated. I was evicted from my office. I put out a call for help, or rather, my wife did, but we were abandoned, miniaturized, desiccated. Prepared for the worst. I often wondered who would internalize me, keep a wallet-sized photo of me in their heart space and form a masochistic bond with my shocking destiny. But I am getting ahead of myself here. We're not there yet.

● ● ●

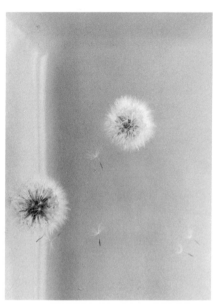

I understand the younger generation's justified hostility against the science of the nineteenth and twentieth centuries. I wrote the book. "In our vital need – so we are told – this science has nothing to say to us." You can look it up in *Crisis*, p. 6.

Can you recall when science was vibrant? Now it is no longer being *vitally* practiced. Let us go back to the times in which modern man and the modern philosopher still believed in themselves and in a philosophy, when, in the context of the transcendental motivation, they struggled for a new philosophy with the responsible seriousness of an inner, absolute calling that one senses in every word of the genuine philosopher. Even after the so-called collapse of Hegelian philosophy, in which the line of development determined by Kant culminated, this seriousness remained intact for a time in the philosophies reacting against Hegel (even though its original force was weakened). Why did transcendental philosophy not achieve the unity of a development running through all its interruptions? Why did self-criticism and reciprocal criticism among those still animated by the old spirit not lead to the integration of compelling cognitive accomplishments, into the unity of an edifice of knowledge that grew from generation to generation, which merely needed perfecting through constantly renewed criticism, correction, and methodical refinement?

In this regard the following general remark must first be made: an absolutely novel procedure such as that of transcendental science, which was lacking any sort of guidance by analogy, could appear to the mind at first only as a sort of instinctive anticipation. An obscure dissatisfaction with the previous way of grounding in all science leads to the setting of new problems and to theories that exhibit a certain self-evidence of success in solving them in spite of many difficulties that are unnoticed or, so to speak, drowned out. This first sheath of self-evidence can conceal within itself more than enough obscurities that lie deeper, especially in the form of unquestioned, supposedly quite obvious presuppositions.

Sure, I understand that the history of transcendental philosophy first had to be a history of renewed attempts, if only to bring transcendental philosophy to its starting point and, above all, to a clear and proper self-understanding of what it actually could and must undertake. Its origin is a "Copernican turn," that is, a turning-away in principle from the manner of grounding in naïve-objective science.

A true beginning, achieved by means of a radical liberation from all scientific and prescientific traditions, was not attained by Kant. I need to start again.

Insurmountable inhibitions, the effects of my faltering health, force me to neglect the elaborations that I had firmly impressed in my mind. I am concerned. I am concerned that we not lose sight of what science had meant and could mean for human existence. The exclusiveness with which the total worldview of modern man, in the second half of the nineteenth century, let itself be determined by the positive sciences and be blinded by the "prosperity" they introduced, meant an indifferent turning-away from the questions that are decisive for a genuine humanity. Merely fact-minded sciences make merely fact-minded people. Anyway, the specifically human questions were not always banned from the realm of science. Positivism, in a manner of speaking, decapitates philosophy. The positivistic concept of science in our time is, historically speaking, a residual concept. It has dropped all the questions that had been considered under the now narrower, now broader concepts of metaphysics, including all questions vaguely termed "ultimate and highest." Examined closely, these and all the excluded questions have their inseparable unity in the fact that they contain, whether expressly or as implied in their meaning, the *problems of reason* – reason in all its particular forms. Reason is the explicit theme in the disciplines concerning knowledge (i.e., of true and genuine, rational knowledge), of true and genuine valuation (genuine values as values of reason), of ethical action (truly good acting, acting from practical reason); here reason is a title for "absolute," "eternal," "supertemporal," "unconditionally," valid ideas and ideals. If man becomes a "metaphysical" or specifically philosophical problem, then he is in question as a rational being; if his history is in question, it is a matter of the "meaning" or reason in history. All these "metaphysical" questions taken broadly – commonly called specifically philosophical questions – surpass the world understood as the universe of mere facts. And they all claim a higher dignity than questions of fact, which are subordinated to them even in the order of inquiry. Positivism decapitates philosophy.

Even the ancient idea of philosophy, as unified in the indivisible unity of all being, implied a meaningful order of being and thus of problems of being. Accordingly, metaphysics, the science of the ultimate and highest questions, was honored as the queen of the sciences; its spirit decided on the ultimate meaning of all knowledge supplied by the other sciences.

But the belief in the ideal of philosophy and method, the guideline of all movements since the beginning of the modern era, began to waver; this happened not merely for the external motive that the contrast became monstrous between the repeated failures of metaphysics and the uninterrupted and ever increasing wave of theoretical and practical successes in the positive sciences. This much had its effects on outsiders as well as scientists who, in the specialized business of the positive sciences, were fast becoming unphilosophical experts. Even among those theorists who were filled with the philosophical spirit, and thus were interested precisely in the highest metaphysical questions, a growing feeling of failure set in – and in their case because the most profound, yet quite unclarified, motives protected ever more loudly against the deeply rooted assumptions of the reigning ideal. There begins a long period, extending from Hume to Kant to our own time, of passionate struggle for a clear, reflective understanding of the true reasons for this centuries-old failure; it was a struggle, of course, only on the part of the few called and chosen ones; the mass of others quickly found and still find formulas with which to console themselves and their readers.

Philosophy became a problem for itself. Yes, philosophy became a problem for itself. At first, understandably, in the form of the problem of the possibility of metaphysics. This concerned implicitly the meaning and possibility of the whole problematic of reason. As for the positive sciences, at first they were untouchable. Yet the problem of a possible metaphysics also encompassed *eo ipso* that of the possibility of the factual sciences, since these had their relational meaning – that of truths merely for areas of what is – in the indivisible unity of philosophy. Can reason and that-which-is be separated, where reason, as knowing, determines what is? This question suffices to make clear in advance that the whole historical process has a remarkable form, one that becomes visible only through an interpretation of its hidden, innermost motivations.

What I'm trying to say is that, ultimately, all modern sciences drifted into a peculiar, increasingly puzzling crisis with regard to the meaning of their original founding as branches of philosophy, a meaning they continued to bear within themselves. This is a crisis that does not encroach upon the theoretical and practical successes of the special sciences; yet it shakes to the foundations the whole meaning of their truth. This is not just a matter of a special form of culture – "science" or "philosophy" – as one among others belonging to European mankind. The crisis of philosophy implies the crisis of all modern sciences as members of the philosophical universe: at first a latent, then a more and more prominent, crisis of European humanity itself in respect to the total meaningfulness of its cultural life, its total "*Existenz.*" Of course, I consider America to be part of Europe but, as I have been subsequently told, I do have somewhat racist views concerning the rest of the world and so-called Eastern philosophies. I am not sure that I am very fond of the trouble-shooting women who disrupt the line of thought I am trying in all earnestness to develop. Yet I can see where and why they come in.

I have written that if man loses faith – the faith in man's freedom, that is, his capacity to secure rational meaning for his individual and common human existence – it means nothing less than the loss of faith "in himself," in his own true being. This true being is not something he always already has, with the self-evidence of the "I am," but something he only has and can have in the form of the struggle for his truth, the struggle to make himself true. True being is *everywhere* an ideal goal, a task of *epistēmē* or "reason," as opposed to being which through *doxa* is merely thought to be, unquestioned and "obvious." More and more the history of philosophy, seen from within, takes on the character of a struggle for existence, that is, a struggle between the philosophy that lives in the straightforward pursuit of its task – the philosophy of naïve faith in reason – and the skepticism that negates or repudiates it in empiricist fashion. Unremittingly, skepticism insists on the validity of the factually experienced [*erlebte*] world, that of actual experience [*Erfahrung*], and finds in it nothing of reason or its ideas. Reason itself and its object become more and more enigmatic.

● ● ●

You see, I still carry around the glint of mission passed on to me by my early mentor, Franz Brentano. It's a struggle. There's an originary temporality, a hint of becoming that is already immediately there, none of that comforting "ergo sum" or the stabilized pretemporality of a mystified Being. I was *called* to this task as a serious philosopher. I have fallen into a painful existential contradiction. The faith in the possibility of philosophy as a task, that is, in the possibility of universal knowledge, is something I *cannot* let go. Ever. How can I avoid this – I am a functionary of mankind. The quite personal responsibility of our own true being as philosophers, our inner personal vocation, assumes within itself at the same time the responsibility for the true being of mankind; the latter is, necessarily, being toward a telos and can come to realization, *if at all,* only through philosophy – through *us, if* we are philosophers in all seriousness. Is there, in this existential "if," a way out? If not, what should we, who believe, do in order to *be able* to believe? We cannot seriously continue our previous philosophizing; it lets us hope only for philosophies, never for philosophy. In his sweet book *En découvrant l'existence avec Husserl et Heidegger* – great, now we're a couple, as if I didn't know what EL has to say about couples – Levinas gets it right when he says that I am pushing the logic of the science of all science, following the lead of Leibniz's *mathesis universalis.*[5] For me, and he saw this, the vain succession of philosophical systems constitutes a distressing spectacle, entirely unworthy of a philosopher. True and real *Philosophie* does not spring from the head of a single thinker. It is, like science, the work of teams and generations of philosophers.

I am beset by the actual situation of the present and see its distress as a sober fact. We need to reflect back in a thorough and *critical* fashion, in order to provide, *before all decisions,* for a radical self-understanding. How this is to be carried out, and what this apodicticity could ultimately be which would be decisive for our existential beings as philosophers, is at first unclear. This is why I introduced my work as a test of which I am the subject. I actually wrote it down this way for everyone to see that I put myself on the line: "In the following I shall attempt to show the paths that I myself have taken, the practicability and soundness of which I have tested for decades. From now on we proceed together, then, armed with the most skeptical, though of course not prematurely negativistic, frame of mind" (*Crisis*, 18). This is what I add to Avital's theory. I worry that her ardent skepticism has introduced an excessive negativistic force to the field. I do not as such quarrel with what she's doing. It's a matter of timing; I don't think that the destructive edge of skepticism should be introduced prematurely. In fact, even though she doesn't come out with it, at least not sufficiently for my taste, I feel that she owes me a lot. I even added, just to please her, in Part IIIB 65 "Testing the legitimacy of an empirically grounded dualism by familiarizing oneself with the factual procedure of the psychologist and physiologist" (224). But she tripped me up. Because from the moment I wrote the word *test* in the subsequent paragraph, I started stumbling. It was not the first time. In Part I, I skip over experimentation, making it look as if my thought were stuttering. Here, from the moment I wrote "as anyone can convince himself who tests our presentation," the editor pasted a footnote. He writes that I had crossed it out but not replaced it by anything (225, footnote 3).

Oh, please. Why make such a big fuss over this trivial caesura? I had already written in "Idealization and the Science of Reality – The Mathematization of Nature," the first *Abhandlung*, about the multiplicity of subjective manners of givenness, focusing the question concerning the flux of being in becoming and concerning the conditions of the possibility of identity of being in becoming, of the identical determinability of an existing real entity as the determinability of intuitively given continuity through the mathematization of continua. This must be independent of accidental subjectivity. What could be clearer? Maybe if she had looked more closely at my *Logical Investigations*, she would have seen the difference on which I lean between evidence and truth in empiricism. Evidence is nothing other than the "lived experience" of truth. The truth is lived. And just as in the realm of perception where not-seeing does not coincide with not-being, then the lack of evidence does not have the same meaning as the absence of truth.

But no, she had to turn to Nietzsche. All these kids run after the irrational ones. Do you see him working with the development of the logic of being as the logic of reality or with the development of apophantic logic as the formal logic of predicative determination? Not on your life. You have that de Man character rooting around in the rhetoric of the promise but that does not exactly lead to the forms of determining predicates, with the possibilities of hypothetical, disjunctive manners of determination, the modal variations, and so forth, which belong to determination. Sometimes I have to wonder what the hell he's up to. It certainly doesn't get us to the attainment of hypothetical truths from hypothetical stipulations, does it? I can see where he belongs in the skeptical critique of science and of all practical norms that lay claim to objective validity. But he could use a dose of the Socratic return to self-evidence, even if this represents a reaction to the fields of pure possibilities, the free variation that upholds the identity of meaning, identity of the object as substrate of determination, and makes it possible to discern this identity. In any case, okay, skepticism forces the critique of the skeptical critique, and since this critique concerns the possibility of truth and of knowable being in general, it forces a radical consideration of the conditions of possible truth and possible being. I am not talking about vague ideas but about radical thinking aimed at the ultimate showing of possible being.

Science is not naïve knowledge in the theoretical interest; rather, to its essence there belongs from now on a certain critique – a critique based on principle, a critique that justifies every step of the knowing activity through "principles," which at every step involves the consciousness that any step of such a form is necessarily a correct one, that in this way the path of cognitive grounding, of the progress of that which grounds and that which is grounded upon it, is a correct path aimed at the goal, so that the resulting knowledge is a genuine knowledge and that the being known is not merely supposed [*vermeintes*] but known in the pregnant sense – she calls it the test drive, thinking she can show how this ground is not as stable as I counted on it being. Nonetheless she, like science in general, makes use of cognitive results of earlier knowledge. For my part, I do not consider that every *change* in the sensible stock of characteristics disturbs identity.

You wonder about my obsession for Galileo, as you indelicately put it. The ubiquity of the term "obsession" is disturbing. You can read Derrida on the significance to all of us of Galileo. Or God forbid, you can read me, really study how it is that the geometrical *eidos* can be recognized by virtue of having withstood the test of hallucination. I won't get into that here, and I will not substitute a few words for your reading practice. Nothing can substitute for reading these things yourself. As concerns your topic, I will say this much about the verificational character of natural science's fundamental hypothesis. Beyond its indisputable significance for the task of physics, the Galilean idea is a *hypothesis,* and a very remarkable one at that; and the actual natural science throughout the centuries of its verification is a correspondingly remarkable sort of verification. It is remarkable because the hypothesis, in spite of the verification, continues to be and is always a hypothesis; its verification (the only one conceivable for it) is an endless course of verifications. It is the peculiar essence of natural science, it is *a priori* its way of being, to be unendingly hypothetical and unendingly verified. Here verification is not, as it is in all practical life, merely susceptible to possible error, occasionally requiring corrections. There is in every phase of the development of natural science a perfectly correct method and theory from which "error" is thought to be eliminated.

Newton, the ideal of exact natural scientists, says "hypotheses non fingo," and implied in this the idea that he does not miscalculate and make errors of method. In the total idea of an exact science, just as in all the individual concepts, propositions, and methods that express an "exactness" (i.e., an ideality) – and in the total idea of physics as well as the idea of pure mathematics – is embedded the *in infinitum,* the permanent form of that peculiar inductivity that first brought geometry into the historical world. So, we have a progression of hypotheses that are in every respect hypotheses *and* verifications. But true nature does not lie in the infinite in the same way that a pure straight line does; even as an infinitely distant "pole," it is an infinity of theories and is thinkable only as verification; thus it is related to an infinite historical process of approximation. When I wrote about this, I hit a wall, and I knew she would get me for it. She wanted me to go on to describe a phenomenology of testing. Instead, I just broke off. Backing down from my own insight, I wrote at the time: "This may well be a topic for philosophical thinking, but it points to questions which cannot yet be grasped here and do not belong to the sphere of questions we must now deal with" (*Crisis,* 42). I swerved and said that our task is "to achieve complete clarity on the idea and task of physics which in its Galilean form originally determined modern philosophy, to understand

it as it appeared in Galileo's own motivation, and to understand what
flowed into this motivation from what was traditionally taken for granted
and thus remained an unclarified presupposition of meaning, as well as
what was later added as seemingly obvious, but which changed its actual
meaning" (42). She learned from me the need to explore that which in
life is taken for granted, the unclarified presupposition of meaning; she
wanted me to go on to the place where I said we cannot build thought.
Not yet. Now she is usually a cautious explorer, but in this case she took it
as a call. This is not to impugn her sometimes exaggerated yet cautious
circumspection. I know that she still thinks in terms – this is what she
takes from me – of the somewhat antiquated form of a task. She thought
it was her task to take the call. That is how she proceeds, her "method." I
was trying merely to show that mathematization is decisive for life, offering a method that grounds formulae logically and compellingly for all.
I wanted to show how arithmetic thinking becomes free, systematic,
a priori thinking, completely liberated from all intuited actuality about
numbers, numerical relations, numerical laws. She liked the politics – or
as she preferred, those days, the ethics – of these assertions. Hence the
hookup with Levinas. Leibniz, though far ahead of his time, first caught
sight of the universal, self-enclosed idea of a highest form of algebraic
thinking, a *mathesis universalis,* as he called it, and recognized it as a task
for the future. Only in our time has it even come close to a systematic
development. In its full and complete sense it is nothing other than a
formal logic carried out universally (or rather *ad infinitum* in its own essential totality), a science of the forms of meaning of the "something-in-
general" that can be constructed in pure thought and in empty, formal
generality. On this basis it is a science of the "manifolds." I was trying to
get at the manifolds that are themselves the compossible totalities of objects in general, which are thought of as distinct only in empty, formal
generality and are conceived of as defined by determinate modalities of
the something-in-general.

At the end of the first part of my *Crisis,* I emphasize the notion of testing.
I write: "We shall attempt to strike through the crust of the externalized
'historical facts' of philosophical history, interrogating, exhibiting and
testing their inner meaning and hidden teleology. Gradually, at first unnoticed but growing more and more pressing, possibilities for a complete

reorientation of view will make themselves felt, pointing to new dimensions. Questions never before asked will arise; fields of endeavor never before entered, correlations never before grasped or radically understood, will show themselves" (18). I know it may seem as though I was on a bit of a manic high, riding the wave of testing, breaking into new dimensions and promising disclosive potentialities.

It may seem that the promise met and matched itself in these utterances, that is to say, it proved its own excessive nature, misspoke, crashed through fences of rational expectation, and momentarily drowned out more subtle reflections. But you must remember that I felt that everything was on the line at this point. I was deeply distressed about the threat of objectivist alienation, which conceals the instituting origins and renders them strange and inaccessible to us. The world had become unintelligible. I was less concerned with the epistemological conflict inherent in the internal development of these sciences than with a divorce between the theoretical and practical activity of science. I was provoking science to remember its sense for life and the possibility of being related to *our* whole world. Besides, in making these promises and by signing the promissory note of which the *Crisis* consisted, *I was testing myself.* In the spirit of the irony of the promise, and as a moment in the elaboration of the test drive, the work remained constitutively incomplete. I claimed no other right than that of speaking according to my best lights, principally before myself but in the same manner also before others, as one who has lived in all its seriousness the fate of a philosophical existence.

• • •

P.S. – There were, of course, other little tests, so many of them, and I was hard on myself. I do not fancy myself to be in a situation similar to that of Goethe, so I am not trying to propose that I stand as a cipher for an epoch – even though I'm the one who put the interruptive *epochē* on the map. I never let much be said about myself, I left few traces, apart maybe from my letters. They form a micronarrative, a historical slice, and maybe they manage to transpose in a way my sense of historicity, my understanding of what makes some remnants and not others of the past stay with us and mean for us, even today.

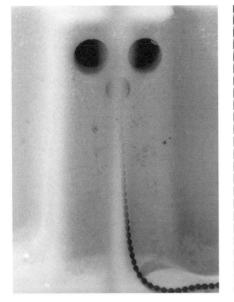

What do we hold on to? Well, some of my tests were marginal at best. I was plagued at one point by a benign, well not so benign as all that, but in those days, anyway, an addiction: In my correspondence I chronicle the ordeal of giving up cigarettes. Between 1 January 1928 and 7 February 1928, I put myself to the test; by then, as I wrote to Martin H., I had quit smoking for nine days. The world and my manuscript seem estranged to me; insomnia turns into *Schlafsucht* – a kind of compulsive, addictive somnolence. I am anxious because I can't think clearly. I end the letter saying, "Man kann doch nicht immer spazieren gehen" – one can't just take strolls all the time, which is what I was doing to keep the cigarettes away. By 7 February, I write that I am holding on to the withdrawal pattern, I'm staying with my resolve (well, not altogether mine: doctor's orders) to quit. My appetite is back and most of the effects of nicotine poisoning are subsiding. The only problem is that I haven't been able to work. What a trial for me, being fogged out from my own work! I have always withstood such trials in my life, small and personal test stations that eventually escalated into institutional and political ordeals. But the tests began early.

In school, I was considered to be only an average student. Yet I aced my tests. I remember it very well. My finals. 30 June 1876. This, my contestable triumph, surprised everyone, especially my teachers. Kind of like the boy in Kafka's story, the one who was pegged as mediocre, even stupid. I was not considered stupid, just spaced out, and, yes, average. Until later on when I met up with my true teachers, whom I adored and emulated. Kronecker, Paulsen; obviously, Weierstrass. I was also psyched for my habilitation thesis examination. My thesis on the concept of number was completed in 1887; my examiners included Carl Stump (my advisor) and also Georg Cantor, the inventor of the theory of sets, as well as the mathematician Hermann Grassmann. But most emphatically, there was, for me among my teachers, Brentano, to whom I was devoted until the end, his end – OK, unlike that Martin H., who did not even deign to visit me as I lay dying. No deathbed scene, no apocalypse of forgiveness or, on the other hand – and he was capable of it – no eerie silent treatment, such as the one with which he had tortured my poetic counterpart, Paul Celan. But even before that, in 1934, as a suddenly Jewish professor emeritus, I was effectively deprived of my library privileges in the university, as they say in *The Cambridge Companion to Husserl,* "by his former colleague Heidegger."[6] Has anyone noticed that there is still no Husserl biography? That's why Malvine had to come up with the sketch of my life, the *Skizze eines Lebensbildes von E. Husserl,* kept in the archives at Louvain (under the Signatur X III 1).[7] Anyway, Franz Brentano was like a solar storm for me, he took me over, converted me to descriptive psychology. Maybe "solar storm" is too dramatic or misses the point, the texture of it all. Because we had a loving, devoted relationship of reciprocal support. I adored him and was led to formulate, though the girls don't go for this I am told, that a true professor is like a father. Avital does not mind this quaint perspective, because she says she upgrades it to the "paternal metaphor"; in any case, her ambition would have her strive to be everyone's father, and she is secretly filing dozens of paternity suits. But she is not the subject, not even the transcendental subject, of my prosopopoeic remembrances . . .

On the subject of putting a face on the voice from the grave, Frau Brentano, who had conceived a passion for painting, began my portrait. She swooned over my blond, blue-eyed, dreamy and timid appearance, comparing me often to a figure from the Italian Renaissance. Guess what? Professor Brentano himself completed the portrait of me as a young scholar! Though I hadn't said so earlier, the making of that portrait was to serve as an allegory of the emergence of the student, at least in the eyes of the pupil, to quote another master. The only thing we ever fought over was my admiration for the Prussian state. My sympathy for the Prussian spirit, my monarchism, confounded poor old Brentano. Eventually my young Polish disciple, Roman Ingarden, and I would share a belief in a supranational ethics. In those days Brentano did not share my feelings of patriotism and military fervor. I don't think he was too crazy about my interest in the religious works of Fichte, either.

When you think about it, I was to be blessed with a number of fine disciples. In Göttingen and Munich alone, I magnetized to the cause of transcendental idealism, yes, already then, A. Reinach, Hedwig Conrad-Martius, Alexander Koyré, Jean Héring, Fritz Kaufmann, and the remarkable Edith Stein. In the end I could count as my disciples Alfred Schutz, Maurice Merleau-Ponty, Jean-Paul Sartre, and far younger analytic phenomenologists such as Dagfinn Føllesdal and, why not, even the Berkeley red-

head Hubert Dreyfus. Others studied with me in Freiburg: Herbert Marcuse, Günther Anders, Rudolf Carnap, Marvin Farber, Aron Gurwitsch,
William Kneale, Aurel Kolnai, Charles Hartshorne. They have each placed
the emphases on different moments in giving an account of the structures of experience. They understood the science of phenomenology as
I had defined it, as the study of the essence of conscious experience,
and especially of intentional experience. What's not to understand? By
the summer semester of 1905 (there is a temporality induced by semesters
which I still intend to get to one day), the famous Munich invasion of
Göttingen had occurred – members of the Munich group, students of
Theodor Lipps, had moved to join me in Göttingen, though they pro-
pounded what they called a "realist" phenomenology, referring in particular to those aspects of the *Logical Investigations* that relate to the
essential structures of acts, meanings, expressions, signs, and entities of
other types. Phenomenology, for the invaders, consists in setting forth in
a non-reductive manner and as faithfully as possible the *a priori* laws that
govern the relations between these different sorts of objects in different
regions of investigations. Adolf Reinach exploited this method in relation
to the essential structures of legal and quasi-legal uses of language (for
example, in promises, commands, requests, etc.). OK, I don't want to
complain, but can someone tell me why Austin and Searle got all the
credit for developing a theory of speech acts exactly of this sort fifty years
later? Hello?

Does anyone do scholarship anymore? You know, the Germanic, philo-
logical, dusty, ball-breaking kind of scholarship where you no longer see
the light of day and dark circles form around your eyes, you have turned
the answering machine off, no one can reach you, you're shivering in the
cold regions of a searing solitude, more absent, more dead, more alone
than ever before, each time more alone – OK, maybe these are my issues,
or even more likely, she is grafting hers onto me . . .

I remember writing a letter to Martin, when was that? Oh yes, here it is,
the letter of – well, it is funny to have trouble finding the letter because
Martin worked for the post office in the first world war; he opened letters
and censored them. That was his job, to act as censor. Rumors had it that
he took the opportunity to read his colleagues' letters. I wouldn't put it

past him, but I can't say for sure. I don't want to add a supplementary fold to the *carte postale* dynamics by slandering him, so I will add only the official data. As functionary of mankind I am in any case prone to add bureaucratic details. He was assigned to censorship duties at the Postal Control Office in Freiburg "with effect from 2 November 1915, with the status of a Landsturmmann or member of the territorial reserve. The posting took place on battalion orders. This period of mail censorship – those assigned to these duties were a very mixed bunch of Freiburg tradesmen, women conscripted for labor, men pronounced unfit for garrison service – remains totally shrouded in mystery as far as the available sources of information are concerned."[8] Later on, Heidegger served with his meteorological observer unit on the Western front, in the sector assigned to the 1st Army. One thinks of the Dylan song about which way the wind blows, or Hölderlin's passages on the Nor'eastern. I like Hölderlin, I write to Martin, but I don't know him that well. I will pack him in my suitcase with the manuscripts and read him on vacation, when I visit my mother. Oh, but I am losing myself. "Frontwetterwarte 414" was under the operational command of the 3rd Army's meteorological observer corps and was stationed in the Ardennes. These meteorological units had been set up to provide advanced weather information in support of poison gas attacks.[9] My letters to "Frontwetterwarte 414" may interest you.

I thought I was being supportive, very keen on seeing the Fatherland win out, very excited by the youthful vigor of my young friend and disciple who, for his part, bitterly complained that he had to lay aside his philosophical work in order to serve. I tried to encourage him and say this was for now more important. I write, "Daß Sie nun einmal die Philosophie ganz bei Seite thun mußten, ist ganz gut" – the fact that you have had to scrap philosophy is totally fine, I say. I cheer him on, saying that the splendid victories we now see mean that the war will soon end. In the meanwhile, write to me from the field. Then I proceeded to describe in detail my advances in philosophical inquiry. She, of course, claims to have detected the strongest expression of ambivalence here. Can she let go of it for just one time? Her "logic" (what a catachresis!) is that while he suffered tremendously from having been torn from his work, I am excitedly exposing the exquisite importance of staying with the work, which is what I manage to do at this time. All I wrote was, In the solitude of the

mountains "ein großes Werk [wächst mir] heran," a great work is emerging – "Zeit u. Individuation, einer Erneuerung einer rationalen Metaph
[ysik] nach den Prinzipien. Herzlichst grüßt Sie, wie auch meine Frau,"
and so forth ("time and individuation, a renewal of metaphysics according to set principles. Heartfelt greetings, also from my wife"). She sees this
as the subtlety of a preemptive attack, telling him that it's okay for him to
set aside his work while mine is lavishly growing. And, naturally, being a
student of rhetoric, she declines the particulars of my emerging work as
the irony of time and individuation, which she claims Martin H. will later
practice on me. In time, *he* will individuate; I will resist. She says it will
reverse: I am renewing metaphysics while leaving him in the ditches; he
will ditch me, revoke my library privileges. This is going far, all this from
a friendly postcard. In the missives I send him, I urge him to grow in the
free outdoors, I support my favorite troop, and tell him that what he is
doing for the Fatherland is of utmost importance. Soon enough he'll find
time for abstract quibbles: "Jetzt ist nicht für Sie die Zeit für abstrakte
Grübeleien" (11.V.1918).[10] I see nothing aggressive in the contents of these
letters. She thinks he'll have something to say about my determination of
time once he crawls out of the trenches. She can't get over the fact that I
say to him "Now is not the time for you." I don't know what drives her
exegetic energies in this unfortunate direction. Of course, on the occasion
of writing these letters, I had given up all psychologistic inroads, well,
most of them. (Let's face it: by the time of the "Prolegomena to Pure
Logic," which constitutes the first volume of my, ahem, magnum opus,
the *Logical Investigations* of 1900–1901, I had delivered a devastating critique of all forms of psychologism in philosophy – of all attempts, that
is, to conceive the subdisciplines of philosophy as branches of empirical
psychology. This critique had a wide influence and beat out even my
friends Bolzano and Frege's critiques.) I will concede, though, that my
relations to Front Weatherman 414 were complicated. Even so, I always
offered him the guest room and implored him to spend a few days with
us. Once Malvine wrote to say he should spend the night so that he could
explain passages of *Sein und Zeit* to me, passages that remained altogether
unclear to me.

● ● ●

Let us not confuse disciples with friends. It rarely works out, though there are some dazzling exceptions. I think. Would you say that Plato and Socrates were "friends"? Of course, Nietzsche and Wagner – now, there's a friendship. Well, let me take a pass here, I'll shelve the question for now and try to keep things separate. My best friend in Berlin, Gustav Albrecht, later on became a science professor. Even though I couldn't have cared less about religious issues, I had started reading the New Testament at the age of 23. Prodded and to no small extent inspired by Albrecht, I converted at the age of 27 to the evangelical religion. I got baptized in Vienna under the name Edmund Gustav Albrecht Husserl. My wife, Malvine Charlotte Steinscheider, had converted shortly before our marriage. . . . Well, these are old stories, and I don't know why she pulls them out of me at this time. I am decidedly reserved, I always was; after my son was sacrificed in the war, I closed myself in for a year, I became even more silent and could not shake the sense of unspeakable disaster. In the end I was resigned, defeated, kicked out, humiliated. I deflated even as my fame grew and I was elected as a member of the British Academy, which in those days was no small honor. My other son was summarily dismissed from his university post, a great blow for me (she seems to be drawn to those among us who suffered uncommonly, but I do not need her, I have my work and legacy, I don't need to be taken into protective custody, she should worry about herself, get some sleep and balance in her life, stop ulcerating over past injustices to which she now adds stupid American policies and admittedly aggressive behaviors, I am not prescribing passivity for her but chronic anxiety cannot be the answer under any circumstances, I see that on some level she does not admit the past, it intrudes upon her presently, the daily invasions that leave her awash in a sea of anguish). As with any darkening, there were sudden flares sent up, gleams – sometimes hallucinatory, at other times closer to the possible. There was one moment when my spirits momentarily roused, in December of 1933 I believe it was, when I contemplated an offer from America. I was offered a chair at USC. (The president of that institution was not an outspoken philosemite from what I hear.) I would have been in California with the others, with Tommy, Teddy, and the post-tonal musicians. But I am German, I cannot leave, I am demobilized in the crash of historical contradiction. According to the spirit of my own work, the question would be why this moment in history still flashes in her head, why she can't get over it and "move on," as the Americans pleasantly say.

I am reminded of a long letter from Marvin Farber, who, after studying with me, went to Buffalo before returning to Cambridge. He wrote of his wish to make his "a work of so high an order to be worthy of the dedication to you."[11] He eventually wrote *The Foundation of Phenomenology*, a fine work. In the letter he poses four major questions of which the third reads: "(3) Have you ever taken a stand, qua phenomenologist, toward the historical materialism of Marx and Engels? If not, would you indicate the general nature of your attitude?" To this portion of his letter I responded without embellishment: "(3). I never had the opportunity to engage such particular historical-philosophical naïvetés as those of Marxism."[12] Maybe that was too bitch-slapping of me but, even in my hour of abandonment and slide into defeat, I was not going to surrender my grasp of the resounding historical task that lay before us; there was no way I was going to give or hang up on what was calling me. No way I could accept the schematizations and false hopes signaled by the marxisms that offered themselves as the other, more complete revolution. Maybe I was too defensive-reactive. Still, I thought that philosophical rigor, despite its relentless difficulty and history-disrupting interrogations, needed to be preserved at all costs. Understanding itself was at stake, even the irony of understanding. As tradition and transmission, as that which is sedimented, history is for us inseparable from its understanding. Understanding history means to seize the living moment of the mutual solidarity and implication of the formation of meaning and the sedimentation of its originary sense. The origin is nothing other than the act by which an event "enters into" history. I have always made it clear that for me it is precisely by means of transhistoricity that we understand history. That's why I emphasize the "ideal formations" such as language and geometry, which, while being historical, nonetheless furnish history with the *a priori* structure without which history would be deprived of sense. Any science of fact presupposes an unassailable ground of evidence. And that evidence is nothing but the continuity until now of the still possible passage of the horizon to the present. This is the intelligible unity against and owing to which particular "cultural figures" are cut. As far as I'm concerned, only transcendental reflection renders explicit the universal structure of history: it permits us to understand why the past is not dead but persists and perpetuates itself in the consciousness that currently runs, speaks, writes, trips, sobs, sings, records. In history, the originary *an sich* is our present.

I am fatigued now. I know that some portions of my universal pathos have been questioned and that others among you have lost patience or lost your work permit, you are harried by a different rhythm, other addresses, mutated desires, increasing responsibilities, a decidedly decreasing appetite for philosophical care. I am not trying to call you to order, just testifying. The testimony comes from one who falls short of the ability to locate the right tact, the ideal addressee. In the end there were so many episodes of nervous exhaustion; at the end, one unrelenting panic attack, a long stretch of breathless anxiety. January 15, 1936, marks the withdrawal of my teaching license. Unlike Heidegger I didn't entertain questions or discussions. Heidegger asked questions in his seminars. As Pierre Aubanque told Avital over a vin rouge Bourgogne, once I offered a particularly intense philosophical soliloquy and ended my class saying "Great discussion today!" This is no reason to pull my license. On June 8, 1937, I was not permitted to participate in the Ninth International Congress of Philosophy in Paris. 1937 was the eviction from Lorrettostrasse. My papers migrated to Louvain. Thanks to Father H. L. Van Bréda, one of the last faithful ones. Eugen, who had helped me prepare my *Nachlass,* eulogized what he called the calm heroism I exhibited in life and death. In April 1939, Malvine Husserl obtained the necessary authorization to transfer my ashes from Freiburg to Louvain. A complete copy of my archives exists at the New School University in New York, two or three blocks from where she lives.

Let two additional letters frame the end of this prosopopoeic appearance. Not that I wish to accord Frau Heidegger any privileges. By all measures her behavior was inexcusable, her rudeness to Celan's wife, Giselle, to Hannah, and so many others, her staunch National Socialist views. Most likely this letter was dictated by him, who held himself in reserve by that time. It was a bizarre collaboration, this final letter. Addressed to my wife, the letter sent on 29 April 1933 by Elfriede Heidegger "in her husband's name" as well as her own asserts, "our gratitude remains unaltered as we think of everything you have given us."[13] They begin on the twin constellations of thanking and thinking. "If my husband had to part ways with yours on his philosophical path, he will nonetheless never forget what he as the pupil of your husband gained as his ownmost task." This does not sound like Elfriede's diction, though once in a while she would write articles such as the one on girls in the Third Reich.[14] In this short letter to a long good-bye, they seem genuinely stirred by the fact that my son, Gerhart, despite having fought on the front lines in World War I, was "beurlaubt," relieved of his post, on 25 April 1933, as Professor of Law at Kiel. Evicted, put on a permanent sabbatical or "vacation" as the official language had it. The Heideggers express the hope that this law will be repealed or that my son will be reinstated. The law was unfairly applied in this instance, they offer, no doubt in a moment of tremulous urgency for the Fatherland. They send me their wishes on this portentous occasion, they write, she repeats, as a sign of unending thankfulness.

I am not one to end on a sour note. Nor will I indulge speculation on the way they inch toward Nietzschean gratitude, an act of violence in the test of friendship. I turn my gaze elsewhere. I also enjoyed uncomplicated relations with disciples, when I could take in, if only to immunize myself against the others – against a whole nation – some cloudless moments of cheerful if hyperbolic deference, prompted by gestures of extreme receptivity. Yosuke Hamada was one such disciple. His letter of 18 August 1928 began, unforgettably, "Highly honored, world-famous and greatest Philosopher of Germany."[15] It was brief, another letter of departure but one indicating interruption without rupture, or at least it located a rupture that was part of the deal from the start: "I think of you always and heartfully thank you for the pure friendship that you showed me during my studies in Freiburg. Today, towards evening, I am going home to Japan. Phenomenology will eternally define my life and also eternally determine [the] Japanese philosophical life. Please take care, Leben [Sie] wohl. With greatest respect, Y. Hamada." I have no final word to offer, just the beginning of a contemplation on the disciple and friendship, on the transgenerational research team and the endless ends of transference. These are figures for the telling of a larger, less manageable story that continues to harass my spirit: If anything, I want you to understand something of the way our work was tested by history and how it was subjected to the incessant violence of subtle philosophical transmission systems. There are more threads, much more residue to be considered in this light. But such work must be left to another exercise in testamentary narration, and to another trial.

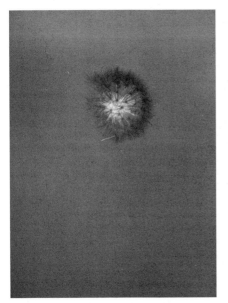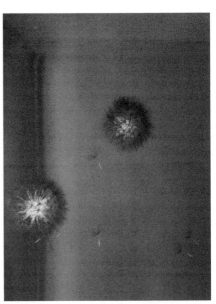

Part 6
Testing Your Love

or: Breaking up

For I was condemned to Germans. If one wants to rid oneself of an unbearable pressure, one needs hashish. Well, I needed Wagner. Wagner is the antitoxin against everything German par excellence – a toxin, a poison, that I don't deny. – Nietzsche

Type of my disciples. – To those human beings who are of any concern to me I wish suffering, desolation, sickness, illtreatment, indignities – I wish that they should not remain unfamiliar with profound self-contempt, the torture of self, mistrust, the wretchedness of the vanquished. –Nietzsche

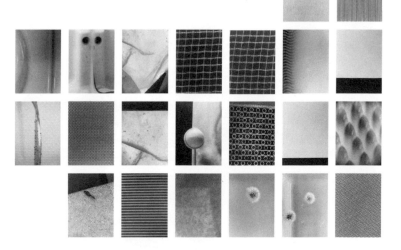

Refrain: One pays heavily for being one of Nietzsche's disciples.

1. The End, My Friend

Supposing I were in love, or, let us say, I am deeply transferentially engaged. Supposing the transference went sour. Well, not sour; I am still transferred onto this other, unavoidably. But I feel betrayed. At some level I don't care about the schoolboyish ideologies of betrayal: my middle name is betrayal. That's another story. I am in love; I am betrayed; the other is my fate. (I am also drawn to the other's partner, but that, too, is another story. I keep on skidding off the other's desire track.) I am amorously caught on an object. Demobilized. The loner and loser Friedrich Nietzsche spins out a story that catches me by surprise. Alfred Hitchcock caught a spark off the transferential machine that Nietzsche installed; he called it <u>Rope</u>. Hitchcock's <u>Rope</u> thematizes the temptation of tying Nietzsche to reference. The same rope that strangles a student is used to tie up the books that are returned, if I recall correctly, to the dead student's father. The purloined rope is meant to name in the end (I know one shouldn't skip to the end when discussing a film; I can't help it, precipitating toward the end whether of art or the relationship) – it is meant to name in the end the way we are roped in by Nietzsche, transferentially duped, told to get lost. Zarathustra does it, Nietzsche does it: they sever transference, thereby tightening the bind. For Hitchcock the Nietzschean love story captures the pedagogical ordeal. It stages the drama of reference, for the murderous students, the perps, read Nietzsche with a passion for the literal. Out of love. For the teacher. The students want to translate Nietzsche into a referential act. It is an offer of love to the teacher, a postcard from the classroom. Jimmy Stewart didn't mean for the students to take Nietzsche as a blueprint for historical action. He takes a swig of whiskey.

An exemplary pedagogy, Stewart's teaching of Nietzsche will have prepared the crime scene: a commencement feast in which a corpse is buried (not yet buried, another "Trouble with Harry" issue of transferring the body-text). The students – one senses that the two men are a gay couple – are in the school of transference and translation. They triangulate onto the teacher, Nietzsche. Stewart, as emissary and purveyor of Nietzsche, is appalled, defeated. His teaching produced a corpse. Dissolve. The perfect crime, this was to be the final exam that the ever-transferring students wrote for the teacher. A term paper that in the end understood everything the teacher had tried to convey. Now they have to transfer the body. Another swig of whiskey. Nietzsche, transference, love. Sirens. Maybe the students had understood something or at least their homework assignment was to redraw the boundary of the pedagogical reach. Who's to say that passion for the literal can be controlled, that gaping and scarring will not break through to the real at any given moment?[1] Who can patrol symbolic territories and assure secure frontiers among levels and systems of transfer? Where Nietzsche teaches severance, Hitchcock refuses the suture, suspends the edit as the long shot of the film goes on, making it to the end of its thematic rope, without a marking cut.[2] That is the shot of transference, the shot of whiskey that burns the teacher's throat in the film experiment induced by Nietzsche's text. Hitchcock's reluctance to cut trails the unbreakable corridor of transference.

At the end of the day, at the end of the semester, the students refuse to mourn. They create an unmournable corpse, a sign of gratitude for the teaching instigated by Jimmy Stewart, who, befuddled and scholarly, has been presented with the mutilated telegraph message that represents the notes taken in his seminar. A question with which the film leaves us, besides the regressive temptation that it tracks, concerns the Nietzschean concept of gratitude: how can one thank the beloved teacher? (I mean, without bringing a dead mouse to the door, as if one were a cat.)

Nietzsche was the most thankful of philosophers, and yet his gratitude, to become what it is, often took the form of violence. There were moments of pause, episodes of recollection, when Nietzsche would take the time to thank and to affirm his life. At such moments he gave thanks to his own life, or to the life that so often dispossessed him of himself, made him sick, gave him headaches. He begins his most autobiographical text, *Ecce Homo*, by offering thanks and preparing, on this birthday, to bury his past: "On this perfect day, when everything has become ripe and not only the grapes are growing brown, a ray of sunlight has fallen on to my life: I looked behind me, I looked before me, never have I seen so many and such good things together" (*An diesem vollkommnen Tage, wo alles reift und nicht nur die Traube braun wird, fiel mir eben ein Sonnenblick auf mein Leben: ich sah rückwärts, ich sah hinaus, ich sah nie so viel und so gute Dinge auf einmal).*[3]

On this perfect day he looks ahead, he looks back, he offers thanks before revving up the engine of critical self-review. That he loses the self in the process is by now undisputed among Nietzsche scholars. Maybe he shouldn't have been so thankful; or, maybe it is only due to the thankfulness starting up the autobiographical gamble that Nietzsche can get over himself, drop himself dead, and move on without dialectical assistance. The paradoxes of Nietzschean gratitude are legion. Gratitude, often in excess, is linked in his work to revenge – very possibly recalling in English the way we mean in American English, "thank you very much" with the decisive intonation given over to "f . . . you very much." This could be a quote from Nietzsche, remastered.

Yet, however torqued and disfigured, gratitude henceforth belongs to the very possibility of thinking: miming prayer, it holds thought. Nietzsche signals a change of address when he thanks his life rather than, say, God. Thanking thinks, we could say, nearing Heidegger, where thanking as thinking puts out a special call. Nietzsche's act of thanking draws close to Heidegger's conjoining of *danken* and *denken* only if one remembers that the kind of mindfulness implied by thanking also involves remembrance, *andenken*, in other words, a certain experience of mourning. (The fellows in Hitchcock's film refuse to mourn; their thank you note is of another order than the one Nietzsche plays out here. They are still students.)

For Nietzsche, saying "thank you" involves the experience of letting go without disavowing that history which has run its course. Thanking sends it on its way, thus allowing it to have arrived. The sendoff is crucial here, for it can follow the trajectory of a missive or missile – not so smart always, not securely on target – making the violence of destination a matter of concern for Nietzsche, of destinal concern. Whom is one addressing when giving thanks? To the extent that one is giving or given to thanks, does the offering imply sacrifice, a sacrificial offering? Or perhaps even the gift of death, as Derrida offers? For Nietzsche, bestowing thanks – something he never lets up on – comes at great cost, even though it cannot be subsumed under any economy but breaks the bank in the spirit of potlatch. It's the great giveaway that lets one start from scratch, detach. It belongs to the repertory of Nietzschean violence. The violence skips over the boundaries of what normally fastens a text down. Even so, I am less interested in Nietzsche's violence as something that was programmed by his work or carried out by his different animals and readers, ideologues, editors, disciples (one pays heavily for being one of Nietzsche's disciples), than – for the moment – in the violence to which Nietzsche submitted himself, as if in the act of thanking he were continually testing himself.

Our study of *The Gay Science* has tried to locate the test drive in Nietzsche's work and link it to the problem of the test site and the bold experiments, the unprecedented improvisational dimensions that open up this space. Now let us consider more closely how Nietzsche posits himself as the test site, putting himself continually at risk, obeying the provisional logic of the test. Even though he dismisses them largely as regressive formations, there are no convictions that will not be put to the test. In the previous section I tried to develop the concept of rescindability, a concept Nietzsche uses to attack racism and all unproven hypotheses concerning determinations of the human and its possible mutations. Nietzsche installs a concept of rescindability within everything he stands for – and falls for. We could say that Nietzsche fell for Wagner. He fell hard. But, to quote Hölderlin, he fell upwards ("man kann auch in die Höhe fallen").[4] This is the fall or pitch that language makes us associate with love. One's fall is pitched upwards, if we follow the chart of Nietzsche's fateful involvement with Wagner. Still, no matter how exalted or in fact enduring – there was something unbreakable about this relation that kept relating itself – it was not spared the hard test of rescindability. Now it turns out that rescindability is more subtle than we could have imagined; it does not amount to mere dismissal, nor does it fully participate in the reassuring restorations of *Aufhebung*, the Hegelian recalls of which sublation consists. Something is taken back, disqualified, without leaving the scene.

It is rescinded with a decisive gesture but nonetheless has a long and prominent shelf life.

The temporal agonies of the Nietzschean duration are well known. In Nietzsche everything will have to stand the test of time.[5] This is one meaning of the eternal return. But, in the case of Wagner, the test of time takes a victory lap, so to speak, extending beyond its official time: the test of time will have been untimeliness – a standard to which Nietzsche holds himself as well. For his part, Wagner, held back by disheartening attachments and embarrassing compromises, was too agglutinated to his time, Nietzsche felt: There was no resistance, finally, to Wagner among Germans, Germans of the Reich. Wagner melted into his time, which was a time clocked by Nietzsche in terms of decadence, weariness, impoverishment. The Wagnerian meltdown was so total (the only thing total about Wagner – even the *Gesamtkunstwerk* was an aggregate of little parts that Wagner managed like a special effects engineer) that he lost the startup quality of being human. The great friend says that he was not a human being *("Ist Wagner überhaupt ein Mensch?")* but, in the end, a sickness.[6]

When Nietzsche takes on Wagner he loads up on gratitude. In fact, his attack is backed by thankfulness, which, in a sense, has forced his hand. On the side of Wagner, Nietzsche feels obligated to take him apart. This is part of the transferential duty, the price he estimates he has to pay for the teacher, friend, love, surrogate father, envied husband, and intensely demanding mother, W . . . But I should back down, take some Distanz and measure, as he everywhere counsels, because I have so quickly found myself in the target zone of a Nietzschean attack. (One pays heavily for being one of Nietzsche's disciples.) With Nietzsche one needs to locate oneself on the map of utterance that he has drawn up; following his writing habits, one is enjoined scrupulously to ascertain for whom and from where one speaks. In sum, one needs to stay aware of the temptation to attack, particularly when it slips into the fast-paced rhythm of a rant, the double and other of the Wagnerian sound off. What does it mean when one's attack is directed by Nietzschean command systems? Such an attack differs from the sniper shots, turkey shoots, or savage polemics that abound in academia. The Nietzschean attack – the one in which one finds oneself inscribed as soon as one tries to say "thank you" – displays a peculiar learning curve. Attack for Nietzsche is more often than not an indication of gratitude. One wants to express gratitude, among other things, for having withstood the hardest tests, for having held one's ground (more or less) and survived (more or less) an experience of merger; the extreme experience of attachment, even attachment to a virtue, easily escalates into a debilitating dependency, as he writes in *Beyond Good and Evil*. One's thankfulness goes to the ability to mourn – more or less, assuming true mourning to be possible. When letting go (a dreadful gift) occurs or arrives or has happened without arriving, thanks are given to mark an almost historical ability to split off from a powerful, a once necessary convergence of forces that held you to the tyranny of promise. It is important to climb into the think tank with him in order to have a sense of what Nietzsche is aiming for, and how he orchestrates the offensive.

Nietzsche, most thankful and most ballistic of philosophers, obeys a restraining order. As unique and shattering as it was and in some ways continues to be, his assault was raised traditionally, trained on a certain relation to truth-telling. His attack and gratitude converge in a figure who says something dangerous, putting himself at risk when addressing the powerful yet deeply troubling other. Like the Greek *parrhesiastes*, he takes a risk in speaking his truth (since the tyrant may become angry, may punish him, may exile him, may kill him).[7] This was Plato's situation with Dionysius in Syracuse, concerning which there are references in Plato's *Seventh Letter* and also in *The Life of Dion* by Plutarch. In *parrhesia* the danger "always comes from the fact that the said truth is capable of hurting or angering the interlocutor. *Parrhesia* is thus always a 'game' between the one who speaks the truth and the interlocutor."[8] To the extent that he performs a parrhesiastic act, he assumes responsibility for himself, runs a risk, and responds to a duty: "To criticize a friend or a sovereign is an act of parrhesia insofar as it is a duty to help a friend who does not recognize his wrongdoing."[9] Even though Nietzsche self-gathers enough to address Wagner, Christianity, the Germans, and other short-listed culprits, without end, he is not so New Age as to think he could elicit an enlightened response or initiate a healing. And yet he proceeds as if healing were not entirely out of the question and the response could come from the future – even Wagner's response might come from the future. Where he stands his ground, Nietzsche mostly attacks only those causes that are victorious. His statement: I attack only when I stand alone. He firms up the parrhesiastic stance. Nietzsche does not go for the jugular of a person or human being, however – he does not go after their aloneness or destitution, or even after their singularity. He pounces where they begin to generalize and dominate, where they bloat up as an idea or harden as a cultural icon. In contrast to the sprawling tendencies of the other, Nietzsche refrains from seducing or conscripting recruits to serve his cause, which remains unsupported by any generality. I attack only when I stand alone *and*: I never attack persons. This sums up the Nietzschean code of ethics for attack.

Wagner became the sign for Nietzsche of that which compels an unavoidable cannonade of gratitude. (One could also say that Wagner demanded gratitude from the disciple Nietzsche, and this is what he got.) He moved in on Wagner deliberately, prepared to rush a particular stage of history and its undocumented events. Still, when he says, "I never attack persons," you may be inclined to suppose Wagner to be a person. Not so, not always or only so. Nietzsche's several postscripts to *The Case of Wagner*, his conclusive inability to finish with finishing off Wagner, are meant to serve as reminders that, despite his abiding love for Wagner, he is bound by duty to attack *his case*. Nietzsche loved Wagner to death. He means "case" the same way we do in English when we say, "he's a case" – a case for psychologists and physiologists. The interlinguistic pun earns some surplus value as well: *der Fall Wagner*, which brings to mind that *casus* is related to falling, even to decadence. Nietzsche, who fell hard, loved Wagner – this point needs to be hammered home; he *had* to give him up ("To turn my back on Wagner was for me a fate. To like anything at all after that, a triumph").[10] Nietzsche loved Wagner, and that is what interests me: what led him to break the friendship of ten years was not intersubjective but ethical. It was not a whim, a mood, an episode, a sense of harm or an account of the other's wrongdoing that instantiated the break – it almost had nothing to do with Mr. Richard Wagner, for what do we care about Herr Wagner and his messy little opinions? Wagner – Nietzsche is emphatic on this point – has become a dashed double of himself; he produces his alias as a sickness, a hysterical actor, a sign of the times with which he coincides. I never attack persons, therefore. But what should we make of the assertion and Nietzsche's investment in the scenography that has him attack only when standing alone? Standing alone is not as such originary; one started off, even in Nietzsche's times, in *Mitsein*, in the sharing and partition of which Jean-Luc Nancy, thinking with Heidegger, writes.[11] In Nietzsche's vocabulary, standing alone suggests that the attack is already preceded by all sorts of breaks. He has taken and dealt the cuts that have him standing alone, positing himself as alien without allowing for the complacencies of saying "I am the other," the sufferer, to which something is owed. Nietzsche wants nothing from Wagner; at most, he wants to thank him. This may be hard for us to understand today where the break tends to be resisted among conflicting forces in favor of consensual hallucinations and the matching profiles of warring parties.

Let us slow down to a Nietzschean pace in order to consider what defines necessary secession and how it might be bound up with gratitude. When I say "Nietzschean pace," I am by the way still caught up in the attack on Wagner to the extent that Wagner, it is claimed, has shown no respect for the pace, the measure, the step – features that Nietzsche assimilates to style. What does this imputation encode? Heidegger reminds us, by looping back to Hölderlin, how Nietzsche means by this censure that Wagner was lawless – the law being precisely that which in Hölderlin's notion of sacred sobriety prescribes measure, the considered step or gait, *Dis-tanz*: the dance of distance. In Wagner one swims or floats. In Nietzsche you're walking, you're dancing the measure, honoring the step. You move in accordance with the frolicking *Wissenschaft*. Thus Nietzsche took measure; he took steps where Wagner sought dissolution, the sheer exaltation of the Dionysian. Nietzsche, on the contrary, concentrated his gaze on "Bändigung und Gestaltung" – boundedness, figuration – taking the step beyond dissolution and, in so doing, anticipates Maurice Blanchot's mildly interdictory *"pas au delà."* (When Nietzsche was on Wagner's case, he was decidedly into the French, behind and ahead of him, preferring even the can-can to Wagner's can't-can't, but this is neither here nor there and Blanchot would be appalled though that has never stopped me before but let me adopt some of that sobriety.)

To the extent that Wagner refused to keep pace, to hold to the fundamental disposition that Hölderlin had recognized as Western sobriety – in other words: the Apollonian – the rupture between them, says Heidegger, was inscribed in their relationship from the very start. Nietzsche's break attests to this aspect of their divide: he positioned himself as the figural resistance to Dionysian complacency and affective abandon. Interestingly, the charges that Nietzsche pressed against his teacher and friend have not been dropped or seriously refuted in the philosophical follow-ups that we have at our disposal. Heidegger retains Nietzsche's principal grief against Wagner: the absence of style. We know from Derrida and subsequent other readings of the styles of Nietzsche – including those of Philippe Lacoue-Labarthe and, more recently, Susan Bernstein – that when a man is caught short on style, there is an indication of trouble, female trouble.[12] A man without a style is, in Lacoue-Labarthe's words, an *"être pénétré,"* turned back on himself into the sappy feminine. This is the other woman, one who fails to coincide with the woman in Nietzsche or rather the women in Nietzsche who spar with truth – those who know ungroundedness and don illusion as a de-essentializing weapon. The other woman-type, the one whom Nietzsche tries to chase down, has invaded the decadent space of Wagnerian ascendancy. As if climbing out of his own masochistic pit to where Wagner time and again escorted him during their friendship, Nietzsche puts Wagner on the side of the passive feminine, aesthetic reception, opium, anesthesia, drugs (all things with which Nietzsche charges Wagner and his *opus hystericum*). Projecting these attributes on Wagner, Nietzsche shakes off crucial attributes of the intoxicated encounter. Whether or not Nietzsche at one point himself embodied these attributes – was he not Mr. Aesthetic Reception to Wagner's mass hysteria and project, "passive feminine," high on musical meaning, and all the rest of the downgrades? – his accusation bears serious philosophical consequences.

Absence of style, which refers to the inability to figure, to produce a figure or figurations *(Gestaltung)* invites the violent imposition of form. *Gestaltung* works against hysteria – against nihilism, that is – against formless pessimism and that which sinks into nothingness. If in his text Heidegger criticizes Nietzsche, he has no criticism to make of the Nietzschean critique of Wagner. He's behind Nietzsche all the way on the question of style – more precisely, on Wagner's lack of style. There's no rhythm here, says Heidegger, recalling that rhythm originally means *Gepräge*: imprint, type. This is where sexual markings occur, because rhythm, imprint, and type set up the conceptual policy that allows for determined oppositions such as action *versus* passivity, virility *versus* the feminine. In fact, these reflections that set up sexual markings sound the first and last words of Western philosophy on the subject of music, notes Lacoue-Labarthe. From Plato to Nietzsche the case is closed: music is rediscovered each time to be unmanned. There is terror behind the musical note and what it performs on the invaginated ear, receptive and labyrinthine at once. The fear of passive identification, of imitation by identification – these "feminine" attributes scoped by Plato, rediscovered by Nietzsche – finally admit only virile and warrior music. What compels interest for us at this point is the fact that the philosophical lexicon of musical anxiety rests on the same principle that governs the break: Wagner is associated with the quality of frazzled nerves, torpor, narcosis, submission, feminine passivity. To fend off Wagner, Nietzsche reaches for the apotropaic composition. Rossini or Bizet are shown, on the contrary, to mark the allegro, the intensification of life, energy, joy and pride of standing: quickening the step, respecting the walk, they overturn Schopenhauer's definition of art as a tranquilizer as they convert music into a life stimulant. This overturning implies nothing less than the transformation of the determination of art in its essence, a *geschichtliche Auseinandersetzung*, a historical explication and a prefiguration, a *Vorgestaltung* of the future. Such a decision, according to Heidegger, offers the affirmation – against Wagner – of style because in style is staked what governs all of history. This is why the stakes are so high when Nietzsche rips into Wagner for lacking style and thus failing art. History depends on art in a crucial way. Art is not only subject to rules or subordinate to other concerns; it is lawgiver, ever enacting the giving that is truly art. The *Gestalt*, missing in action in Wagner's opus, is understood as the presentation of the law. Art art-iculates (which comes from *ars*) the relation of *physis* (the inexhaustible, earth) and *technē* (the creatable, to be created World). This law is historiality itself, the opening of history in its possibility.

All this – the drama of historial opening, the preeminent rule of law in art, genuine pride and the affirmation of life – is what Nietzsche decisively marked when he broke with Wagner. This was not a private squabble but reached beyond its apparent contingencies to inflect the way we think about and live the relation to history and the future. Heidegger considers this break decisive – for all of us – and historial. For him, a need to read the epochal decision in these terms may be compelled politically as well as "philosophically," suggesting their overdetermined nature; his own reading of Nietzsche is informed by an *Auseinandersetzung* with blind political attachments and his attempted break with National Socialism. Nietzsche serves not only to stage the necessity of breaking up, supplying the legislation of the rift with narrative and content, but also ironizes any reciprocal appropriation, driving a wedge between his reader and the cathected political object. Nietzsche makes one break the story, interrupt a continuous narrative, lose the fusional desire. He hammers the reader, splintering stagnant allegiances. The breakup that Nietzsche endured but also continues to provoke is worked by effects of textual fissuring: his text relentlessly administers "the hardest test." The claim that Nietzsche's life-and-works makes on us today involves this installation of something like a break-up machine, a textual apparatus that still needs to be reviewed according to different and uncompromising perspectives.

One would be mistaken to try to locate the fissuring apparatus strictly in what might be considered the work; Nietzsche led the way by marking the breach within and outside the boundaried parameters of writing. Where his writing lands and whom it seduces or repels is quite another story with which we are still dealing. The hardest test was in any case not limited to a site in a given book or among its aphoristic neighbors, in this or that letter or as one of the medical reports that Nietzsche's signatures also produced. He was thrown by the breaks that befell him (even if he initiated them), yet he threw himself into them, enacting and embracing the break, if this connection is bearable, as his *Geworfenheit*, his thrownness. It is not an exaggeration to state that Nietzsche broke like no one before or after him. It was as if his writing steered his life or as if his life circumscribed the proving grounds of what he was to offer up in writing. The severance policy was unyielding, infiltrating the terms of every possible equation: what we understand by life gets broken up – who can measure Nietzsche's lifespan? – and, despite the excellent editions available to us, the work remains to this day uncontained. The experience of breach proliferates in what we know of his life, which is quite a bit: regardless of minor thematic divergences, the narrations all agree, without really making a case of it, that Friedrich Nietzsche broke with everyone and everything that tried to have a substantial hold on him. In his life and in his afterlife Nietzsche broke the code of any program that tried to hold him to its truth. The list of Nietzsche's breakups remains impressive: moving to Basel and then on to Italy, he broke with the German areas of the world map; insisting that his origins were Polish, he broke away from a "racially" codified contract with national identity; in his first book he broke with philology, his official academic discipline and job description; as a philosopher, he refused to found a school and as a teacher he told his disciples to lose him; in his work he broke with the human and tried to figure the transhuman; in his time he broke with his time. No doubt there are more examples and themes to exploit here. His *relation* to the break is perhaps equally significant, however.

Not one to hide behind the overturning momentum of events, Nietzsche announced and explained the break; he did not slither away or forget. He was responsible for his breaks, more often than not he initiated them, and he took responsibility for them. The break was itself a contract; it did not escape the confines of an ethical assignment but exerted quasi-legal pressures on the sensitive philosopher who paced and posed its stipulations at every juncture. An acquaintance of his, Resa von Schirnhofer, even interprets the famous *Peitsche-Foto* as an effort to pose the break: "Lou Salomé showed me the often discussed posed photograph in which she, sitting in a handcart with a whip (if I remember correctly), steers the two harnessed friends, Dr. Rée and Nietzsche. The team is pulling in two different directions, as if it were trying to break apart."[13] The inverse of a ghost whose presence cannot be observed in a photograph, Nietzsche's relation to the break shows up to make its claims in the most material instances. It is the steadiness of the break that remains uncanny in the Nietzschean family album, and the way it develops its light out of an apparent negative.

When Nietzsche comes out of the darkroom, he brightens up our earth with the news of a breakup, something he splices into the notion of "great health." Health, which might be thought to depend on wholesomeness for its substance, is shown to hinge on a capacity for fissuring – for enduring the necessity of breaking off from a figure of wholeness, seen to be finite and fragile, if not illusory from the start. But Nietzsche doesn't want to pull the rug out from under a moment of experienced wholesomeness, which would resemble the ploy of a resentful lover ("it was never that good anyway"), the aggressive effacer of a story that despite it all deserves to be affirmed. Great health embraces the crash, plunges into the undertow if it means to rise up again as a sign of itself, becoming what it is: healthful. In the part of the life that became indistinguishable from the work, these themes and lacerations were perhaps most dramatically played out in relation to Wagner. The case of Wagner did not come from or happen to someone for whom friendship was foreign or remote. His title is not "in case of Wagner." What I mean to say by this is that friendship was not a contingency for Nietzsche and his work, something that you could take or leave, blow off or restrict, like limiting the phone calls you make or deciding to go out only two evenings a week.

Nietzsche knew friendship, he understood and nurtured it, articulated it, lived it, which is why his politics of breaking up is so poignant. The end was written into friendship as its ownmost possibility and its finite ground. Had the experience of friendship been able to hold its own, it would not have required the special attunement that Nietzsche felt he could offer.[14] Nietzsche recognized that friendship was not itself a stable substance but split into so many hetero- and homogeneities, occupied by a multitude of personae and sub-personalities, a gift that life offers, which is dealt significant blows and revised itineraries by time. In the case of his Wagner, it was often a mimetic hideaway for the philosopher who fancied himself a musical composer. If the temptation to merge hadn't been so great, Nietzsche would not have had to devise a test and instate a fissuring machine to get himself out of the mess. So identified was he with Wagner that for a long while he wanted to draw Cosima close – he drafted musical compositions in her honor, and he took several other routes of desiring Richard's desire. Becoming Richard Wagner, he began the labor of break-ing off. If Nietzsche proved capable of wrenching apart from Wagner, as well as from that part of himself that was cleaved to Richard Wagner, Wagner, for his part, was to be designated henceforth as a restorer, a uni-fier; he tried like no other to produce a unity of the arts. Nietzsche, he would no longer stand for any theater of reunification.

In addition to what was noted by Heidegger and considered by Lacoue-Labarthe, style means something else. It involves the ability to end. So when Nietzsche charges Wagner with lacking style, I think he also means what he says he means: absence of style points not only to the inability to figure, but also crucially means the failure of rhythm to meet or make its end; in Nietzsche's vocabulary bad rhythm can run interference in mat-ters concerning the walk, the step, and *cadence*. Cadence, Nietzsche re-minds us, together with the walk, the step, is a matter regarding man, if not outright the ends of man. The man who knows truly how to live the cadence does not exist yet, however; he is not even the last man, perhaps no longer a man. In principle this is what makes or breaks a man, given a situation in which breaking is no longer bound to a structure opposed to making, but can break into another form. There should be something like the art of the cadence, Nietzsche's text advises, calling for a realm to se-cure the ending that is linked to healthfulness. Not any break, for a bad break could mean decadence or pity or resentment. In *Nietzsche contra Wagner*, Nietzsche lists Heinrich von Kleist among several authors martyred by such a break in need of healing.

So. This is what I want to thank Nietzsche for today: for teaching how to break, for initiating the break of so many oppressive holds, including the stranglehold of man, for letting us translate his thought in congruence with the word and work *Daybreak,* for the unprecedented breaking free that he accomplishes in the preface to *Human, All Too Human,* for a break that is not naïve yet may demand the impossible. I want to express my gratitude to Nietzsche for thinking the necessity of a break that tries to dodge what he diagnosed as decadence: the debilitating expiration, the ending decreed by life impoverished, the will to the end, the great weariness – these qualities, effects of depletion, lie behind morality, under its most sacred names and values. All right, then, a breakup that would not be decadent: what would this look like?

Splitting up in the style of Nietzsche would entail a break without *ressentiment* on the one hand ("It's all your fault"); on the other hand, it would have to be accomplished without the excess called bad conscience ("It's my fault"). For Nietzsche, breaking up would be, and was, an engagement, a commitment – a vow that does not restrict itself to the acknowledgment of a fact but that firmly invokes a responsibility. Breaking up has to assert itself as actual, as a commitment, which is to say, in Nietzschean terms, that it requires the affirmation of breakage by submitting itself to the test of the eternal return. The Nietzschean break does not indulge a regression in the sense of a falling back or return to a prior unity before the relation (that would be Wagnerian). When carried out, it holds the *zweideutige,* double-binding or ambivalent horizon under which it occurs. Nor does it provide much space for exemptions such as indifference or the excuse of drifting apart. It derives its force, on the contrary, from being about difference, the condition of having a difference, being different, which explains in part why the Nietzschean break is a machine that produces so many rhetorical effects of difference: Beginning with the play of sexual difference, Wagner aligns himself – or herself – with the feminine, whereas I am on the side of the masculine; Wagner replicates the passive, whereas I mark the active (although Nietzsche will have a lot to say against the presumptions of the man of action, and the values of the heroic active, which merely reasserts that we are dealing with a program and machine of difference, not substantial difference). He/she/Wagner is an opiate, whereas I am a stimulant; he is a Christian, whereas I am a pagan; he is a German, whereas I am anything but German (however, some differences last only a minute, for the first of only two footnotes in *The Case* swerves in the opposite direction: "War Wagner überhaupt ein deutscher?" Was Wagner actually German?), and so on and so forth. If we have anything in common, Wagner and I have our differences, which it is my task to name, explicate, enact, and affirm.

Nietzsche never finishes his explications with Wagner: he never finishes affirming the break, returning to it or turning it on the axis of its many facets. Naming the break, *The Case of Wagner* can however not be closed, performing as it does a closure without end. Textually, it is trailed by two postscripts and an epilogue, holding in place a structure of continuance that appears to belie a will to termination. Posing an interminable end, it takes up where it leaves off, never really abandoning Wagner but over and over renewing the commitment to the break. As our language insists, the break charts an upward fall, it is a break *up* sketching a movement of ascendancy that is carried forward only to return eternally, each time marking that the past is passing, making a passage through you time and again and so it comes to pass.

"One pays heavily . . ."

2. Falling for Wagner

The first postscript appended to *The Case* bears the title, "The Price We Are Paying for Wagner." In case we did not receive the invoice, the text repeats as its refrain no less than five times, "One pays heavily for being one of Wagner's disciples." It is small wonder that Nietzsche had to establish a credit account in *Ecce Homo*; the burden of debt is considerable for the disciple Nietzsche. Still, Nietzsche is not one to default on his student loans. He finds himself transferring accounts in an effort to meet it. The ledger is predictably complicated but still available to review. As it turns out, he is not so much indebted to Wagner, although this debt is never disputed by Nietzsche, as he is indebted by Wagner; and since on some level he can never truly dissociate himself from the Master, he is still paying interest. The way he manages his debt bears Nietzsche's signature. One sees the Dionysian payment plan at work.

The first postscript to the case study, "The Price We Are Paying for Wagner," reclaims Wagner by reminding the resentful reader of the Master's irreplaceability. Anyone who thinks that Wagner belongs to the drama of exchange value has understood nothing. In essence unmournable, Wagner can never be substituted. To the suggestion that he might have gleefully supplanted Wagner with Brahms, Nietzsche retorts: "When in this essay I declare war on Wagner – and incidentally upon German 'taste' – when I use harsh words against the cretinism of Bayreuth, the last thing I want to do is start a celebration for any other musicians. *Other musicians don't count compared to Wagner.*"[15] Or, "I admire his work [*Parsifal*]. I wish I had written it myself."[16] His last word on the subject: "The case of Wagner is a windfall for the philosopher – this essay is inspired, you hear, by gratitude."[17] This is why we need to stay close to the ground of gratitude, especially where it is linked to war. Even though Nietzsche himself proposed Bizet in lieu of Wagner or railed against the embarrassment called *Parsifal*, probity requires that he keep Wagner strictly out of the range of a resentful politics. To prove that *The Case* was not produced in the heat of passion, as uncontrollable anger, resentment, as an act of malice, Nietzsche later writes, renewing his vows, *Nietzsche contra Wagner*. His final effort, *Nietzsche contra Wagner* was finished in 1888, only a few days before his total collapse. *The Case of Wagner* was the last book whose publication he himself experienced.

Nietzsche continually exposes himself to the end without however *accomplishing* this end. Another way of seeing this is that Nietzsche proceeds without benefit of a dialectical apparatus that would at once sublate and exalt the end. Dialectics reabsorbs what it separates and cuts; what it holds on to changes its character, accommodating the severance as part of its unfolding. Nietzsche stares the severance in the face, takes it straight, so to speak, without transforming Wagner into something more "tasteful" or dialectically assimilable. Nietzsche, the great vomiter, can't even throw him up (the reverse of dialectics). The loss stays with him. The multiplication of texts around him tells us that Wagner is here to stay, if only as the pressure point of loss. Nietzsche cannot simply write off this loss but continues henceforth to count the losses ("Other musicians don't count compared to Wagner"). Driving him into his own abysses, Nietzsche somehow still holds on to Wagner. The friendship has to be surrendered on historical demand – only weakness and a lacking integrity would vote to keep it – but there is no question as to which of the two might be seen as having survived the friendship in the sense of overcoming it. Nietzsche stayed with the departed friend the way he kept the memory of his father close. The circuitry of mourning is interrupted by the canceled friendship. In the case of the father, death took the beloved other away. The hardest test, though, is self-administered, so to speak; implying resolve, a supplement of determination, it is something you do to yourself.

Nietzsche had a hand in calling Wagner off and everywhere suggests that he has lost the rights to the melancholic sheltering by which he guarded his father's phantom (sometimes he hallucinated his father crouching behind him as he wrote). Calling off the friendship, graduating early (or too late) from the apprenticeship – he is still paying heavily, he says, for being a Wagner disciple – Nietzsche creates the disturbingly arid circumstances of the other's deathless death, which inhibits friendly or stark phantomizations, and introduces another site on the fringe of mourning, where one is called upon to liquidate the transference. Dissolving the Wagner account while maintaining the debt, Nietzsche embarks on what Goethe famously calls, with regard to the suffering Werther, "a long insomnia." Roland Barthes writes something that may help us grasp the fringe mourning that Nietzsche undergoes:

> In real mourning, it is the "test of reality" which shows me that the loved object has ceased to exist. In amorous mourning, the object is neither dead nor remote. It is I who decide that its image must die (and I may go so far as to hide this death from it). As long as this strange mourning lasts, I will therefore have to undergo two contrary miseries: to suffer from the fact that the other is present (continuing, in spite of himself, to wound me) and to suffer from the fact that the other is dead (dead at least as I loved him). Thus I am wretched (an old habit) over a telephone call which does not come. . . .
>
> Though justified by an economy – the image dies so that I may live – amorous mourning always has something left over: one expression keeps recurring: "What a shame!"[18]

No reality-testing controls the sensibility of one who has had to call off the friendship. The lost friend still travels the surface of a world that is meant to wound or trouble the decision that continues to be negotiated in some back room of last hope, even where the decision to shred the already introjected image has been announced and partially enacted. The writing on internal walls "What a shame!" indicates that an alternate history always threatens to break through, weaken the resolve, or force a recount. "Quel dommage!" – the French for "What a shame!" – stays within an economy, as when saying What are the damages? we ask to see the check at the end of a meal. Nietzsche would want to have *dommage* rhyme with *homage*, because, remember, he pays with gratitude. "What a shame!" indicates that the history could have gone otherwise and lives on in that place of precarious unfulfillment. The friendship taken off the agenda, Nietzsche refines the experience of the break. With Wagner he made it a clean break to the extent that it can never be done with but offers residue and return. It is a clean break only in the transvaluated sense; Nietzsche is not so naïve as to think that he could walk away under the protection of erasure. Cleanliness means staying in touch with the history and pain from which you've bolted, particularly where it transcends your own particularity.

Nietzsche subjects himself endlessly to this end that resists closure or appropriation. Becoming addressee, Wagner passes beyond himself, is at once exalted and limited by the signatory Nietzsche. A destiny, he becomes the destination of Nietzsche's writing. But even when the destination appears to be reached it refrains from offering a stop or pause: the destination Wagner proves never to be terminal but prompts a persistent destinal rerouting, never as such suitable or exhausted enough for the sender, Nietzsche. Nietzsche cannot stabilize his position as a sender whose function would be separable from the one who receives the break. He may well receive the break as an order to be carried out by necessity, as something that befalls him and for which he must answer. In any case, Nietzsche does and does not *own* the break. It is true that many interpreters have seen the breakup with Wagner as a triumphal act of self-reappropriation: Losing Wagner, Nietzsche has finally come into his own; the student has trumped the Master; he has achieved the sublimity of self-overcoming. Nietzsche at no point corroborates such a rendering, however. Even if he were capable of controlling the break, it could not maintain its status as a particularly strong moment in his *Bildung*. Signing for it, Nietzsche nevertheless does not own the break; he cannot contain its effects – in fact, it can be seen at times to break him – but he at every juncture owns up to the break. One reason that he cannot own the break is because as a self with a history, Nietzsche is scarcely involved in the break. These are the terms at least of the contract that he has himself countersign time and again. The contract is up for renewal almost every time Nietzsche declares war on Wagner, in part because the temptation to create a suffering self around the break must have been great.

When Nietzsche writes *Nietzsche contra Wagner* he is poised in a battle of names: Nietzsche, Wagner. He rises above the contingencies of self and its rallying tropes in order to pit these names against each other. As Derrida has shown, Nietzsche exercises the fate of the name with strategic precision.[19] Pluralized, the names of Nietzsche define the playing field where everything is staked. It was a duty for Nietzsche to offer and honor his names. One should look closely when Nietzsche reports for duty, however. For when Nietzsche says he is duty-bound, often giving to understand that what he is saying goes against his instinct, he does violence to himself because he does duty toward this other, the duty of his name. Something else happens when Nietzsche turns over the files on Wagner to the authority of the name. Having decided to let the names fight it out, Nietzsche already enters the death zone where the surviving names will outrun their owners. In this way what happens between Wagner and Nietzsche is not only a fight unto death but has leapt onto the site where neither subjectivities rigorously matter – their material densities will have been crushed by a battle that has long removed them from the scene. Putting up his name for battle, Nietzsche walks. When Nietzsche walks, he is dead man walking.

Nietzsche's death cued an impossible spectacle of unending cessation that remains to this day somewhat of a philosophical event. One could say that his death was itself a multiplication of the end, figuring the break without end. Nietzsche did not simply expire; there was no sure boundary separating the here from the hereafter. Nietzsche's collapse staged the absolute precession of death to itself. His collapse, diagnosed as a paralysis, did not consist primarily in a cessation, an annulment, or destruction. It was, as Jean-Luc Nancy observes, above all a presentation, presenting nothing, nothing less than the becoming-dead of God. Nietzsche, taking on the posture and figure of God, assumes a death with no resurrection.

In contrast to Christ, he is the incarnation of the dead and not the living God. Nietzsche's collapse poses as death itself, presenting and preceding itself in paralysis. Until that moment God had always signified that death *is not*. Just as God could not present himself as living, he could not present himself as dead but could only emit the cry of him who sees himself not being. Slumped, vacant, mute, Nietzsche after 1889 is the site where death precedes itself infinitely, "for only death is capable of such preceding."[20] For Nancy, this precession inscribes a new spacing.

Though later on in his writing Nancy, following Derrida's concerns, will back off on the linking of community with politics, at this point he writes toward the new spacing of a bountiful community, whose *history* does not consist in accomplishing an *end* but in letting new names and new songs arise unendingly. With each name of history a finitude is marked "whose limit puts into play, each time anew the whole spacing of the world. It simply exposes itself to an end."[21] Each name holds a finitude, opening and closing world according to the rhythm of the Nietzschean cadence – the exposition to the end that Nietzsche lived out or steadily died out to the end. Still, one could say that Nietzsche's passing had passed through him from very early on, even before 1889, which is why he was always also a decadent and, like Zarathustra, started out by carrying a corpse on his back. Or many corpses: his brother, Josef, his father, Europe, the last man, and, at this point, the Wagner who no longer coincides with Wagner. In a letter remembering their friendship, Ida Overbeck writes: "he was deeply depressed by the consciousness that as a sick man he was not one of the strong, and could not say the last word to mankind; he was excluded from too much; to a certain extent he was already dead."[22] Remembering her friend, she indicates that the friendship was already lived in remembrance to the extent that Nietzsche presented himself as not being – as, we could say, the unbeing.

3. Loving Your Enemy

In the finite but passionate moment when Nietzsche was a Wagnerian, when in the fourth Untimely Meditation he became the ticket master for Bayreuth, extolling the virtues of Wagner's insight, Friedrich Nietzsche claimed that he was able to distill Wagner to one concept, one name. If one were to situate "Richard Wagner in Bayreuth" (the title of the fourth Meditation) today, just to get the true flavor of its historicity, one would have to imagine a teenaged Friedrich Nietzsche on the eve of the ur-Woodstock explaining to the nation the meaning of an ecstatic musical event: The altogether unprecedented gathering at Bayreuth-Woodstock would imply social revolution, peace, love, hope, and would be bound to rock the stagnant music scene.[23] The bourgeois thought police were put on alert. Let us flash back with Nietzsche to their moment of greatest accord. Nietzsche's Untimely Meditation announces what is to come; the future has a name: it is Richard Wagner. Eventually Nietzsche will come to see this future as a false one, a mere detention of the present. When it's about to be initiated on the grounds of Bayreuth, Wagner's music promises to fight the power; it will slam the philistines, Nietzsche argues, and break up the bourgeois monotony of quiet, easy listening, or what Theodor Adorno will call regressive listening (Adorno includes Wagner in this genre and later changes his mind). The abundance of texts produced around them – from the Meditation to subsequent tracts, books, and articles on Wagner and Bayreuth – leaves no doubt that this was the first media-technical event, the first music event with special effects, with people coming from miles around, high on ecstasy and other drugs (Nietzsche will later come clean and denounce Wagner as a bad drug, a dangerous hallucinogen).

Nietzsche's essay "Richard Wagner in Bayreuth" was scheduled to appear a few weeks before the opening of the Bayreuth festival. Wagner represented for Nietzsche at this point a courageous outcast, a solitary genius who, having been exiled from the German domains by the forces of *ressentiment*, was coming back to make serious trouble. As far as a future genealogy of landmark concerts goes, Bayreuth was a bust to the extent that it became a tremendous success. Politically and philosophically, it folded in on itself, co-opted by the meanest ideological orders of the day – something that Wagner welcomed, and for which he was without a doubt himself responsible. Some lasting points were scored by the Wagner camp: The relation of mass concerts to national political playing fields was put on the map. Backed by musical programs, national aesthetics henceforth saw a number of coded accompaniments as a crucial supplement to the political scene. Wagner would supply the death knell of background music not only to political movements; he would lay down the soundtrack for cinema. The deception and disappointment that Nietzsche recorded at the time is related to the fact that the music fest became an institution, an excuse for national complacency and the launching pad of self-congratulatory mythologemes. Bayreuth quickly became the appropriated site for the Reich, Nietzsche contended in bitter disappointment. Bayreuth's one cheerleader found himself run over by crowds of conservative nationals, happy to see their views mirrored and mythologized. The wave of vulgar nationalism occurs, of course, after Nietzsche's announcement of the good news of Bayreuth's inaugural performance, which he had offered before the ring was recycled into the loop of another contract. Still, to the extent that Nietzsche infiltrates the Wagner compound, it becomes difficult to put a date on the true beginnings of the war effort.

The war that Nietzsche declares on Wagner, too, was to precede itself, because the young philosopher gets on Wagner's case from the minute he starts writing about him. Maybe the writing ran ahead of Friedrich, on a kind of unconscious reconnaissance mission. But whatever one says, however one measures the proximities and scopes out the love – these are not being disputed – Nietzsche's writing was already there, ready to take apart Wagner from the start. Nietzsche sounds the war cry early on, even before he openly declared war on Wagner. He prepares his rhetorical forces when he has Wagner in his sights. (Just because he gives his word on avoiding a ressentimental payback does not mean that Nietzsche's revenge will not be devastating.) Let us observe the way Nietzsche amasses his considerable forces against the cause of Wagner. In the fourth Untimely Meditation, Nietzsche, setting up the Wagner war machine, is able to distill Wagner to a single concept, to one word, which becomes a fetish-word: loyalty (*Treue*):

What secret does the word loyalty hold for his whole being? For the image and problem of loyalty is impressed upon everything he thought and created; there exists in his works a virtually complete series of all possible kinds of loyalty, the most glorious and rarest among them: loyalty of brother to sister, of friend to friend, of servant to master, Elizabeth to Tannhäuser, Senta to the Dutchman, Elsa to Lohengrin, Isolde, Kurwenal and Marke to Tristan, Brünhilde to Wotan's innermost desire – to make only a start on the series. [Loyalty] is the most personal primal event that Wagner experienced within himself and reveres like a religious mystery.[24]

Loyalty will spin on the axis of possible meanings, because this is Nietzsche, remember, for whom there will be a stock of noble and decadent types of loyalty, and its value is going to turn bad sooner rather than later. Loyalty will have to stand the test, that is to say, true loyalty requires its own repulsion: it belongs to the register of attachment that has to be repelled. But hold on. Someone or something needs to intervene, wanting to go on record. When I read this passage on Wagner and the secret of the word "loyalty," I felt like a detective who had come upon a crucial piece of evidence, but evidence of what? It took me days to calm down and gather myself around this missing piece of evidence that emerged as absolute revelation but kept its meaning in the dark, playing off the decisive tone of concealment. This cannot come as a surprise once one recognizes that Nietzsche initiated the passage on Wagner's innermost truth as a secret, even though it displays the qualities of an open secret – after all, Wagner had staged his secret and repeated its disclosure in every major music drama after *Rienzi*; he had aired his secret, yet it was hidden and disseminated among other objects and languages until the philosopher pinpointed it. Or rather, breached it. For Nietzsche avows Wagner's secret as if it were protected, part of a privileged communication. Now look who's singing. Nietzsche spills what he knows. When most emphatically on Wagner's side, then, as his disciple and adulator, Nietzsche claims to uncover a personal and primal experience that he locates *within* Wagner. Nietzsche plants himself both inside and alongside Wagner. He knows him inside out, as we easily say; he claims to know his secret, or, more disturbingly, the secret code word to his entire being ("What secret does the word loyalty hold for his whole being?") We are given to understand by this strategic chip that when Nietzsche turns against Wagner, he does not merely signal an aversion to this or that aspect of the Wagner phenomenon; he conducts an absolute and precise destruction, targeting a break within the whole being that gathers itself under the name Wagner.

There are a number of battlefields in the war on Wagner, for Nietzsche does not limit the destruction to the affiliations and identitary policies that Wagner signed. Some of the battles continue to rage. Nietzsche turns against Wagner and the Germanies that this name was evermore to call forth, against the philosophical hazards released by the music without rhythm or style (Adorno tries to limit the damages by reducing the whole matter to a squabble of ears, a grave default in music theory: he says, Well, if Nietzsche didn't get with the rhythm of Wagner, then he was listening with Biedermeier ears). The battlefields naturally appear to narrow in scope when things get personal. In this area there is quite a bit that Nietzsche must dispose of or subdue. Among other things, Nietzsche must carry out his break with the teacher and father figure, the one who won and kept Cosima's devotion – Nietzsche was caught in an embarrassingly transparent Oedipal drama with Wagner and Cosima – he must lay waste to the extreme forms of attachment of which he proved capable; he has to produce a noble "no" to repel the man who considered him little more than a propagandist for himself and who thought nothing of having Nietzsche do the shopping, including the Xmas shopping for him, and while you're at it, get me a pair of underwear, and rewrite "Schopenhauer as Educator" in which you forgot to mention me. It is small wonder, by the way, that Nietzsche was one of the few sensibilities to appreciate Eckermann, Goethe's abject secretary, because, in the beginning of his own *Lehrjahre* (apprenticeship), he found himself in a phase of full on Eckermania. As with Eckermann – yet he, Nietzsche, was to find a way out of the interminable transference though never altogether over and out with Wagner – recalling Eckermann, he committed terrible blunders, was responsible for inappropriate invasions, and provoked border disputes with the Master (Wagner was called by him, and in fact by everyone, Master). Wagner was no Goethe, so the invasions were not always welcome or in the first place designed by a master who thrived on the parasitic invasion. And Nietzsche was no Eckermann, which means that his mimetic raids tended to backfire: after all, Nietzsche was beginning to be "Nietzsche" and Eckermann was meant only to replicate and fade.[25]

One example of a sadly typical blunder: Wagner had surprised Cosima on her birthday with a morning concert, presenting her with a new piece of chamber work he had just composed: the *Siegfried Idyll*. Exactly a year later, Nietzsche offers as his own birthday gift a new piece he had composed: "The Echoes" (no kidding), a piano duet for four hands. Echoing Wagner. Nietzsche was himself too shy to present the gift in person, so none of his hands performed the piece. When Cosima and the conductor, Hans Richter, played the composition that day, Richard became fidgety and restless; he could not sit still but finally burst out laughing.[26]

TAKE TWO   Another account of the same episode says that Wagner got up hastily and left the parlor; when a guest followed him out, he found the Master rolling on the floor in an uncontrollable fit of laughter. We can surmise that Nietzsche's quotation in his own composition of a passage from the *Siegfried Idyll* precipitated the laughing fit. Nietzsche's musical career did not end here. It concluded when, in 1872, Nietzsche sent a copy of his recently completed Manfred Meditation to Hans von Bülow, one of the leading musicians of the age, and the former husband of Cosima, not long divorced. Apparently it was not enough for Nietzsche to provoke only one of Cosima's husbands but, as always, he had to multiply the trajectories. Von Bülow, who was in any case notorious for his invective, delivered a devastating reply. He speculated in writing that the work was "some kind of joke," "a parody of the Music of the Future." "Have you no better way to kill time?" – we'll return to this question, for Nietzsche will kill time hereafter – and, most appallingly, von Bülow wrote, "You have raped the muse of music."[27] A more psychoanalytic reading of this violent utterance might want to decode "the muse of music" as Cosima. Friedrich Nietzsche was beginning to get the sense that maybe he wasn't cut out to be a musician. He virtually stopped composing, concluding his efforts with the "Hymnus an die Freundschaft," composed in 1874, essentially his final musical work. Friendship, *Freundschaft*, ended Nietzsche's musical career.

When Nietzsche turned decisively against Wagner, it was prompted by these lacerations and by still more reasons. Others have found the cause for the break to lie in the protofascist alignments of institutional Wagnerism; Adorno, in Wagner's music itself (he later qualifies himself on this point). There was the question of Nietzsche's upcoming autonomy. Yet Nietzsche's writing offers a different set of clues. It shows him to be bent on repelling the innermost and secret name of Wagner. When he was with the program, Nietzsche burrowed deep in Wagner's soul – somewhere in his work he defines love in this way, as a parasitic burrowing – and seized on the true name. He goes in there to extract something from the friend, to set up temporary residency. Nietzsche begins the fourth Meditation by tracking an increasingly inward movement; after scanning the rainy site on the day Wagner was to christen Bayreuth, Nietzsche zooms in on Wagner's deepest inner thought. He codes the narrative to suggest that he has the inside story; this is an inside job, he can read inside Wagner ("er schwieg und sah dabei mit einem Blick lange in sich hinein. Was aber Wagner an jenem Tage innerlich schaute . . .").[28] No matter how lofty, necessary, painful, and justifiable, Nietzsche catches Wagner's secret in order to destroy him. His method of destruction? Transvaluation. Nietzsche will have to transvaluate loyalty. In the meantime, back at Tribschen, Wagner is Treue, he is loyalty, which is not far from truth, as when we say, "a true friend," a true or loyal friend.

Let us go over what we have already bagged. Heidegger, Lacoue-Labarthe, and others have disclosed some of Nietzsche's motives for the breakup. Mazzino Montinari, by the way, pins it on the "tödliche Beleidigung," the wounding insult that Nietzsche suffered at Wagner's hands. This makes reference to Wagner's unsolicited letter to Nietzsche's doctor, where the Master expresses solicitude but adds his own diagnosis. It was obvious to the great etiologist, Richard Wagner, that Nietzsche was having eye trouble, with the increasing possibility of going blind, because of excessive onanism. Elizabeth heard this rumored at Bayreuth (Wagner did write the letter) but as usual muddled everything and conveyed to her brother that Wagner had accused him of pederasty rather than of masturbation. (Well, someone accused him of pederasty because that rumor is still alive.) The circulation of this letter provides Montinari with the motive to attribute the break. Réné Girard locates the necessity of the rupture in mimetic rivalry. The break attracted the heavies and put them to work. We are left with quite an impressive scope of investigative clues ranging from the letter on onanism, to historical appointment, and – somewhat more of a matter for the theoretical bureau of internal affairs – to philosophy's inability to read music.

Let us return to the scene. From the start there are deep ambivalences, and the manuscript version of the *Untimely Meditations* reveals harsh criticisms as well. Nonetheless, at this point, Nietzsche's hero worship is unwavering. Before the break, Nietzsche interprets Richard Wagner as a historical event (later he said he had misread him as a beginning when in fact he was an end, the total corruption and decadence of an era). On and at Wagner's side he discloses in the friendly fire of his supportive text Wagner's most primal signifier, "loyalty." All the thematizations that girdle his operas are but so many metonymies of this primal impulse. There is a discernible logic according to which it can be shown that Nietzsche cannot simply break with someone or something whose entire being is staked on loyalty. Everything that Wagner thought and created is concentrated on this signifier. This includes the disciple Nietzsche. On the one hand, Nietzsche cannot easily turn against Wagner since he was tuned by the Master to loyalty, to its exigencies. Moreover, Wagner covers the range of aberrations and extensions that loyalty encounters: he has studied and mastered the "image and problem" of loyalty, acculturating his disciple to its repertoire.

On the other hand, loyalty does not present itself as a shield that one can pierce or toss off. Nietzsche cannot separate from loyalty but has to enter its domain even more deeply in order to effect a rupture. Betraying Wagner, he would have to become the lord of loyalty. Loyalty is what Nietzsche learned from Wagner, the secret to which he alone had access, even though it was there at all times, like a purloined letter. It was a letter addressed to him, Friedrich Nietzsche. To the extent that he has and knows the other's secret, he is already involved in a politics of betrayal, however. The vertiginous abysses of this logic are productive of a series of ambivalent cycles to which Nietzsche submits. His job will be to detect a way out of the pull of loyalty. As Nietzsche knows early on, there will be no outside of the essentially loyal. The only way out will eventually be in: his mission retraces the fate of the labyrinth. From another perspective, the concept itself holds the key to its internal dismantling. Nietzsche will approach the problem of loyalty from two sides. Obviously, they will be contradictory, self-annulling, and yet potent. First, he will show himself to be truly a disciple of Wagner by maintaining his relation to loyalty: his betrayal was commissioned by loyalty (this is why he is still paying heavily as Wagner's disciple). As a true Wagnerian, he had to do it. In this way Wagner will have "created and thought," authored Nietzsche's disloyalty: it is a destiny that Wagner had scripted. Second, Nietzsche launches a philosophical campaign against the very notion of loyalty, undermining its safe-hold on the repertoire of presumed virtues. Nietzsche pulverizes the personal and primal code word that he associates with Wagner's entire being: he strikes at the Master's secret name, *Treue*. The very means by which Nietzsche attacks Wagner guarantees that they will be locked in an unbreakable embrace. Reminiscent of the end of Goethe's drama *Torquato Tasso*, it will remain strictly undecidable whether the embrace of the great agons portrays an adversarial lock or a lover's hold.

Attacking Wagner, Nietzsche also cosigns a shared if troubled text. He takes on the inevitable snares of declaring war on Wagner pumped with the mixed energy of warrior pride and brokenhearted resolve. We are now able at least to translate the titles of the works addressed to, against, and even, to the extent that he initiated the thought, by Wagner. *The Case of Wagner* or *Nietzsche contra Wagner,* and already the fourth of the *Untimely Meditations,* call out to be read, translated in supratitles, as "The Case of Loyalty" or "Nietzsche contra Loyalty." Can one truly be against loyalty? Nietzsche enters the contra as a crucial and liberatory possibility that has everything to do with time, with becoming and time, with resisting the restraints of old convictions that, rigid, unchanging, depend upon no proof outside themselves. Another twist in the logic of loyalty needs to be countenanced with before we move on. When Nietzsche establishes Wagner as the predicate for loyalty, he already fills the zone of an essential loyalty with the name, Wagner. Anything or anyone else risks falling short of the essence of loyalty that Wagner's name embodies. At the same time, we can see the early – untimely – maneuverings of a defense team build-up: namely, "it's not my fault, because it's not me but Wagner who is loyalty." But much like the distinction Lacan draws between being and having the phallus, loyalty, as Nietzsche states it, holds a secret for Wagner. It is at no point clear that Wagner has access to his unassailable core – only Nietzsche can break this code.

When Nietzsche attacks loyalty, he takes aim at the secret core of Wagner's being. Where his work submits loyalty to the genealogical test, it engages the extensive *Auseinandersetzung* with his teacher and mentor. To the extent that he continues to pay the price for the school of discipleship in which he was enrolled, Nietzsche remains to a certain degree dependent on the relation that exacts punctual tax returns. He is still paying the interest. Identified with Wagner, loyalty invites a philosophical showdown. On one level, we can see that Nietzsche needs to explain to himself the concept of loyalty that was toppled in service of a higher loyalty. However, Nietzsche's integrity does not allow for a calculation so transparent that it would give him the advantage in a battle of values that come to describe loyalty. This is war, not a lame manipulation of thought. What's more, loyalty admits of another problem. It always implies a relation to an other, whether that other is under surveillance or under oath. Loyalty, no matter how internally set, exposes a limit of relation or an outward form of relatedness. Loyalty involves *presentation* – a type of dependency that, at least for Wagner, entails representation, constant staging, proof, and manifestation. The loyalty test is something that Wagner never ceased administering on this side of metaphysics. Nietzsche's goal is to pass and detonate the test at once, but also to keep the relation to the other somehow going, even if the relation needs to be transgressed, exploded in the name of the other.

If we open the dossier we find that Nietzsche's case against loyalty is in fact as portentous as it is provocative. It has wide-reaching implications. Pulling away from Wagner momentarily and focusing on the nature of loyalty, let us consider Nietzsche's argument on its own merits. The short version goes something like this: when you made a vow of loyalty (no doubt time-canceling and eternal), you were in the throes of passion, in a hysterical conversion scene, you flung yourself at someone's knee – at God, an ideal, a country, a thinking or its thinker – and made an oath of eternal loyalty to this entity. Are they really going to hold you to it? Are you really going to be bound to an oath made in so plain a state of pathological imbalance and aberrancy? This description more or less sums up the short version. Something about its occurrence should not be overlooked. Very often the instantiation of loyalty requires an oath. You swear loyalty. You posit and institute it on the balance of a promise. Things get rhetorically tricky, which is what allows some tyrants to decide arbitrarily that loyalty isn't happening. To the extent that loyalty is often attested to by some sort of speech act – a promise, an oath, a pledge – it is not natural but conventional and prey to all the rhetorical disruptions, parasitism, and static that have been signaled in those works on or by Husserl, Derrida, Austin, de Man, and Butler, among others, that concern the structure of the promise, its legality and inherent fragility.

Well, let us examine what Nietzsche is up against. What is loyalty? An event? A contract? Does the question even hold water? Are we right in thinking we can go after the essence of loyalty ("what *is* . . .?")? Or does loyalty hover in the vicinity of nonbeing? In the Nietzschean scheme of things, loyalty does not appear to invite affirmation. He gives us to understand that the break and breach, what Heidegger elsewhere calls the *Riss*, can be affirmed. In Nietzsche, *dis*loyalty deserves and is in need of support. Perhaps loyalty is that which cannot – even, should not – be expressed or affirmed, as in the precincts of loyalty's great test case – in *King*

Lear, where Cordelia, most loyal of daughters, can say only "nothing." Literature takes us where saying meets its limit, and this is where Nietzsche goes in order to fortify his argument, such as it is. Dependability, loyalty, steadfastness, all these qualities have to fall beneath their masks; if they do exist as something graspable, they need to be freed from the concept that claims to have identified their essential features. The most loyal of daughters is gravely misunderstood because she cannot *say* loyalty, she cannot *act* loyally, and we could go so far as to say that King Lear founders on this impossible facet of loyalty. His fatal mistake was to have issued an invitation, to call for a command performance to which only the counterfeit loyalists were able to respond. Loyalty cannot present itself as presence, fulfilling itself in the present; yet it is about nothing other than this flash of presencing in the night of abandonment. For Nietzsche, the other madman who could be seen to founder on the fringes of loyalty's severe recalcitrance, the nothing and silence to which Cordelia is committed is an unbearable parable of nihilistic dissolution. She presents the aporias of loyalty by dissolving before its importunities. Nietzsche closes down *King Lear*, however, and reads another Shakespeare to get traction on this question. Cut to Caesar.

In *The Gay Science* Nietzsche mysteriously, if emphatically, asserts that Shakespeare loved Brutus best of all. Of all his characters, Shakespeare identified with Brutus. He recognized himself in the courage to betray. The betrayal enacted by the disciple Brutus is absolute, for it comes bounding from *inside* Caesar. The great Caesar, touched to the core, can only die from the closest bond, naming Brutus as he falls, falling only because he has been cut by Brutus. Nietzsche, for his part, knows without need of demonstration or scholarly leveraging that Shakespeare identified with Brutus. The proof? The dramatist has cleverly hidden this identificatory pathos by naming the tragedy *Julius Caesar*. Nietzsche goes so far as to assert that Brutus and Shakespeare had "secret relations," perhaps even that Brutus dominated Shakespeare. "But whatever . . . secret relationships there may have been [between Shakespeare and Brutus]: before the whole figure and virtue of Brutus, Shakespeare prostrated himself."[29] Staking out Brutus's undisputed position of sovereignty among Shakespeare's cast of exalted characters, Nietzsche goes a step further: he demotes the other contender, Hamlet. He boldly asks, or rather declaims: "What is all of Hamlet's melancholy compared to that of Brutus?"[30] There are two points to be underscored in the domain of this rhetorical question. Perhaps a third. "Brutus" operates almost as an anagram of Bayreuth, "bereits bereut" in Nietzsche's decryption. His name – let us not forget that this is a battle of names – overlays the script of betrayal that has conscripted Bayreuth. The first two points concern the contestatory positions occupied by Hamlet and Brutus with a view to fringe mourning. Nietzsche's depreciation of Hamlet is, of course, quite nervy and serves to underscore the adulation of Brutus on which he places his bets. The difference that Nietzsche introduces supports the need we felt earlier to try to distinguish, within the topologies of mourning, between the loss of a beloved other and the cancellation of a friendship.

Reduced to schematic bare bones and strategic usefulness, *Hamlet,* which Nietzsche pushes off the stage, offers the tears of a "true" mourning; allegiance and a bouquet of neurotic slipups are pledged to the dead father to whom Hamlet swears remembrance. Brutus, on the other hand, cannot ascribe the cause of the beloved's death outside of himself – not a trace of neurotic feints in this guy – but must assume and affirm the murderous act. Where Hamlet received penalties for holding back, he, Brutus, must *do* the deed, become its cause. Nietzsche is very clear about aligning himself with Brutus, which returns him to the hardest test. It is well worth citing him on this point:

> Independence of soul! – that is at stake here. No sacrifice can be too great for that: one must be capable of sacrificing one's dearest friend for it, even if he should also be the most glorious human being, an ornament of the world, a genius without peer – if one loves freedom as the freedom of great souls and he threatens this kind of freedom. That is what Shakespeare must have felt . . . he raises beyond measure Brutus's inner problem as well as the spiritual strength to cut *this knot.*[31]

As bold as it is young, the passage gains on poignancy to the extent that it is capable of sustaining a fast turnover of posited values. About this moment, we can say that the passage turns in on itself, mimicking the inner swerves and external lunges that it traces. When Nietzsche presumes to get inside Shakespeare's head, who himself has attained to Brutus's inner problem, before which the poet is said to prostrate himself, the passage ironically rescinds its own assertion. Let us revisit a few knots that Nietzsche did not manage to cut in the texture of an exalted insight. Every microflash appears to be reined in by a macrostructure that snuffs it. Thus the very movement of thought that is headlined by "independence of soul" reverts, in order to urge its point, to a figure of extreme submissiveness, that of prostration.

Another Hamletian moment, deserving of a more hesitating reading, occurs at the ostensible dénouement of the passage, when Nietzsche names "the spiritual strength that was able to cut this knot." In other words, at the very place where Nietzsche wishes to put his weight behind the strength applied to cutting *this knot*, his language slips into the trap already set by the tragedy (which powerfully ponders the name, acts of naming, and false naming) – irrepressibly encrypting Caesar in the triumph of cutting. The very thing meant to do away with Caesar reasserts his name. If Brutus was able to cut Caesar down, his act could not amount to a cut initiated by him, one might say, because the cut is Caesar in his defiant totality; from his very birth Caesar bears the naming name of the cut. The act of independence was prescribed by the name of the other. I now cut to the chase.

The crucial place that Brutus assumes in the Nietzschean corpus can hardly be overstated. A quotation from Nietzsche's notebooks reads, "In that which moved Zarathustra, Moses, Mohammed, Jesus, Plato, Brutus, Spinoza, Mirabeau – I live, too."[32] This represents quite a lineup. Brutus is up there with the other great positors and sacred initiators. Each one of these figures turned on his people, overturned the tables. These names form the energy lineage ("in that which moved" them) to which Nietzsche responds, and the community of solitaries whose counsel he keeps.

4. Rules of Engagement

In the section of *Human, All Too Human* entitled "On Convictions and Justice," Nietzsche asks, "Why do we admire the man who remains faithful to his conviction and despise the one who changes it?"[33] In other words, why do we tend to distrust those who change their minds, alter their positions, withdraw their cathexes, and break commitments? Nietzsche proposes: "Let us test how convictions come into being and observe whether they are not vastly overrated."[34] This test is devised to arbitrate a matter of great urgency. The stakes are high, involving the history of sacrifice and the status of truth in philosophical thought. Conviction, something for which people sacrifice themselves, die and kill in so many words, gathers momentum on knowledge and powers itself on truth: "conviction is the belief that in some point of knowledge one possesses absolute truth. Such a belief presumes, then, that absolute truths exist." Thus "the man of conviction . . . stands before us still in the age of theoretical innocence, a child."[35] Nietzsche, neither a child nor a theoretical innocent, has by now overcome his attachment to the thrall of conviction and the proximity to truth that it presupposes. Having asserted and acted on this always renewable effort of desistance in so many ways, he profiles, on the contrary, a parolee who has served time for convictions that keep one shackled to a narrow space of confinement. "On Convictions and Justice" lays the groundwork for his theory of the transformation of the spirit that later will be developed in *Thus Spoke Zarathustra* (Part One, "Of the Three Metamorphoses"). "To carry out later," the section begins "in coolness and sobriety, what a man promises or decides in passion: this demand is among the heaviest burdens oppressing mankind." The irony of the passionate pledge holds consequences for our ability to understand or carry out justice. Detaching from the oppressive weight of conviction, Nietzsche joins Flaubert in dissecting its pernicious logic:

> Because we have vowed to be faithful, even, perhaps, to a purely imaginary being, a God, for instance; because we have given our heart to a prince, a party, a woman, a priestly order, an artist, or a thinker in the state of blind madness that enveloped us in rapture and let those beings appear worthy of every honor, every sacrifice: are we then extricably bound? . . . Was it not a conditional promise, under the assumption (unstated to be sure) that those beings to whom we dedicated ourselves are the beings they appeared to be in our imaginations? Are we obliged to be faithful to our errors, even if we perceive that by this faithfulness we do damage to our higher self?[36]

A number of the leitmotifs (as much as Nietzsche detested the figure of the leitmotif) that are textured into the breakup with Wagner recur in the interrogation of conviction. When and under what conditions a vow was made should not be excluded from the understanding we may have of the genesis of an unwavering conviction. Nietzsche introduces a mood nar-

rative to help scan the contractual urge. The bond was forged, the promise made, he surmises, in a state of rapturous assent – under the influence,
in other words, of the opiate that Nietzsche associated throughout his life
with Wagner, the great intoxicator. Does a promise made in a mood of
rapture, under a musical narcosis, count when you can't count 'til twenty?
Will you be bound evermore by a contract on whose line you can't walk,
much less sign? These questions carry over to the purported sobriety of
rhetorical inquiry to the extent that Nietzsche makes one wonder, Is there
ever a promise that is not made in blindness and rapture? Of course, every
promise by its very structure is excessive – how could it not be so when it
speaks for all futures, of every mutation, positing eternity within the limits of a necessarily finite utterance: Is not every promise – I do, I will for-
ever and ever – not a little drunk with itself, dipped in some witches' brew
or Dionysian concoction? Nietzsche implies – no, he actually says – that
one cannot make a promise that obligates or commits one in the same
way as do those words that must be kept in a state of sobriety. This opens
another dossier that can be indicated at this point, another interrogatory
bend, namely, are not all declarations, utterances, textual gestures part of
the promising community?

In relation to the formation of conviction, the promise seems to pivot
unevenly on the tonal modulation of Western sobriety and Greek rapture. One eventually wakes up from such a promise – truly, the greatest
indulgence, committing as it does all eternity – one wakes up from the
night of promising with a hangover, a headache, which is another way of
saying an obligation, an oppression that locks in the future: the promise
portends madness. Thus Nietzsche sets up the promise in such a way as to
let us escape its imperial purchase. In the first place promise, as Heidegger
later intimates, entails the act of *versprechen*, which means both mis-
speaking and promising.[37] By necessity, one will have misspoken when
making the promise. The essential trip-up bears interesting consequences for Nietzsche's definition of man as the promising animal. Second, Nietzsche lets time take apart the temporal adhesive of the promising offer. He does so by underscoring the noncoincidence of the being to
whom we promise loyalty as that being appears to us in our imagination
and the way they turn out "really" to be. In other words, the transferential
structure of our relation to others gives us a way out, involving the experience of mourning. Projection offers the possibility for liberatory ejec-
tion, and, once the transference de-intensifies, the other proves no longer

to be the same, no longer in any case the miraged One to whom we have committed. They have changed, we have changed – an observation that is usually made in the form of a reproach, though not in the case of a Nietzschean couple that charges itself up by undergoing constant transformation, even where there is always a hint of otherness within sameness. Mutability dominates the scene of relatedness, such that the promise necessarily reaches the wrong address. They will change, you will change, Nietzsche will change – also when nothing has changed; yet, even so, things *will* have changed, and they changed perhaps more perceptibly the minute you locked onto the transferential target. Nietzsche feels that we suffer altogether too much from this law of change. The excess of pain brought on by the rule of mutability causes us to build virtues on disavowal. For the purpose of guarding against the ineluctability of change, we praise the dependable person of unwavering conviction, we approve the faithful and demand constancy. Such values continue to have contemporary religious resonance in their extolling of family values of constancy, abhorrence of divorce, and confirmation of the righteously faithful of identity politics.

Nietzsche asks if we are obligated to the promise made, "even if we perceive that by this faithfulness we do damage to our higher self." The locus of responsibility splits off into a higher self, making the addressee of accountability vulnerable to damage by a non-ironic lower self that believes what it says and holds itself unblinkingly to the said. Nietzsche legislates between the two offices of self, answering the question of obligation thus:

> No – there is no law, no obligation of that kind; we must become traitors, act unfaithfully, forsake our ideals again and again. We do not pass from one period of life to another without causing these pains of betrayal, and without suffering from them in turn.[38]

If we are to pass the test or pass to another stage of life, our relation to the promise needs to be a broken one. The promise can be counted on only to enforce its breakability. Nietzsche asks whether we construe ourselves as being obligated to the promise made. "No," he answers, or rather, No – dash, sending up a diacritical mark that can be read as an absence of a link, operating simultaneously as severance and connector: No, dash, there is no law. In a place where no law is asserted to stand, he posits law.

In fact, law appears in two manifestations of utterance: the "No" itself comes down as law; additionally, Nietzsche piles on a prescriptive utterance that, establishing law, repeals and reinstates the very law with which it purports to break: we *must* break the law, the promise of the law, and we must do this (become traitors) not once, as if it were a matter merely of an aberration or slipup, but we must do it recurrently in such a way that it each time returns to sender, that it comes back to be stamped again, affirmed, held, and taken on as a responsibility that makes me suffer.

Nietzsche famously ends *Human, All Too Human* by raising up the wanderer – a figure propelled by the effects of breakup. The wanderer, an early generation of nomad, travels in shifts and ruptures, intellectually torn from any lasting habitat by an experience of homelessness tied to time. To the extent that time is, the wanderer moves on, moving away from positions grazed or occupied: "We then stride on, driven by the intellect, from opinion to opinion, through the change of sides, as noble traitors to all things that can ever be betrayed – and yet with no feeling of guilt."[39] The figure of the noble traitor, brought into the picture at the end of this work, is not introduced by Nietzsche simply as a mask of backbiting betrayal, as a common coward or weakling. Nietzsche says and appears to mean a noble traitor, indicating someone or something capable of sustaining a highly developed sensibility for betrayal – not just a reactive or resentful someone who lets you down with a decadent and degenerate thud. By no means resuscitating the flake or disappointment we have all known and may have been at one or another time, he points up the figure of the *noble* traitor as the wanderer who knows when to fold, when to leave, "though not as a traveler towards a final goal. . . . But he does want to observe, and keep his eyes open for everything that actually occurs in the world; therefore he must not attach his heart too firmly to any individual thing; there must be something wandering within him, which takes its joy in change and transitoriness."[40] The wandering occurs, in the first place, internally, finding its correlate in more external forms of transitoriness that correspond to and change places with a more inner being.

Wandering, in Nietzsche's sense, assures vigilance, keeps one's eyes open. This all gets very complicated when one considers the possibility that the noble traitor comes closest to what Nietzsche means by loyalty, something we should provisionally oppose to Wagner's apotheosis of fealty in *Treue*. Loyalty implies a play of near and far, a capacity for letting go. Some distance is required. If you have someone on a short leash, you cannot seriously assert your own or their loyalty (whether you are a government, a person, or a god). Loyalty presupposes suspension, distance. As with trust, the less loyalty can rely on a host of givens and certitudes, the more it approaches the noble nature of a nearly incalculable attachment, and the more unconditional it appears. Unconditional loyalty *needs* distance in order to draw closer to its essential nature, becoming what it is. Its essential nature is to flow away from essence, to elude a common and blind level of dependence and dependability. Even though Nietzsche situates blind loyalty's turn into disloyalty within the parameters of the hardest test, the capacity for discerning loyalty cannot be tested in the present or be settled by the requirement of any loyalty oath. Loyalty cannot give itself up to the present. Or, when pressed, like Cordelia, loyalty can say nothing short of "nothing." It is never quite ready for its close-up. This is why, perhaps, in Nietzsche, that is, in *Zarathustra*, the friend is the farthest and the future. Zarathustra does not teach "the neighbor" but "the friend," the farthest and the future. According to Zarathustra the friend is the presentiment of the Overman. Loyalty hence becomes a matter of temporal relatedness in terms of the temporal slack that friendship cuts. One is asked to remain loyal to the presentiment lodged in the friend, not to the friend now or, should this be possible, to the friend present as himself. ("Himself": Derrida asks why it is that friendship has been based historically on brotherly love, *fraternité* and *égalité;* the *Übermensch* may allow a slip for transgendering affiliation, for a way out of the often deadly brotherhood of friendship.)

Given time, loyalty may have the chance of showing itself. For Nietzsche, loyalty also concerns the mapping of spatial relations. The instability of the topographical determinations of Nietzsche's declaration of war on Wagner complicates matters concerning the place where loyalty or disloyalty can be enacted. When Nietzsche uses figures of interiority to describe Wagner ("Was aber Wagner an jenem Tage innerlich schaute ... in sich hinein," and so forth), as though Nietzsche were himself speaking or ventrilocating from inside Wagner, this indicates that the boundary between Nietzsche and Wagner is neither clear nor finished: Nietzsche declares war on the Wagner locked inside Nietzsche. Even Heidegger allows that there was something *inside* young Nietzsche that responded to the Dionysian call of Wagner. The breakup, at every point also an operation that he performs on himself, does not act merely to separate a form of exteriority that should be removed and disposed of. There is a secret congregation of names whose designated meeting place is in Nietzsche. At times they form a merger. Or, as he says in *Ecce Homo* about the *Untimely Meditations*, " – Schopenhauer and Wagner or, in one word, Nietzsche."[41] Moreover, when attacking the apparent other, Nietzsche allows, "I would not wish to deny that fundamentally [these essays] speak only of me."[42] Nietzsche can get very far on this logic; he can end up subsuming Wagner altogether, making him a kind of linguistic boy toy, using him as a sign, much in the same way Plato made Socrates bend over: "It was in this way that Plato employed Socrates, as a semiotic for Plato" – he invites us, in very clear terms, to use "Wagner" as a semiotic for Nietzsche.[43]

The subsumption of names cuts both ways, at once honoring and demeaning the other, assuming responsibility for the other and letting the other disappear under the weight of one's own name. You choose. We are suddenly notified that Nietzsche goes by the name "Wagner"; he wanders into this other territory. The name tag does not stop here, for Nietzsche pulls out a name like a switchblade. He switches names, as in the first dedication of *Human, All Too Human*, to wound Wagner with the slash of a French accent. Not only will he take up with Paul Rée and convert to "Réelism," but, pushing beyond Wagner's objections to his object choice, he inscribes "the name of Voltaire on a writing by me – that really was progress – towards myself." To get anywhere at all it seems as though Nietzsche has to hitch a ride on the name of the other, a name that he uses both to cut himself loose on the way to himself and to cut a wound into a now offending name. At the same time, Nietzsche is not cut out for this survival camp exercise of cutting through a thicket of names. He has to do it as part of his test, but sometimes, depleted and weak, he borrows another name to do the cutting work for him. Thus when Nietzsche really wants to censure Wagner he pulls out the big-gun name of Goethe to judge and condemn him. "What Goethe might have thought of Wagner?" – he then proceeds to have Goethe indict *Parsifal*.[44] Still, he ends up, he feels, mostly alone, having cut himself off from his other names, his many other names and signs for whom he refuses evermore to sign.

> "Why so apart, so alone? Renouncing everything I admired, even admiration? Why this severity, this suspicion, this hatred of one's own virtues?" But now he dares to ask it loudly, and already hears something like an answer.

5. On Anticipatory Bereavement

Human, All Too Human marks the break with Wagner, without mentioning his name. The lowest blow. At this point Nietzsche also cuts the ties to his romantic past, and, moving toward a monistic position, he returns to the pronounced materialism that had impressed him earlier in Friedrich Albert Lange's work, *The History of Materialism* – a work also espoused by his new best friend, Paul Rée. The preface to *Human, All Too Human* struggles with the history of a difficult rupture, figuring a decapitation that heads up the new work after the break. In the first edition, Nietzsche marked the absence of a preface by citing, in lieu of a preface, Descartes. One can hardly overestimate the nerve of such a citation in the context of historical and philosophical Franco-Prussian wars – Descartes was enemy territory – and of Wagner's explicit censure of anything French. Nietzsche continues the sweep.

The first aphorism of the book, "A chemistry of concepts and feelings," takes a swipe at Schopenhauerian romanticism in favor of a scientific approach associated with Descartes that regards the search for knowledge as the sanctioned way to meaning and joy. *Human, All Too Human* presents a turning point in Nietzsche's understanding of style; it also gives birth to the "Free Spirit," Zarathustra's precursor. Independent of recognizable conventions, the Free Spirit embodies the friend Nietzsche would have wanted to call to his side; by means of the "semiotic" of Free Spirit, Nietzsche posits the future and invents the friend. The friend becomes the conduit to the future. As friend, the future speaks to Nietzsche with a decidedly French accent. Taking a deliberate turn westward, his work relocates the Greeks to France, signaling a change of plans and a new itinerary. The Greeks had made a wrong turn when they were heading toward the German language and terrains. They should never have been directed to that Autobahn.

In the fourth Meditation Nietzsche had compared the Germans to the Greeks and saw in Wagner's art the rebirth of Dionysus; in this work, he contends that the French have inherited the birthright of the Greeks. The

Greek spirit has veered off to the left and reincarnated in France. In case we didn't get the point, Nietzsche backs up Descartes with another French insult. From the point of view of Wagner and his circle, Nietzsche's extreme act of apostasy began with the dedication to Voltaire, anticipating the one hundredth anniversary of the French skeptic's death. Our troubleshooting philosopher's French allegiance of 1876 served at least two purposes as it continued to honor his self-testing imperatives. The Voltaire dedication – truly an insolent change of address – was a way of hurling defiance at Wagner; it also enables him to fend off, he thinks, the widespread chauvinism of the years following the Franco-Prussian War. He is in warrior pose, detached from national adherences, resolutely averting his gaze from the great Teutonic mentor. But the pose dissolves – perhaps even strengthens – as he lets go of Voltaire as well. His removal of the dedication in the 1886 edition has suggested to scholars that it had committed Nietzsche to too radical a turn westward. He waffles on the French connection as he tries to negotiate a peace for his own private Franco-Prussian war effort. The loosening of French ties admits another interpretation as well. It seems in keeping with the commandments that culminate in the hardest test – his policy of rigorous detachment – that Nietzsche would *have to give up* anything that simply opposed itself to a first degree of attachment; strictly speaking, he could not allow himself or his work to stay in the methadone clinic of substitute dependency for a very long while. The trick for him is to avoid oppositional logic while opposing Wagner, or to prevent himself from trading in one musician or country or ideal for another – the sort of economy that keeps you miserably hooked on the very thing you are trying to shake. The logic is infernal. Still, Nietzsche emphasizes that he at no point seeks a solution to Wagner, or an exteriority; all the while he is scoping for an exit. Nietzsche crushes the dedication but does not forget it. Storing it in *Ecce Homo*, he offers that his honoring Voltaire by dedicating the work to him is in truth a step toward his self-discovery. "Voltaire": another name, he repeats, a temporary stop and semiotic for "Nietzsche."

Human, All Too Human resembles in its way a rhetorically converted medical report. A nearly clinical document translated into the tropes of Nietzschean thought, it charts the course of an acute episode of separation. In the preface Nietzsche traces a "history of the great separation." It tells of someone who, "burdened with an absolute *difference of viewpoint*," displays occasional symptoms of the "chills and fears stemming from isolation."[45] Surviving separation without however overcoming the condition of separateness, the "I" that describes the course of a model healing deliberately moves from one type of experimental existence – from the desert – to another level of experimental life, that of abundance and renewal. The narrative voice that molds the mystery of separation has moved "a long way from this morbid isolation, from the desert of these experimental years, to that enormous, overflowing certainty and health which cannot do without even illness itself, as an instrument and fish-hook of knowledge; to that *mature* freedom of the spirit which is fully as much self-mastery and discipline of the heart, and which permits paths to many opposing ways of thought."[46] Illness embraced, the great health borne of the tremendous separation allows for life lived experimentally:

> It is a long way to the inner spaciousness and cosseting of a superabundance which precludes the danger that the spirit might lose itself on its own paths and fall in love and stay put, intoxicated, in some nook; a long way to that excess of vivid healing, reproducing, reviving powers, the very sign of great health, an excess that gives the free spirit the dangerous privilege of being permitted to live experimentally and to offer himself to adventure: the privilege of the master free spirit! In between may lie long years of convalescence, years full of multicolored, painful-magical transformations, governed and led by a tough will to health which already often dares to dress and disguise itself [*sich zu kleiden und zu verkleiden*] as health.[47]

The excess described by Nietzsche involves, as its midpoint (if one can posit a measure), a letting go of every yes and every no; freed of determinant affect, it runs up into the sky, flying and fluttering, moving and avoiding, as he says; avoiding in such a way as to call up a new multiplicity that appears beneath the soaring body:

> No longer chained down by hatred and love, one lives without Yes, without No, voluntarily near, voluntarily far, most preferably slipping away, avoiding, fluttering on, gone again, flying upward again; one is spoiled, like anyone who has ever seen an enormous multiplicity beneath him – and one becomes the antithesis of those who trouble themselves about things that do not concern them. Indeed, now the free spirit concerns himself only with things (and how many they are!) which no longer *trouble* him.[48]

Living "without" the axis of yes/no, and unchained, one for the first time lives with the possibility of disappearing and returning, with nearing and distancing oneself at will. Surprisingly, the "without" accommodates a supplement of will. A questioning being, the free spirit does not begin the research trip with an existential bump or a proposition, the inquiry of which begins, "I'm having trouble with . . . ," but moves past the yeses and noes that trigger resentful question marking. Enabled to be "gone again," one gathers the momentum to effect returns and probe new concourses of surrounding proximities. The history of convalescence opens out as a movement toward what is near, prompting in a Heideggerian sense an attunement to that which is most hidden. A new approach, a cautious return: "Another step onward in convalescence. The free spirit again approaches life, slowly, of course, almost recalcitrantly, almost suspiciously. . . . He almost feels as if his eyes were only now open to what is near. He is amazed and sits motionless: where *had he been*, then? These near and nearest things, how they seem to him transformed!"[49] Previously self-absent, removed from world and things, the free spirit stops in its imaginary tracks to experience amazement, the primal philosophical affect that Nietzsche henceforth associates with science. Amazement at what is turns the free spirit toward the past.

A moment of looking back anticipates *Ecce Homo*. Nietzsche writes back in forward motion. The backward glance calls to the future without simply unloading the past. Nearing and thanking, the backward glance offers a moment tying the great separation, convalescence, to gratitude:

> He glances backward gratefully – grateful to his travels, to his severity and self-alienation, to his far-off glances and bird flights into cold heights. How good that he did not stay "at home" "with himself" the whole time, like a dull, pampered loafer! He was beside himself – and what surprises he finds there! What untried terrors! What happiness even in weariness, in the old illness, in the convalescent's relapses. . . . There is wisdom, practical wisdom in it, when over a long period of time even health itself is administered only in small doses.[50]

Administering an ethics of small doses, the text embraces even the positivity of health as discreet apportionment, as the *Mitteilung*, the imparting that separates and returns only in small measure, like interest drawn from years of terrific severity. When the free spirit arrives at this point of wisdom, it will have accomplished a history of breaking away. The free spirit offers a fiction with which Nietzsche pumps the impoverished history of friendship. A design for the future, this fictional supply of spirit helps Nietzsche "to cure and restore" himself.[51] "I invented when I needed them, the 'free spirits' too, to whom the heavyhearted-stouthearted [*schwermütig-mutig*] book with the title *Human, All Too Human* is dedicated. There are no such 'free spirits,' were none – but, as I said, I needed their company at the time, to be of good cheer in the midst of bad things (illness, isolation, foreignness, sloth, inactivity); as brave fellows and specters to chat and laugh with, when one feels like chatting and laughing, and whom one sends to hell when they get boring – as reparation for lacking friends."[52] These spirits are set as the true addressees of the work that has borne the other, troubled and more referentially anchored dedication; they not only contour the future friend, they already dwell in Nietzsche, taking responsibility for an "unsuspected pregnancy." The future, the friend, and pregnancy start showing after the experience of separation: "It may be conjectured that the decisive event for a spirit in whom the type of the 'free spirit' is one day to ripen to sweet perfection has been a great separation [*Loslösung*]."[53] At this point the narrative voice has itself passed into a spirit who bears the imprint and seed of the free spirit. Pregnant with this other, the spirit roams, evicted and alienated, crossing deserts, seeking and probing. The free spirit grows into becoming and nomad thought: "Behind his ranging activity (for he is journeying restlessly and aimlessly, as in a desert) stands the question mark of an ever more dangerous curiosity."[54]

As the mutating free spirit evolves, we learn that its history begins where others (Hegelian and Goethean others) end, arrive. The Nietzschean spirit, coming from the other end of Hegelian spirit, originates in the phrase universe of reason and obligation. Its history shows obligation to come first; that is, it departs from the established priority of an ethical bind that must first be loosened. First, the law and its prohibitions, followed by a state of savagery, transgression, a thicket of sensation. The unrelenting sense and regimen of obligation belong to youth, to the sublimity, perhaps simplicity of youth. The decisive event of a great separation describes the drama of a bond that cuts. Nietzsche goes to the heart of a bond that can "almost" not be torn, that of obligation. The bond, loosened by traumatic separation, comes suddenly, "like the shock of an earthquake." Commanded by a voice, it is steered by an imperative. Unlike the Kantian version but every bit as prescriptive, this voice seduces *away* from the obligatory realm:

> It may be conjectured that the decisive event for a spirit in whom the type of the "free spirit" is one day to ripen to sweet perfection has been a *great separation*, and that before it, he was probably all the more bound a spirit. . . . What binds most firmly? Which cords can almost not be torn? With men of a high and select type, it will be their obligations: that awe which befits the young, their diffidence and delicacy before all that is time-honored and dignified, their gratitude for the ground out of which they grew, for the hand that led them, for the shrine where they learned to worship – their own highest moments will bind them most firmly and oblige them most lastingly. For such bound people the greatest separation comes suddenly, like the shock of an earthquake: all at once the young soul is devastated, torn loose, torn out – it itself does not know what is happening. An urge, a pressure governs it, mastering the soul like a command: the will and wish awaken to go away, anywhere, at any cost: a violent, dangerous curiosity for an undiscovered world flames up and flickers in all the senses. "Better to die than to live *here*," so sounds the imperious and seductive voice. And this "here," this "at home" is everything which it had loved until then! A sudden horror and suspicion of that which it loved; a lightning flash of contempt toward that which was its "obligation"; a rebellious, despotic, volcanically jolting desire to roam abroad, to become alienated, cool, sober, icy: a hatred of love, perhaps a desecratory reaching and glancing *backward*, to where it had until then worshipped and loved; perhaps a blush of shame at its most recent act, and at the same time, jubilation *that* it was done; a drunken, inner, jubilant shudder, which betrays a victory – a victory? over what? over whom? a puzzling, questioning, questionable victory, but the *first* victory nevertheless: such bad and painful things are part of the history of the great separation. It is also a disease that can destroy man, this first outburst of strength and will to self-determination, self-valorization, this will to free will: and how much disease is expressed by the wild attempts and peculiarities with which the freed man, the separated man, now tries to prove his rule over things! he wanders about savagely with an unsatisfied lust; his booty must atone for the dangerous tension of his pride; he rips apart what attracts him [er zerreisst, was ihn reizt].[55]

In this rendering or reversioning, the experimental disposition comes about traumatically, accompanied by the shock of loss, the unavoidable residue of which creates an expanse of anxious ambivalence. Values turn in on themselves and pivot on undecidable qualities, the distress of split attributes. Glancing backward invites a "desecratory" remembrance, love turns to hatred, worshipful adherence to shame, obligation to disgust. And so on. One is exposed to the severe regions of ambivalence, the unsteadiness of a ground that can no longer hold the illusory conciliations of blind existence.

Henceforth one is on one's own, trying and proving, ripping into the very thing that soothes and attracts, caught in the undecidable border areas of health and disease. The release into more autonomous playing fields is, Nietzsche writes, "also a disease" – it can destroy a man. The excess and advent of freedom does not round itself out on the side of health. The separated, freed being is condemned to the solitary spheres of a perpetual proving grounds. Unavoidably, desire rules these grounds, which is to say that an economy built on the missing other, a stressful borrowing system, overtakes the being who has accomplished separation. Surviving the hardest test, this being now needs the unending compensations of contest and rupture.

In partial compensation for the excruciating pain and mystery of separation, the one who has cut loose finds some solace in an impossible operation: that of converting the extreme particularizations of wounded singularity into generality. The free spirit ends it all by generalizing his case, as if capable of offering a cut or rendering a decision: "'As it happened to me,'" the story goes, "'so must it happen to everyone in whom a task wants to take form and 'come into the world.'"[56]

- • • •
- •
- • "No tests!"
- • Pepper, in the film *What a Woman*
  (1943)

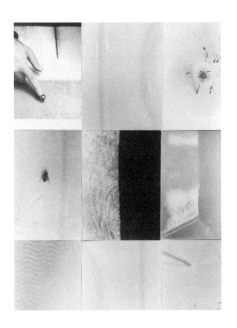

Notes

Part 1. Proving Grounds

Epigraphs: Emerson, *Diary,* 1852. Benjamin, *One Way Street* (London: New Left Books, 1979), 158. Acker, *My Mother: Demonology* (New York: Pantheon, 1993).

1. Immanuel Kant, "On the Miscarriage of All Philosophical Trials in Theodicy," in *Religion and Rational Theology* (Cambridge: Cambridge University Press, 1996), translated and edited by Allen W. Wood and George Di Giovanni, 24–37, "Über das Mißlingen aller philosophischen Versuche in der Theodizee," in *Immanuel Kant Werkausgabe XI: Schriften zur Anthropologie, Geschichtsphilosophie, Politik und Pädagogik I* (Frankfurt: Suhrkamp, 1981), edited by Wilhelm Weischedel, 105–24, which begins by affirming tests within tests when stating that "the human being is justified, as rational, in testing all claims, all doctrines which impose respect upon him, before he submits himself to them, so that this respect may be sincere and not feigned" (24).

2. Hannah Arendt understands the camps in these terms as well, as "laboratories in which the fundamental belief of totalitarianism that everything is possible is being verified. Compared with this, all other experiments are secondary in importance." *The Origins of Totalitarianism* (Cleveland: Meridian Books, 1958), 437. Consider also her assertion that what is practiced there constitutes the "testing ground in which [ideological indoctrination] must prove itself" whereas the camps themselves are "supposed to furnish the 'theoretical' verification of the ideology" (438). They also "serve the ghastly experiment of eliminating, under scientifically controlled conditions, spontaneity itself as an expression of human behavior" (438). The camps form the center of "the experiment of total domination" (438). However, Arendt does not interrogate what it is that made this experimental turn possible. In *Ce qui reste d'Auschwitz: L'archive et le témoin Homo Sacer III* (Paris, Editions Payot & Rivages, 1999), translated by Pierre Alferi, Giorgio Agamben considers experimentation in the camps and on U.S. prisoners in terms of the suspension of legal rights.

3. Friedrich Nietzsche, *The Gay Science, Die Fröhliche Wissenschaft,* KSA (Berlin, New York: de Gruyter, 1988), edited by Giorgio Colli and Mazzino Montinari, 384:

"Vielleicht ist sie [die Wissenschaft] jetzt noch bekannter wegen ihrer Kraft, den Menschen um seine Freuden zu bringen, und ihn kälter, statuenhafter, stoischer zu machen." Translated with commentary by Walter Kaufmann (New York: Vintage Books, 1974).

4. Edmund Husserl, "The positivistic reduction of the idea of science. The 'crisis' of science as the loss of its meaning for life," §2, in *The Crisis of European Sciences and Transcendental Phenomenology* (Evanston: Northwestern University Press, 1970), translated by David Carr, 5.

5. See Jacques Derrida, *Mémoires: For Paul de Man* (New York: Columbia University Press, 1986) translated by Cecile Lindsay, Jonathan Culler, and Eduardo Cadava, edited by Avital Ronell and Eduardo Cadava.

6. *Jacques Lacan, The Ethics of Psychoanalysis, The Seminar Book VII, 1959–1960* (New York: W. W. Norton, 1992), edited by Jacques-Alain Miller, translated by Dennis Porter.

7. Husserl, *Crisis*, 56.

8. Ibid.

9. Ibid.

10. Ibid.

11. Ibid.

12. Ibid., 57.

13. Ibid.

14. Consider in this light what Derrida states in *Aporias:* "In order to be responsible and truly decisive, a decision should not limit itself to putting into operation a determinable or determining knowledge, the consequence of some preestablished order. . . . One must avoid good conscience at all costs." *Aporias: Dying – Awaiting (One Another at) the "Limits of Truth"* (Stanford: Stanford University Press, 1993), translated by Thomas Dutoit, 8.

15. Ibid., 24.

16. There are too few activists but there are some, such as Steve Potter's team at the Laboratory for Neuroengineering, shared by Emory University and Georgia Tech. Potter's robotic creations – for instance, the Hybrot, a machine controlled by rat neurons sealed in a patented dish spiked with micro-electrodes – have become an object of desire of the U.S. military and Department of Defense, with which Potter refuses to deal. For a succinct review of further listings, see Erik Baard, "Some Scientists Refuse to Get Paid for Killer Ideas" in the *Village Voice*, 10–16 September 2003, 39–43.

17. The repression of the destructive edges of irony in the works of Szondi and Booth is one of the concerns of Paul de Man in "The Concept of Irony," in *Aesthetic Ideology* (Minneapolis: University of Minnesota Press, 1996), edited by Andrzej Warminski.

18. Edmund Husserl, "The Vienna Lecture," in *Crisis*, 297.

19. See Martin Heidegger's discussion of this utterance in *What Is Called Thinking?* (New York: Harper & Row, 1968), edited by Ruth Nanda Anshen, 51ff. *Was Heisst Denken?* (Tübingen: Max Niemeyer Verlag, 1954).

20. Ibid., 297.

21. Jacques Derrida, "Interpretations at War," *New Literary History* 22.1 (Winter 1991): 56.

22. Cohen after Derrida, "Interpretations," 56.

23. Ibid., 57.

24. Ibid.

25. Ibid.

26. Ibid., 58.

27. Ibid.

28. Ibid.

29. Ibid.

30. Ibid., 59.

31. Ibid.

32. *Daubert v. Merrell Dow Pharmaceuticals, Inc.,* 509 U.S. 579 (1993). Let us situate the cases in question. *Frye v. United States,* 293 F. 1013, 1014 (D.C. Cir. 1923) held, in the context of a case involving the admissibility of opinion evidence based upon use of a precursor of the polygraph, that scientific evidence would be admissible only after the thing from which the deduction is made had been sufficiently established to have gained general acceptance in the particular field in which it belongs. This decision was the birth of what ultimately became known alternatively as the *Frye* test or the general acceptance test. While ignored initially by other courts, the *Frye* test would, by the end of the 1990s, become the majority test for the admissibility of novel scientific evidence. As for *Daubert v. Merrell Dow Pharmaceuticals, Inc.,* based upon relevant reviews of extensive published scientific literature, it originated in a famous case of birth defects. Petitioners, two minor children and their parents, alleged in their suit against respondent that the children's serious birth defects had been caused by the mothers' prenatal ingestion of Bendectin, a prescription drug marketed by respondent. I would like to thank Antje Pfann-kuchen for her help in gathering the research materials that describe these cases.

33. *Frye v. United States,* 293 F.1013 (D.C. Cir. 1923).

34. Paul C. Giannelli, "Forensic Science: Frye, Daubert, and the Federal Rules," *Criminal Law Bulletin,* vol. 29, 428 (1993).

35. Black, Ayala, Saffran-Brinks, "Science and Law in the Wake of Daubert: A New Search for Scientific Knowledge," *Texas Law Review* 72.4 (March 1994): 715, 745. See also Edward J. Imwinkelried, "The Daubert Decision, Frye Is Dead: Long Live the Federal Rules of Evidence," *Trial,* September 1993, 60, 61.

36. Ibid.

37. This feature of facts was noted time and again by Goethe when conducting his scientific experiments.

38. Adina Schwartz, "A 'Dogma of Empiricism' Revisited: *Daubert v. Merrell Dow Pharmaceuticals, Inc.* and the Need to Resurrect the Philosophical Insight of *Frye v. United States,*" *Harvard Journal of Law & Technology* 10.2 (Winter 1997): 237.

39. Ibid., 154.

40. Ibid.

41. Interestingly, neither Schwartz nor the courts revert to more recent theories linking testing with evidentiary materials. Clark Glymour's *Theory and Evidence* (Princeton: Princeton University Press, 1980), a key work on testing and relevant evidence, investigates the methodology of theory testing and points out the flaws in hypothetico-deductivism as well as Bayesianism. For meta-rhetorical considerations of evidence and probability, see Ruediger Campe, *Das Spiel der Wahrscheinlichkeit: Literatur und Berechnung zwischen Pascal und Kleist* (Göttingen: Wallstein, 2002).

42. See Karl R. Popper, *Conjectures and Refutations: The Growth of Scientific Knowledge* (New York: Basic Books, 1965).

43. Ibid., 165.

44. Ibid., 133.

45. Karl R. Popper, "Science: Conjectures and Refutations," in *Conjectures and Refutations,* 33–37.

46. Schwartz, "Dogma," 165.

47. Karl R. Popper, *The Logic of Scientific Discovery* (New York: Harper & Row, 1968), 19.

48. Schwartz, "Dogma," 166.

49. Ibid.

50. Popper, *Conjectures,* 33, note 49.

51. Schwartz, "Dogma," 166.

52. Ibid., 155.

53. Ibid., 152.

54. Ibid., 153.

55. Carl G. Hempel, "Empiricist Criteria of Cognitive Significance: Problems and Changes," in *Aspects of Scientific Explanation, and Other Essays in the Philosophy of Science* (New York: Free Press, 1965), cited in Schwartz, "Dogma," 168.

56. Schwartz, "Dogma," 171.

57. Imre Lakatos, "Falsification and the Methodology of Scientific Research Programmes," in *Can Theories Be Refuted?* (Dordrecht-Holland, Boston: D. Reidel, 1976), edited by Sandra G. Harding, 205–59; Hilary Putnam, "The 'Corroboration' of Theories," in *Mathematics, Matter, and Method,* Philosophical Papers, volume 1 (Cambridge: Cambridge University Press, 1979), 255–58. Cited in Schwartz, "Dogma," 152, whose view is largely aligned with that of Lakatos.

58. A Letter from Albert Einstein, 1935, Appendix 12, "The Experiment of Einstein, Podolsky, and Rosen," in Karl R. Popper, *The Logic of Scientific Discovery* (London: Routledge, 1997).

59. Popper, *Logic,* 16.

60. Ibid., 12–13.

61. Ibid., 17.

62. Ibid., 27.

63. Ibid.

64. See his "Testability and Meaning," *Philosophy of Science* 3 (1936), especially 427.

65. Popper, *Logic,* 27.

66. Ibid.

67. Ibid., 252.

68. Ibid., 251.

69. Ibid.

70. Ibid., 252.

71. Ibid., 152.

72. Ibid., 278.

73. Ibid.

74. See especially Francis Bacon, *Novum Organum,* I, XXVI–XXXIII.

75. Discussed in Popper, *Logic,* 279. See also Mary Poovey on Bacon and experimentation in *A History of the Modern Fact: Problems of Knowledge in the Sciences of Wealth and Society* (Chicago: University of Chicago Press, 1998), 98ff.

76. Ibid.

77. Ibid.

78. Ibid., 280.

79. Ibid.

80. Ibid., 280–81.

81. Hans-Jörg Rheinberger, "Experiment, Difference, and Writing: Tracing Protein Synthesis," *Studies in History and Philosophy of Science* 23, no. 2 (1992): 305–31, 330. This argument is extended in his book *Experiment, Differenz, Schrift* (Marburg: Basiliskenpresse, 1992).

82. Rheinberger, "Difference," 310.

83. Ibid.

84. Ibid.

85. Ibid.

86. Gaston Bachelard, *La formation de l'esprit scientifique* (1938; reprint Paris: Vrin, 1969), 13.

87. (Boston: Beacon Press, 1984), 6.

88. Ibid.

89. Rheinberger, "Difference," 309.

90. Jacques Derrida, "La Différance," in *Marges de la philosophie* (Paris: Minuit, 1972), 7.

91. Rheinberger, "Difference," 319.

92. Jacques Derrida, *Psyché: Inventions de l'autre* (Paris: Gallilée 1987).

93. Rheinberger, "Difference," 321.

94. Ibid.

95. Ibid.

96. George Kubler, *The Shape of Time: Remarks on the History of Things* (New Haven: Yale University Press, 1962), 125.

97. Rheinberger, "Difference," 323, footnote 57: "In the everyday language of the laboratory scientist the 'result' is that unit with which the dynamics of an experimental system are measured. The 'result' is not a final scientific statement. . . ."

98. Ibid., 323.

99. Ibid.

100. Ibid.

101. Ibid., 329–30.

102. Ibid.

103. Ibid., 319.

104. François Jacob, *The Statue Within* (New York: Basic Books, 1988), 279.

105. Johann Wolfgang von Goethe, "The Experiment as Mediator between Object and Subject," in Johann Wolfgang von Goethe, *Scientific Studies* (New York: Suhrkamp, 1988), edited and translated by Douglas Miller, 17.

106. Rheinberger, "Difference," 319. On the problem of evidence in rhetoric and science, see Ruediger Campe, *Wahrscheinlichkeit*.

107. Bruno Latour, "The Force and Reason of Experiment," in *Experimental Enquiries* (Dordrecht: Kluwer, 1990), edited by Homer le Grand, 65.

108. Rheinberger, "Difference," 323.

109. Andrew Hodges, *Alan Turing: The Enigma* (New York: Simon and Schuster, 1983), 176. I wish to thank Jean Lasségue of the CNRS, Paris, for sharing with me his research and far-reaching papers on Turing, including his work on testing and sexual difference.

110. See especially Alan Turing, "Intelligent Machinery: A Heretical Theory," in Sara Stoney Turing, *Alan M. Turing* (Cambridge: W. Heffer & Sons, 1959).

111. The paper, in which Turing defines his logical machine, in fact appeared in *Proceedings of the London Mathematics Society* (London: C. F. Hodgson, 1936), 2d ser., 42:230–65.

112. Hugh Whitemore, *Breaking the Code* (Oxford: Amber Lane Press: 1987), 33.

113. See *Alan M. Turing: Intelligence Service, Schriften,* edited and introduced by Bernhard Dotzler and Friedrich Kittler (Berlin: Brinkmann & Bose, 1987); also see Friedrich Kittler, "Die künstliche Intelligenz des Weltkriegs: Alan Turing," in *Arsenale der Seele: Literatur- und Medien-Analysen* (München: Fink, 1989), edited by Friedrich Kittler and Georg Christoph Tholen, 187–202.

114. Hodges, *Turing,* 464. See also Adrian MacKenzie's "Undecidability: The History and Time of the Universal Turing Machine," *Configurations* (1997): 359–79.

115. Hodges, *Turing,* 473.

116. I suggest a more substantial understanding of the event or catastrophe at the root of scientific discovery in *The Telephone Book: Technology, Schizophrenia, Electric Speech* (Lincoln: University of Nebraska Press, 1989).

117. Whitemore, *Code,* 50.

118. See in particular the works of Nicolas Abraham, Maria Torok, Jacques Derrida, Laurence Rickels, Werner Hamacher, and Nicolas Rand on the fate of cryptonymy in literature, psychoanalysis, and philosophy.

119. Douglas Hofstadler, *Gödel, Escher, Bach: An Eternal Golden Braid* (N.Y.: Vintage Books, 1980), 411.

120. Hodges, *Turing,* 534.

121. Jeremy Bernstein, *The Analytic Engine: Computers, Past, Present, and Future* (New York: Random House, 1964), 101.

122. Alan Turing, "Computing Machinery and Intelligence," *Mind* 49 (1950): 433–60, later published under the title "Can a Machine Think?" in *The World of Mathematics,* volume 4 (New York: Simon & Schuster, 1956), edited by James R. Newman, 2099–2123.

Part 2. Trial Runs

1. John Llewelyn, "Amen," in *Ethics as First Philosophy: The Significance of Emmanuel Levinas for Philosophy, Literature, and Religion,* edited by Adrian T. Peperzak (New York: Routledge, 1995). Interview in Salomon Malka, *Lire Lévinas* (Paris: Cerf, 1984), 108.

2. In *Return to Freud: Jacques Lacan's Dislocation of Psychoanalysis* (Cambridge: Cambridge University Press, 1991), translated by Michael Levine, Samuel Weber organizes his reflections around the concept of experimentation. Lacan's laboratory is linked to "the laboratories of experimental science" and shown to be, in comparison, "as unstable as the margins of a text: not entirely inchoate, to be sure, but also never completely under his control" (xiii). While no scientific lab can be said to be fully under control, the rhetorical ploy is apt. Psychoanalysis belongs to the "epistemic thing" subsumed under the notion of experiment. (It is nearly amusing to note that narrow-minded opponents of psychoanalysis oppose it to science precisely where it shares structures of risk-taking, epistemological uncertainty, and the community of trials with scientific endeavor.) Weber continues: "It is this instability that distinguishes what Lacan calls 'l'expérience psychanalytique' – a phrase which *also* means psychoanalytical *experiment* – from its scientific homonym. To make one's way under conditions that can never be entirely controlled is a part of what constitutes psychoanalytic truth." Historically, beginning with Goethe and ranging to Hans-Jörg Rheinberger, the lab is no longer the stable entity that can duck the tendencies of sci fi or psy fi annexations of its functional purpose.

3. *Standard Edition of the Complete Works of Sigmund Freud* (London: Hogarth Press and the Institute of Psycho-Analysis, 1953–1974), VII, 7.

4. Ibid., 10.

5. Ibid.

6. For Karl Popper, Freud is a pseudo-scientist to the extent that nothing can disprove his claims; see note 27.

7. Freud, *S.E.* 1933, 22:7–30.

8. Freud, *S.E.* 1915, 14:265–66.

9. Adolf Grünbaum, "Retrospective Versus Prospective Testing of Aetiological Hypotheses in Freudian Theory," in *Testing Scientific Theories* (Minneapolis: University of Minnesota Press, 1983), edited by John Earman, 323.

10. Freud, *S.E.* 1915, 14:265–66.

11. Ibid., 265.

12. Grünbaum, *Testing,* 321.

13. Ibid., 325.

14. Ibid.

15. Ibid.

16. Ibid., 341.

17. The heuristic and probative dimension of Freud's work, with special attention to the Rat Man case, is discussed by Adolf Grünbaum in "Retrospective Versus Prospective Testing of Aetiological Hypotheses in Freudian Theory," in *Testing Scientific Theories*, 315–49, and Paul E. Meehl, "Subjectivity in Psychoanalytic Inference: The Nagging Persistence of Wilhelm Fliess's Achensee Question," ibid., 349–411. Grünbaum writes: "The strategy involved in the Rat Man case is essentially the same as a strategy very frequently used in testing physical theories." Glymour himself had pointed out that the major argument of this case is similar to the one underlying Book III of Newton's *Principia*.

18. I analyze these sessions more closely in "The Sujet Suppositaire," in *Finitude's Score: Essays toward the End of the Millennium* (Lincoln: University of Nebraska Press: 1994), 105–29.

19. Freud, *S.E.* 14:243.

20. Ibid.

21. Ibid., 258.

22. Ibid., 244.

23. Freud, *S.E.* 23:198.

24. "Mourning and Melancholia," in Freud, *S.E.* 14:244.

25. Ibid., 254.

26. Ibid., 233.

27. That Freud submitted his work to relentless testing hardly needs to be restated, though the testability of his observations has of course been famously contested. Popper views Freud as a pseudo-scientist since nothing can disprove his claims; even resistance is said to prove the hypothesis, if not the thesis, he puts forward. This tendency of psychoanalysis to find its own truth, to "recognize" itself as Derrida later says, pointing to the prearranged and proper place of the phallus in Lacan, poses significant problems for those who assert a science free of its pregivenness or science without compromising presuppositions. Yet Grünbaum makes a reasonable argument for the probative role of tests, clinical testability, and examples of falsifiability in the work of Freud. One such example is "A Case of Paranoia Running Counter to the Psychoanalytic Theory of the Disease" (Freud, *S.E.* 1933, 22:7–30); another example is furnished by the lecture "Revision of the Theory of Dreams" (Freud, *S.E.* 1915, 14:265–66). Grünbaum shows that "the psy-

choanalytic aetiology of paranoia is empirically falsifiable (disconfirmable) *and* that Freud explicitly recognized it (Grünbaum, *Testing,* 323).

28. Franz Kafka, "Die Prüfung," in *Kritische Kafka-Ausgabe: Nachgelassene Schriften und Fragmente II* (Frankfurt am Main: S. Fischer Verlag, 1992), 327; "The Test," in *Description of a Struggle* (New York: Schocken Books, 1958), 207.

29. "Die Prüfung," 328.

30. "The Test," 208.

31. Ibid., 209.

32. Ibid.; "Die Prüfung," 329.

33. "Die Prüfung," 327.

34. "The Test," 207.

35. I have offered a reading of this poem in relation to the problem of cognitive deficit in *Stupidity* (Urbana: University of Illinois Press, 2002), 7–10. It is interesting to note that, in *The Origin of the Art Work,* Hölderlin is viewed throughout by Heidegger as a test to be stood for historical destiny.

36. Franz Kafka, *Wedding Preparations in the Country and Other Posthumous Writings,* with notes by Max Brod (London: Secker and Warburg, 1954), 223. These texts and notes open the dossier on a facet of stupidity that I had not considered before and want to explore here in terms of the largely conceptual pressures of testing. The reader will forgive me if I have not finished with Stupidity, yes?

37. Ibid., 218.

38. Ibid.

39. Ibid.

40. Ibid.

41. Ibid.

42. Ibid.

43. Ibid., 219.

44. Ibid.

45. Ibid.

46. Ibid.

47. Friedrich Nietzsche, *Beyond Good and Evil: Prelude to a Philosophy of the Future* (Cambridge: Cambridge University Press, 1990), translated by R. G. Hollingdale, §9.

48. Page duBois, *Torture and Truth* (New York: Routledge, 1991), 25.

49. Ibid., 35.

50. *Oedipus at Colonus,* 834–35. Cited in duBois, *Torture,* 24.

51. DuBois, *Torture,* 24.

52. For more on torture, see Romuald Turasiewicz, *De servis testibus in Atheniensium iudiciis* (Wroclaw: Zaklad Narodowy, 1963).

53. DuBois, *Torture*, 25.

54. Ibid., 36.

55. Ibid., cited by duBois as legal expert.

56. Ibid., 37.

57. See Douglas M. MacDowell, *The Law in Classical Athens* (London: Thames and Hudson, 1978), 8, cited in duBois, *Torture*, 37.

58. Demosthenes 30.37, cited in duBois, *Torture*, 49–50.

59. Ibid., 69.

60. Aristotle, *Politics* 1255b; see duBois's discussion of this section, *Torture*, 66.

61. Aristotle, *Rhetoric* 1376b–1377a, cited in duBois, *Torture*, 67.

62. Herodotus, *Histories* 5.35, cited in duBois, *Torture*, 70.

63. DuBois, *Torture*, 112.

64. Cited in duBois, *Torture*, 113.

65. Ibid., 115.

66. Ibid.

67. Ibid.

68. These Heideggerian titles have been and can be translated as *The Question of Being* and *What Is Called Thinking?* Heidegger stresses the question over any eventual answer. We need to stay with the question, he urges. An answer can too readily make disappear the question to which we must attune ourselves.

69. See in particular Jessica Mitford's 1973 exposé *Kind and Usual Punishment: The Prison Business* (New York: Alfred A. Knopf, 1973) and Allen Hornblum's *Acres of Skin: Human Experiments at Holmesburg Prison: A True Story of Abuse and Exploitation in the Name of Medical Science* (New York: Routledge, 1998). The film *Miss Evers' Boys* (television, 1997, director: Joseph Sargent) treats the infamous Tuskegee syphilis study.

70. In *Negotiations: 1972–1990* (New York: Columbia University Press, 1995), 3.

71. Steven Shapin and Simon Schaffer, *Leviathan and the Air-Pump: Hobbes, Boyle, and the Experimental Life* (Princeton: Princeton University Press, 1985), 20.

72. Ibid., 24.

73. Ibid.

74. Charles Coulston Gillispie, *The Edge of Objectivity: An Essay in the History of Scientific Ideas* (Princeton: Princeton University Press, 1960), 103.

75. Cited in ibid., 59.

76. Ibid., 57.

77. Shapin and Schaffer, *Air-Pump*, 59.

78. Ibid., 18. In this context, see also Svetlana Alpers, *The Art of Describing: Dutch Art in the Seventeenth Century* (London: John Murray, 1983), which examines the critical convergences of universal language projects, the experimental program in science, and painting in the Netherlands and England.

79. Shapin and Schaffer, *Air-Pump*, 158.

80. Ibid.

81. Ibid.

82. Ibid., 159.

83. Ibid., 163. See also Lisa Jardine, *Francis Bacon: Discovery and the Art of Discourse* (Cambridge: Cambridge University Press, 1974), and Karl R. Wallace, *Francis Bacon on Communication and Rhetoric* (Chapel Hill: University of North Carolina Press, 1943). For a contemporary review of the stakes of the experimental narrative, see Friedrich Ulfers, "Von der Skepsis zur Utopie: Musils Idee des 'Essayismus'" in *Skeptizismus und literarische Imagination,* edited by Bernd Hüppauf und Klaus Vieweg (Frankfurt am Main: Wilhelm Fink Verlag, 2003), 210–12, where testing and the essay form are brought into conjunction and the present is posited by Musil as sheer hypothesis.

84. Shapin and Schaffer, *Air-Pump*, 24.

85. Ibid. See "Understanding Experiment," 19ff.

86. See the discussion in ibid., 19–20.

87. Ibid., 20.

88. Ibid., 25.

89. See "Prototype .09," below.

90. A. Rupert Hall, *From Galileo to Newton* (New York: Dover Publications, 1981), 254, and idem, *The Revolution in Science, 1500–1750* (London: Longman, 1983), 262.

91. Hall, *Galileo,* 29.

92. See in particular Ian Hacking, *The Emergence of Probability: A Philosophical Study of Early Ideas about Probability, Induction, and Statistical Inference* (London: Cambridge University Press, 1975), and Barbara Shapiro, *Probability and Certainty in Seventeenth-Century England: A Study of the Relationships between Natural Science, Religion, History, Law, and Literature* (Princeton: Princeton University Press, 1983).

93. Shapin and Schaffer, *Air-Pump*, 23.

94. For more traction on Nietzsche's "noble traitor," see Part 6: "Testing Your Love, or: Breaking Up," below.

95. "Two Essays on the Unsuccessfulness of Experiments," in *The Works of the Honourable Robert Boyle* (London: J & F Rivington, 1772), edited by Thomas Birch, vol. 1 (1661), 318–53.

96. Shapin and Schaffer, *Air-Pump*, 64.

97. Ibid., 65.

98. Cf. ibid.

99. Ibid.; also Robert Boyle, "Proemial Essay," 301–307, 300; cf. idem, "Sceptical Chymist," 469–70, in Boyle, *Works*.

100. Shapin and Schaffer, *Air-Pump*, 66.

101. Ibid.; Boyle, "Proemial Essay," 318, 304. See also Hans Aarsleff, *From Locke to Saussure: Essays on the Study of Language and Intellectual History* (London: Athlone Press, 1982), 225–77.

102. Boyle, "Proemial Essay," cited in Shapin and Schaffer, *Air-Pump*, 67; on "wary and diffident expressions," see the discussion of Boyle's text, "New Experiments," 68ff.

103. See the discussion of "Some Specimens of an Attempt to make Chymical Experiments Useful," in Shapin and Schaffer, *Air-Pump*, 68.

104. Cited in ibid.

105. Ibid., 74.

106. Ibid.

107. In significant articles devoted to Lyotard, Rodolphe Gasché defines the phrase event by distinguishing the phrase from a proposition: "Phrases, first and foremost, are occurrences. They are events before they are beholden to specific regimens, such as, for instance, the logical and cognitive regimen to which propositions belong." "The Sublime, Ontologically Speaking," in *Yale French Studies 99: Jean-François Lyotard: Time and Judgment* (New Haven: Yale University, 2001), edited by Robert Harvey and Lawrence R. Schehr, 118.

108. Jean-François Lyotard, *The Differend: Phrases in Dispute* (Minneapolis: University of Minnesota Press, 1988), translated by Georges Van Den Abbeele, 72; see also Gasché's discussion of this statement, *Yale French Studies 99*, 139.

109. Rodolphe Gasché, "Saving the Honor of Thinking: On Jean-François Lyotard," *Parallax* 6.4 (2000): 135.

110. Lyotard, *Differend*, 8.

111. Ibid.

112. Ibid.

113. See Gasché's discussion of *logon didonai* in *Saving the Honor*, 135ff.

114. Ibid., 138.

115. Lyotard, *Differend*, 25–26.

116. Ibid.; see also Gasché's discussion along these lines in *Saving the Honor*. However, I must add a word of caution. If we allowed the weaker "argument" to prevail in the *stronger* sense, then testimonial arbitration would not pose such a consternating problem – the inability in some cases of the weak to produce argument or admissible language requires attentive analysis here.

117. Derrida works with the relationship of gravity, weighing, and thinking in *Béliers: Le dialogue ininterrompu: entre deux infinis, le poème:* "... si le commerce du remerciement risque toujours de rester une compensation, nous avons, dans nos langues latines, cette amitié entre penser et peser (*pensare*), entre la pensée et la gravité. Entre la pensée et la portée. D'où l'*examen*. Le poids d'une pensée appelle et s'appelle toujours l'*examen* . . ." (Paris: Galilée, 2003), 28–29.

A Heideggerian consideration of the relation of weighing to testing is offered by Michiko Tsushima: "Being tested means being brought forward, scrutinized, and examined. Whatever is being tested is put at risk. That is to say, it risks its secret. So testing entails exposing the secret while keeping it. . . . To consider the testing of language in this sense, one could say that the secret of language is exposed and put at stake. . . . Testing marks the site in which the relation between man and Being, which reveals itself as language, is ceaselessly put on trial, if you will, in its musical and 'theatrical' essence. . . . Heidegger holds that the thinker who is learning to think must 'think of testing the saying of reflective thinking.' And he himself attempts to 'test the saying of reflective thinking.' 'A Dialogue on Language' clearly reveals this." *The Space of Vacillation: The Experience of Language in Beckett, Blanchot, and Heidegger* (Bern, Switzerland: Peter Lang, 2003), 194–95.

118. See Lyotard, *Differend*, 70.

119. Gasché, *Saving the Honor*, 134.

120. Ibid.

121. Ibid., 139.

122. Ibid.

123. Lyotard, *Differend*, 5.

124. Ibid.; see also Gasché, *Saving the Honor*, 139–40.

125. Jean-François Lyotard, *The Inhuman: Reflections on Time* (Stanford: Stanford University Press, 1991), translated by Geoffrey Bennington and Rachel Bowlby, 202.

126. Gasché, *Saving the Honor*, 127.

127. Ibid.

128. Shoshana Felman and Dori Laub, M.D., *Testimony: Crises of Witnessing in*

Literature, Psychoanalysis, and History (New York: Routledge, 1992). See also Ulrich Baer's haunting discussions of medical testimony in *Spectral Evidence: The Photography of Trauma* (Cambridge: MIT Press, 2002).

129. The land of Descartes rather unavoidably has shown a receptivity to casting doubt on disaster-formation. Thus the best-selling *L'Effroyable Mensonge* by Guillaume Dasquié and Jean Guisnel (Paris: Découverte, 2002) put an undermining spin on the destruction of the World Trade Center. But dialectical turnovers being what they sometimes are, the so-called French have also put out the most compelling probes, setting up unavoidable question marks and in a certain unwearying way keeping the pain alive, on the agenda.

130. Jacques Derrida, *Demeure: Fiction and Testimony* (Stanford: Stanford University Press, 2000), translated by Elizabeth Rottenberg, 35. Compelled by a rhetoric of testing, Derrida also writes of the "test of the instant," "the linguistic test," and submits a number of hypotheses to the test in this work.

131. Ibid., 27.

132. Ibid., 27–28.

133. Ibid., 29.

134. Ibid., 30.

135. Maurice Blanchot, *The Step Not Beyond* (Albany: State University of New York Press, 1992), translated by Lycette Nelson, 76. See also Derrida's discussion of this passage in *Demeure*, 31 ff.

136. "The Mahayana Sutras," in Heinrich Demoulin, *Zen Buddhism: A History* (New York: Macmillan, 1974).

137. *Dropping Ashes on the Buddha: The Teaching of Zen Master Seung Sahn* (New York: Grove Press, 1976), edited by Stephen Mitchell, 134.

138. Maurice Blanchot, *Ecriture du Désastre* (Paris: Gallimard, 1980), 37; *The Writing of the Disaster* (Lincoln: University of Nebraska Press, 1986), translated by Ann Smock, 20. See also Christopher Fynsk's discussion of this passage in terms of the Heideggerian "es gibt" of Being.

139. See Christopher Fynsk's treatment of these questions in *Infant Figures: The Death of the "Infans" and Other Scenes of Origin* (Stanford: Stanford University Press, 2000).

140. Blanchot, *Désastre*, 43; *Disaster*, 24.

141. For a discussion of related forms of non-knowledge in Eastern and Western thought, see Keiji Nishitani, *Religion and Nothingness* (Berkeley: University of California Press, 1982), translated by Jan van Bragt, 162ff.

142. Oxford English Dictionary (Oxford: Oxford University Press, 2000–).

143. See Ruth Benedict, *The Chrysanthemum and the Sword* (Boston, Houghton Mifflin, 1946), xi, 246.

144. Ibid., 19.

145. Ibid., 258. See also the introduction to Hsing-hsiu, *Book of Serenity* (New York: Lindisfarne Press, 1990), translated and introduced by Thomas Cleary, ix–xli, and Koun Yamada, *Gateless Gate* (Tucson: University of Arizona Press, 1979), 93–169.

146. Benedict, *Chrysanthemum*, 258. Heinrich Dumoulin, *Zen Buddhism, a History: India and China with a New Supplement on the Northern School of Chinese Zen* (New York: Macmillan, 1994), translated by James W. Heisig and Paul Knitter.

147. Cited in Benedict, *Chrysanthemum*, 382.

148. Ibid.

149. Ibid.

150. Ibid., 259.

151. Ibid.

152. Ibid.

153. Ibid., 260.

154. Ibid.

155. Ibid.

156. Ibid.

157. While the contradictions and disputes between the two principal schools appear to be bound by a differend – the irreconcilable differences between "silent-illumination Zen" (*mokusho-zen*) and "kōan-gazing zen" (*kanna-zen*) cannot be resolved – it is perhaps of some consequence that each school also regarded the other as a genuine form of Zen Buddhism. Zen histories refer to documents that reveal the consistently friendly, cordial relations enjoyed by Hung-chi and Ta-hui. "When Hung-chih died in the monastery of Mount T'ien-t'ung, which through his persevering efforts had become one of the important centers of Zen Buddhist monasticism, Ta-hui hastened to attend the funeral rites of his deserving colleague, and we can be certain that Hung-chih would not have hesitated to show the same respects to Ta-hui." Ibid., 260.

158. Ibid., 262.

159. Ibid.

160. Martin Buber, *Werke III, Schriften zum Chassidismus* (Munich, Heidelberg: Kösel-Lambert Schneider, 1963), vol. 3 of the collected works, 993ff., also 883–94.

161. See his introduction to Daisetz Teitaro Suzuki's *Introduction to Zen Buddhism* (New York: Philosophical Library, 1949), also included in C. G. Jung, *Collected Works*, vol. 2 (London: Routledge and Kegan Paul, 1969), 538–57.

162. Zen Master Torei Enji, *The Discourse on the Inexhaustible Lamp of the Zen School* (Boston: C. E. Tuttle, 1996), with commentary by Master Daibi of Unkan, translated by Yoko Okuda, 254.

163. The advice comes from Chinese Zen Master Ta-hui: "The thousand and ten thousand doubts that well up in your breast are really only one doubt, all of them burst open when doubt is resolved in the kōan. As long as the kōan is not resolved, you must occupy yourself with it to the utmost. If you give up on your kōan and stir up another doubt about a word of scripture or about a sutra teaching or about a kōan of the ancients, or if you allow a doubt about worldly matters to come up – all this means to be joined to the evil spirit. You should not too easily agree with a kōan solution that you have discovered, nor should you think about it further and make distinctions. Fasten your attention to where discursive thinking cannot reach." Ibid., 257–58.

Part 3. On Passing the Test

Epigraphs: Nietzsche, *Beyond Good and Evil: Prelude to a Philosophy of the Future* (New York: Vintage Books, 1966), translated by Walter Kaufmann, §1. Bataille, *On Nietzsche* (New York: Paragon House, 1994), translated by Bruce Boone, xxii.

1. Friedrich Nietzsche, *Beyond Good and Evil,* §14.

2. Ibid., §42.

3. Ibid., §133.

4. Ibid., §210.

5. Ibid.

6. Ibid.

7. Jacques Derrida, *Negotiations: Interventions, and Interviews 1971–2000* (Stanford: Stanford University Press, 2002), edited by Elizabeth Rottenberg.

8. Ibid., 245.

9. Ibid., 253.

10. This is also a theme of a colloquium in Cerisy-la-Salle (2002) organized around the political thought of Derrida under the title "The Coming of Democracy (regarding Jacques Derrida)."

11. Derrida, *Negotiations,* 251.

12. Ibid.

13. Ibid.

14. Jacques Derrida, *The Ear of the Other: Otobiography, Transference, Translation* (Lincoln: University of Nebraska Press, 1985), translated by Peggy Kamuf and Avital Ronell.

15. Nietzsche, *Beyond Good and Evil,* §210.

16. Ibid., §211.

17. Ibid.

18. Ibid.

19. Ibid.

20. Ibid., §205.

21. Ibid., §24.

22. Ibid., §41.

23. Ibid.

24. Ibid.

25. Jacques Derrida, "Desistance," in Philippe Lacoue-Labarthe, *Typography: Mimesis, Philosophy, Politics* (Cambridge: Harvard University Press, 1989), edited by Christopher Fynsk, 41.

26. This view diverges from some of Nietzsche's earlier pronouncements on the nobility of overflow that marked, by means of a redescription of Aristotle's "great-souled man," the valorization of self-expenditure. For Nietzsche and for the Greeks, writes Babette E. Babich, "generosity and kindness are benedictions bestowed on others not in response to the imperatives of duty or as gifts in a structural economy of exchange. Rather, like a star's shining exuberance, like the sun dripping gold, the gold of light, sparkling reflection, of unreal shining glory, the greatness of will or benevolence cannot be withheld. The noble, great-souled individual is compelled to and is capable of an excess that makes its own measure." *Nietzsche's Philosophy of Science: Reflecting Science on the Ground and Art of Life* (Albany: SUNY Press, 1994), 178. Whoa! Hold your horses! Something has happened to Nietzsche that makes him want to rein in the unfettered drive. At this point the other Greek value, moderation, sets the bar and disrupts the unregulated flow of a self-offering that too soon turns into sacrifice.

27. See Paul Rabinow, *Making PCR: A Story of Biotechnology* (Chicago: University of Chicago Press, 1996).

28. Friedrich Nietzsche, *Jenseits von Gut und Böse,* KSA (Berlin: de Gruyter, 1988), edited by Giorgio Colli and Mazzino Montinari, §41.

29. Jacques Derrida, "The Law of Genre," *Glyph: Textual Studies* 7 (1980), translated by Avital Ronell, 202–29.

30. Nietzsche, *Beyond Good and Evil,* §42.

31. Ibid., Preface.

32. See Derrida's discussion of the "dangerous perhaps" in *Politics of Friendship* (London: Verso: 1997), translated by George Collins, 26–49.

33. Jacques Derrida, *Spurs: Nietzsche's Styles* (Chicago: University of Chicago Press, 1978), translated by Barbara Harlow.

34. Nietzsche, *Beyond Good and Evil*, §292.

Part 4. The Test Drive

Epigraph: William Gibson, *Neuromancer* (New York: Ace Books, 1984), 35.

1. "L'absence de l'oeuvre" is the formulation of Philippe Lacoue-Labarthe in *Le sujet de la philosophie* (Paris: Aubier-Flammarion, 1979), 178. In *The Infinite Conversation* (Minneapolis: University of Minnesota Press, 1993; translated by Susan Hanson), Maurice Blanchot writes repeatedly of Nietzsche's "broken work." I am also moving with the flow of Derrida's reading of Nietzsche's styles and signatures in his many works devoted to Friedrich Nietzsche. Most recently, for Derrida, when linked to the technological grid, "the name of Nietzsche could serve as an 'index' to a series of questions that have become all the more pressing since the end of the Cold War." *Negotiations: Interventions, and Interviews 1971–2001* (Stanford: Stanford University Press, 2002), translated by Elizabeth Rottenberg, 253.

2. *The Gay Science: With a Prelude in Rhymes and Appendix of Songs* (New York: Vintage Books, 1974), translated by Walter Kaufmann, 243. Contrary to scholarly habit, I have decided to quote from the most popular edition of *The Gay Science*, so that the reader can sing along.

3. One wonders why Kaufmann felt compelled to translate "fröhlich" as "gay" if the decision was clearly disturbing to him, as his introduction to the most available English edition of the work indicates. He could have kept it straight and settled down with "joyous" or, for that matter, "frolicking."

4. Nietzsche, *The Gay Science*, §345.

5. See Jacques Derrida, *Psyché: L'invention de l'autre* (Paris: Galilée, 1987).

6. Nietzsche, *The Gay Science*, §300.

7. Ibid., §337.

8. Ibid., §370.

9. Ibid., §343.

10. Ibid., §51.

11. Walter Kaufmann, *Nietzsche: Philosopher, Psychologist, Antichrist*, 4th edition (Princeton: Princeton University Press, 1974), 92.

12. Nietzsche, *The Gay Science*, §366.

13. Blanchot, *Infinite Conversation*, 32.

14. See Gilles Deleuze's discussion of the "test of the eternal return" (86) and his

working statement: "Subjecting truth to the test of the base, but also subjecting falsity of the test of the high: this is the really critical task and the only way of knowing where one is in relation to 'truth.' When someone asks 'what's the use of philosophy?' the reply must be aggressive, since the question tries to be ironic and caustic" (105–6). In *Nietzsche and Philosophy,* translated by Hugh Tomlinson (New York: Columbia University Press, 1983). Nietzsche links testing to willing and decline in several passages of his posthumous writings, especially in *Nachgelassene Fragmente,* Herbst 1885 bis Herbst 1887, KSA 12.62, KGW VIII–1.58; *Nachgelassene Fragmente,* Anfang 1888 bis Anfang Januar 1889, KSA 13.615, KGW VIII–3.425; *Kritische Studienausgabe,* Band 15, Chronik zu Nietzsches Leben Nizza, Oktober–Dezember 1887, Brief an Carl Fuchs.

15. For an aerial snapshot of his views of unlimited finity, see *The Deleuze Reader* (New York: Columbia University Press, 1993), edited by Constantin V. Boundas, 100.

16. I have further elaborated this aspect of testing with regard to virtual and other advanced as well as nano-technologies in *Finitude's Score: Essays toward the End of the Millennium* (Nebraska: University of Nebraska Press, 1994).

17. Nietzsche, *The Gay Science,* §357.

18. Ibid., §346.

19. Paul de Man, *Allegories of Reading: Figural Language in Rousseau, Nietzsche, Rilke, and Proust* (New Haven: Yale University Press, 1979), 82.

20. Søren Kierkegaard, *Fear and Trembling* (New York: Viking Penguin, 1985), translated by Alastair Hannay, 53.

21. I have written differently about Abraham, mostly from the point of view I impute to Isaac, whose sacrificial desire was cut off when, in silent complicity with his father's need, he was benched in the last minute. Abraham's passing of the test failed Isaac. I organized another dimension of these questions around a reading of Kafka's parable "Abraham" in *Stupidity* (Urbana: University of Illinois Press, 2002). For other Abrahams, see Derrida, "Abraham, l'autre," in *Judéités: Questions pour Jacques Derrida* (Paris: Galilée, 2003), 11–42. See also Gil Anidjar, "Derrida, le Juif, l'Arabe" in *Judéités.* In the same volume, Hent de Vries adds an important chapter to his own magisterial oeuvre, "Autour du théologico-politique," when he discusses the related structures of diagnostics, affirmation, and critique. For a supplement to theories of testing, or what contemporary technology calls "NDT" – non-destructive testing – see in particular the sections on the virtues of "Vernunftskepsis" in de Vries, *Theologie im Pianissimo & Zwischen Rationalität und Dekonstruktion* (Amsterdam: Kampen, 1989) 92ff.

22. By means of a delicate operation, Carlo Ginzburg studies the predicament or trials of interrogators, persecutors, and executioners. Without confounding the two positions, he nonetheless sees how the tester is being tested. While the executioner may be seen to "play God," it is not clear that God should need to test Himself, even though He seems to come out to do so at appointed times. See Carlo Ginzburg, *History, Rhetoric, and Proof* (Hanover, N.H.: University Press of New England, 1999) and *The Judge and the Historian: Marginal Notes on a Late-Twentieth-Century Miscarriage of Justice* (London: Verso, 1999), translated by Antony Shugaar.

23. The status of the Gulf War as test is a working thesis in *Finitude's Score*.

24. In the case of the Gulf War, weapons were deployed that had been amassed against the Soviet Union but fell under the risk of never being tried out. As clear as the logic of engagement may have seemed with the justificatory chatter of a New World Order, the Gulf War was, strictly speaking (in terms of the essence of technology that is pushing these buttons), a closely supervised field test. While the unstoppable relation of technology to testing may still require considerable theoretical scrutiny, it comes as no surprise to the so-called military establishment (the distinction between military and civil technologies blurs increasingly). The trade fair held directly after the Gulf War tagged certain weapons as "combat proven," boosting sales. Finally, war, as it increasingly becomes the technological and tele-topical test site par excellence, has lost its metaphysical status as meaningful production – at least when compared to Hegel's discussion of war as a sort of pregnancy test for historical becoming. If we no longer know how to wage war, in other words, how to legitimate and justify its necessity in history's unfolding (we desist at times from calling our interventions war – they have become police actions or humanitarian runs), we still hold out the hope that it may yield some test results.

25. Nietzsche, *The Gay Science,* §377.

26. Ibid.

27. Ibid., §380.

28. Ibid., §107.

29. Ibid., §41.

30. Ibid., §324.

31. Ibid., §345.

32. Ibid.

33. Ibid., §296.

34. Ibid., §307.

35. Michel Foucault, "Nietzsche, Genealogy, History," in *Language, Counter-*

Memory, and Practice: Selected Essays and Interviews (Ithaca: Cornell University Press, 1977), edited by Donald F. Bouchard, 163.

36. Nietzsche, *The Gay Science*, §58.

37. Ibid., §307.

38. "Introduction," in *Philosophy and AI: Essays at the Interface* (Cambridge: MIT Press, 1991), edited by Robert Cummins and John Pollock, 1.

39. Ibid.

40. Ibid.

41. Ibid., 2–3.

42. Ibid., 4.

43. Ibid.

44. Ibid., 4.

45. Ibid.

46. Ibid., 7.

47. Ibid.

48. Ibid.

49. Ibid., 8.

50. Douglas Hofstadter, *Gödel, Escher, Bach: An Eternal Golden Braid* (New York: Vintage Books, 1980), 414.

51. Ibid., 408.

52. I offer a reading of these works in conjunction with Derrida's discussion of "Force of Law" in "Activist Supplement: Papers on the Gulf War," in *Finitude's Score*, 293–304.

53. See the fairly straightforward discussion in Hofstadter, *Gödel*, 18–19.

54. Nietzsche, *The Gay Science*, §357.

55. In *Frankenstein, a Modern Prometheus* (London, 1818), Shelley figures the discovery of America that, when compared with the invention of the fiend, figures as the more grievous monstrosity.

56. Nietzsche, *The Gay Science*, §356.

57. For an admirable update of the syntax of improv and experiment, see Fred Moten, *In the Break: The Aesthetics of the Black Radical Tradition* (Minneapolis: University of Minnesota Press, 2003) and J. M. Lozano, "Aistheticon," Ph.D. thesis (Switzerland: European Graduate School, 2003), who discusses the experimental staging of contemporary thought.

58. Nietzsche, *The Gay Science*, §356.

59. Ibid., §295.

60. Ibid.

61. The meaning of the personal trace in the logic of scientific discovery is a problem that has been tried by Derrida in his analysis, for instance, of Freud's place in the discovery of *fort/da* as well as in the trajectories of Lacan's return to Freud, or Foucault's massive reading of desire and power. Derrida's relation to improvisation and invention is something that still needs to be understood *scientifically*, if one can still say so.

62. Max Weber, *Wissenschaft als Beruf* (Munich: Duncker und Humblot, 1919), 3–15, and Max Weber, *On Universities: The Power of the State and the Dignity of the Academic Calling in Imperial Germany* (Chicago: University of Chicago Press, 1976), translated by Edward Shils.

63. Weber, *On Universities*, 149–50.

64. Ibid., 141.

65. Ibid., 141–42.

66. Ibid., 142.

67. Ibid.

68. Ibid., 143.

69. Ibid.

70. Ibid., 146.

71. See in particular Derrida's "Nietzsche Machine," in *Negotiations*.

72. Nietzsche, *The Gay Science*, §370.

73. Ibid.

74. Ibid.

75. Ibid., §338.

76. Ibid., §319.

77. Cited in Kaufmann, *Nietzsche*, 19; also 423.

78. Nietzsche, *The Gay Science*, §344.

79. Ibid.

80. Ibid., §107.

81. Ibid.

82. Ibid.

83. There is no absolute justification for clearing Nietzsche of the uses to which his name lent itself historically. We can let the destinal machine of double programming keep running, just as we can keep it running with Hegelianisms, Marxisms, and theologies of the left and right. See Jacques Derrida, *The Ear of the Other: Otobiography, Transference, Translation* (Lincoln: University of Nebraska Press, 1985), translated by Peggy Kamuf and Avital Ronell, for further instructions on the installation of such a machine and archive.

84. Nietzsche, *The Gay Science,* §4.

85. Ibid., §6.

86. Ibid., §327.

87. Ibid., §7.

88. Ibid., §283.

89. Ibid., §343.

90. Ibid., §293.

91. Ibid., §.281.

92. Desire for privation is something that Lacan explores through the figure of the troubadour in the *Ethics of Psychoanalysis, The Seminar of Jacques Lacan, Book VII, 1959–1960* (New York: W. W. Norton, 1992), edited by Jacques-Alain Miller, translated by Dennis Porter.

93. *The Gay Science,* §293.

94. The work of Judith Butler has famously and importantly tracked the fate of parading gender the way Nietzsche does: the more macho his puffs and huffs, the more he shows up in drag, etc. See in particular *Gender Trouble: Feminism and the Subversion of Identity* (New York: Routledge, 1990) and *Excitable Speech: A Politics of the Performative* (New York: Routledge, 1997).

95. Nietzsche, *The Gay Science,* §221. In *The Psychopathology of Everyday Life* (*S.E. 6*), Freud writes of the miracle of St. Januarius whose blood, kept in a vial in a church in Naples, liquefies on his feast day.

96. Nietzsche, *The Gay Science,* §276.

97. I discuss this painful moment in "Hitting the Streets: *Ecce Fama,*" in *Finitude's Score,* 63–83.

98. Nietzsche, *The Gay Science,* §277.

99. Ibid.

100. Carl G. Hempel, "Studies in the Logic of Confirmation," *Mind* 45 (1945): 104, raises a similar point as an objection to defining the "confirmation" of a hypothesis in terms of what can be deduced from the hypothesis in conjunction with observable propositions. Richard B. Braithwaite, *Scientific Explanation: A Study of the Function of Theory, Probability, and Law in Science* (New York: Harper, 1960), 19, who looks for the place of probability on our language-map, does not give a precise definition of "confirmation" but believes the limitation of hypotheses to be themselves general propositions. There is an elaborate discussion of these problems in Rudolf Carnap, *Logical Foundations of Probability* (Chicago: University of Chicago Press, 1950), §§87ff. Braithwaite points out that a probability statement cannot be identified with any statement of frequencies in any set of actual in-

stances. This "view can properly be called a 'frequency view of probability' in that the meaning of the probability statements are all given in terms of their reject-ability (albeit provisional rejectability) by observable frequencies," *Scientific Explanation*, 195.

101. Werner Hamacher, "Lectio: de Man's Imperative," in *Premises: Essays on Philosophy and Literature from Kant to Celan* (Cambridge: Harvard University Press, 1996), translated by Peter Fenves, 196.

102. The irony of this passage is that, after writing it, I set about to spin off the section on "The Rhetoric of Testing" in the book that ended up preceding this one, *Stupidity*. In that work I look at entirely different aspects of some of the same materials. It would be impossible to write about Nietzsche and the test drive without giving thought to the status of irony. Hence the return of irony as a truly permanent parabasis in these works.

103. The aporias of promising have been investigated thoroughly in several works by Derrida, including *Mémoires: For Paul de Man* (New York: Columbia University Press, 1986), translated by Cecile Lindsay, Jonathan Culler, and Eduardo Cadava, edited by Avital Ronell and Eduardo Cadava, and *Limited, Inc.* (Evanston: Northwestern University Press, 1988).

104. In *Aesthetic Ideology* (Minneapolis: University of Minnesota Press, 1996), edited by Andrzej Warminski, 163–84.

105. Ibid., 178.

106. Ibid., 179.

107. Ibid.

108. Ibid., 177.

109. Ibid., 182.

110. Ibid., 183.

111. Ibid.

112. Carol Jacobs, *In the Language of Walter Benjamin* (Baltimore: Johns Hopkins University Press, 1999), 8.

113. Walter Benjamin, "The Destructive Character," in *Walter Benjamin: Selected Writings*, volume 2, 1927–1934 (Cambridge: Belknap Press, 1996–), translated by Rodney Livingstone and others, edited by Michael W. Jennings, Howard Eiland, and Gary Smith.

114. See de Man's commentary in *Concept of Irony*, 169.

115. Kierkegaard's *Journal* (cited without page reference) by Walter Lowrie in his notes to Kierkegaard, *Concluding Unscientific Postscript* (Princeton: Princeton University Press, 1968), translated by David Swenson and Walter Lowrie, 558.

116. De Man, "Concept of Irony", 170.

117. Ibid.

118. De Man, *Allegories of Reading,* 197.

119. Ibid., 5.

120. Nietzsche, *The Gay Science,* §46.

121. Paul Valéry, *Monsieur Teste* (Princeton: Princeton University Press, 1973), translated by Jackson Mathews, 5.

122. Ibid.

123. Ibid., preface of the 1925 edition, 6–7.

124. Ibid., 13.

125. Ibid., 14.

126. Ibid.

127. Jean-Luc Marion, *God without Being: Hors-Texte* (Chicago: University of Chicago Press, 1991), translated by Thomas A. Carlson.

128. Ibid., 113.

129. Ibid., 112.

130. Ibid.

131. Ibid.

132. Ibid., 113.

133. Ibid.

134. Ibid.

135. Ibid., 11–12.

136. While he doesn't directly link the increasing problem of experienceability to experiment or test, Benjamin expresses concern that the spectacle of the Olympics is turning into a test rather than a contest and, in *Illuminations,* he writes that the camera helps us to scope out another politics of detestation, fascism, because it creates an "aesthetic" experience that, nonauratic, is critically testing the type of narcissism on which fascism depends. Walter Benjamin, *Illuminations* (New York: Schocken Books, 1969), edited by Hannah Arendt, translated by Harry Zohn, 229. On the conjunction of tyranny, sport, and the test, Simone de Beauvoir offers in *The Second Sex* (New York: Vintage Books, 1974), 222: "Woman is sport and adventure, but also a test."

137. Marion, *God without Being,* 112.

138. Ibid., 115.

139. Freud, *S.E.* 11:197.

140. Marion, *God without Being,* 116.

141. I offer a more sustained reading of the yawn of boredom, melancholia, and

being in *Crack Wars: Literature, Addiction, Mania* (Lincoln: University of Nebraska Press: 1992).

142. Rorty, *Contingency, Irony, and Solidarity* (Cambridge: Cambridge University Press, 1989).

143. Ibid.

144. Ibid., xv.

145. Ibid.

146. Ibid., xvi.

147. Ibid.

148. Ibid., 104.

149. Ibid.

150. Ibid., 97.

151. Ibid., 99.

152. Ibid., 101.

153. Ibid.

154. Ibid., 102.

155. Ibid., 120–21.

156. See Paul de Man's discussion of Booth's wish to stop irony in *Concept of Irony.*

157. *Review of Metaphysics* 36 (1983): 677–78.

158. Rorty, *Contingency,* 123.

159. Ibid., 105–6.

160. Ibid., 106.

161. In one case, monkeys, tested for normal mothering and infant response, i.e., variables in "maternal efficiency," were evaluated in an engineering frame. "So there duly appeared among the maternal androids a cloth surrogate with ice water pumped through 'her' body (named predictably the 'ice cold mother'). This creature's opposite was the 'warm woman' or 'hot mamma.' Neonatal monkeys preferred the warm surface; and in the case of the icy cloth surface, they recoiled to a far corner of the cage and never approached it ('her') again. 'There is only one social affliction worse than an ice-cold wife, and that is an ice-cold mother,'" 240. Cited in Donna Haraway, *Primate Visions: Gender, Race, and Nature in the World of Modern Science* (New York: Routledge, 1989), 237–38.

162. Ibid.: "Harlow's lab's creativity in generating testing technology . . . was the development of the Wisconsin General Test Apparatus (WGTA), which allowed efficient presentation and variation of discrimination problems to experimental subjects. The backbone of monkey intelligence tests . . . were integrated with cor-

tical localization and lesion studies and with ontogenetic studies of motivation and learning. . . . The testing situation allowed Harlow and his colleagues to bring into and resolve in their laboratory a previously heterogeneous lot of questions and claims about learning that had been vexatious to many animal and human psychologists. The WGTA embodied the central logic of the laboratory: a means of multiplying, displacing, and condensing phenomena so as to interest diverse constituencies. In enlisting these constituencies, the WGTA moved from the Harlow lab and into other worlds, e.g., in the testing of learning deficits among retarded human children. The WGTA was prolific and reliable, generating an endless and varied progeny of scientists and science. The discovery of learning sets justified Harlow's election to the National Academy of Sciences in 1951."

163. Ibid., 220: In the normal ribald humor of the laboratory, granted over $1 million by the National Institutes of Mental Health to study the nature of primate love, this piece of lab equipment was, in print, called the "rape rack": "we resorted to an apparatus affectionately termed the rape rack, which we leave to the reader's imagination." After this "procedure," the female monkey then became a natural-technical object of knowledge called the "motherless monkey mother," the most effective in a sorority of "evil mothers" engineered by the Harlow lab to study psychopathologies for the NIMH. The isolated and technologically raped rhesus mothers were members of the family of maternal surrogates; they were constructs for the literal translation of metaphors into hardware – or in 1980s techno-speak, wetware. "Not even in our most devious dreams could we have designed a surrogate as evil as these real monkey mothers."

164. Ibid., 237–38.

165. See in particular "Support Our Tropes" and "Activist Supplement," in *Finitude's Score.*

166. Haraway, *Primate Visions,* 420.

167. Nietzsche, *Twilight of the Idols and the Anti-Christ* (London: Penguin, 1990), translated by R. J. Hollingdale, §47, 174.

168. Ibid., 175–77.

169. Nietzsche, *The Gay Science,* §110.

Part 5. Trial Balloon

1. "Husserl an Heidegger," 9.V.1928 (1), in Edmund Husserl, *Briefwechsel,* Band IV, Die Freiburger Schüler (Dodrecht: Kluwer, 1994), 143.

2. Jonas Cohn, *Theorie der Dialektik: Formenlehre der Philosophie* (Leipzig: Meiner, 1923).

3. Husserl, *Briefwechsel,* 139.

4. Ibid., 153–54.

5. Emmanuel Levinas, *En découvrant l'existence avec Husserl et Heidegger* (Paris: Vrin, 2001), 12–13.

6. *The Cambridge Companion to Husserl* (Cambridge: Cambridge University Press, 1995), edited by Barry Smith and David Woodruff Smith, 8. On Heidegger's legacy of silence, including the apologies offered belatedly to Frau Husserl concerning his withholding shutdown during the master's illness and death, Levinas writes that Heidegger's persistent refusal to speak out even after the war ended was interrupted only by traces and utterances on technology. Levinas cites Wolfgang Schirmacher's book, *Technik und Gelassenheit: Zeitkritik nach Heidegger* (Freiburg: Verlag Karl Alber, 1983), which reveals unpublished lectures on the production of corpses in the death camps. Emmanuel Levinas, "Wie ein Einverständnis gegenüber dem Schrecken," *Zeitmitschrift: Journal für Ästhetik* 5 (Herbst 1988).

7. We also have some indices from Karl Schuhmann, *Husserl-Chronik: Denk- und Lebensweg Edmund Husserls* (Den Haag: Martinus Nijhoff, 1977); Ludwig Binswanger, "Dank an Edmund Husserl," in *Edmund Husserl 1859–1959: Recueil commémoratif publié à l'occasion du centenaire de la naissance du philosophe* (La Haye: Martinus Nijhoff, 1959), 64–72; Dorion Cairns, *Conversations with Husserl and Fink* (Den Haag: Martinus Nijhoff, 1976); "Persönliche Aufzeichnungen. Herausgegeben von Walter Biemel," *Philosophy and Phenomenological Research* 16 (1956): 293–302; as well as Roman Ingarden's "Meine Erinnerungen an Husserl," in Edmund Husserl, *Briefe an Roman Ingarden* (Den Haag: Martinus Nijhoff 1968), edited by Roman Ingarden, 106–84, and "Edith Stein on Her Activity as an Assistant of Edmund Husserl," *Philosophy and Phenomenological Research* 23 (1962): 155–75.

8. Hugo Ott, *Martin Heidegger: A Political Life* (New York: Basic Books, 1993), translated by Allan Blunden, 83.

9. Ibid., 105.

10. Husserl, *Briefwechsel,* 131.

11. Ibid., 80.

12. Ibid., 83.

13. Ibid., 160–61.

14. The article is mentioned in Philippe Lacoue-Labarthe, *La fiction du politique: Heidegger, l'art et la politique* (Paris: C. Bourgois, 1987). I consider its possible significance in *The Telephone Book: Technology, Schizophrenia, Electric Speech* (Lincoln: University of Nebraska Press, 1989) 412.

15. Ott, *Heidegger*, 117.

Part 6. Testing Your Love

Epigraphs: Friedrich Nietzsche, *Ecce Homo,* in Nietzsche, *On the Genealogy of Morals: Ecce Homo* (New York: Vintage Books, 1967), translated and edited by Walter Kaufmann, §II, 6. See discussion of this passage in Walter Kaufmann, *Nietzsche: Philosopher, Psychologist, Antichrist,* 4th edition (Princeton: Princeton University Press, 1974), 31–33. Nietzsche, *The Will to Power* (New York: Random House, 1969), translated by Walter Kaufmann and R. J. Hollingdale, §910.

1. Shireen R. K. Patell writes of the "violence of hyperliteralist or fundamentalist reading practices" in "The Violence of Reading: Levinas, Hawthorne, and the Ethics of Allegory" (textscript).

2. Alenka Zupancic briefly discusses the unique narrative and technical aspects of *Rope,* including the fact that the film unfolds "with no dissolves and no time lapses," in "A Perfect Place to Die: Theatre in Hitchcock's Films," in *Everything You Always Wanted to Know about Lacan (But Were Afraid to Ask Hitchcock)* (London: Verso, 1992), edited by Slavoj Zizek, 78. I owe thanks to John Muse for discussions of loyalty and testing, and the case of Leopold and Loeb, which Hitchcock's film reprised. Two delinquents obsessed with Nietzsche's philosophy, they were determined to upgrade to *Übermensch* status through the murder of Bobby Franks. The plot thickens: Defense attorney Clarence Darrow tried to call Sigmund Freud as an expert witness, but he declined, due to failing health.

3. Nietzsche, *Ecce Homo,* flysheet.

4. Friedrich Hölderlin, "Reflexion," in Hölderlin, *Werke und Briefe* (Frankfurt am Main: Insel Verlag, 1969), edited by Friedrich Beißner and Jochen Schmidt, 602.

5. For another inflection of time-testing, see William H. Gass, *The Test of Time: Essays* (New York: Alfred A. Knopf, 2001).

6. Friedrich Nietzsche, *The Case of Wagner. Turiner Brief vom Mai 1888,* in *The Birth of Tragedy, and The Case of Wagner* (New York: Vintage Books, 1967), translated by Walter Kaufmann.

7. Michel Foucault, *Fearless Speech* (Los Angeles: Semiotext(e), 2001), edited by Joseph Pearson, 16.

8. Ibid., 17.

9. Ibid., 19.

10. Nietzsche, *Case of Wagner*, 143.

11. See Jean-Luc Nancy's *Being Singular Plural* (Stanford: Stanford University Press, 2000), translated by Robert D. Richardson and Anne E. O'Byrne.

12. Philippe Lacoue-Labarthe, *Musica Ficta: (Figures of Wagner)* (Stanford: Stanford University Press, 1994), translated by Felicia McCarren, 111. See also the relevant essays by Susan Bernstein, "Fear of Music? Nietzsche's Double Vision of the 'Musical Feminine,'" Laurence Rickels, "Insurance for and against Women: From Nietzsche to Psychotherapy," as well as Sarah Kofman, "A Fantastical Genealogy: Nietzsche's Family Romance," and Kelly Oliver, "Nietzsche's Abjection," in *Nietzsche and the Feminine* (Charlottesville: University Press of Virginia, 1994), edited by Peter J. Burgard.

13. *Conversations with Nietzsche: A Life in the Words of His Contemporaries* (New York: Oxford University Press, 1987), edited by Sander L. Gilman, translated by David J. Parent, 147.

14. For another rhetoric of philosophical friendship, where the distinction is established between mastering and testing the friend ("the friend is not *gemeistert* [mastered] but, rather, *gemustert* [tested]"), see Peter Fenves's reading of hypocrisy and hypercritique in Kant in *Late Kant: Towards Another Law of the Earth* (New York: Routledge, 2003), 122.

15. Nietzsche, *Case of Wagner*, 184.

16. Ibid.

17. Ibid.

18. Roland Barthes, *A Lover's Discourse: Fragments* (New York: Farrar, Strauss and Giroux, 1978), translated by Richard Howard, 106–8.

19. Jacques Derrida, *The Ear of the Other: Otobiography, Transference, Translation* (Lincoln: University of Nebraska Press, 1985), translated by Peggy Kamuf and Avital Ronell.

20. Jean-Luc Nancy, "Dei Paralysis Progressiva," in Nancy, *The Birth to Presence* (Stanford: Stanford University Press, 1993), translated by Brian Holmes, 55.

21. Ibid., 56.

22. *Conversations with Nietzsche*, 144.

23. Nietzsche continues to play a role in the unfolding histories of rock and roll. Breaking on through to the other side of the Wagnerian eruption, Jim Morrison, the other presencing of Dionysus out of the spirit of music, wanted to have Dionysian feasts and excess; he cites the *Birth of Tragedy* and gave birth to a series of

Nietzsche-Morrison wannabes. The relation of Wagner, rock and roll, and Hollywood musical scores is not (yet) a part or partition of Heideggerian readings of Nietzsche.

24. Friedrich Nietzsche, "Richard Wagner in Bayreuth," 203.

25. Johann Peter Eckermann's relation to Goethe and Nietzsche's recognition of the largely effaced secretary is the topic of my *Dictations: On Haunted Writing* (Lincoln: University of Nebraska Press, 1992) and *Der Goethe-Effekt* (Munich: Wilhelm Fink Verlag, 1986), edited by Friedrich Kittler, translated by Ulrike Dünkelsbühler.

26. On the relation between philosophically resonant laughter and breaking up, see the aptly titled *Breaking Up [at] Totality: A Rhetoric of Laughter*, by D. Diane Davis (Carbondale: Southern Illinois University Press, 2000), and Peter Rehberg, "*Lachen/lesen*" (Ph.D. diss., New York University, 2001). The model text for testing limits, laughter, and transgression is Blanchot's "The Laughter of the Gods," most recently published in *Decadence of the Nude: Pierre Klossowski* (London: Black Dog Publishing Ltd., 2002).

27. Ronald Hayman, *Nietzsche: A Critical Life* (Oxford: Oxford University Press, 1980), 155.

28. Friedrich Nietzsche, *Unzeitgemäße Betrachtungen, Viertes Stück: Richard Wagner in Bayreuth,* KSA I, 431.

29. Friedrich Nietzsche, *The Gay Science: With a Prelude in Rhymes and Appendix of Songs* (New York: Vintage Books, 1974), translated by Walter Kaufmann, 151. On Hamlet's melancholy and anamorphoses, see Anselm Haverkamp, *Hamlet: Hypothek der Macht* (Berlin: Kulturverlag Kadmos, 2001).

30. Ibid.

31. Ibid., 150.

32. Friedrich Nietzsche, *Nachgelassene Fragmente Frühjahr 1881 bis Sommer 1882,* KSA IX, 642.

33. Friedrich Nietzsche, *Human, All Too Human: A Book for Free Spirits* (Lincoln: University of Nebraska Press, 1984), translated by Marion Faber, with Stephen Lehmann, §629.

34. Ibid.

35. Ibid.

36. Ibid.

37. Derrida discusses de Man's interest in the fate of *versprechen* in *Mémoires for Paul de Man*. See also Hamacher's discussion of the self-misspeaking promise in Werner Hamacher, *Premises: Essays on Philosophy and Literature from Kant*

to Celan (Cambridge: Harvard University Press, 1996), translated by Peter Fenves, 196.

38. Nietzsche, *Human, All Too Human*, 261.

39. Ibid., §637, "On Probabilities."

40. Ibid.

41. "The Untimely Ones," in *Ecce Homo* (New York: Vintage Books, 1969), translated by Walter Kaufmann, 277.

42. Ibid., 281.

43. The inversion of this scene launches Derrida's *Post Card: From Socrates to Freud and Beyond* (Chicago: University of Chicago Press, 1987).

44. Nietzsche, *Case of Wagner*, 162.

45. Nietzsche, *Human, All Too Human*, 6.

46. Ibid., 7.

47. Ibid., 8.

48. Ibid.

49. Ibid.

50. Ibid.

51. Ibid., 4.

52. Ibid., 5.

53. Ibid., 6.

54. Ibid., 7.

55. Ibid., 6–7.

56. Ibid., 10.

Index

Index

Index

Index

Index

Index

knowledge: *Aporias* (Derrida) and, 328n14; Boyle's fallibilistic conception of, 98; and cognition, 101; *epistēmē* (certainty) as, 41; life as means for, 176; necessity of risk and, 217–18; nihilism and, 159–60; non-, 119, 341n141; origin, 244; philosophy/science rift and, 17; pleasure and, 173; and quest for truth, 38; reality-testing and, 165–67; reason and, 257; rejected, 96; reputation of those seeking, 178–79; stupidity and, 75–78; and the systematists, 100–101

kōans: athletics and, 126–27; completion of, 122–24; emptiness of Zen and, 116–17; enlightenment and, 113–15; and perception, 120; Rinzai/Soto schools and, 125–26; scale of danger and, 128–29; Zen and, 342n157, 343n163

Kolnai, Aurel, 268

Koyré, Alexander, 267

Laboratory for Neuroengineering, 328n16

Lacan, Jacques, 7, 19; *Ethics of Psychoanalysis*, 7

Lacoue-Labarthe, Philippe, 142–43

Lakatos, Imre, 30

language/lexicon: academic speech as, 200–201; accountability of science through, 154, 156; anacoluthon and, 224; art universally and, 338n78; BlooP tests and, 187; Boyle and, 99–100; Bush, George W. and, 167–68; cryptonymy and, 333n118; developed by Boyle, 95; experimentation and, 45; as feminine, 238–40; and gender, 236–37; irony and, 227–28, 235, 237–38; Kafka and, 74–75; kōan practice and, 128–29; of a liberal ironist, 237–38; Nietzsche's use of definitions and, 180–81; phrase events and, 102–3; testimony and, 87–88; testing and importance of, 31, 34; "third eye" and, 120; Turing Test and, 51–52

Late Kant: Towards Another Law of the Earth (Fenves), 357n14

Latour, Bruno, 50

law: Athenian, 83; *Daubert v. Merrell Dow Pharmaceuticals, Inc.* and, 26–29; and expert testimony as scientific, 29; *Frye v.*

United States and, 26–29; hypothesis verification and, 36–37; nonexistence of, 13–14; phrase events and, 102; Turing, Alan and, 53–56. *See also* testimony

"The Law of Genre" (Derrida), 147

L'Effroyable Mensonge (Dasquié & Guisnel), 341n129

Leibniz, Gottfried Wilhelm, 263–64

"Letter to a Harsh Critic" (Deleuze), 88

Leviathan and the Air-Pump (Shapin and Schaffer), 94

Levinas, Emmanuel: 9, 119, 251, 253, 263; on Blanchot and passivity, 118; and *blessure*, 252; *The Cambridge Companion to Husserl* (Smith & Smith) and, 355n6; épreuve vs. expérience, 63; on Heidegger, 355n6; Husserl on, 251–52; on Jewish identity, 252; logic of science and, 260; verification and, 63

The Life of Dion (Plato), 284

limit determination, 145–46

Linus, Franciscus, 101

Lipps, Theodor, 268

logic: as articulated by *The Gay Science*, 156; artificial intelligence (AI) and, 182–83; Christianity and, 207; experimental disposition and, 19; kōan of testing and, 116–17

Logical Foundations of Probability (Carnap), 350–51n100

Logical Investigations (Husserl), 261, 268, 270

Lorenz, Paul (Rat Man), 66–67, 335n17

love: friendship and, 315; Nietzsche and, 174, 177–78, 279–80; Nietzsche/Wagner relationship and, 286–88, 291–93; primate, 354n163; and technologization of human relations, 216

loyalty, 300–301, 305–8, 312, 315

Lozano, J. M., 348n57

Lyotard, Jean-François, 102–3, 105–7, 109–10; *The Differend*, 102–3, 109–10

MacDowell, D. M., 83

Marcuse, Herbert, 268

Marion, Jean-Luc, 230–33; *God without Being*, 230–231

Index

Index

ture, 344n26; and Wagner, 142, 283–88, 291–93, 295–96, 298–305, 316–21; *The Will to Power*, 162; woman-hating and, 237; *Zarathustra*, 315

Nietzsche contra Wagner (Nietzsche), 297

Ninth International Congress of Philosophy, 273

non-destructive testing (NDT), 346–47n21

nothingness: kōan of testing and, 116–17, 122–24; Marion, Jean-Luc and, 231–33; pre-existing conditions and, 116; stupidity through trauma and, 108–9; threat of, 105. *See also* reality-testing

number theory, 189

objectivism, 17

The Origins of Totalitarianism (Arendt), 327n2

Outline of Psycho-Analysis (Freud), 69

parrhesia, 284

Parsifal (von Eschenbach), 114–16

Parzifal (Wagner), 116

passivity, 125–26, 143

Patell, Shireen R. K., 356n1

Paulhan, Jean, 229

Perceval (de Troyes), 114–16

personality: accountability and, 175; morality and, 177; strength of, 209–10

Pestalozzi, Johann H., 201

phenomenology: *The Crisis of European Sciences and Transcendental Phenomenology* (Husserl), 328n4; *The Foundation of Phenomenology* (Farber), 272; as intentional experience, 268

phrase events, 102–3

physical activity: kōan practice and, 126–27; Nietzsche's equestrian abilities, 218; Olympics as test, 352n136

physics, 94–96, 263

place: destiny/destination as, 174–77; homelessness, 172, 175–76; relation of testing to, 171–73; wandering and, 314–15

Plato: and *elegkhos* (elenchus), 86; and law, 23; *parrhesia* and, 284; passivity and, 125; *The Sophist*, 86; verification and, 105–6

pleasure: Nietzsche and, 173; and pity, 143;

science and, 218–19. *See also The Gay Science* (Nietzsche)

political institutions: America (Nietzsche) and, 191–92, 194, 196–97; evil and, 215; experimental testing and, 18–19; future experimentation and, 134–35, 146–49, 203; irony and, 234; reality-testing and, 167–68

Popper, Karl: critical attitude of, 32–37; falsifiability and, 27–31; and Freud, 335–36n27; *The Gay Science* and, 156; justice of dismissal and, 27–31; scientific quest for truth and, 38–42

positivism, 257–58

Potter, Steve, 328n16

predictability: as articulated by *The Gay Science*, 157; in psychoanalysis, 66; scientific, 179. *See also* probabilities

prejudices and scientific quest for truth, 39–40

"Preludes of Science" (Nietzsche), 157

primitive recursive functions/predicates, 187

"The Principal of Mental Functioning" (Freud), 68

Principia Mathematica (Whitehead & Russell), 189

private interview (Zen), 127–28

probabilities: as articulated by *The Gay Science*, 156; frequency view of, 350–51n100; hypothesis concept and, 35–36; truth and, 41

"Prolegomena to Pure Logic" (Husserl), 270

Promenades of a Solitary Walker (Rousseau), 126

Proust, Marcel, 225

psychoanalysis: controls for testing and, 64–70; finding truth through, 335n27; *Return to Freud: Jacques Lacan's Dislocation of Psychoanalysis* (Weber) and, 334n1

purity, 37, 39–40

Putnam, Hilary, 30

questioning and divinity, 13

racism: anti-Semitism (Nietzsche), 214;

368

Index

Index

knowledge, 38; in the sense of science, 249; and slave torture, 83–85; and testing, 23, 25–26; and testing of falsity, 346n14
Tsushima, Michiko, 340n117
Turing, Alan, 51–57, 333n109–111
Turing Test, 51–52, 220
Tuskegee syphilis study, 337n69

United States, Frye v., 26–29, 329n32
"Unsuccessfulness of Experiments" (Boyle), 99

Valéry, Paul, 229–30
values: Boyle and, 92, 94–96; gender and, 149; irony and, 238; and Nietzsche view on philosophers of the future, 136, 146–49; rationalization and, 202
Van Bréda, H. L., 273
veracity, 104. *See also* truth
verification: Freud and, 64; Levinas and, 63; reality-testing and, 103–4; torture victims and, 105
Verleugnung, 69
Versuch, 6, 18, 133, 142, 160–61, 327n1
violence, 188–89. *See also* torture

Wagner, Cosima, 302
Wagner, Richard: gratitude and, 283–88; loyalty and, 300–301, 307; and Nietzsche,

142, 283–33, 291–93, 295–96, 298–305, 316–21; opiates and, 312; *Parzifal,* 116; "Richard Wagner in Bayreuth" (Nietzsche), 298–99; test of no pre-existing conditions and, 116; and war, 300–301. *See also* Nietzsche, Friedrich: *The Case of Wagner*
war: Gulf War as test, 347n24; Wagner and, 300–302. *See also* violence
Weber, Max, 197, 200–203
Weber, Samuel, 334n1
Weltanschauung, 197–98, 203
What Is Called Thinking? (Heidegger), 15, 102, 118–19
What Is Metaphysics? (Heidegger), 118
Whitehead, Alfred North, 189
Whitemore, Hugh, 52
The Will to Power (Nietzsche), 162
Wisconsin General Test Apparatus (WGTA), 353–54n162
witness, 109–11. *See also* reality-testing
Wu-men Hui-K'ai, 124

yogic teachings, 113–15
Yosuke Hamada, 252, 274

Zarathustra (Nietzsche), 315
Zen: kōans and, 342n157, 343n163; physical activity and, 126–27; private interview of, 127–28; Rinzai/Soto schools and, 125–26; and testing, 113–15. *See also* kōans

AVITAL RONELL is a professor of German, English, and comparative literature at New York University, where she also chairs the German department. She is author of *Stupidity, Finitude's Score, Crack Wars,* and other books.

The University of Illinois Press is a founding member of the Association of American University Presses.

Composed in Adobe Minion with Myriad display. Typeset and designed by Richard Eckersley. Manufactured by Thomson-Shore, Inc.

University of Illinois Press
1325 South Oak Street
Champaign, IL 61820-6903
www.press.uillinois.edu